Management Accounting

An Introduction

Management Accounting
An Introduction

Pauline Weetman

Professor of Accounting
Heriot-Watt University

PITMAN PUBLISHING

London · Hong Kong · Johannesburg · Melbourne · Singapore · Washington DC

PITMAN PUBLISHING
128 Long Acre, London WC2E 9AN
Tel: +44 (0)171 447 2000
Fax: +44 (0)171 240 5771

A Division of Pearson Professional Limited

First published in Great Britain in 1996

© Pearson Professional Limited 1996

ISBN 0 273 62362 1

British Library Cataloguing in Publication Data
A CIP catalogue record for this book can be obtained from the British Library

10 9 8 7 6 5 4 3 2 1

Typeset by Land & Unwin (Data Sciences) Ltd
Printed and bound in Great Britain by Clays Ltd, St Ives plc

The Publishers' policy is to use paper manufactured from sustainable forests.

Contents

Part 2
Applying the basic tools of management accounting

Preface

Introduction

The importance of communication between a business and its stakeholders increases as organisations become larger and more complex. One very significant group of stakeholders is the internal management of the organisation. Managers have access to a wealth of detailed financial information and a responsibility for the careful management of the assets and operations of the organisation. The way in which the managers of an organisation use financial information is very much contingent on the purpose for which the information is intended. Management accounting is a specialist area of study within accounting more generally. Ideally, management accounting and financial accounting would coalesce if the external users could be given access to all internal information, but that might damage the competitive position of the business and would probably swamp the external users in detail. For some, management accounting is a means of earning a livelihood but for a much wider range of managerial interests it is an essential tool of planning, control and decision making.

First level degree courses in accounting are increasingly addressed to a broad base of potential interest and this book seeks to provide such a broad base of understanding of management accounting whilst also supplying a sound technical base for those intending to pursue specialised study of the subject further.

Aim of the book

This book aims to establish a firm understanding of the basic techniques, recognising that the wider aspects of management accounting will be explored in subsequent years of study by those seeking to specialise. A contingency approach is adopted which emphasises that the selection of management accounting techniques is conditional on management's purpose. To meet this purpose the management accountant performs the roles of directing attention, keeping the score and solving problems. These themes are reiterated throughout this book. A student who has completed this first level study of management accounting will be aware of many of the day-to-day practices of management accounting in business and the relevance of those practices.

In particular

Concepts of management accounting are presented in early chapters and applied consistently thereafter.

User needs in respect of management accounting are discussed by including first-person commentary from a professional consultant who gives insight into the type of interpretative comment which students of management accounting often find difficult.

Practical illustration is used in specific examples in each chapter and by the case studies discussed by the consultant. Reinforcement is provided by end-of-chapter cases which have a real-world application.

Interpretation is a feature of all the management accounting chapters where the use of first-person commentary by the consultant allows more candid discussion than would be appropriate in the usual dispassionate style of the academic text.

Current developments in management accounting are outlined in Chapter 11 as an indication of the exciting prospects for those seeking more advanced study and for those who may in future employment find themselves applying those developments. In many businesses these current developments are already standard practice but they have evolved from, or as a reaction to, the traditional approach explained in the text. An understanding of the basic approach remains a prerequisite for those embarking on the new ideas.

Self-evaluation is encouraged by setting learning objectives at the start of each chapter and placing activity questions at various stages throughout each chapter. Self-testing questions at the end of the chapter may be answered by referring again to the text. Group activities are suggested at the end of each chapter with the particular aim of encouraging participation and interaction. Further end-of-chapter questions provide practice in practical applications. Answers are available to all computational questions, either at the end of the book or in the lecturer's supplement.

A sense of achievement is engendered in the reader by providing a general understanding of the basic tools of analysis in Chapters 1, 2 and 3 through use of simple illustrations. Thereafter the lecturer who wishes to truncate a first level course may select chapters for application, depending on whether decision making or planning and control are key features of the particular course. The sense of achievement is created in being able to participate in the group activities and to solve the end-of-chapter problems.

Logic in analysis is encouraged by presenting computations so as to match as closely as possible the reasoning process represented by the computations. Ledger accounts are not used, so that the student concentrates on solving the problem with a methodical form of presentation which suits the particular circumstances, rather than trying to memorise ledger accounting recording.

Flexible course design

In teaching and learning management accounting various combinations are possible depending on course design aims. Chapters 1, 2 and 3 provide an essential set of basic tools of analysis but thereafter some flexibility is feasible. For a sample of planning, control and decision-making aspects, Chapters 4, 6, 9 and 11 would provide a range of material. For concentrating on decision making and awareness of current developments, Chapters 6, 9, 10 and 11 would be recommended. For concentrating on planning and control Chapters 6, 7, 8 and 11 would give students experience of the variety of techniques in use.

Target readership

This book is targeted at a broad-ranging business studies type of first level degree course. It provides comprehensive material for one full semester of 12 teaching weeks. The book has been written with undergraduate students particularly in mind, but may also be suitable for professional and postgraduate business courses where management accounting is taught at an introductory level. Chapter 1 provides an outline of the accounting equation for students who have not studied financial accounting.

Acknowledgments

I am grateful to academic colleagues and to reviewers of the text for helpful comments and suggestions. I am also grateful to undergraduate students of five universities who have taken my courses and thereby helped in developing an approach to teaching and learning the subject. Ken Shackleton of the University of Glasgow helped plan the structure of the book. The Institute of Chartered Accountants of Scotland gave permission for use of the end-of-chapter case study questions. I am grateful to Pat Bond at Pitman Publishing for his considerable patience, to Julianne Mulholland for overseeing the editing of the text, and to Ron Harper at Longman Australia for initiating the project.

Part 1

Setting the scene and defining the basic tools of management accounting

Functions of management accounting

Contents			

Learning objectives	After studying this chapter you should be able to: 1 Understand the nature of judgement in management accounting. 2 Identify some of the decisions for which management accounting information is useful. 3 Form ideas of your own on how management accounting may contribute to decision making situations. 4 Form ideas of your own on how such decisions may be monitored for success or failure.

1.1 Introduction

There is no single 'official' definition of accounting but for the purposes of this text the following wording will be used:

Definition	*Accounting* is the process of identifying, measuring and communicating financial information about an entity to permit informed judgements and decisions by users of the information[1].

Many would argue that the foremost users of accounting information about an organisation must be those who manage it on a day-to-day basis. This group is referred to in broad terms as *management*, which is a collective term for all those persons who have responsibilities for making judgements and decisions within an organisation. Because they have close involvement with the business, they have access to a wide range of information (much of which may be confidential within the organisation) and will seek those aspects of the information which are most relevant to their particular judgements and decisions. Because this group of users is so broad and because of the vast amount of information potentially available, a specialist branch of accounting has developed, called management accounting, to serve the particular needs of management.

Activity 1.1	*Before reading any further, take a piece of paper and write down what you think management accounting means. What do you expect to learn in a course on management accounting? Keep the list safe in your file. Later in this chapter you will be asked to look back to the list and say whether your expectations are being met.*

Those who manage a business are described as the internal users of information. They may be contrasted with external users who form judgements on the overall performance of the organisation and make judgements on their own relationship with the organisation. Their decisions are of the type: 'Shall I invest money in this business?' 'Shall I continue to be an investor in this business?' 'Shall I supply goods to this business?' 'Shall I continue to supply goods to this business?' 'Shall I become a customer of this business?' 'Shall I continue to be a customer of this business?'

The internal users make different types of judgements and different types of decisions. They may have to judge the performance of the various products of the organisation as compared with those of competitors. They may have to judge the performance of different divisions within the organisation. Their decisions are of the type: 'Shall I invest in manufacturing more soap powder, or do I switch resources into toothpaste?' 'Shall I continue offering a television repair service as support for my sales of televisions?' 'Is it cost effective to have three separate locations at which my tenants can pay their rent?' 'Will this investment in a new factory pay for itself over the next ten years?' There is great variety in the judgements and decisions made by those who manage the business. Their needs are so wide ranging that management accounting has developed as a separate discipline, within the overall 'accounting' umbrella, in order to serve the particular needs of management.

In thinking of accounting as a tool which will assist in the management of a business, two significant questions emerge:

1 What types of informed judgements are made by management and about management?
2 What types of decisions are made by management?

It is presumed that many of those reading this text for the first time may not have a great deal of experience of the types of judgements and decisions made in business. This chapter therefore devotes space to four case study illustrations of management situations where management accounting will have a contribution to make. The case studies are uncomplicated so that the management accounting applications are intuitively obvious. After each case study outline there is a comment on the management accounting aspects. You will then meet Fiona McTaggart, a management accounting consultant, who explains how she sees the management accountant's contribution to the management issues raised in each of the four case studies.

Before exploring the case studies, this chapter sets out, in section 1.3, some basic categories of management functions and then outlines, in section 1.4, the role of management accounting in helping to meet the information needs of those management functions. For those who are meeting accounting for the first time, section 1.2 explains the main ideas and technical words on which accounting relies, all of which flow from the financial aspects of business represented by the accounting equation.

1.2 The accounting equation

Those who manage a business need a full understanding and knowledge of the *resources* available to the business and the *obligations* of the business to those outside it. They will also have to be confident that the business has an adequate flow of cash to support the continuation of the business. Accounting has traditionally applied the term *assets* to the resources available to the business and has applied the term *liabilities* to the obligations of the business to persons other than the owner.

The owners of the business have a claim to the resources of the business after all other obligations have been satisfied. This is called the *ownership interest* or the *equity* interest. From time to time the managers of a business must show the owners how the operation of the business is increasing or decreasing the ownership interest. A textbook on financial reporting will contain a substantial section on accounting aspects of the ownership interest. A textbook on management accounting concentrates on the management of the assets and liabilities. Assets and liabilities are reported in a financial statement called a *balance sheet*. The balance sheet is a *statement of the financial position* of the entity at a particular point in time. It may be described by a very simple equation.

Assets minus **Liabilities**	equals	**Ownership interest**

The ownership interest is the residual claim after liabilities to third parties have been satisfied. The equation expressed in this form emphasises that residual aspect.

Another way of thinking about an equation is to imagine a see-saw on which two containers are balanced. In one container are the assets minus liabilities. In the other is the ownership interest.

If anything happens to disturb the assets then the see-saw will fall out of balance unless some matching disturbance is applied to the ownership interest. If anything happens to disturb the liabilities then the see-saw will fall out of balance unless some matching disturbance is applied to the ownership interest. If a disturbance applied to an asset is applied equally to a liability then the see-saw will remain in balance.

The ownership interest will increase if assets grow (provided liabilities do not grow faster). Achieving that growth is an essential skill of management. The ownership interest will increase if capital (cash or other assets) is contributed by the owner and it will decrease if capital is withdrawn by the owner. Those actions of the owner are not in the control of management. Consequently this book concentrates on the activities of making use of assets and controlling liabilities. The words *revenue* and *expense* are used to describe the results of actions which increase or decrease the ownership interest through the management of assets and liabilities.

Change in ownership interest	equals	Capital contributed/withdrawn by the owner plus **Revenue** minus **Expenses**

The difference between revenue and expenses is more familiarly known as *profit*. So a further subdivision of the basic equation is:

Profit	equals	**Revenue** minus **Expenses**

1.2.1 Reporting profit

An expense is caused by a transaction or event arising during the operations of the business which causes a decrease in the ownership interest. It could be due to an outflow or depletion of assets such as cash, trading stock, or fixed assets. It could be due to a liability being incurred without a matching asset being acquired.

Revenue is created by a transaction or event arising during the operations of the business which causes an increase in the ownership interest. It could be due to an increase in cash or debtors, received in exchange for goods or services. Depending on the nature of the business, revenue may be described as sales, turnover, fees, commission, royalties or rent.

Definition

> *Revenue* is created by a transaction or event arising during the ordinary activities of the business which causes an increase in the ownership interest.
>
> An *expense* is caused by a transaction or event arising during the ordinary activities of the business which causes a decrease in the ownership interest.

In management accounting it is common to use the word *cost*, rather than *expense* which is more commonly encountered in financial accounting. For the purposes of this book the word cost may be taken as equivalent to expense. Financial accounting takes a broad view in deciding the categories of expense (e.g. selling expense, administrative expense). Management accounting delves much deeper into the various types of cost (e.g. selling expense is subdivided into costs of commission paid to sales staff, costs of travel in selling goods, costs of paperwork in recording orders and sales, and costs of goods or services rejected by customers).

1.2.2 The matching, or accruals, concept

One very important aspect of accounting practice is that it is based on the idea that costs of any period should be matched against the sales which have been earned through the activity causing those costs. When a product is manufactured using electricity, the cost measured should include the cost of electricity used for that item. However, the electricity may not be paid for until some time later. So the amount of cash paid at one point in time will relate to the use of electricity in an earlier period.

The matching concept of accounting (also called the accruals concept) requires the management of a business to estimate the cost of resources used during a period in producing the goods or services of the period. Returning to the electricity example, management would be expected to keep records of electricity consumed and to estimate the costs from that information. That cost would appear in a profit and loss account, matched against the sales created during the period. The cash payment made to the electricity supplier would be reported separately in a cash flow statement.

1.2.3 The prudence concept

The preparers of financial statements have to contend with uncertainty surrounding many events and circumstances. The existence of uncertainties is recognised by the disclosure of their nature and extent and by the exercise of prudence in the preparation of the financial statements. Prudence means that there will be a degree of caution in the exercise of the judgements needed in making estimates. In particular there will be a wish to ensure that income or assets are not overstated and that expenses or liabilities are not understated. The need for prudence should not, however, be regarded as justification for deliberate understatement of assets and revenue or deliberate overstatement of liabilities and expenses. That would lead to a situation which was not reliable. Take as an example the costs of repair work lasting over more than one accounting period. It might be argued as prudent to report all the repair cost in the first period but that would give a wrong impression of the cost of repairs if the activity is in fact spread over the two periods. One example of the application of prudence in this text is the reporting of profit on a partly-completed contract. A portion of profit is reported in order to reflect the economic activity of the period and to apply the matching concept, but some portion of profit is kept back until a later period as a prudent precaution against unforeseen events.

1.2.4 Ensuring good accounting practice

One important difference from financial accounting is that there is no official regulatory process governing management accounting. This is very different from the framework of company law, accounting standards and other regulatory processes which are found throughout financial reporting to external users. Consequently there is relative freedom in management accounting to tailor the accounting process to the management function. That does not mean that management accounting is any less rigorous professionally than other forms of accounting reporting. In the UK there is a professional body, the Chartered Institute of Management Accountants (CIMA), which provides guidance to its members on good practice in management accounting. That guidance includes a wide range of publications ranging from definitions of terminology to reports on newly emerging techniques. Similar professional bodies having a management accounting specialism exist in other countries.

1.2.5 Financial statements

The various financial statements produced by enterprises for the owners and other external users are derived from the accounting equation. There is a view that there are three purposes of external financial reporting, in producing information about the financial position, performance and financial adaptability of the enterprise. The three most familiar primary financial statements, and their respective purposes, are:

Primary financial statement for external users	Purpose is to report	Main contents
Balance sheet	financial position	assets, liabilities, ownership interest
Profit and loss account	performance	revenue (also called turnover or sales), expenses (also called costs), profit for period
Cash flow statements	financial adaptability and ability to meet need for cash	cash flow in and cash flow out, cash position at end of period

These are the financial statements produced by management when reporting to the external users of accounting information. Management uses similar financial statements for internal purposes but designed to provide much more information. This textbook will show examples in the subsequent chapters. If you have studied financial accounting previously, you will find that management accounting reports look quite different because they are produced for different purposes. Those different purposes relate to the variety of functions which management carries out. These functions are described in the next section.

1.3 Management functions

This section describes three management functions: planning; decision making; and control.

To be effective, each of these functions requires the application by management of communication and motivation skills. To ensure that the entity's operations are effective, those who work in the entity must be persuaded to identify with its objectives. Managers require the skills to motivate those for whom they are responsible, creating a sense of teamwork. The communication process is a vital part of creating a sense of teamwork and ensuring that all the players understand the role they play in achieving targets. They must also be motivated to want to achieve the targets. Management accounting has a particularly important role in that process of communication and motivation.

1.3.1 Planning

Managers have to plan ahead in making major decisions on sales, production and capital expenditure. Such planning is required for the immediate future and for the longer term. Businesses will typically make a detailed plan for the year ahead and a broader plan for a two to five-year period. Plans for sales require decisions on which products to sell, which markets to target, and what price to charge. Plans for production require decisions on the mix of resources, including labour, the source of raw materials or component parts, the level of stock of raw materials and finished goods to hold, and the most effective use of productive capacity. Plans for capital expenditure require a longer-term perspective, taking into account the expected life of the capital equipment acquired. As well as investing in fixed assets, the business will need working capital as a base for a new project. Decisions will be required on the level of working capital which is appropriate. If the enterprise is to move ahead, plans must lead to decisions.

1.3.2 Decision making

Decision making is central to the management of an enterprise. The manager of a profit-making business has to decide on the manner of implementation of the objectives of the business, at least one of which may well relate to allocating resources so as to maximise profit. A non-profit-making enterprise (such as a department of central or local government) will be making decisions on resource allocation so as to be economic, efficient and effective in its use of finance. All organisations, whether in the private sector or the public sector, take decisions which have financial implications. Decisions will be about resources, which may be people, products, services, or long-term and short-term investment. Decisions will also be about activities, including whether and how to undertake them. Most decisions will at some stage involve consideration of financial matters, particularly cost. Decisions may also have an impact on the working conditions and employment prospects of employees of the organisation, so that cost considerations may in making a final decision be weighed against social issues. Where the owners are different persons from the manager (for example, shareholders of a company as separate persons from the directors), the managers may face a decision where there is a potential conflict between their own interests and those of the owners. In such a situation cost considerations may be evaluated in the wider context of the responsibility of the managers to act in the best interests of the owners.

1.3.3 Control

Once a decision has been taken on any aspect of business activity, management must be in a position to control the activity and to have a view on whether the outcome is in accordance with the initial plans and with the objectives derived from those plans. This might involve identifying areas in the business where managers are in a position to control and account for costs and, in some cases, profit. To implement the control process, individual managers will require timely, relevant and accurate information about the part of the business for which they are responsible. Measurement, including cost measurement, is therefore an important ingredient in carrying out the control function.

The information provided to individual management is an essential part of the communication process within a business. For effective communication, there must be an organisational structure which reflects the responsibility and authority of management. Communication must cascade down through this organisational structure and the manner of communication must have regard for the motivation of those who are part of the control process. For control to be effective there must also be a reverse form of communication upwards so that management learn of the concerns of their staff. Motivation, expectations and personal relationships are all matters to be considered and to be harnessed effectively by the process of control.

<table>
<tr><td>**Activity 1.2**</td><td>*Think of an organised activity in which you participate at college or at home. To what extent does this activity involve planning, decision making and control? Who carries out the planning? Who makes the decision? Who exercises control?*</td></tr>
</table>

1.3.4 An organisation chart

Exhibit 1.1 presents a simple organisation chart showing various types of relationships in a manufacturing company. It illustrates line relationships within the overall finance function of the business, showing separately the management accounting and financial accounting functions. In most medium to large companies, the management accounting function will be a separate area of activity within the finance function. The term 'management accountant' is used here as a general term, but a brief perusal of the 'situations vacant' pages of any newspaper or professional magazine advertising accountancy posts would indicate the range of titles available and the versatility expected (*see* Case 1.1 at the end of the chapter). Two other functions have been shown in the chart as 'project accountant' and 'systems accountant'. Such specialists have specific roles in the internal accounting process within the enterprise which are relevant, although not exclusive, to the management accounting function.

The organisation chart shows individual people, each with a different job to do. Each person has a specialisation indicated by the job title, but he or she also has responsibilities to others higher in the structure and with authority over others lower in the structure. In the interests of the business as a whole, individuals must communicate up and down the line relationships and also across the horizontal relationships.

Taking one line relationship as an example, the finance director must make plans for the year ahead which are communicated to the financial controller. The financial controller must consult the systems accountant to ensure that the accounting systems are in place to record and communicate these plans within the organisation. The financial controller must also consult the project accountant to ensure that there is an evaluation of any capital investment aspects of the finance director's plans. The management accountant will prepare accounting statements showing how the plans will be implemented. The financial controller will bring together the details supplied by each person,

Exhibit 1.1
Part of an organisation chart for a manufacturing company, illustrating line relationships within the overall finance function of the business

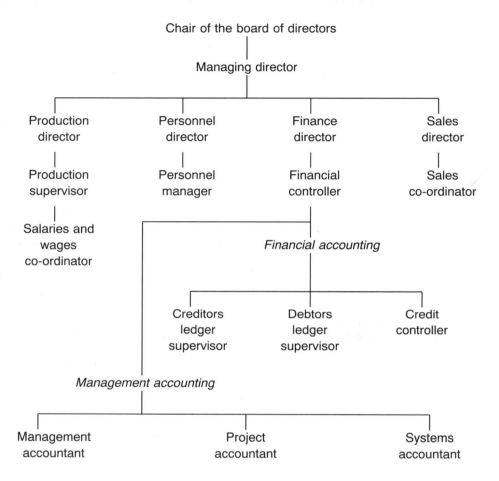

summarising and evaluating the main factors so that the results may be relayed to the finance director.

Horizontal relationships can be more difficult when communications channels are being planned, because there are so many potential combinations. It is a responsibility of management to decide which horizontal relationships have the greatest communication needs. Continuing the planning theme, the finance director will be expected to communicate the financial plan to the other members of the board of directors, who in turn will want to see that it fits the board's overall strategy and that it is compatible with the capacity of their particular areas of activity in the business. The financial plan will depend on the projected level of sales and will reflect strategy in production and personnel management. The plan will therefore need to be communicated to the sales co-ordinator, the production supervisor and the personnel manager. The sales co-ordinator, production supervisor and personnel manager will in turn provide feedback to the financial controller. The detailed analysis of the plans for the period, and the expected impact of those plans, will be evaluated by the management accountant, project accountant and systems accountant. They will report back to the financial controller who in turn will channel information to the finance director and the rest of the board of directors.

Activity 1.3

Think again about the organised activity which you identified in Activity 1.2. Prepare an organisation chart to include all the persons involved in the activity. Draw green lines with arrows to show the direction of communication. Draw red lines with arrows to show the direction of responsibility. What does the pattern of red and green lines tell you about communication and co-ordination in the organisation? What is the mechanism for motivation? Does it use the communication network?

1.3.5 Illustration of the interrelationships

The three management functions of planning, decision making and control are all interrelated in the overall purpose of making judgements and decisions. Exhibit 1.2 shows how a company owning a chain of shops supplying motor-cycle spares might go about the business of planning to open a new shop in the suburbs of a city. The shop will sell motor-cycle spares and will also provide advice on basic repair work which motor cyclists can safely undertake themselves.

Exhibit 1.2
Managing a decision on the location of a new business

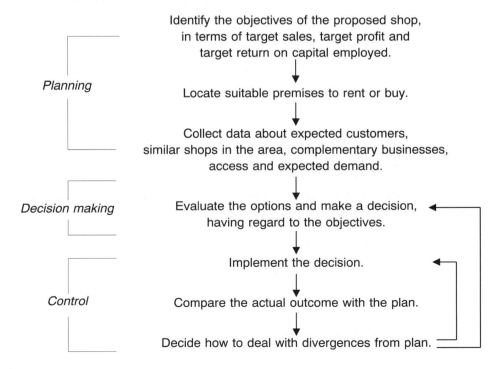

The shop's objectives will be concerned with achieving target sales and profit, and with making an adequate return on the capital invested in establishing the shop. Because of the desire to offer an advice service as well as selling spare parts, there will be non-financial objectives expressed in terms of customer satisfaction. These non-financial objectives will have indirect financial implications because satisfied customers will lead to increased sales and increased profits. The location of the shop, other types of shop close by, hours and days of opening and approach to stock control are all factors which are considered in the planning process. The choice of shop premises will depend upon the rent to be paid, any costs associated with the property, such as refurbishment and repairs, access for delivery and collection, and security. If the shop is to trade successfully there will need to be parking facilities, good access by road, and preferably public transport backup for those who need spare parts but whose motor cycles are too much in need of repair to be used as transport to the shop. Location requires careful consideration. Is it preferable to have the shop in a neighbourhood where a high proportion of residents own motor cycles or to locate it on a main road along which they travel to work? Evaluation for decision making purposes will require information about planned costs and revenues, although non-cost factors may also influence the decision.

Knowing the objectives and planning to meet those objectives will result in a decision, but the decision to start up the shop is not the end of the story. There has to be a continuing judgement as to whether the shop is successful and, eventually, there may be another decision on expanding or contracting the shop's activity. The continuing exercise of judgement will require a management accounting information outcome of the judgement. Any future decision to expand or contract will similarly include a requirement for information on planned costs and revenues.

Planning, decision making and control are shown on the diagram in exhibit 1.2 as separate parts of the total activity. Communication is shown by arrows from one stage to the next. Motivation is not easily shown on a diagram, so there is no attempt to do so, but it remains an important part of the communication process. The greater the number of communication trails built into the process, the more effective will be the understanding and motivation of those who carry out the work of the business at various levels of management. Ideally, the diagram would be criss-crossed with communication trails so that all participants are well informed.

Activity 1.4

> *Find again in your file the list which you prepared as the first activity of this chapter. Use that list to make a further list of the ways in which you think that management accounting could help the operations of the new shop selling motor-cycle spare parts. Read the next section and compare your answer with the text.*

1.4 Role of management accounting

In the previous illustration of planning where to open a new shop, there is work for the management accountant: first, in directing attention to accounting information which is relevant to making plans and taking the decision; second, in keeping the score for making judgements on the effectiveness of decisions; and third, in helping to solve problems which arise when the results of decision making do not work out as expected. So there are three roles that management accounting could play in this exercise that will be found to be general features of any decision making situation encountered by management. These are: directing attention; keeping the score; and solving problems.

1.4.1 Directing attention

Directing attention is a matter of being able to answer questions such as 'Who should take action?' or 'Whose responsibility is this loss?' or 'Who is to be congratulated on this favourable result?' Managers are busy people. They do not always have time to consider every detail of cost information about the operation or process they control. They look to the management accountant to direct their attention to the exceptional points of interest, be these good or bad. One way of carrying out that function is to highlight those costs which have departed from expectations – provided everyone understands at the outset what the expectations are. Words such as *fairness* and *timeliness* are almost bound to be involved in attention-directing processes.

Managers are also sensitive people. They do not like being blamed unjustly for something they see as being beyond their control. So the management accounting information has to be presented in such a way as to relate to the level of responsibility and degree of authority held by the manager concerned. On the other side of the coin, managers enjoy being praised for achievements and may welcome management accounting information which helps them to demonstrate their accountability for the resources entrusted to them.

1.4.2 Keeping the score

Score keeping is very much a case of being able to answer the questions 'How much?' or 'How many?' at any point in time. It requires careful record keeping and a constant monitoring of accounting records against physical quantities and measures of work done. The emphasis is on *completeness* but also on *fairness*. Questions such as 'How much?' may involve sharing, or allocating, costs. Accounting is concerned with allocations of various types, all concerned with aspects of *matching*. That could require matching costs to a time period, matching costs to an item of output, or matching costs against revenue for the period. For this matching process to be effective, information must be complete and the basis of allocation must be fair.

1.4.3   Solving problems

Solving problems involves a different type of question. It might be 'Why did that plan go well?' or 'Why did that action fail?' or 'Which of these three choices is the best to take?' In solving problems of this type, *relevance* is an important issue. People who have taken a decision are often reluctant to admit that it has not turned out as expected and may continue making worse mistakes unless someone points out that past events are of little or no relevance to decisions on future action. Where choices are concerned, those choices will involve people, each of whom may have different motives for preferring one choice above others. Management accounting information may have a role in providing an objective base for understanding the problem to be solved, even where at the end of the day a decision is based on non-accounting factors.

Some problems resemble making a jigsaw, or perhaps deciding which piece of the jigsaw has gone missing. Other problems are like solving crosswords where the answers must interlock, but some of the clues have been obliterated. In solving any problem of that type, logical reasoning is essential. No one can memorise the answer to every conceivable question which might arise. You will find that management accounting tests your powers of logical reasoning in that every problem you encounter will never entirely resemble the previous one.

Exhibit 1.3 illustrates a combination of the management accounting functions of directing attention, keeping the score and solving problems. It shows the cycle of profit planning and control, starting with the measurement of existing

Exhibit 1.3
Stages in the cycle of profit planning and control

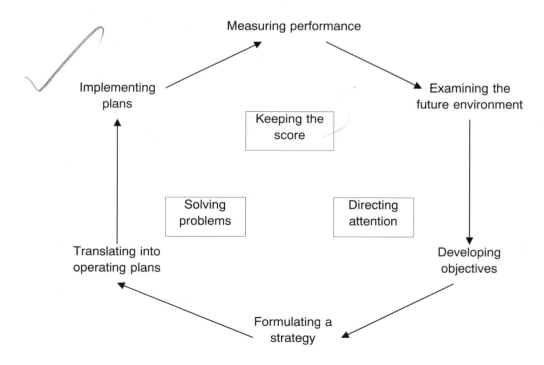

performance, which is an example of the score-keeping aspects of management accounting. From the measurement of existing performance the cycle moves through an examination of the future environment of the business, where techniques of economic analysis would be used. In developing objectives, the management accountant would provide accounting information on targets to be achieved. Formulating a strategy is a management task but the management accountant is then expected to provide detailed budgets which translate that strategy into operating plans. When the plans are implemented the management accountant must be ready to measure the results and compare these with the outcome expected when the operating plans were set. From there the cycle is repeated.

Activity 1.5	*Find your list of initial thoughts on what management accounting means. Having read this far, do you have the same views? Have you added anything new to your expectations? Have you removed something from your list which now seems overambitious?*

1.5 Judgements and decisions: case study illustrations

You are now presented with four cases in which there is a need for decisions and for judgements. After each case study there is a brief analysis of the decisions and judgements which will arise in each. You are then introduced to Fiona McTaggart who will explain what the management accountant can contribute to the decisions and judgements required.

Activity 1.6	*Read the text of the case study (set out in the box at the beginning of each case) and then make a note of the way in which you think management accounting may help each person. Compare your answer with the discussion which follows each case.*

> John Smith has taken early retirement at the age of 50 in order to develop his hobby of model shipbuilding into a full-time business. He has several models already assembled and has advertised in the model builders' weekly journal. Interested enquiries are starting to come in and he realises that he does not know what price to charge for the models.

John Smith needs to make a decision about pricing policy. That will involve many factors such as looking at what competitors are charging, having regard to the type of customer he expects to attract, and making sure that the price covers the cost of making and selling the models. After he has decided on a pricing policy he will need to measure its success by making judgements on the level of sales achieved and on the profitability of the product in relation to the capital he has invested in the business.

> Jennifer Jones has been operating a small hairdressing business for several months. She would like to expand by employing an assistant and by purchasing new dryers and washing equipment. She cannot decide whether the investment would be justified.

Jennifer Jones will be taking a longer-term view in making a decision about investing in new equipment. That equipment must generate cash flows over its expected life. Jennifer's decision to invest will take into account the number of customers she expects, the prices she is able to charge them, and the cost of paying the proposed assistant, projected ahead for several years. It will also take into account the percentage return expected on the capital invested in the equipment.

If she decides to invest, she will need to monitor the success of that investment by making judgements on the profitability of the product in relation to the capital she has invested in it, and on whether the return on the investment is adequate in the light of having expanded the business.

> Central Ltd is a small business manufacturing and assembling plastic components for use in car manufacture. It has been drawn to the attention of the financial controller that one of the plastic components could be purchased elsewhere at a price less than the cost of manufacture. What action should the production director take?

The production director of Central Ltd needs to decide whether to continue manufacturing the component within the business or to cease production and buy the component elsewhere. To make that decision requires a knowledge of the full cost of manufacture and reassurance that the cost has been calculated correctly. It also depends on the relative aims and objectives of the financial controller and the production director, who may be in conflict and who may be putting their own point of view at the expense of the overall good of the business. Costs of ceasing manufacture will also need to be taken into account. Beyond the accounting costs there are human costs and business risks. Is there alternative employment for the staff released from this internal production? Will there be redundancy costs? Is it safe to rely on this outside supplier? What are the risks to Central Ltd if supplies dry up?

Whatever decision is taken, there will be a subsequent need for judgement in monitoring the effectiveness of the decision and its impact on profitability. In the decision and in the subsequent judgements of the effectiveness of that decision, there will be a need for communication and interaction between the financial controller and the production director.

> Ann Brown is a hospital manager having responsibility for ensuring that the cost of treatment is recovered in full by invoicing the patient or the appropriate organisation which is financing the patient care. Pricing policy is dictated at a more senior level.

Ann Brown has no direct decision making responsibility but the information she collates and the records she keeps, in relation to identifying costs and charging these costs to patients, will be used in the decision making process at a more senior level. It will also be used as a tool of judgement on the effectiveness of the hospital's cost control and charging policy for the various treatments and services provided. In this case the criteria for the judgement may be rather different in that there may be less emphasis on profitability and more on the quality of service in relation to the cost of providing that service.

1.6 Case studies explored

These four cases indicate areas where management accounting could serve as a tool to provide information which is relevant to decision making and to the formation of judgement at all levels within an organisation. Hopefully, you will have recognised some situations in each case where accounting information will be of help.

The organisation chart in exhibit 1.1 includes an expert management accountant. It has already been explained that most medium to large companies include specialist management accountants on their staff. However, from time to time a consultant may be called in to give a wider and more frank appraisal than might be feasible for a paid employee. In this and subsequent chapters you will meet Fiona McTaggart, a freelance management accountant, who is prepared to offer advice on a variety of case study situations. In practice, the management accountant within the organisation might provide similar advice, but this text uses the management consultant so that her comments are not unduly constrained by existing limitations within the business.

Fiona now explains what she could offer from her management accounting experience in each of these four case study situations. Read her explanations and in each case identify the places where she is hinting at directing attention, keeping the score, or solving problems.

1.6.1 Case study: John Smith

FIONA: *John Smith needs to know the cost of the models he is making. That sounds easy – he has a note of the money he has spent on materials for the models and he has detailed plans which tell him exactly how much material is used for each one. But that's not the end of the story. John puts a tremendous amount of time into the model building. He says it is all enjoyment to him, so he doesn't treat that time as a cost, but I have to persuade him that making the models represents a lost opportunity to do something else. The cost of his time could be measured in terms of that lost opportunity.*

Then there are his tools. He has a workshop at the end of the garage and it's stacked high with tools. They don't last for ever and the cost of depreciation should be spread over the models produced using those tools. He needs heat to keep the workshop warm, power for the electric tools, and packing material for the models sent in response to a postal enquiry. He has paid for an advertisement in the model builders' magazine and there is stationery, as well as postage and telephone calls, to consider.

Costs never seem to end once you start to add them up. It can all be a bit depressing, but it is much more depressing to sell something and then find out later that you've made a loss. I could help John work out his costs and make sure the price he charges will leave a profit so that he builds up his investment in the business.

Making the decision on selling price would not be the end of my involvement. I would continue to measure costs each month and compare these with sales. I would give John reports on profit and cash flow and warnings if working capital was starting to build up. If he gives credit he'll need to keep an eye on the level of debtors, and there will always be a stock, either of raw materials or finished goods or both. Trade creditors will fund some of the stock but working capital mismanagement has been the downfall of many a business which tried to expand too fast.

In advising John Smith, Fiona McTaggart will direct attention to the costs which are relevant to the pricing decision, she will keep the score by calculating profits once the business is in production, and will help solve problems by monitoring the working capital position.

1.6.2 Case study: Jennifer Jones

FIONA: *Jennifer Jones needs help in taking a longer-term perspective. To assess the profitability of the new equipment and the assistant, I'll first of all need Jennifer to tell me how many customers she can realistically expect and what she will be able to charge them. I'll need those estimates over the life of the equipment, which will probably be around five years.*

Once I have the estimates of cash inflows from customers over the five years, I can set against that the cash outflows in terms of payments for all the costs of providing the service, including the wages of the intended assistant. Then I will apply to those cash flows a factor which makes an allowance for uncertainty in the future and also takes account of the rate of interest Jennifer could earn if she invested her money in financial markets rather than hairdryers. I'll then compare the expected cash flows with the initial cost of acquiring the equipment, to see whether it's a good idea. Of course, if Jennifer gets the cash flow estimates wrong, then the answer won't mean very much, but that's not my problem.

If Jennifer makes the decision to invest, I'll be needed after that to monitor the success of the project. I can measure the cash flows after the event and give an indication of how well they met expectations. I can compare the cost of the assistant with the revenue generated by the extra work available.

Problems might arise if there is a change of fashion and everyone decides they prefer short straight hair. That could cause chaos in the hairdressing industry and might make some of the washing equipment surplus to requirements. There is a great temptation in such situations to hang on to the past because of the cash which was sunk into it. That's often the wrong thing to do because it brings disaster ever closer. It may be better to cut off the activity altogether and limit the losses. I can give a dispassionate view based on cost rather than sentiment and emotion.

Fiona McTaggart will provide information which is relevant to the investment decision by drawing attention to the cost in comparison with the expected cash inflows. She will keep the score on the cash inflows and outflows once the project is established and she will help in problem solving by evaluating the losses arising if an unsuccessful project continues in operation.

1.6.3   Case study: Central Ltd

FIONA: *Central Ltd is an example of the football game situation where sometimes the players in a team forget that they are on the same side. I saw a game last week when the home team won on the away team's own goals. The same thing could happen for Central. When people have a defined role in an organisation they can be too closely involved in their own work to see the bigger picture. The financial controller sees the costs of manufacturing and assembling the parts and has identified a cost saving based on a simple comparison. It's hard for the production director to fight the logic of that argument but I can see he's worried.*

What I can do is turn his worries into cost arguments which should be considered alongside the direct make-or-buy comparison. The costs may not be capable of such precise calculation but I'll give estimates of the risk to the business and the sensitivity of the situation. I'll give particular attention to the quality issues and to the risk of disruption of supply. It's more than likely that the financial controller and the production director will still not agree even when they have the information, so I'll present my information in a way which the board of directors can relate to the overall objectives and strategy of the company. Whatever decision is taken, I'll establish a monthly reporting system, to be operated by the financial controller, which will give the earliest possible warning of whether the decision remains in the best interests of the company.

Fiona McTaggart will provide information directly relevant to the make-or-buy decision. She will help in problem solving by setting out the information in such a way that others in the organisation can be satisfied that a decision will be in the best interests of the company as a whole. Finally, she will establish a score-keeping system which continues to monitor the effectiveness of the decision taken.

1.6.4   Case study: Ann Brown

FIONA: *Ann Brown doesn't have direct decision making responsibility. She is a smaller cog in a large machine. However, the efficiency with which she carries out her job will have a direct impact on the performance of the hospital and will have an impact on future decision making at a more senior level. Charging out to patients the cost of their care is a difficult matter and requires very careful record keeping. Patients who are ill don't question their treatment at the time, but when they are convalescing they have lots of time to look through the bill, especially if the medical insurance company is asking questions. Some patients may be paid for through the health service but at the end of the line there is a fundholder who wants to ensure that the funds are used to best advantage.*

The cost of, say, major surgery can be the least difficult to work out because the time in theatre will be known, the staff on duty will be listed and their salary costs can be apportioned over the time taken. But when the patient is back on the ward recovering, there have to be records kept of the type of nursing care, the specialist equipment and supplies, food costs and the hotel-type services associated with providing a bed. Then there have to be charges to cover the overhead costs of heating, maintaining and cleaning the buildings.

Ann Brown needs an effective recording system which is accurate in terms of care for each patient but is not so cumbersome to apply that the nurses' time is entirely taken up with clerical recording. Many costs can be applied to patient care on a predetermined charge-out rate based on previous experience. A computerised cost recording system, with a carefully thought out coding system for each cost, is essential. Of the four cases I have considered here, this will be the most time-consuming to set up, but it will give satisfaction all round when it is working and seen to be fair to patients in terms of individual charge-out costs as well as giving the hospital reassurance that all costs are being recovered.

The cost recording system will provide information for the decision making process in relation to future pricing policy and also for the more difficult decisions as to which specialised medical functions at the hospital are cost effective and which functions do not fully cover costs. There are bound to be problems within the hospital if decisions are needed on expanding or cutting back. Everyone hates the accountant at those times, but at least I can design a system which provides an objective starting point even though non-financial factors are eventually the determining factor.

Fiona McTaggart is describing here the score-keeping aspects of management accounting. That score keeping will be used as information for the decision making process and may also have a problem-solving aspect if disputes arise where medical decisions have a cost impact.

1.6.5 Comment

These case study discussions have given some insight into how the management accountant has a role to play in contributing to the management of an organisation. Three general themes have been explored, namely, keeping the score, directing attention and solving problems. The case studies have shown that within each of these three themes there are many different approaches to be taken, depending on the circumstances. By way of illustration of the scope of management accounting activity, Fiona McTaggart has the following list of special studies she has undertaken, as an adviser on management accounting, where problem-solving skills have been required:

- product cost comparisons
- evaluation of product profitability
- alternative choices of resource usage
- asset management
- labour relations
- capital investment
- investigation on behalf of customer for contract pricing purposes.

All of these, and other problem situations, will be encountered in subsequent chapters. This chapter ends with a warning that there will be some new terminology to learn and a summary of the role of the management accountant.

1.7 Matching the management accounting approach to the situation

It should be apparent, through reading these case studies, that there is no single management accounting system which may be applied to all circumstances. In that respect, you will find management accounting more diverse in its nature, and sometimes more puzzling, than financial accounting where there is a well-defined framework of statutes and accounting standards. For management accounting there will be a choice of approach which in each instance will depend on matching the features of the problem to the most suitable accounting approach. The management accounting approach is therefore conditioned by (or contingent upon) the situation to be dealt with. In the academic literature, this view of matching the technique to the needs is referred to as 'contingency theory'. The academic debate on contingency theory need not detain us here, but throughout the following chapters you will find repeatedly the concept that the management accounting approach is dependent on the purpose to be served. That concept will be reinforced by the case studies presented by Fiona McTaggart, who will show the way in which the formal technique comes to life when applied to a specific situation.

1.8 Terminology of management accounting

Management accounting is not a difficult subject but to understand it requires a logical mind. To be successful, methods of management accounting must reflect a reasoned approach to a judgement on a situation problem and a logical basis for making decisions. If reason and logic are strong, then it should not be difficult to understand the approach.

Unfortunately, as with most specialist subjects, management accounting has grown a language of its own, which is helpful to those who work closely with the subject but can sometimes cause problems at the outset for newcomers. This chapter has avoided using specialist terminology relying on intuitive ideas. However, progress in understanding management accounting will be limited without the use of that terminology, so subsequent chapters will introduce the technical terms, each of which will be explained. End-of-chapter questions will help you to test your understanding of new terminology before you move on to each new chapter.

1.9 Summary

This chapter has introduced three functions of management:

1 planning;
2 decision making; and
3 control;

and three roles that management accounting plays in helping to fulfil these functions:

1 directing attention;
2 keeping the score; and
3 solving problems.

Four case studies have been examined in which the role of management accounting is explained and illustrated. Those case studies have demonstrated the importance of matching the management accounting technique to the situation. In the remaining chapters of this textbook you will meet the various techniques that have been developed in management accounting for keeping the score, directing attention and solving the problems.

Accounting relies on words as well as numbers, and therefore you will need to look out for, and understand the meaning of, the language of management accounting.

Notes and references

1   AAA (1966), *A Statement of Basic Accounting Theory*, American Accounting Association, Evanston, Illinois, p. 1.

Further reading

CIMA, *Management Accounting Official Terminology*, Chartered Institute of Management Accountants (1996).

Emmanuel, C. R., Otley, D. T. and Merchant, K. (1991), *Accounting for Management Control*, Chapman & Hall.

Horngren, C. T., Foster, G. and Datar, S. (1993), *Cost Accounting: A Managerial Emphasis*, Prentice Hall.

Wilson, R. M. S. and Chua, W. F. (1992), *Managerial Accounting: Method and Meaning*, Chapman & Hall.

Self-testing on the chapter

1   Give four types of management decision in a profit-oriented organisation where management accounting is likely to be useful.

2   Give four types of management decision in a non-profit-oriented organisation where management accounting is likely to be useful.

3 Explain why management decisions will normally require more than a management accounting input alone.

4 Explain why it is unlikely that a management decision could be taken without having any regard whatever to management accounting information.

5 Explain, giving a suitable example in each case, what is meant by the management functions of:

(a) planning;
(b) control; and
(c) communication and motivation.

6 Explain, giving a suitable example in each case, how management accounting may serve the purpose of:

(a) directing attention;
(b) keeping the score; and
(c) solving problems.

Activities for study groups

1 Form a study group of four to six persons who are to act out the role of the finance director and related staff on the accounting team of a company which is planning to open a new supermarket chain at an out-of-town location. Give a ten-minute presentation to the rest of the class explaining the major issues you will be expected to deal with in making a contribution to the decision and the subsequent monitoring of that decision.

2 Form a study group of four to six persons who are to negotiate the development of a new production line to process canned peas. The canned peas will replace an existing product, canned carrots. Half of the team will argue on behalf of the canned peas while the other half will argue on behalf of the canned carrots. Give a ten-minute presentation to the class (five minutes for each half of the team) explaining how management accounting information will help you to justify the decision you propose and to monitor the implementation of the decision.

Case study

Case 1.1
Set out here is a selection of advertisements for posts in management accounting. Read the text of the advertisement and relate the specified requirements to the three management accounting roles set out in this chapter, namely:

(a) directing attention;
(b) keeping the score; and
(c) solving problems.

GROUP FINANCIAL CONTROLLER
(company recently listed on the Stock Exchange)

Responsibilities will include monthly management reports, quarterly and annual accounts, budgets, treasury and foreign currency risk management, and systems development. The ability to manage, motivate and delegate in an established team is important.

FINANCIAL CONTROLLER
(company selling accounting software)

Reporting to the board of directors, you will be responsible for business plans, budgets and management reporting, as well as the preparation of statutory accounts and interim reporting. In addition you will be accountable for short-term cash management, systems development, company secretarial duties and building commercial relationships.

HEAD OF MANAGEMENT ACCOUNTS
(the finance office of a university)

You will be responsible for the setting, monitoring, control and reporting on budgets and the regular production of management accounts. In addition, you will ensure the provision of a comprehensive payroll service and be responsible for arranging and accounting for capital finance.

MANAGEMENT ACCOUNTANT
(a merchant banking company)

Working as part of a team covering a number of profit centres, you will be playing a key part in assisting with the decision making and in contributing to future pricing policies.

MANAGER – FINANCIAL APPRAISAL
(a property company)

Reporting to the head of finance and heading up a team of four, your varied brief will include leading projects, advising on key transactions including joint ventures and providing detailed analysis on property investment proposals. You will additionally be responsible for managing and motivating your team.

SYSTEMS ACCOUNTANT
(company in retail sector)

You will:
- Play a leading role in the development and integration of the Group's financial systems.
- Continually develop the financial information to reflect the business in a changing environment.
- Integrate operating and financial systems to ensure compatibility and accuracy of data and compliance with accounting standards.
- Extend existing functions and develop future strategy in information technology to serve business needs.
- Implement and gain full acceptance of changes and enhancements, providing training where required.

Chapter 2

Classification of costs

<table>
<tr><td>

</td><td>

After studying this chapter you should be able to:

1 **Analyse the behaviour of costs and revenues over a range of activity levels.**

2 **Define and explain each of the cost terms contained in the chapter.**

3 **Explain why cost classification for planning and control differs from cost classification for decision making.**

4 **Suggest ways of classifying costs in practical situations.**

</td></tr>
</table>

2.1 Definition of a cost

The cost of an item of input or output may be analysed in terms of two measurements:

1 a physical quantity measurement

multiplied by

2 a price measurement.

Where a production process uses 100 kg of material which has a price of £5 per kg, the cost is £500. Where a production process uses 200 hours of labour time at a rate of £3 per hour, the cost is £600. That may appear to be a statement of the obvious, but the breaking down of cost into physical quantity and price is frequently essential for the application of management accounting methods where the physical flow of inputs and outputs may sometimes be recorded separately from the unit price. The analysis of the separate elements of quantity and price will be dealt with in more detail in Chapter 7.

2.2 The need for cost classification

Cost classification systems in practice are as varied as the businesses they serve. In Chapter 1 the functions of management are described as: planning, decision making, and control. For purposes of classification it is convenient to take planning and control as a combined function because the classifications required by each are similar. For decision making, particular care has to be taken to use classifications of cost which are relevant to the decision under consideration.

This chapter will first explain three types of cost classification:

1 fixed costs and variable costs;

2 direct costs and indirect costs; and

3 product costs and period costs.

Each of these cost classifications will then be related to the management functions of planning, decision making and control. It is important to emphasise here that the three types of cost classification are *different ways* of looking at costs. Any particular item of cost could have more than one of these classifications attached to it, depending on the purpose of the classifications being used.

Finally, the chapter will explain the importance of correct coding of costs in a computer-based system, and will show how costs are selected and reported according to the unit of the business for which information is required.

2.3 The meaning of 'activity'

The word 'activity' will be used in this textbook in a general manner to refer to any measure of the physical operations of the organisation. It could be measured by, for example, units of output produced by a manufacturing business, units of sales by a retail store, hours worked by employees in an advertising agency, miles driven by a road haulage business, households served by a refuse disposal company, students taught in a school, or passengers carried by an airline. (In Chapter 11, the word 'activity' takes on a particularly significant meaning in the context of 'activity-based costing', a phrase coined to acknowledge that management accounting is most effective when it is most closely linked to the activity of the business.)

2.4 Variable costs and fixed costs

Costs behave in different ways as the level of activity changes. Some costs increase in direct proportion to the increased level of activity. These are called *variable costs*. Some costs do not vary, whatever the level of activity. These are called *fixed costs*. Some show elements of both features. These are called *semi-variable costs*.

2.4.1 Variable costs

Exhibit 2.1 shows the costs of clay used by a pottery company for various levels of output of clay vases for garden ornaments. It may be seen from the data in exhibit 2.1 that the clay required for each vase costs £10.

Exhibit 2.1
Costs of clay related to activity levels

Output (number of vases)	100	200	300
Cost (£s)	1,000	2,000	3,000

The *total cost* increases by £10 for every vase produced, and is described as *variable*. The *unit cost* is £10 per vase and is *constant*. Sometimes students find it a little confusing at this point to decide whether they should be thinking about the *total cost* or the *unit cost*. It may help you to think of yourself as the owner of the business manufacturing the vases. If you were the owner, you would be most interested in the *total cost* because that shows how much finance you will need in order to carry on production. You will only recover the cost of buying the clay when you sell the finished goods to the customers. Until then you need finance to buy the clay. The more you produce, the more finance you will need. If you approach the bank manager to help you finance the business you will be asked 'How much do you need?', a question which is answered by reference to *total cost*.

Exhibit 2.2 shows, in the form of a graph, the information contained in exhibit 2.1. It plots activity level (number of vases produced) on the horizontal axis and total cost on the vertical axis. The graph reinforces the idea that the total cost is a variable cost. It shows a straight line moving upwards to the right. The fact that the line is straight, rather than curving, means that the total cost increases in direct proportion to the increase in activity (that is, total cost increases by £10 for every unit of output).

Exhibit 2.2
Graph of variable cost measured as activity increases

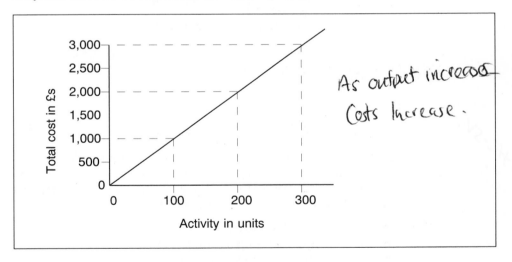

Examples of variable costs are:

- materials used to manufacture a unit of output or to provide a type of service
- labour costs of manufacturing a unit of output or providing a type of service
- commission paid to a salesperson
- fuel used by a haulage company.

Definition

A *variable cost* is one which varies directly with changes in the level of activity, over a defined period of time.

2.4.2 Fixed costs

Exhibit 2.3 sets out the cost to the pottery company of renting a building in which to house its kiln and other production facilities. It may be seen from the data in exhibit 2.3 that the *total cost* remains *fixed* at £3,000 irrespective of how many vases are produced. The *unit cost* is *decreasing* as output increases, as shown in exhibit 2.4, because the fixed cost is spread over more vases. Here again, it is more important usually to think about *total cost* because unless the pottery can pay its rent it cannot continue in business. This type of cost is therefore described as a *fixed cost*. The cost of rent is shown in graphical form in exhibit 2.5.

Exhibit 2.3
Costs of rental related to activity levels

Output (number of vases)	100	200	300
Cost (£s)	3,000	3,000	3,000

Exhibit 2.4
Unit cost of the pottery rental

Output (number of vases)	Unit cost (£)
100	30
200	15
300	10

A fixed cost is by definition unchanged over a period of time, but it may vary in the longer term. Rent, for example, might be fixed for a period of one year, but reviewed at the end of every year with the possibility of an increase being imposed by the landlord. Other examples of fixed costs are:

- salary paid to a supervisor
- advertising in the trade journals
- business rates paid to the local authority
- depreciation of machinery calculated on the straight line basis.

Definition

A *fixed cost* is one which is not affected by changes in the level of activity, over a defined period of time.

Exhibit 2.5
Illustration of fixed cost

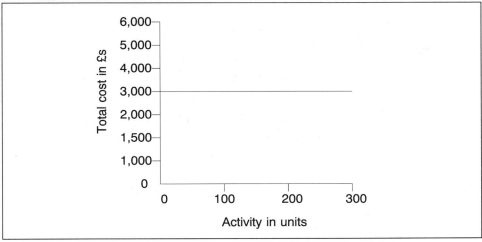

2.4.3 Semi-variable costs

Exhibit 2.6 sets out the costs incurred by a telephone sales company which pays a fixed rental of £2,000 per month and a call charge of £1 per telephone sale call. This total cost has a mixed behaviour, which may be described as *semi-variable*. It has a fixed component of £2,000 and a variable component of £1 per telephone sale.

The graph of this semi-variable cost is shown in exhibit 2.7. The fixed cost is shown by the point where the line of the graph meets the vertical axis. The variable component is shown by the slope of the graph. The fixed component of £2,000 is shown as the point where the line of the graph meets the vertical axis. The slope of the graph shows the total cost increasing by £1 for every extra unit of activity.

Exhibit 2.6
Telephone rental costs

Activity (number of calls)	100	200	300
Cost (£s)	2,100	2,200	2,300

Examples of semi-variable cost are:

● office salaries where there is a core of long-term secretarial staff plus employment of temporary staff when activity levels rise
● maintenance charges where there is a fixed basic charge per year plus a variable element depending on the number of call-outs per year.

Exhibit 2.7
Illustration of semi-variable cost

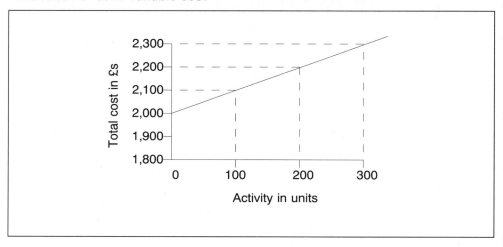

2.4.4 Importance of the time period chosen

The extent to which a cost varies with activity depends on the period of time chosen. In manufacturing picnic tables, the cost of the plastic frame and the table top are variable costs, as is the labour cost of assembly. The annual rent of the warehouse where the tables are assembled is a fixed cost for the year, but will be a *stepped* cost over a period of several years if there is a rent review each year. Exhibit 2.8 shows a *stepped* cost of rent increasing annually over five years. The rental starts at £1,000 and increases by £100 each year.

Exhibit 2.8
Stepped cost for five-year period, with annual increase

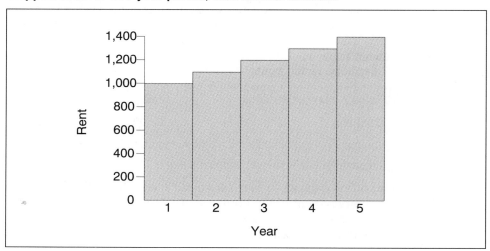

The graph in exhibit 2.8 is different from those shown earlier in the chapter because the horizontal axis measures time rather than activity. However, it is also possible to estimate the activity levels expected over the five-year period. Whatever the expected activity level, the relationship between total cost and activity level will be more complex than the simple fixed, variable and semi-variable relationships already shown. For the purposes of the rest of this textbook all the costs you meet will be simplified as fixed, variable or semi-variable, within a defined period of time.

Activity 2.1

> *At this point, be sure that you are comfortable with the idea of variable costs, fixed costs and semi-variable costs. These will appear frequently in later chapters and it is important to understand them. If you are not familiar with graphs, go back through the section and try to draw the graph from the data presented. If you are familiar with graphs, make up some cost patterns and plot these on graph paper to confirm that you can link the graphic presentation to the pattern of numbers.*

2.5 Direct costs and indirect costs

The costs of a business activity may also be classified as direct costs and indirect costs. Direct costs are those which are directly related to the activity, while indirect costs are incurred in respect of all activities of the type and have to be allocated on a basis of sharing which is as fair as can be devised.

The word 'activity' is used here in a very broad sense. It could refer to a major operating division of the organisation, a department within a larger segment of the business, an individual working within a department, or a unit of output which could be a product or a service.

The first question you should ask, whenever you see the words 'direct' or 'indirect' is 'Direct or indirect in which respect?' This will remind you that the words have no meaning in isolation. An item which is a direct cost for a department could be an indirect cost for the units of output produced by the department. Take the example of electricity consumed in a department. If the department has a meter, then the amount of electricity used may be identified directly with the department. However, if all items produced within the department share the benefit of the electricity supply, then the cost will need to be shared among them as an indirect cost so far as products are concerned.

Definitions

The definition of direct and indirect costs depends on the purpose for which the cost will be used.

Direct costs are directly traceable to an activity of the business for which costs are to be determined.

Indirect costs are spread over a number of activities of the business for which costs are to be determined.

Fiona McTaggart gives an example of how she would distinguish direct costs and indirect costs in a particular situation.

FIONA: *I was working recently with a publishing firm about to bring out a new children's magazine series based on a popular cartoon programme. The publisher had already incurred market research costs in respect of the new magazine series and it looked like a good idea.*

The magazine is to be produced in a department where there are already ten other magazines in production. Writers work freelance and are paid fees on a piecework basis for each item they write. Graphic artists are employed full-time in the department, producing designs and drawings for all the magazines. Once the magazine production is completed, it is sent to external printing at another company which charges on the basis of volume of output. I was asked to help design a monthly cost analysis statement for the new magazine.

I pointed out that some costs were easy to identify because they were directly traceable to the product. Working back from the end of the story, the external printer's charge would be a direct cost of the new magazine because it is directly related to that specific output. The work of the freelance writers is also a direct cost of the new magazine because it is easy to make a list of fees paid to them in respect of particular work on the new magazine.

The work of the graphic artists is an indirect cost so far as the product is concerned, because their time is spread over all magazines produced. They do not keep detailed records of every design they produce. Many designs can be used in more than one magazine title. I suggested that a fair basis of allocation would be to share their cost across all magazines in proportion to the number of illustrated pages in each. That turned out to be a bad idea because some illustrated pages may contain full-size pictures while others may contain a quarter-page design, so it was eventually decided to apply a factor to each page depending on whether it was fully illustrated or partly illustrated.

Although the graphic artists are an indirect cost so far as the product is concerned, they are a direct cost for the department, because they don't work in any other department. I suggested that the full cost of the new magazine would only be known when it was also carrying its share of the direct costs and indirect costs of the department as a whole. Direct costs for the department could include heat and light, maintenance of the operating equipment, machine depreciation and supervisor's salary, while indirect costs could include a share of administration costs and a share of rent and business rates. It is not easy to ensure that all costs are included for purposes of planning and control.

In her explanation, Fiona has repeatedly used the words 'direct' and 'indirect', but at the start of the explanation she is referring to the direct and indirect costs of the new magazine while at the end she is referring to the direct and indirect costs of the whole department. The departmental costs, taken together, are all indirect costs so far as the *products* of the department are concerned.

Activity 2.2

Think of some activity observed in your everyday life where costs are involved. (It could, for example, be travelling on a bus, watching the sales assistant in a shop, or asking the television repair service to call.) Write down five types of cost which might be incurred in that activity. How would you decide which types of cost are fixed and which are variable?

2.6 Product costs and period costs

Another way of looking at the cost of a business activity is to distinguish product costs and period costs. Product costs are those which are identified with goods or services intended for sale to customers. These costs belong to the products and stay with them until they are sold. If goods remain unsold, or work-in-progress remains incomplete, then the product costs stay with the unsold goods or work-in-progress under the heading of stock. Period costs are those costs which are treated as expenses of the period and are not carried as part of the stock value.

Definitions

Product costs are those costs associated with goods or services purchased, or produced, for sale to customers.

Period costs are those costs which are treated as expenses in the period in which they are incurred.

In a manufacturing organisation, all manufacturing costs are regarded as product costs and all costs beyond the completion of manufacturing, such as administration and selling costs, are regarded as period costs. In a service organisation, all costs incurred in providing the service, up to the point of completion of the service, would be product costs, while any costs incurred outside the service activity, such as advertising the service or collecting cash from customers afterwards, would be a period cost. The distinction can be important for external reporting, where there may be an accounting standard which requires that only manufacturing costs are applied to unsold stock. The distinction is preserved in management accounting on occasions where the aim is to calculate the total cost of the product.

However, for many decision-making purposes the period costs are seen as being non-controllable in the short term, so that attention may focus on the product costs.

Chapter 9 deals with the management accounting aspects of this subject further under the heading of 'absorption costing and variable costing'.

2.7 Costs for planning and control

For planning and control, the approaches to classification described in sections 2.4, 2.5 and 2.6 could all be useful, depending on the circumstances. Set out on the left-hand side of exhibit 2.9 are two planning questions and two control questions which might be asked by management. In the right-hand column there is an indication of the cost classification which is appropriate to that particular question.

Exhibit 2.9
Cost classification for planning and control problems

Planning question	*Cost classification which may be appropriate*
What is the cost impact of a change in levels of production over a period of time?	Fixed and variable costs
What is the cost effect of planning operations in a particular location?	Costs directly and indirectly associated with the location

Control question	Cost classification which may be appropriate
Are the costs of each product within the targets set?	Costs directly and indirectly associated with the product
Is the value of stock stated correctly?	Period and product costs

The managers of the business set the questions but the management accountant chooses the most appropriate classification of costs to provide answers to the questions. Depending on the question asked, fixed and variable, direct and indirect, or person and product classifications may all be important.

Activity 2.3

Imagine you are the manager of a departmental store in the centre of town. Write down one planning question and one control question which you might ask in respect of information about costs.

2.8 Costs for decision making

For decision making purposes, the key word is *relevance*. The costs used in the decision making process must only be those which are relevant to the decision. In this respect, the classification into variable and fixed costs is particularly important. That is because, in the short term, little can be done by a business in relation to fixed costs, so that the need for a decision may focus attention on the variable costs. Fiona McTaggart explains how she would use such a classification to present information for decision making.

FIONA: *The Garden Decor Company is thinking of making two garden ornaments, gnomes and herons. The variable cost of making a gnome would be £12 and the variable cost of making a heron would be £7. Market research indicates that garden ornaments of similar types are selling in the shops for around £10 each. Output up to the level of 20,000 garden ornaments, in any combination of output of each, would lead to fixed rental and insurance costs of £3,000.*

My recommendation would be that the company should not even contemplate the garden gnomes because the expected selling price of £10 will not cover the variable cost of £12 per unit. The company will make a loss as it produces each item. The selling price of the herons would cover their variable cost and make a contribution of £3 each (£10 minus £7) to the fixed cost. If they can sell 1,000 herons or more, the £3 contribution from each will cover the £3,000 additional fixed costs and any further herons sold will give a profit clear of fixed costs.

Fiona has used the word 'contribution' in this discussion. You can probably guess its meaning from the context in which it is used, but you will meet the word again as a technical term in Chapter 9.

2.9 Cost coding

We will now look in more detail at an approach to cost recording that allows classification systems to be applied accurately and speedily.

Most costing systems are computerised. For these, the coding is critical to effective use of the cost information. Computers allow selective retrieval of information quickly, but only if the coding is correctly designed to suit the needs of the organisation.

A code number must be unique to the cost which it identifies. The code should be as short as possible and it is preferable to have a code structure which creates consistent images in the mind of the user. The code may be entirely numerical or may have a mixture of letters and numbers (an *alphanumeric* code).

The design of the coding system and the assignment of code numbers should be carried out centrally so that the system is consistent throughout the organisation. The code system may have built into it the structure of the organisation, so that the code starts by specifying a major unit of the organisation and gradually narrows down to a particular cost in a particular location. Here is Fiona McTaggart to explain a cost coding system she has recently designed.

FIONA: *This company, producing and selling books, has 15 different departments. Within each department there are up to six cost centres. There are three different types of book – reference, academic and leisure. The list of costs to be coded contains 350 items, down to detail such as bindings purchased for special strength in reference works.*

The coding is based on a six-digit alphanumeric code. The department is represented by the first digit of the code, taking one of the letters A to Z (except that the company decided not to use letters I and O because of the confusion with numerical digits). Each cost centre has a letter code, which appears in the second position. (Again the letters I and O are not used.) The next digit is the letter R, A or L depending on whether the book is reference, academic or leisure. The last three digits are numbers taken from a cost code list which covers all 350 items but which could in principle expand up to 999 items in total. Within those three digits, there is further grouping of costs by code – for example, 100 to 199 are reserved for fixed asset items; 200 to 399 are various types of material cost; 400 to 599 are various types of labour cost; 600 to 899 are a whole range of production overhead costs; and 900 to 999 are administration and selling costs.

So, under code number HCA246, it would be possible to find the cost of paper used in printing an academic textbook on the new printing machine. Working backwards through the code, item 246 is paper, letter A is an academic book, letter C denotes the new printing machine (which is itself a cost centre) and letter H indicates the printing department.

Activity 2.4	*Create a six-digit coding system which would allow you to classify all the items of expenditure you make in a year. (You will need to write down the items of expenditure first of all and then look for patterns which could be represented in a code.) To test your code, ask a friend to write down three transactions, converting them to code. Then use your knowledge of the code to tell your friend what the three transactions were.*

2.10 Cost selection and reporting

Once the costs have been coded, a computerised accounting system can be programmed to retrieve the costs in a systematic manner for reporting purposes. The code structure must include alphanumeric characters that cover each of the purposes for which cost is required.

The code structure outlined by Fiona McTaggart above would allow classification of cost by reference to items of output and would allow classification of cost by reference to cost centre. A cost centre is only one of the units into which an organisation is subdivided for cost collection purposes. Two others are a profit centre and an investment centre. The chapter ends with definitions of the following terms that will be encountered in subsequent chapters in relation to cost selection and reporting: cost of a unit of output; cost centre; profit centre; and investment centre.

2.10.1 Cost of producing a unit of output

Product costs have been defined earlier in the chapter as those costs associated with goods or services purchased, or produced, for sale to customers.

For manufactured products it is usual to collect costs together in a statement of the type shown in exhibit 2.10. There is one term in this statement which has not yet been defined in this chapter: that is the term 'production overhead'. It is defined as indicated in exhibit 2.10, consisting of indirect material, indirect labour and other indirect costs of production. Such indirect costs of production could include depreciation of machinery, insurance of the factory premises and rental of warehouse storage space for raw materials. There are many other types of overhead costs which you will encounter in your progress through later chapters. They all consist of indirect cost of some type, with the type of cost determining the particular name given to the overhead cost.

Exhibit 2.10
Statement of cost of a production item

	£	£
Direct materials		xxx
Direct labour		xxx
Other direct costs		xxx
Prime cost		xxx
Indirect materials	xxx	
Indirect labour	xxx	
Other indirect costs	xxx	
Production overhead		xxx
Total product cost		xxx

Definition

Production overhead cost comprises indirect material, indirect labour and other indirect costs of production.

2.10.2 Cost centre

A cost centre is a unit of the organisation in respect of which a manager is responsible for costs under his or her control. A cost centre could be a location (e.g. a department) or a function (e.g. the manufacture of a product), or it could even be a production machine or group of similar machines. One essential feature of a cost centre is that it must be a homogeneous unit carrying out a single form of activity. A second essential feature is that it must correspond to an identifiable managerial responsibility.

Identification of a cost centre with managerial responsibility leads to a further type of cost classification, namely, controllable and non-controllable costs. Costs allocated to a cost centre should be classified according to whether they are controllable or non-controllable by the manager of that cost centre.

Definitions

A *cost centre* is a unit of the organisation in respect of which a manager is responsible for costs under his or her control.

A *controllable cost* is one which is capable of being managed by the person responsible for the cost centre, profit centre or investment centre to which the cost is reported.

2.10.3 Profit centre

A profit centre is a unit of the organisation in respect of which a manager is responsible for revenue as well as costs. In practice an operating division would be a profit centre if it produced output whose selling price could be determined in some manner. The selling price could be based on an internal transfer between departments at an agreed price. It would not necessarily require a sale to a third party outside the business entity.

A profit centre is similar to a cost centre in that it must relate to an area of managerial responsibility, although the activity may be less homogeneous than that of a cost centre. The profit centre, though, is likely to contain more than one cost centre.

Definition

> A *profit centre* is a unit of the organisation in respect of which a manager is responsible for revenue as well as costs.

2.10.4 Investment centre

An investment centre is a unit of the organisation in respect of which a manager is responsible for capital investment decisions as well as revenue and costs. These decisions could be related to such matters as purchase and disposal of equipment or acquisition of premises. The investment centre will be undertaking business activity in such a way that it will probably carry out an operation which is significant to the overall profit-earning capacity of the organisation. As is the case with a profit centre, the investment centre must relate to an area of managerial responsibility, but the activities of the investment centre need not be homogeneous. There will probably be a number of cost centres and profit centres within the investment centre.

Definition

> An *investment centre* is a unit of the organisation in respect of which a manager is responsible for capital investment decisions as well as revenue and costs.

2.11 Summary

In this chapter we have presented the basic range of terminology you will require in order to be able to continue reading the remaining chapters of the book. You will not remember them all at once and you will need to look back to this chapter many times in the early stages. One measure of your growing confidence will be the decrease in the number of times you need to return to this chapter.

In particular, you have seen the distinction between variable and fixed costs and you are aware of the difference between direct and indirect costs. As a particular example of the way in which indirect costs are collected together under a useful overall description, you have encountered the production overhead cost. You have seen that some costs relate to products while others are perceived as being more closely linked to a period of time. Finally, you are aware that costs may be allocated to areas of the business which may be cost centres, profit centres or investment centres, depending on the authority and responsibilities of those managing the particular areas. It may be important that the managers' attention should be drawn particularly to the controllable costs which they may be able to influence.

Further reading

The following references are provided so that you may delve more deeply into any one of the cost aspects outlined in this chapter. You should, however, be aware that there is no standard terminology in the field of management accounting, so every author will have a slightly different form of wording to define a given concept.

CIMA, *Management Accounting Official Terminology*, Chartered Institute of Management Accounting (1996).

Drury, C. (1992), *Management and Cost Accounting*, Chapman & Hall.

Horngren, C. T., Foster, G. and Datar, S. (1993), *Cost Accounting: A Managerial Emphasis*, Prentice Hall.

Morse, W. J. and Roth, H. P. (1986), *Cost Accounting: Processing, Evaluating and Using Cost Data*, Addison-Wesley.

Self-testing on the chapter

1 For each of the following cost classification terms, give a definition and give one example of how the definition applies in practice:
   (a) variable cost;
   (b) fixed cost;
   (c) direct cost;
   (d) indirect cost;
   (e) product cost; and
   (f) period cost.

2 For each of the following cost items, explain how it could be classified under more than one of the headings given in question 1:
   (a) raw materials to be used in production;
   (b) subcontracted labour in a special contract; and
   (c) rent of a warehouse for one year to allow temporary expansion of output.

3 Classify each of the following as being primarily a fixed cost or a variable cost, and, if necessary, explain why you think such a classification would be difficult without more information being provided:
   (a) direct materials;
   (b) factory insurance;
   (c) production manager's salary;
   (d) advertising of the product;
   (e) direct labour;
   (f) indirect labour;
   (g) depreciation of machinery;

(h) lubricants for machines;

(i) payment of a licence fee for the right to exclusive manufacture; and

(j) canteen manager's salary.

4 Explain why cost classification for planning and control may differ from cost classification for decision making.

5 Explain the importance of an unambiguous system of cost coding.

6 What are the component costs of the total cost of production?

7 What are:
(a) a cost centre;
(b) a profit centre; and
(c) an investment centre
and how do they differ?

Activities for study groups

1 You are the management team in a business which makes self-assembly kitchen units and sells them to large do-it-yourself stores. One person should take on the role of the financial controller but the rest of the team may take any managerial roles they choose. Each manager will have responsibility for a cost centre. The group should decide, at the outset, on the name and purpose of each cost centre.

In stage 1 of the team exercise, each manager should write down the name of the cost centre and a list of the costs for which the manager expects to have responsibility. A copy of the cost centre name and the list of costs should be supplied to each member of the team.

In stage 2, each manager should separately write down his or her requirements from a company-wide cost coding system, yet to be designed, which has been specified in outline as having six alphanumeric characters. Each manager should also make a note of any costs which are shared with another manager or managers.

While the managers are carrying out the second stage, the financial controller should prepare a cost coding system which would meet the needs as specified on the lists of costs provided by each manager from stage 1.

In stage 3, the group should come together for a management meeting at which the financial controller will provide his or her cost coding system and each manager will respond with his or her ideas. If possible, a mutually agreed solution should be found but, at the very least, the group should identify the areas where further negotiation will be required. Finally, the group should make a five-minute presentation to the class describing the negotiations on the coding system and commenting on the practical problems of such negotiation.

2 The group is the management team of a supermarket chain operating ten shops in out-of-town locations. Each member of the group should choose a management role, one of which must be the financial controller. Work together to prepare a proposal for establishing one profit centre, together with three cost

centres within the profit centre for which each manager will be responsible, writing a definition of the responsibilities of each profit centre and cost centre.

Then work together further to produce a list of costs for each cost centre, in a table as follows:

Type of cost	Fixed/variable cost	Direct/indirect for the cost centre	Product/period cost

Set out *one* question relating to planning, *one* question relating to control and *one* question relating to decision making. Explain how the table of cost classification will help answer each of these questions.

Practical questions

1 (a) Identify the cost behaviour in each of the following tables as:
  (i)   fixed cost; or
  (ii)   variable cost; or
  (iii) semi-variable cost.

  (b) Draw a graph for each table to illustrate the cost behaviour.

Cost x

Output (units)	100	200	300	400	500
Total cost (£)	600	600	600	600	600
Unit cost (£)	6.00	3.00	2.00	1.50	1.20

Cost y

Output (units)	100	200	300	400	500
Total cost (£)	300	600	900	1,200	1,500
Unit cost (£)	3.00	3.00	3.00	3.00	3.00

Cost z

Output (units)	100	200	300	400	500
Total cost (£)	660	720	780	840	900
Unit cost (£)	6.60	3.60	2.60	2.10	1.80

2 Tots Ltd manufactures babies' play suits for sale to retail stores. All play suits are of the same design. There are two departments: the cutting department and the machining department. You are asked to classify the costs listed below under the headings:

(a) Direct costs for the cutting department.
(b) Direct costs for the machining department.
(c) Indirect costs for the cutting department.
(d) Indirect costs for the machining department.
(e) Direct costs for the play suits.
(f) Indirect costs for the play suits.

List of costs

(i)   towelling materials purchased for making the play suits;
(ii)   reels of cotton purchased for machining;
(iii) pop-fasteners for insertion in the play suits;
(iv)   wages paid to employees in the cutting department;
(v)   wages paid to employees in the machining department;
(vi)   salaries paid to the production supervisors;
(vii) oil for machines in the machining department;
(viii) rent paid for factory building;
(ix)   depreciation of cutting equipment;
(x)   depreciation of machines for sewing suits;
(xi)   cost of providing canteen facilities for all staff.

3   Oven Pies Ltd plans to buy a delivery van to distribute pies from the bakery to various neighbourhood shops. It will use the van for three years. The expected costs are as follows:

	£
New van	15,000.00
Trade-in price after 3 years	600.00
Service costs (every 6 months)	450.00
Spare parts, per 10,000 miles	360.00
Four new tyres, every 15,000 miles	1,200.00
Vehicle licence and insurance, per year	800.00
Fuel, per litre[1]	0.70

Note: [1] Fuel consumption is 1 litre every five miles.

(a) Prepare a table of costs for mileages of 5,000, 10,000, 15,000, 20,000 and 30,000 miles per annum, distinguishing variable costs from fixed costs.
(b) Draw a graph showing variable cost, fixed cost and total cost.
(c) Calculate the average cost per mile at each of the mileages set out in (a).
(d) Write a short commentary on the behaviour of costs as annual mileage increases.

4   During the month of May, 4,000 metal towel rails were produced and 3,500 were sold. There had been none in store at the start of the month. There were no stocks of raw materials at either the start or end of the period. Costs incurred during May in respect of towel rails were as follows:

	£
Metal piping	12,000
Wages to welders and painters	9,000
Supplies for welding	1,400
Advertising campaign	2,000
Production manager's salary	1,800
Accounts department computer costs for dealing with production records	1,200

(a) Classify the list of costs set out above, into product costs and period costs.

(b) Explain how you would value stock held at the end of the month.

Chapter 3

Accounting for materials, labour and overheads

Learning objectives	After studying this chapter you should be able to:

1 State the main components of the cost of a unit of output.
2 Explain how materials costs, labour costs and production overheads are recorded.
3 Understand the problems of overhead cost allocation.
4 Solve problems which require the measurement of total product cost.

3.1 Introduction

Some businesses manufacture goods, while others perform a service. Whatever the nature of the business, all will at some stage use materials, they will employ labour and they will incur overhead costs (the name given to other costs which are necessary to the operation of the manufacturing or service process).

In this chapter we outline traditional procedures for recording the costs of materials, labour, and production overheads and indicate some of the problems which are encountered. Many of these procedures remain a corner-stone of present day management accounting but others, particularly those related to overhead costs, have caused management accountants to look for new procedures, some of which will be explained in later chapters.

3.2 Keeping the score: total product cost

In Chapter 2, you have seen a statement showing all the elements of the cost of production of one item of product. That statement of the cost of a unit of output provides a useful starting point for this chapter in setting out a list of items to be explained in more detail (*see* exhibit 3.1).

Exhibit 3.1
Statement of cost of a production item

	£	£
Direct materials		xxx
Direct labour		xxx
Other direct costs		xxx
Prime cost		xxx
Indirect materials	xxx	
Indirect labour	xxx	
Other indirect costs	xxx	
Production overhead		xxx
Total product cost		xxx

This chapter explains the procedures for recording materials, labour and production overhead costs in the context of a *job costing system*. A job costing system for recording the cost of output is appropriate to a business which provides specialised products or makes items to order, so that each customer's requirements constitute a separate job of work. Job costing is appropriate in manufacturing industries such as shipbuilding, bridge building, construction, property development and craft industries. Job costing would also be used in costing the provision of services by professional persons such as lawyers, doctors, architects and accountants. It could also be used for repair contracts, or specialist service contracts.

Definition

A *job costing* system is a system of cost accumulation where there is an identifiable activity for which costs may be collected. The activity is usually specified in terms of a job of work or a group of tasks contributing to a stage in the production or service process.

In a job costing system there will be a job cost record for each job, showing the costs incurred on that job. An illustration of a job cost record is shown in exhibit 3.2.

3.2.1 Collecting the details for the job cost record

The job cost record shows the costs of materials, labour and overhead incurred on a particular job. The accounts department knows from the stores requisition the quantity of materials issued to production and knows from the invoice the price per unit charged by the supplier. This allows the cost of materials to be recorded as the materials are used. Each job will have a job number and that number will be entered on all stores requisitions so that the materials can be traced to the job cost record.

Direct labour costs will be calculated using hours worked and the hourly rate for each employee. The hours worked will be collected from employee time sheets which show each job under its own job number. Hourly rates for the employee will be available from personnel records.

Other direct costs will be charged to jobs by entering on the expense invoice the appropriate job number. The invoices will be used as the primary source from which information is transferred to the job cost record.

Production overhead costs are much more troublesome because, by definition, they are not directly attributable to any specific product. One section of this chapter is given to explaining how overhead costs are shared among the jobs to which they relate.

In the remainder of this chapter you will meet with more detailed aspects of costs of materials, labour and production overheads.

Exhibit 3.2
Illustration of a job record

JOB COST RECORD JOB NO..............		Customer reference .... Product description.................		Product code	
DATE	CODE	DETAILS	Quantity	£	p
		Direct materials:			
		Type A	kg		
		Type B	kg		
		Type C	litres		
		Direct labour:			
		Employee A	hrs		
		Employee B	hrs		
		Employee C	hrs		
		Other direct costs			
		PRIME COST			
		Indirect materials			
		Indirect labour			
		Other indirect costs			
		Total production overhead			
		TOTAL PRODUCT COST			

Activity 3.1

You have been employed as the management accountant at a car repair garage. Write down a list of the types of costs you would expect to find on a job cost record for a car service and repair. (You don't need to put any money amounts into the list.)

3.3 Accounting for materials costs

Exhibit 3.3 shows the sequence of activities which control the ordering, delivery, and safekeeping of materials, together with the subsequent payment of suppliers. Information which is useful for accounting purposes will be collected from the documentation that is created during these procedures.

It is not difficult to see that with so many procedures involved there needs to be careful control over materials moving into, and out of, store. Each stage in the

Exhibit 3.3
Materials control procedures

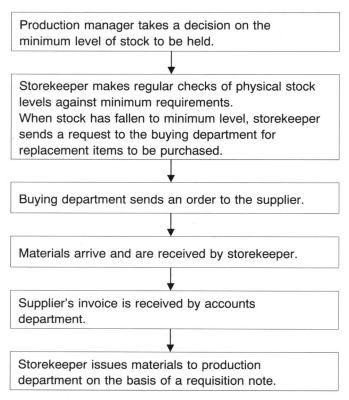

process requires a document as evidence that the transaction or process has been completed correctly. Every business has a different system of documentation which suits its particular needs. The following description is typical of the documents encountered in materials handling and control. Italics are used to indicate each document.

3.3.1 Materials handling and control documentation

When the storekeeper notes that the stock has fallen to the minimum level, triggering a reorder requirement, a *purchase requisition* will be sent to the buying department. The buying department will have a list of items which the production manager wishes to have available in store and the quantity to be reordered. Provided the item is on that list, the buying department will send a *purchase order* to the supplier. In some cases the production manager may have issued a purchase requisition directly because a new item of materials, not previously held in store, is required. It is the responsibility of the buying department to choose a supplier who provides reliable service and a high quality product at a competitive price. A copy of the purchase order will be sent to the storekeeper as notification that the materials have been ordered.

When the goods arrive from the supplier, the driver of the delivery vehicle will bring a *delivery note* which the storekeeper will sign, after checking against the quantities receive and noting any discrepancies. The storekeeper will then prepare a *goods received note*, sending one copy to the buying department and another to the accounts department. Soon after the goods arrive, the accounts department will receive the *supplier's invoice*, showing the quantities of the goods supplied and the price charged for them. The accounts department will check the quantities against the goods received note and will check the invoice price against an agreed price list provided by the buying department. If all is correct, the accounts department will pay the supplier.

Finally, the materials will be needed by the various production departments. To release the goods from store, the production departments will produce a *stores requisition* which the storekeeper will check and will then pass on to the accounts department for use in keeping the management accounting records.

Exhibit 3.4
Documentation in materials control procedures

Document	Origin	Destination	Use
Purchase requisition	Storekeeper or production manager	Buying department	Authority for purchase of materials from supplier
Purchase order	Buying department	1 Supplier 2 Storekeeper	Authority to supply goods Indication that goods will arrive
Delivery note	Delivery driver	Storekeeper	Check on quantity received, in good state
Goods received note	Storekeeper	1 Buying department 2 Accounts department	Confirmation that buying process is complete Evidence of quantities for checking against invoice
Supplier's invoice	Supplier	Accounts department	Shows quantities received and **unit price**
Stores requisition	Production departments	1 Storekeeper 2 Accounts department	Authority to release goods from store Record of **quantities used** in production

Exhibit 3.4 provides a summary of the various documents, their origin, destination and use for recording purposes. The two essential pieces of information for determining the cost of materials used in production are the price per unit and the quantity of materials issued. These are highlighted in bold printing in exhibit 3.4. As you will see, the price and quantity are taken from different documents, the supplier's price being taken from the invoice while the quantity of materials used is taken from the stores requisition.

The documents listed in exhibit 3.4 are referred to as *primary sources* because they form the first evidence that a transaction or event has taken place. From these primary sources the accounting records are created. Clearly, the accuracy of the accounting records is heavily dependent on careful and accurate processing of the primary documents.

3.3.2 Materials costs when input prices are changing

One problem faced by the accounts department is that suppliers change their prices from time to time. Goods held in store may have arrived at different times and at different unit prices. How does the accounts department decide on the unit price to be charged to each job when all the materials look the same once they are taken into store? The usual procedure is to assume, for pricing purposes, that the first goods to arrive in store are the first ones to leave. This is usually abbreviated to 'FIFO' (first-in-first-out).

Some businesses prefer to use the average cost of all items in stock as the basis for pricing issues. For management purposes the best method for the purpose should be applied. Management accounting escapes the constraints of statute law, accounting standards and tax law which restrict practice in financial accounting.

3.3.3 Costs of wastage and scrap

In the ideal situation, all goods received into stores are issued to production. Real life is not always like that, because stores may disappear before they have a chance to be used in the production process. The disappearance may be caused by deterioration or damage in store, the goods may become obsolete or unsuitable for use in production, or they may be stolen. Sometimes goods may appear to have gone missing when in reality it is the accounting records which are incorrect because a stores requisition note has been lost or an item has been allocated to the wrong job cost record, or perhaps there is a calculation error on a stores list. It is always worthwhile to check the accuracy of the accounting records before assuming that stores have disappeared.

For the management accountant the loss of goods creates another cost problem. The cost must be charged somewhere in the system but it cannot appear on a job cost record as a direct cost because the materials never reached the production department. The cost of wastage therefore has to be noted as a separate indirect materials cost, to be spread over the cost of all jobs. If any cash can be recovered by selling obsolete or damaged goods, then the proceeds of sale may be recorded as reducing the overall cost of wastage.

3.3.4 Cost classification and materials costs

As explained earlier, job costing is concerned primarily with planning and control. The cost classification system is required primarily to show whether costs are direct or indirect costs and whether they are fixed or variable costs.

How are direct and indirect materials costs distinguished?

The earlier description of materials costing procedures has shown how multiplying unit price by the quantity of materials used will give a measure of cost, although there may need to be a choice of unit price to be applied (*see* section 3.3.2). Materials issued to production are usually made available on the basis of a stores requisition, so there should be no problem in identifying direct materials costs for the job in question.

Some materials costs may be spread over a range of products and activities, each of which must take a share. The case of wastage before the goods are issued to production has already been discussed. Other examples would include transportation costs and all the costs of receiving, issuing and handling stores (such as the storekeeper's wages). It is preferable to record materials costs as direct costs, identified with the job, wherever possible. On the other hand, the cost of spending time on keeping records must be weighed against more productive uses of that time.

How are fixed and variable materials costs distinguished?

Most materials costs will be variable costs, irrespective of whether they are direct or indirect so far as the job is concerned. If output is not being achieved, then materials will not be used and will be held in store for use in a future period.

To be a fixed cost, the materials would have to be required for use in a period irrespective of whether or not production takes place. That is an unlikely situation in most business operations.

Activity 3.2	*You have been employed as a storekeeper at a superstore selling vehicle accessories. Write down the main procedures you would carry out to ensure that:* • *the goods in store are held securely;* • *the accounting records of stock are accurate; and* • *the goods are issued only to authorised persons.*

3.4 Accounting for labour costs

The cost of any resource used in a business is the product of the amount of resource used and the price per unit of the resource. For the resource of labour, the amount of resource is usually measured in terms of hours worked and the price is usually expressed as a rate paid per hour.

3.4.1 Types of pay scheme

The first problem which the management accountant meets in dealing with labour costs is that different employees are on different pay schemes. Some employees receive a monthly salary, paid at the end of the month worked. They are expected to work whatever number of hours is necessary to complete the tasks assigned to them. This type of remuneration is most commonly found in the case of administrative staff where the emphasis is on undertaking tasks which are necessary to the overall duties and responsibilities of the post. Other employees receive a basic salary per week, or per month, which is augmented by extra payments depending on output levels or targets achieved. This type of pay scheme has a 'loyalty' element in the basic salary together with a reward for effort in the output-related extra payments. Other employees may be paid an hourly rate based on actual hours worked, receiving no payment where no hours are worked. Finally, there may be some employees paid on a piecework basis, receiving a fixed amount for every item produced, regardless of time taken. To add to the problem, there may be labour costs of the business which are not paid to the employee in the form of wages or salary. These would include the provision of a car, free medical insurance, clothing allowances, rent allowances, relocation and disruption payments, inducements to join the company and lump sum payments on leaving the company. There are also the employer's labour costs, such as employer's contributions to national insurance, which are part of the total labour cost as far as the business is concerned.

3.4.2 Determining the labour cost in an item of output

The differences outlined in section 3.4.1 all add to the problems of the management accountant in converting the variety of schemes to a uniform basis for costing purposes. Usually, calculating a rate per hour is sufficient to provide such a uniform basis, provided the number of hours worked is known. The cost of labour used on any job may then be determined by multiplying the hourly cost by the number of hours worked.

3.4.3 Cost classification and labour costs

Cost classification in job costing is mainly aimed at planning and control, so the classification system is mainly concerned with whether costs are direct or indirect and whether they are fixed or variable.

How are direct and indirect labour costs distinguished?

Multiplying unit cost by the number of hours worked is fine provided there is a time record and provided that time can be allocated exclusively to one product at a time. In some businesses it might be feasible to keep track of specialist labour time spent on each product. This part of the labour cost is regarded as the direct cost.

Some labour costs may never be allocated directly to a specific job because they are spread over a range of jobs and activities, each of which must take a share (for example, supervisor's salary, cleaner's wages, or non-productive time when skilled employees are not able to work because equipment needs attention). Indirect labour costs also include holiday pay, bonus payments and overtime pay. That gives the management accountant a further problem in deciding on a fair basis of allocation of indirect labour costs. Allocation of indirect costs will be dealt with in the section on production overhead costs.

How are fixed and variable labour costs distinguished?

One quite difficult question with labour costs is to decide whether they are fixed or variable costs. If the employee is on a contract which provides a fixed basic salary, then the total salary is a fixed cost for the organisation. The employee will then spend time on producing output and that amount of time will vary depending on the level of output. Thus the *direct* labour cost attributable to that employee will be a variable cost, depending on level of output. The remaining time, when the employee is not producing output, will be classed as an *indirect* cost of unproductive labour.

3.4.4 Recording labour costs

The system for recording labour costs must be capable of dealing with the payroll aspects (keeping track of how much is paid to each employee) and with the cost allocation aspect of tracing those payroll costs, together with other labour costs, to the products of the business. That in turn requires a careful recording of the total time worked by the employees each week, analysed into the time spent on each job of work and the amount of non-productive time.

Exhibit 3.2 shows how the labour cost might be recorded in a very simple job cost record. Direct labour costs will be calculated using hours worked and the hourly rate for each employee. The hours worked will be collected from employee time sheets which show each job under its own job number. Hourly rates for the employee will be available from personnel records, based on the cost of employing that particular person.

In practice, it is likely that job costing records will be kept by computer, with employees entering data on-line, but the computer output might resemble the record illustrated in exhibit 3.2.

Activity 3.3

> You are employed in the personnel department of a large organisation. Explain how the records kept by the personnel department would be useful to the accounting department in preparing the monthly payroll.

3.5 Production overheads

Production overhead was defined in Chapter 2 as comprising indirect materials, indirect labour and other indirect costs of production. Indirect materials and indirect labour have been explained earlier in this chapter. Other indirect costs will include any item which relates to production and which is not a materials cost or a labour cost. The type of indirect cost will depend on the nature of the business and, in particular, on whether it is a manufacturing business or a service business. Examples are:

- In a manufacturing business: repair of machinery; rent of factory buildings; and safety procedures.
- In a service business: cost of transport to jobs; replacement of tools; and protective clothing.

Whatever their nature, all the production overhead costs have to be allocated to the products.

Normally the management accountant has to devise an allocation scheme. There are some essential features for any successful allocation scheme. It must be:

- fair to all parties involved in the allocation process
- representative of the benefit each party gains from the shared cost
- relatively quick to apply so that provision of information is not delayed
- understandable by all concerned.

This chapter will use arithmetically simple models for illustrative purposes, although the allocation mechanism does not have to be arithmetically simple provided a computer can be used.

The process to be described here has three stages:

1 sharing (apportioning) overhead costs across cost centres;
2 allocating service department costs to production cost centres;
3 allocating costs to products.

3.5.1 Sharing overhead costs across cost centres

There are two main types of cost centre in any business, namely, service cost centres and production cost centres. The production cost centres are those directly involved in the production activity. The service cost centres are not directly involved in the production activity but provide essential backup. To sustain long-term profitability, the products of the business must sell at a price which makes a profit after covering the costs of the service cost centres as well as those of the production cost centres.

The management accountant will first of all divide the overhead costs into two categories: those which are directly attributable to each cost centre; and those which have to be shared (or apportioned) over a number of cost centres according to how the cost centres benefit from the cost incurred. Exhibit 3.5 sets out some common methods of apportionment where costs are regarded as indirect so far as each cost centre is concerned.

If the records were sufficiently detailed, then most of the costs in exhibit 3.5 could be turned into direct costs for each cost centre, avoiding the need for apportionment. Electricity meters could be installed in each cost centre to measure directly the cost of heating and lighting. Employees could be given tickets for the canteen which could be collected and recorded for each cost centre. The production supervisor could keep a diary of time spent in each cost

Exhibit 3.5
Examples of methods of apportionment of costs to cost centres

Cost item	Method of apportionment to cost centres
Rent of building	Floor area of each cost centre
Lighting	Floor area of each cost centre
Power for machines	Number of machines in each cost centre
Production supervisor's salary	Number of employees in each cost centre
Canteen costs	Number of employees in each cost centre
Depreciation and insurance of machinery	Value of machinery in each cost centre

centre. Depreciation could be calculated for each machine. The insurance company could be asked to quote a separate premium for each machine. However, all these procedures would in themselves create a new cost of administration which the business might decide was too high a price to pay for a marginal improvement in the accuracy of allocation of costs.

3.5.2 Allocating service department costs to production cost centres

As explained earlier, service cost centres exist to support production but do not make a direct contribution to the product. Once the costs of the organisation have been channelled into the various cost centres, they must be reallocated from service cost centres to production cost centres. The essential features remain the same, namely, that the method chosen must be:

- fair to all parties involved in the allocation process
- representative of the benefit each party gains from the shared cost
- relatively quick to apply so that provision of information is not delayed
- understandable by all concerned.

Exhibit 3.6 sets out the titles of some service cost centres and gives examples of some methods by which their costs could be reallocated to production cost centres.

3.5.3 Allocating costs to products

You have now reached the final stage of the allocation process where all the costs are collected in the production cost centres, ready to be allocated to products. The essential features, as before, are that the method must be:

- fair to all parties involved in the allocation process
- representative of the benefit each party gains from the shared cost
- relatively quick to apply so that provision of information is not delayed
- understandable by all concerned.

To allocate a fair share of overhead to each product, the allocation method must make use of the best measure of work done on a product. The best measure is usually labour hours or machine hours, depending on whether the production process is labour intensive or machinery intensive.

Exhibit 3.6
Examples of methods of allocating total costs of service cost centres to production cost centres

Service cost centre	Method of allocation to production cost centres
Maintenance department	Number of machines in each cost centre
Employees' restaurant and coffee bar	Number of employees in each cost centre
Stores department	Total value of stores requisitions from each cost centre
Finished goods quality inspection	Value of goods produced by each cost centre
Safety inspectors	Number of employees in each cost centre

A calculation of an overhead cost rate might be set out as in exhibit 3.7, which shows a statement of overhead cost rate for an organisation having two production cost centres, the Assembly Department and the Finishing Department, and one service cost centre, the Maintenance Department. In exhibit 3.7, the indirect costs incurred by the business are set out in table 3.1. These costs related to some or all of the three departments and must be shared among them on a fair basis. Table 3.2 sets out information about each department which will be helpful in this fair sharing. The remaining tables of exhibit 3.7 show the sharing process, step by step.

Exhibit 3.7
Illustration of the calculation of an overhead cost rate

Table 3.1 sets out the indirect costs incurred by the business on behalf of all departments taken together. Table 3.2 sets out relevant information about each department which will be used in the process of determining an overhead cost rate.

Table 3.1
Indirect costs incurred by the business

Cost item	Total cost this month
	£
Indirect materials	36,000
Indirect labour	40,000
Rent	1,000
Insurance	1,600
Depreciation	2,000
Total	*80,600*

Exhibit 3.7 continued

Table 3.2
Information about each department

	Assembly	Finishing	Maintenance
Direct materials used for production (£)	400,000	500,000	not applicable
Number of employees	10	25	5
Floor area (sq ft)	300	600	300
Value of machinery (£)	30,000	50,000	20,000
Number of direct labour hours worked on production	55,000	64,000	not applicable

There are four steps in calculating the overhead cost to be allocated to each job.

Step 1: Allocating costs to departments, using a suitable method for each cost
In table 3.3, each of the cost items contained in table 3.1 is shared across the three departments on an appropriate basis chosen from table 3.2.

Table 3.3
Sharing of cost items across the three departments

	Total £	Assembly £	Finishing £	Maintenance £
Indirect materials[1]	36,000	16,000	20,000	nil
Indirect labour[2]	40,000	10,000	25,000	5,000
Rent[3]	1,000	250	500	250
Insurance[4]	1,600	480	800	320
Depreciation[5]	2,000	600	1,000	400
Total	80,600	27,330	47,300	5,970

Notes:
[1] The cost of indirect materials is likely to be dependent on direct materials so the proportions applied in sharing out the indirect materials costs are 4 : 5. The direct materials are used only in Assembly and Finishing, so the indirect materials will relate only to these two departments.
[2] The cost of indirect labour is likely to be dependent on the total number of employees working in the organisation, so the proportions applied in sharing out the indirect labour costs are 10 : 25 : 5.
[3] Rent costs may be shared out on the basis of floor space occupied by each department, in the proportions 3 : 6 : 3.
[4,5] Insurance and depreciation may both be shared out by reference to the value of the machinery used in each department, in the proportions 3 : 5 : 2.

Step 2: Allocating service department costs to production departments on the basis of value of machines in each department

The maintenance department provides service in proportion to the machinery used in each department, so it is appropriate to share out the maintenance costs on the basis of value of machinery in Assembly and in Finishing, in the proportions 30,000 : 50,000:

$$\frac{30,000}{80,000} \times 5,970 = 2,239$$

$$\frac{50,000}{80,000} \times 5,970 = 3,731$$

Table 3.4
Share-out of maintenance costs between Assembly and Finishing

	Total	Assembly	Finishing	Maintenance
	£	£	£	£
Total cost per dept (from table 3.3)	80,600	27,330	47,300	5,970
Transfer maintenance costs to Assembly and Finishing		2,239	3,731	(5,970)
Total per department	80,600	29,569	51,031	nil

Step 3: Allocating total overhead costs of each production department to units produced during the period

By dividing the total cost of each department by the number of direct labour hours, we obtain the following:

Assembly: £29,569/55,000 hours = 53.76 pence per direct labour hour

Finishing: £51,031/64,000 hours = 79.74 pence per direct labour hour

Step 4: Finding the overhead costs of any job

Now the overhead cost rate may be used to determine how much overhead cost should be charged to each job. The answer will depend on the number of direct labour hours required in each production department, for any job. Take as an example job S, which spends 2 hours in the assembly department and 3 hours in the finishing department. The overhead cost allocated to job S is calculated as follows:

Table 3.5
Example of the allocation of overhead cost to a job

Department	Calculation	£
Assembly	53.76 pence × 2 hours	1.075
Finishing	79.74 pence × 3 hours	2.392
Total overhead cost		3.467

That's all there is to it. The process of cost allocation takes time because every cost has to be traced through to the product, but it is systematic in that all costs eventually find their way through to a product.

> *Return to the start of exhibit 3.7 and try to work the example for yourself. It is very important for later chapters that you understand the purpose of exhibit 3.7 and the method of calculation used. There are some features of the tables in exhibit 3.7 which are worth noting for future reference. First, it is important to keep totals for each column of figures and a total of all the column totals in order to ensure that there are no arithmetic errors that result in costs appearing from nowhere or disappearing to oblivion. Second, it is important to show working notes at all times because there are so many variations of possible method that the person who reads your calculations will need the working notes to understand the method chosen.*

3.5.4 Methods of allocating overhead costs to jobs

In step 4 of exhibit 3.7 the overhead costs of each production department are allocated to jobs based on the number of direct hours worked. Direct hours of labour are used because in general the overhead cost is incurred because people are working. The longer they work, the more overhead is incurred.

Sometimes direct labour hours are not the best measure of work performed. In a machinery-intensive environment, machine hours may be preferred to labour hours as a basis for allocating overhead.

There are occasions when the direct labour hours worked on a job are not known because they are not recorded. In such circumstances a cost per £ of direct labour could be applied. This is acceptable but has a disadvantage in that a change in the labour rate could affect the amount of labour cost and hence the allocation of overhead.

Where all products are identical, a cost per unit would be sufficient. However, in a job costing system such identical products are unlikely.

In summary, four possible methods of allocating overhead costs to products are:

- cost per direct labour hour;
- cost per machine hour;
- cost per £ of labour cost;
- cost per unit.

It would be usual to calculate a variable overhead cost rate and a separate fixed overhead cost rate. This separation becomes particularly important when predetermined overhead cost rates (i.e. cost rates set in advance) are used.

3.5.5 Predetermined overhead cost rates

Because the total overhead cost rate is not known until after all costs have been collected, there may be practical problems in estimating the cost of a job for, say, pricing purposes. Many businesses will therefore use *predetermined overhead cost rates*, estimated at the start of a reporting period. At the end of the period there will be an adjustment to bring the estimated overhead cost into line with the actual overhead cost.

Estimates abound in accounting and part of the reporting process involves explaining why the actual out-turn did, or did not, match up to the estimate. Chapter 7 will introduce the techniques of standard costing and variance analysis, which provide a formal means of analysing and investigating differences between estimated and actual amounts. Provided the estimation process is carried out with care, the benefits of using predetermined overhead costs, in terms of having information early rather than late, by far outweigh the possible negative aspects of having to explain differences between estimated and actual overhead costs charged to products.

The use of predetermined overhead cost rates can cause particular problems where there is a fixed overhead cost, because the volume of activity for the period ahead has to be estimated as well as the amount of the cost. Exhibit 3.8 sets out some data to explain the problems of applying a predetermined fixed overhead cost rates to products. Exhibit 3.8 shows, before the reporting period commences, the manager has estimated that there will be 10,000 labour hours worked, under normal activity conditions, and that fixed overhead of £50,000 will be incurred. The predetermined fixed overhead cost rate is therefore £5 per labour hour. In the event, the costing records show fixed overhead of £40,000 applied because only 8,000 hours were worked and £5 was charged to those records in respect of each hour. The cash book shows fixed overhead expenditure of £50,000, corresponding exactly to the estimated amount. The management accounts will therefore have two items in the profit and loss account, namely the fixed overhead applied (£40,000) and the underapplied fixed overhead (£10,000), giving a total charge for the period of £50,000 (which is as it should be).

Exhibit 3.8
Use of a predetermined fixed overhead cost rate

Estimated direct labour hours for normal activity	10,000 hours
Estimated fixed overhead cost in total	£50,000
Predetermined overhead cost rate	£5 per direct labour hour
Actual direct labour hours worked on jobs	8,000 hours
Overhead costs applied to jobs (costing records)	£40,000
Actual fixed overhead incurred (cash book)	£50,000
Underapplied fixed overhead	£10,000

3.5.6 More questions about overhead cost rates

Overhead cost is one of those topics which make you want to ask a new question every time you have an answer to the previous question. Here are some of the questions which might have occurred to you in thinking about overhead cost rates:

1   Is it necessary to have an overhead cost rate for each cost centre or could there be one rate to cover all production?
2   How is it possible to calculate an overhead cost rate per direct labour hour for fixed overhead costs, when these do not vary with direct labour hours?
3   What is the best way of ensuring that cost allocation to products most closely represents the behaviour of those costs?

The answers to all these questions will be found in thinking about the four conditions for determining a suitable overhead cost rate:

● fair to all parties involved in the allocation process
● representative of the benefit each party gains from the shared cost
● relatively quick to apply so that provision of information is not delayed
● understandable by all concerned.

The answers are therefore as follows.

Is it necessary to have an overhead cost rate for each cost centre or could there be one rate to cover all production?

If there is a wide product range and products spend different amounts of time in different cost centres, it would be undesirable to have one rate to cover all production because that single rate would average out the time spent in the different departments. Thus it is said that 'blanket overhead cost rates' or 'plant wide rates' should be avoided where possible, or used with great caution. The overhead cost rate to use will be one which can be used with confidence that it meets the four conditions stated earlier.

How is it possible to calculate an overhead cost rate per direct labour hour for fixed overhead costs when, by definition, fixed costs do not vary with direct labour hours?

This question is more difficult to answer and the best starting point is a reminder that accounting is often based on estimates. The fixed overhead costs will have to be allocated to products eventually. However, this can only be achieved accurately after production is completed. Job cost estimation cannot always wait that long. Therefore, a predetermined fixed overhead cost rate is applied to each job on the basis of some measure of work done, such as direct labour hours. If the estimating process is accurate, the estimated hours to be worked will equal the actual hours worked and there will be no problem. If the actual hours are greater than, or less than, the estimate, then there will be a difference, referred to as overapplied or underapplied fixed overhead. Exhibit 3.8 has set out an illustration of underapplied fixed overhead.

What is the best way of ensuring that cost allocation to products most closely represents the behaviour of those costs?

This question has aroused considerable excitement in management accounting circles in recent years, as some thinking people realised that too much time had been spent in reading textbooks and theorising. Researchers had omitted to find out whether the actual practice of management accounting was so bad after all. They therefore went out to look, and found that some practical management accountants were having some very good ideas but that those ideas were not finding their way into textbooks.

As a result of those investigations, many articles and books have been written on the importance of *cost drivers*, which are the events that are significant determinants of the cost of an activity. If an oil company has an offshore platform where the supervisor is constantly calling up the helicopter for unplanned visits ashore, the total transport cost for the oil company will rise. The helicopter flight is the cost driver and the platform supervisor needs to be aware that the flight cost is part of the cost of running the platform. If a stores department is receiving frequent deliveries of small quantities, the cost driver for the stores department is the number of deliveries. Cost drivers are not an earth-shattering discovery in themselves, but they have been built into a description of activity-based costing (ABC) which you will find in Chapter 11. Activity-based costing has led many companies to re-examine their approach to allocating overhead costs to products, based on finding a method which most closely models the factors driving the cost.

3.6 Summary

The costs of materials, labour and overheads will be found in almost any costing exercise. In this chapter we have explained how each cost is recorded and how it becomes part of the cost of a product. Illustrations have been provided in the context of a product costing system, but the costs of materials, labour and overhead will be encountered in all the remaining chapters of this book.

The traditional approach to overhead costs has been explained, showing how overhead costs are apportioned to cost centres and then allocated to products. The subjective nature of this process is seen in the variety of methods of allocating overheads to products (e.g. direct labour hours, machine hours, direct labour cost, or number of items produced). The problem of using predetermined overhead costs has been explained.

Finally, in this chapter we pointed away from the traditional approach to overhead costs and towards current thinking on the best methods of accounting for those costs. Despite that current thinking, the traditional approach remains widely applied in practice and it is important for students to understand the basis of calculation.

Further reading

Drury, C. (1992), *Management and Cost Accounting*, Chapman & Hall.

Horngren, C. T., Foster, G. and Datar, S. (1993), *Cost Accounting: A Managerial Emphasis*, Prentice Hall.

Morse, W. J. and Roth, H. P. (1986) *Cost Accounting: Processing, Evaluating and Using Cost Data*, Addison-Wesley.

Wilson, R. M. S. and Chua, W. F. (1992), *Managerial Accounting: Method and Meaning*, Chapman & Hall.

Self-testing on the chapter

1 What is the definition of a job costing system?

2 What are the main items in a statement of the cost of production of an item of output?

3 How may a system of materials control procedures ensure accurate accounting information for job costing purposes?

4 Which source documents should be used to create the accounting record for direct materials costs?

5 What information would appear on a job cost record in a bus company where each job consists of hiring out a luxury coach and a driver to an organised group which is travelling to a particular event?

6 What is meant by the term 'FIFO', when used in deciding on the cost price of goods-issued to production?

7 What are the problems of accounting for wastage and scrap?

8 Is direct labour cost a fixed cost or a variable cost?

9 Give three examples of production overheads in:
   (a) a manufacturing business; and
   (b) a service business.

10 For each of your answers to question 9, say whether the cost is a fixed cost or a variable cost.

11 What are the important features of any successful overhead allocation scheme?

12 For each of the following overhead costs, suggest one method of apportioning cost to cost centres:
   (a) employees' holiday pay;
   (b) agency fee for nurse at first-aid centre;
   (c) depreciation of floor-polishing machines used in all production areas;
   (d) production manager's salary;
   (e) lighting;
   (f) power for desktop workstations in a financial services business;
   (g) cost of servicing the elevator;
   (h) fee paid to professional consultant for advice on fire regulation procedures.

13 Explain how each of the following service department costs could be allocated to production centres:

   (a) Cleaning of machines in a food-processing business.
   (b) Vehicle maintenance for a fleet of vans used by service engineers.
   (c) Canteen services for a company operating a large bus fleet.
   (d) Quality control department of an engineering business.
   (e) Planning department of a bridge-building company.
   (f) Research department of a chemical company.

14 State the principles to be applied in allocating costs to products.

15 What are the benefits and what are the possible problems of using overhead cost rates estimated in advance of the actual costs being recorded?

16 Using your answer to question 14, compare the relative merits of calculating overhead costs per unit of products using each of the following methods:
(a) Cost per direct labour hour.
(b) Cost per unit of output.
(c) Cost per direct machine hour.
(d) Cost per £ of direct labour.

Activities for study groups

1 Obtain the annual report of a large public company in a manufacturing business and read the description of the operating results. Make a list of the main divisions of the business and assign each member of the group to the role of divisional management accountant (or work in pairs if there are insufficient divisions). Working separately, prepare:

(a) A list of cost centres which might exist in such a division.
(b) A detailed list of the types of costs you would expect to appear in an operating statement for the cost of any one product item of the division.
(c) Recommendations on how overhead costs should be allocated to cost centres and to products.

After that stage is completed, come together as a group, circulate your working papers around the group and form a collective opinion on the extent of similarities and differences in your answers. From this analysis, make a list of the items on which you think it would be important to agree to a company-wide approach and the items where a different perspective in each division would be desirable.

2 Obtain the annual report of a large public company in a service business (e.g. road haulage, advertising, insurance) and repeat the exercise set out in question 1 in this section.

Case studies

Case 3.1

Set out below is a table of the planned selling prices and costs in the coming year of a business which manufactures toy pedal cars and toy pedal tractors. Each item is manufactured in two separate production departments, namely, the moulding and the painting departments. The employees have a canteen on the premises, which is treated as a separate cost centre.

Plans for the coming year

	Cars	Tractors
Sales	£	£
Selling price of one toy	120	140
Sales volume expected (units)	3,000	6,000
Direct materials		
Expected cost of one toy	16	10
Direct labour (rate £3 per hour)		
Hours spent on one toy in Moulding department	5	6
Hours spent on one toy in Painting department	4	4

Production overhead costs are expected as follows:

Type of cost	Moulding £	Painting £	Canteen £	Total £
Variable	52,000	18,000	nil	70,000
Fixed	84,000	60,000	32,000	176,000
	136,000	78,000	32,000	246,000

Required:

1 Set out:
    (a) a statement of total cost of production for toy pedal cars; and
    (b) a statement of total cost of production for toy pedal tractors,
    over the coming year. Show detailed schedules of workings to support each of your statements.

2 Estimate the profit or loss which will arise on each product line.

3 Explain how the information you have produced may be of help to management in relation to aspects of planning and control.

Case 3.2

Florence Ltd is a manufacturing company with a financial year ending on 31 December 19X1. The company manufactures wooden storage units for schools and colleges, each job being planned to meet a customer's specific order.

A predetermined overhead rate based upon direct labour hours is used to apply overhead to individual jobs. The flexible budget of overhead costs for the year is:

| Fixed overhead | £476,000 |
| Variable overhead | £3.25 per direct labour hour |

Normal activity for a full year is 120,000 direct labour hours.

During the month of November orders were begun and completed for three customers:

Job A: Southern college
Job B: Northern school
Job C: Eastern university

The following information has been extracted from the company's records in respect of the month of November:

(a) *Stocks at 1 November:*
    Raw materials   £10,500

(b) *Purchases of raw materials:*
    Raw materials   £135,000

(c) *Materials requisitioned for production:*
    Job A: Southern college   £45,000
    Job B: Northern school   £37,000
    Job C: Eastern university   £25,000

(d) *Factory direct-labour hours:*
    Job A: Southern college   3,500
    Job B: Northern school   3,000
    Job C: Eastern university   2,000

(e) *Labour costs:*
    Direct-labour wages   £51,000
    Indirect-labour wages (for 4,000 hours)   £15,000
    Supervisors' salaries   £6,000

(f) *Costs of heat, light and depreciation of buildings:*
    Factory facilities   £6,500
    Sales office   £1,500
    Administration office   <u>£1,000</u>
                                   <u>£9,000</u>

(g) *Other factory costs:*
    Power   £4,000
    Repairs and maintenance   £1,500
    Depreciation   £1,500

Required

1 Calculate the predetermined fixed overhead cost rate to be applied to individual jobs during 19X1.

2 Set out a job cost statement showing the total cost of each of the three jobs started and completed during the month of November.

Part 2

Applying the basic tools of management accounting

Chapter 4

Job costing and contract costing

<table>
<tr>
<td>

Learning
objectives
</td>
<td>

After studying this chapter you should be able to:

1 **Prepare job cost records showing direct material, direct labour and production overhead.**

2 **Analyse transactions involved in job costing, using the accounting equation.**

3 **Prepare job cost records for a long-term contract.**

4 **Understand the method of reporting profit on a long-term contract.**
</td>
</tr>
</table>

4.1 Introduction

In Chapter 3 the elements of a job costing system (direct materials, direct labour and production overheads) were explained. In this chapter the various elements of a job costing system are brought together and analysed to calculate the cost of jobs undertaken during a period of time. The cost of each job is recorded on a *job cost record*. The transactions of the period are analysed and recorded using the accounting equation. This chapter also explains and illustrates the job cost record for a major contract.

<table>
<tr>
<td>

Definition
</td>
<td>

A *job costing* system is a system of cost accumulation where there is an identifiable activity for which costs may be collected. The activity is usually specified in terms of a job of work or a group of tasks contributing to a stage in the production or service process.
</td>
</tr>
</table>

4.2 Job cost records: an illustration

An illustration of a job cost record is provided in Chapter 3. It shows sufficient details of direct materials, direct labour and other direct costs to give the *prime cost* of production. Addition of indirect costs (*production overhead*) gives the *total product cost* of a job.

<table>
<tr>
<td>

Definitions
</td>
<td>

Prime cost of production is equal to the total of direct materials, direct labour and other direct costs.

Production overhead cost comprises indirect materials, indirect labour and other indirect costs of production.

Total product cost comprises prime cost plus production overhead cost.
</td>
</tr>
</table>

The explanation of the elements of a job cost record is given in Chapter 3. These elements are now brought together in the example of Specialprint, a company

Exhibit 4.1
Specialprint: transactions for the month of June

Date	Symbol	Transaction
1 June	✧	Bought 60 rolls of paper on credit from supplier, invoiced price being £180,000. The rolls of paper acquired consisted of two different grades. 40 rolls were of medium-grade paper at a total cost of £100,000 and 20 rolls were of high grade at a total cost of £80,000.
1 June	♣	Bought inks, glues and dyes at a cost of £25,000 paid in cash. The inks cost £9,000 while the glue cost £12,000 and the dyes £4,000.
2 June	⊗	Returned to supplier one roll of paper damaged in transit, £2,500. The roll of paper returned was of medium grade.
3 June	†	Rolls of paper issued to printing department, cost £120,000. 20 high-grade rolls were issued, together with 16 medium-grade rolls. There were three separate jobs: references 601, 602 and 603. The high-grade rolls were all for job 601 (notepaper); 12 medium-grade rolls were for job 602 (envelopes) and the remaining 4 medium-grade rolls were for job 603 (menu cards).
4 June	ø	Issued half of inks, glues and dyes to printing department, £12,500. Exactly half of each item of inks, glue and dyes was issued, for use across all three jobs.
14 June	ψ	Paid printing employees' wages £8,000. Wages were paid to 10 printing employees, each earning the same amount.
14 June	λ	Paid maintenance wages £250. Maintenance wages were paid to one part-time maintenance officer.
16 June		Paid rent, rates and electricity in respect of printing, £14,000 in cash. Payment for rent was £8,000, rates £4,000 and electricity £2,000.
28 June	ϖ	Paid printing employees' wages £8,000. Wages were paid to the same 10 employees as on 14 June.
28 June	φ	Paid maintenance wages £250. Maintenance wages were paid to the same maintenance officer as on 14 June.
30 June	♥	Employee records show that: 5 printing employees worked all month on job 601; 3 printing employees worked on job 602; and 2 printing employees worked on job 603.
30 June	ξ	It is company policy to allocate production overheads in proportion to labour costs of each job.
30 June	#	Transferred printed stationery to finished goods inventory at a total amount of £160,000, in respect of jobs 601 and 602, which were completed, together with the major part of job 603. There remained some unfinished work-in-progress on one section of job 603, valued at £3,000. Separate finished goods records are maintained for notepaper, envelopes and menu cards.
30 June	≈	Sold stationery to customer on credit, cost of goods sold being £152,000. The customer took delivery of all notepaper and all envelopes, but took only £7,600 of menu cards, leaving the rest to await completion of the further items still in progress.

which prints novelty stationery to be sold in a chain of retail stores. The company has only one customer for this novelty stationery. Exhibit 4.1 contains relevant information for the month of June in respect of three separate jobs, 601, 602 and 603. Symbols are attached to each transaction so that the information may be traced through the job cost records.

4.2.1 Information for the job cost record

The job cost record requires information on direct materials, direct labour and production overhead. This information must be selected from the list of transactions for the month of June. Care must be taken to extract only that information which is relevant to each job.

Activity 4.1

From Exhibit 4.1 note the transactions which you think are directly relevant to the cost of jobs 601, 602 and 603. Then read the rest of this section and compare your answer with the text. (Use exhibit 3.1 to remind yourself of the information needed for a job cost record.)

Direct material

Materials are purchased on 1 June and taken into store but that is of no relevance to determining the cost of a job. For job cost purposes what matters is the issue of paper on 3 June. That is entered on each of the job cost records using the detail given for the event on 3 June.

Direct labour

Employees are paid during the month and there are records (time sheets) of the jobs on which they work. It is only at the end of the month that the employee records are checked to find where the work was carried out. At that point the relevant direct labour costs are entered on each job cost record.

Production overhead

Production overhead comprises indirect materials (ink, glue and dyes), indirect labour (maintenance wages), rent, rates and electricity.

		£
Indirect materials	ø	12,500
Indirect labour	λ φ	500
Rent	‡	8,000
Rates	‡	4,000
Electricity	‡	2,000
Total production overhead	ξ	27,000

An overhead cost rate is required to determine how much production overhead should be allocated to each job. We are told in exhibit 4.1 that it is company policy to allocate production overheads in proportion to the direct labour costs of each job. The total direct labour cost for the period is £16,000 and so the overhead cost rate must be calculated as:

$$\text{overhead cost rate (in £ per £ of direct labour)} = \frac{27,000}{16,000}$$

$$= £1.6875 \text{ per £}$$

This rate is then applied to the amounts of direct labour cost already charged to each job (which was £8,000 for job 601, £4,800 for job 602 and £3,200 for job 603). The resulting amounts are recorded in the relevant job records.

Job number	Calculation	Production overhead
		£
Job 601	8,000 × £1.6875	13,500
Job 602	4,800 × £1.6875	8,100
Job 603	3,200 × £1.6875	5,400
		27,000

4.2.2 Presentation of the job cost records

The job cost records are set out in exhibit 4.2. Jobs 601 and 602 are finished in the period and this is shown on the job cost record by a transfer to finished goods of the full cost of the job. Job 603 has a problem with unfinished work- in-progress but the rest of that job is completed and transferred to finished goods. That information is recorded on the job cost record card as shown in exhibit 4.2.

The total work-in-progress record is useful as a check on the separate job costs and is also useful for accounting purposes in providing a total record of work-in-progress at any point in time. It is created by using the totals of the direct materials issued to production, the total direct labour used on jobs and the total production overhead incurred during the month. Exhibit 4.3 shows the total work-in-progress record.

4.3 Job costing: applying the accounting equation to transactions

The job cost record cards used only a part of the information contained in exhibit 4.1. All the transactions must be recorded for purposes of preparing financial statements, using the accounting equation as shown in Chapter 1. This section analyses the transactions of exhibit 4.1 using the accounting equation and

Exhibit 4.2
Job cost records for jobs 601, 602 and 603

	Job cost record: Job 601	
3 June	Direct materials	80,000 †
30 June	Direct labour	8,000 ♥
	Prime cost	*88,000*
30 June	Production overhead:	13,500 ξ
	Total production cost	*101,500*
	To finished goods	(101,500)
	Work-in-progress	nil

	Job cost record: Job 602	
3 June	Direct materials	30,000 †
30 June	Direct labour	4,800 ♥
	Prime cost	*34,800*
30 June	Production overhead:	8,100 ξ
	Total production cost	*42,900*
	Finished goods	(42,900)
	Work-in-progress	nil

	Job cost record: Job 603	
3 June	Direct materials	10,000 †
30 June	Direct labour	3,200 ♥
	Prime cost	13,200
30 June	Production overhead:	5,400 ξ
	Total production cost	18,600
	Finished goods	(15,600)
1 May	*Work-in-progress*	3,000

Exhibit 4.3
Record of total work-in-progress for month of June

	Total work-in-progress	
3 June	Direct materials	120,000 †
30 June	Direct labour	16,000 ♥
30 June	Production overhead	27,000 ξ
		163,000
30 June	Finished goods	(160,000)
1 May	Work-in-progress	3,000

concludes with a spreadsheet record of the transactions for the month. The symbols contained in exhibit 4.1 are used throughout to help follow the cost trail.

Here is Fiona McTaggart to point out the difference between financial accounting and management accounting in the recording of costs.

FIONA: *For financial accounting purposes the cost of materials used, the payment of wages and the payment of various expenses such as rent, rates and electricity will be recorded as expenses which reduce the ownership interest. In the financial accounting records the costs would be reported as separate elements of the cost of goods sold. Management accounting arrives at the same amount for cost of goods sold by a different*

Exhibit 4.4
Routes to reporting cost of goods sold in management accounting and in financial reporting

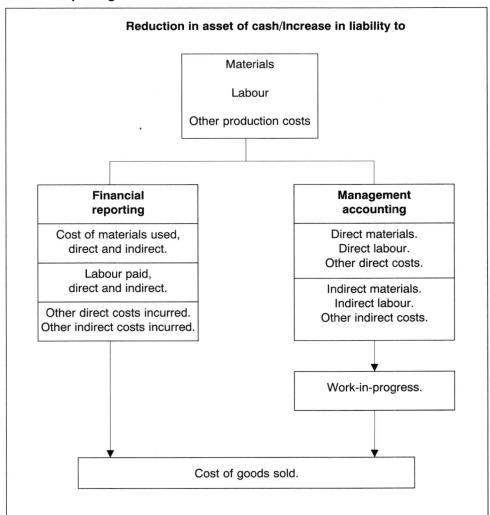

recording route. It collects all costs of material, labour and production overhead within the asset of work-in-progress and then transfers the completed work-in-progress to the asset of finished goods stock. The cost of goods taken from the finished goods stock becomes the cost of goods sold for the profit and loss account. (See exhibit 4.4.)

The management accounting practice follows the pattern of operations while the financial accounting practice is primarily concerned with collecting costs to arrive at total profit. They serve different purposes but arrive at the same answer overall. Where accounting records are held in computerised form, code numbers attached to cost items mean that the information can be used to generate more than one form of accounting report.

✧ ♣ ⊗ 4.3.1 Acquisition of inventory: direct and indirect materials

✧ In purchasing the rolls of paper, the business acquires an asset. In taking credit from the supplier it incurs a liability.

> **Asset ↑ – Liability ↑** = Ownership interest

♣ In purchasing the inks, glue and dyes, the business acquires a further asset. In paying cash, the asset of cash is diminished.

> **Asset ↑↓** – Liability = Ownership interest

⊗ Returning the damaged roll of paper reduces the asset of materials inventory and reduces the liability to the trade creditor.

> **Asset ↓ – Liability ↓** = Ownership interest

† 4.3.2 Converting raw materials into work-in-progress: direct materials

† When the rolls of paper are issued from the stores to the printing department, they become a part of the work-in-progress of that department. Since this work-in-progress is expected to bring a benefit to the enterprise in the form of cash flows from sales when it is eventually finished and sold, it meets the definition of an asset. There is an increase in the asset of work-in-progress and a decrease in the inventory of materials.

> **Asset ↑↓** – Liability = Ownership interest

ø 4.3.3 Issuing indirect materials to production

ø   Inks, glue and dyes are indirect materials. The indirect cost is part of the production overhead cost, to be accumulated with other indirect costs and later added to work-in-progress as a global amount for production overhead. In this case, only half of the indirect materials have been issued (£12,500), the rest remaining in inventory. There is a decrease in the asset of materials inventory and an increase in the asset of work-in-progress.

> **Asset ↑↓ – Liability = Ownership interest**

ψ λ ϖ φ 4.3.4 Labour costs

ψϖ   There are two amounts of direct labour costs paid during the period in respect of the printing employees; and

λφ   two amounts of indirect wages in respect of maintenance.

In practice, it will only be after analysis of the labour records for the period that an accurate subdivision into direct and indirect costs may be made. Although it is assumed here that all wages of printing employees are direct costs, it could be that enforced idle time through equipment failure would create an indirect cost. Taking the simplified illustration, the direct wages paid become a part of the prime cost of work-in-progress while the indirect wages paid become part of the production overhead cost within work-in-progress.

For the purposes of this illustration it is assumed that the manager of the business knows that all printing employees' wages are direct costs (♥) and so may be recorded immediately as direct costs of work-in-progress. The asset of cash decreases and the asset of work-in-progress increases.

> **Asset ↑↓ – Liability = Ownership interest**

It is further assumed that the manager of the business knows that all indirect labour costs will become production overheads (ξ) and hence added to the value of work-in-progress.

> **Asset ↑↓ – Liability = Ownership interest**

‡ξ 4.3.5 Production overhead costs

‡ξ   Rent, rates and electricity costs (‡) paid from cash in respect of printing are production overhead costs (ξ). For management accounting purposes they are regarded as part of the cost of the asset of work-in-progress.

> **Asset ↑↓ − Liability = Ownership interest**

For financial reporting purposes the overhead costs paid are regarded immediately as reducing the ownership claim because they are part of the expense of production overhead. Exhibit 4.4 shows that in both financial reporting and management accounting the production overhead costs eventually emerge as a component of the expense of cost of goods sold.

4.3.6 Transferring work-in-progress to finished goods

When the asset of work-in-progress is completed, it changes into another asset, the inventory of finished goods. In the accounting records the asset is removed from work-in-progress and enjoys a new description as the asset of finished goods.

> **Asset ↑↓ − Liability = Ownership interest**

≈ 4.3.7 Sale of goods

≈ When a sale is made to a customer, that part of the asset of finished goods inventory is transformed into the expense of cost of goods sold. Any finished goods remaining unsold continue to be reported as an asset.

> **Asset ↓ − Liability = Ownership interest ↓ (expense)**

4.3.8 Spreadsheet analysis

The transactions are brought together in spreadsheet form in exhibit 4.5. The entries on each line correspond to the detailed analyses provided in this section. The totals at the foot of each column represent the amounts of the various assets, liabilities and ownership interest resulting from the transactions of the month. Cash has decreased overall by £55,500. The asset of stock of materials (paper, inks, glues and dyes) has increased by £70,000 and the asset of work-in-progress has increased by £3,000. The asset of finished goods has increased by £8,000. The liability to the creditor stands at £177,500. Overall the transactions of the month, as recorded here, have decreased the ownership interest by £152,000, the amount which is recorded as the cost of goods sold.

	£
Overall increase in assets	25,500
Overall increase in liabilities	177,500
Difference	(152,000)
Decrease in ownership interest	(152,000)

Exhibit 4.5
Spreadsheet to show analysis of transactions for the month of June, using accounting equation

Date	Transaction	Symbol	Cash £	Stock of materials £	Work-in-progress £	Finished goods £	Creditor £	Cost of goods sold £
							(Liability)	(Ownership interest)
June 1	Bought 60 rolls of paper on credit from supplier, invoiced price being £180,000.	✧		180,000			180,000	
June 1	Bought inks, glue and dyes, cost £25,000 paid in cash.	♣	(25,000)	25,000				
June 2	Returned to supplier one roll, damaged in transit, £2,500.	⊗		(2,500)			(2,500)	
June 3	Rolls of paper issued to printing department, cost £120,000.	†		(120,000)	120,000			
June 4	Issued half of inks, glues and dyes to printing department, £12,500.	∅		(12,500)	12,500			
June 14	Paid printing employees' wages £8,000.	ψ	(8,000)		8,000			
June 14	Paid maintenance wages £250.	λ	(250)		250			
June 16	Paid rent, rates and electricity in respect of printing, £14,000, in cash.	‡	(14,000)		14,000			
June 28	Paid printing employees' wages £8,000.	ϖ	(8,000)		8,000			
June 28	Paid maintenance wages £250.	φ	(250)		250			
June 30	Transferred printed stationery to finished goods inventory, valued at cost of £160,000.	#			(160,000)	160,000		
June 30	Sold stationery to customer on credit, cost of goods sold being £152,000.	≈				(152,000)		(152,000)
	Totals		(55,500)	70,000	3,000	8,000	177,500	(152,000)

4 · Job costing and contract costing

83

4.4 Contract accounts

One specific application of job costing is to contracts such as engineering or construction projects which usually require more than one accounting period for completion. Such large 'jobs' are normally carried out under a legal contract which sets out the conditions of performance required of the enterprise and the conditions of payment to be imposed on the customer.

Because of the size and significance of such a contract, it is common practice to open a separate job cost record in which to collect all costs and revenues of the project so that the document eventually also records the profit on the contract.

4.4.1 Main features of a contract

Before moving on to the accounting aspects, it is necessary to set out some of the main features of most contracts. The contract is usually for some substantial work based on building or engineering applications, but could be a contract for services such as cleaning a building or providing security cover. Because the contract is agreed in very specific terms, most costs will be directly related to the project. Materials, labour and direct expenses will be identifiable with the project. Labour requirements may be provided by employees of the organisation or may be subcontracted to other businesses. Special equipment may be required for the project. The head office of the organisation will seek to charge overhead costs to the project.

Incomplete contract

If the contract is incomplete at the year-end a *portion of profit* may nevertheless be recognised on the basis that the work has been done and the profit on that work is earned. To refrain from reporting profit as the contract progresses would give a very distorted picture of the activity of the business. In order to achieve a measure of objectivity in assessing the amount of profit earned on a partly completed project, it is normal to seek the opinion of an expert (architect, surveyor or engineer, for example) on the *value of work completed* to date. Any work not certified as being completed at the balance sheet date is carried forward as work-in-progress.

Taking profit as the work progresses is attractive as an application of the *accruals concept* but is felt to be risky in the context of the *prudence concept*. In the case of contracts, this has led to a wide range of practice across and within the various industries. However, it would be safe to assume that most companies would seek to make some provision against being overoptimistic on a long-term contract.

Payments by the customer

Where the contract lasts over a longer period of time, it is quite usual for the enterprise to ask the customer to make *payments on account of progress*. Invoices for these progress payments are made as soon as the technical expert has certified as complete a stage of the project. When the customer makes a progress payment in advance, the sum is effectively a liability from the point of view of the company receiving the payment. If for any reason the contract were not to be completed, the payment would have to be refunded to the customer.

4.4.2 Recording transactions for a contract

Because a contract is usually a significant activity for the business, the job cost record is used to show every aspect of the contract, including all costs incurred, whether for the current or a later period, and the periodic profit.

Costs incurred during the accounting period

The materials, labour, direct and indirect costs of a contract job are recorded on the job card when paid for or when acquired from a supplier who becomes a creditor of the business.

Items remaining at end of accounting period

At the end of the accounting period the value of equipment and materials remaining on site is estimated. The difference between the original cost and the valuation equals the amount of material and equipment consumed by the contract. Items remaining on site are regarded as assets for the next period.

Matching costs with revenues of the accounting period

In the revenue section of the job cost record, an entry will be made for the sales value of work certified by an expert as being complete. Deducting costs of the project from the estimated sales value of work certified will give a profit figure for the period. There are no firm rules as to how much of this profit should be reported for the period, but many companies would report less than the full amount, as a prudent measure. Various formulae are used to decide how much profit to report. A useful rule of thumb at this stage might be to suggest reporting around two-thirds of the profit calculated.

4.5 Illustration of contract accounting

The following pages set out the calculation of periodic profit on a contract which lasts fifteen months in total and straddles two accounting periods. Office Builders Ltd undertook a contract to build the Western Office Complex for a fixed price of £390,000 during the period from May 19X1 to July 19X2.

Exhibit 4.6 gives information for 19X1 which is presented as a job cost record in exhibit 4.7, leading to a statement of profit in exhibit 4.8. Exhibit 4.9 gives information for 19X2 which is presented as a job cost record in exhibit 4.10 and a statement of profit in exhibit 4.11. The overall profit on the contract is presented in exhibit 4.12 and explained in terms of the profit reported in the two separate reporting periods.

Exhibit 4.6
Office Builders Ltd: contract for Western Office Complex – transactions up to the company's year-end in December 19X1

Transactions during 19X1		£000s
May	Materials purchased and delivered to site	87
May	Equipment delivered to site	11
July	Architect's fee	6
June–Dec.	Materials issued from store	51
May–Dec.	Wages paid on site	65
September	Payment to subcontractors	8
May–Dec.	Direct costs	25
December	Head office charges	7
At the end of 19X1		
December	Value of equipment remaining on site	7
December	Value of material remaining on site	32
December	Sales value of work certified	240
December	Amount due to subcontractors	5
December	Direct costs incurred but not yet paid	8

4.5.1 Recording the transactions

In respect of materials, £87,000 was purchased and £51,000 recorded as being issued. It might be expected that would leave £36,000 to be carried forward in store. But only £32,000 of materials were found at the end of the year, implying that £4,000 of materials has either been scrapped because of some defect or has been removed without authority. In practice this would probably lead to an investigation of the control system to discover why some materials have apparently disappeared. The profit calculation for 19X1 assumes that any material not contained in the physical check at the end of the year must have been used on the contract.

The equipment delivered to the site had a cost of £11,000 and an estimated value of £7,000 remaining at the end of the year. Depreciation is therefore £4,000.

The cost of work certified is the total of the costs incurred to date on that portion of the work approved by the architect. In this case the work has been certified at the end of the accounting year, so there is no problem in deciding which costs to treat as cost of goods sold and which to carry forward. If the work had been certified before the end of the financial year, any subsequent costs would also need to be carried forward to be matched against future estimated sales value of work done.

An architect's fee would be quite common on contract work of this type. Provided the fee is specific to the project, it forms a direct cost which must be included in the calculation of contract profit.

All further expenditure of the period, such as wages, other direct costs and payments to subcontractors, is included in the calculation of the profit on the contract because it is, or will become, part of the costs of the contract. At the end of the accounting period a count is taken of everything remaining unused on the site and this count forms the basis for determining how much of the 'expense' should be carried forward as an asset for the next period.

Any costs not carried to the next period will become part of the cost of goods sold, to be compared with the value of work certified in determining the profit for the period. Those managing an enterprise prudently might decide to hold back on reporting some of the profit calculated in the early stages of a project, as a precaution against unforeseen problems later. Various formulae are in use for calculating this 'prudent amount' but this example will take a 'rule of thumb' approach in suggesting that taking credit for two-thirds of the profit calculated might be a reasonably prudent approach.

Exhibit 4.7
Office Builders Ltd: job cost record of Western Office Complex for 19X1

Contract job cost record 19X1 Western Office Complex		
19X1		*£000s*
May	Materials purchased	87
May	Equipment at cost	11
May	Architect's fee	6
May–Dec.	Wages paid	65
September	Subcontractors	8
May–Dec.	Direct costs	25
December	Head office charges	7
December	Due to subcontractor	5
December	Direct costs incurred	8
	Total costs charged 19X1	222
	Carry to next period:	
December	Materials on site	(32)
	Equipment on site	(7)
December	Cost of work certified for 19X1	183

The costs for 19X1 include all recorded payments plus costs incurred but not paid at the end of the period. These include liabilities to the subcontractor £5,000 and direct costs £8,000, which must be settled early in 19X2. Equipment on site and material on site have been paid in 19X1 but will not be used in earning revenue until 19X2. The overall cost of the work certified as completed during 19X1 is therefore £183,000 (*see* exhibit 4.7).

4.5.2 Reporting the profit of the period

In the profit and loss statement for 19X1 (exhibit 4.8), Office Builders Ltd will calculate a total profit of £57,000 resulting from the matching of costs with the value of work certified. That total profit will then be reported in two components. Two-thirds of this amount, £38,000, will be reported in the profit and loss account for 19X1. One-third, £19,000, will be held back until 19X2 as a precaution against unforeseen problems causing additional costs and reducing the overall contract profit.

Exhibit 4.8
Statement of contract profit to be reported in 19X1

	£000s
Value of work certified	240
Cost of work certified	183
Profit of the period	57
Less: portion not reported this period (one-third of calculated profit)	19
Profit to be reported for 19X1	38

4.5.3 Transactions for the following period

To show the complete picture on the contract it is necessary to consider 19X2 also. Exhibit 4.9 sets out the transactions undertaken during 19X2.

Exhibit 4.10 sets out the statement of costs for the second year, and shows that the cost of work certified for 19X2 is £141,000.

The statement of contract profit for 19X2 is set out in exhibit 4.11. It shows that the calculated profit for 19X2 is £9,000 (£150,000 value of work certified minus £141,000 costs incurred for the period). The profit 'held back', £19,000, is added to the profit and loss section of the contract account to give an overall profit of £28,000 reported in 19X2. With the benefit of hindsight it probably was a wise precaution to hold some of the 19X1 profit back from the reported profit and it would appear possible that some of the costs incurred in 19X1 were providing a benefit to the work of 19X2.

At the end of 19X2 all of the remaining profit can be reported since the outcome is certain. In practice, there will be a further period during which the builder has responsibility to put right any defects. It could therefore be prudent to make provision again for possible losses on repairs needed before the hand-over date, but that has not been done in this illustration.

Exhibit 4.9
Office Builders Ltd: contract for Western Office Complex – transactions up to the company's year-end in December 19X2

Transactions during 19X2		£000s
January	Paid subcontractor amount due	5
January	Paid direct costs due at end of 19X1	8
February	Materials purchased and delivered to site	24
June–Dec.	Materials issued from store	56
May–Dec.	Wages paid on site	31
September	Payment to subcontractors	17
May–Dec.	Direct costs	15
December	Head office charges	7
At the end of 19X2		
December	Value of equipment remaining on site	nil
December	Value of material remaining on site	nil
December	Sales value of work certified	150
December	Direct costs incurred but not yet paid	8

Exhibit 4.10
Office Builders Ltd: job cost record of Western Office Complex for 19X2

Contract job cost record 19X2 Western Office Complex		
19X2		*£000s*
January	Material on site b/d	32
January	Equipment on site b/d	7
Jan.–July	Materials purchased	24
Jan.–July	Wages paid	31
March	Subcontractors	17
Jan.–July	Direct costs paid	15
July	Head office charges	7
July	Direct costs incurred	8
	Cost of work certified	141

Exhibit 4.11
Statement of contract profit to be reported in 19X2

	£000s
Value of work certified	150
Cost of work certified	141
Profit of the period	9
Add: portion not reported in previous period	19
Profit to be reported for 19X1	28

4.5.4 Total contract profit

Exhibit 4.12 shows an overall statement of profit. It reports the full contract price, against which are matched all the costs of the contract. The total contract profit is shown to be £66,000, reported as £38,000 in 19X1 and £28,000 in 19X2.

Exhibit 4.12
Western Office Complex: statement of total contract profit

	£000s	£000s
Contract price		390
Direct costs		
Materials (87 + 24)	111	
Labour (65 + 31)	96	
Direct costs (25 + 8 + 15 + 8)	56	
Payments to subcontractors (8 + 5 + 17)	30	
Depreciation of equipment	11	
Architect's fee	6	
	310	
Indirect costs		
Head office charges (7 + 7)	14	
		324
Total contract profit (reported as £38,000 in 19X1 and £28,000 in 19X2)		66

4.6 Summary

In this chapter we have drawn on the information and definitions contained in Chapter 3 to show the method of preparing job cost statements and contract cost statements. It has explained the differences between management accounting and financial reporting in the approach to reporting the cost of goods sold, but has also emphasised that both use the same basic data, so that suitable coding of accounting data on input should allow different reporting formats for different user requirements.

Contract costs have been used to illustrate the issues in cost recording and profit reporting where a contract operates over more than one accounting period. The accruals concept is the principle applied in calculating the profit of a period but the prudence concept also applies in deciding how much of the calculated profit should be reported. Over the entire contract the total profit must be reported, but the example shows there is scope for flexibility while the contract remains incomplete.

Self-testing on the chapter

1   Explain how each of the following transactions is dealt with in a job costing system:

   (a)   The production department orders 16 components from store at a cost of £3 each, to be used on job 59.
   (b)   An employee (A. Jones) receives a weekly wage of £600. In week 29 this employee's time has been spent two-thirds on job 61 and one-third on job 62.
   (c)   On 16 June, job 94 is finished at a total cost of £3,500. The job consisted of printing brochures for a supermarket advertising campaign.

2   The following transactions relate to a dairy, converting milk to cheese, for the month of May:

1 May	Bought 600 drums of milk from supplier, invoiced price being £90,000.
1 May	Bought cartons, cost £6,000 paid in cash.
2 May	Returned to supplier one drum damaged in transit, £150.
3 May	500 drums of milk issued to cheesemaking department, cost £75,000.
4 May	Issued two-thirds of cartons to cheesemaking department, £4,000.
14 May	Paid cheesemakers' wages, £3,000.
14 May	Paid wages for cleaning and hygiene, £600.
16 May	Paid rent, rates and electricity in respect of dairy, £8,000, in cash.
28 May	Paid cheesemakers' wages, £3,000.
28 May	Paid wages for cleaning and hygiene, £600.
30 May	Transferred all production of cheese in cartons to finished goods inventory. No work-in-progress at end of month.

Required

Prepare a calculation of the cost of production transferred to finished goods at the end of May.

3   Restoration Ltd buys basic furniture units and creates period layouts in clients'
     homes. The following transactions relate to jobs 801, 802 and 803 in the month of
     May. Prepare job cost records for each job.

1 May	✧	Bought 70 furniture units on credit from supplier, invoiced price being £204,000. The furniture units acquired consisted of two different grades. 50 units were of standard size at a total cost of £140,000 and 20 units were of king-size at a total cost of £64,000.
1 May	♣	Bought stain, varnish and paint at a cost of £30,000 paid in cash. The stain cost £12,000 while the varnish cost £14,000 and the paint £4,000.
2 May	⊗	Returned to supplier one furniture unit damaged in transit, £2,800. The furniture unit returned was of standard size.
3 May	†	Furniture units issued to finishing department. 40 standard size units were issued, together with 14 king-size units. There were three separate jobs: references 801, 802 and 803. The standard size units were all for job 801 (Riverside Hotel); 10 king-size units were for job 802 (Mountain Lodge); and the remaining 4 king-size units were for job 803 (Hydeaway House).
4 May	ø	Issued stain, varnish and paint to finishing department, £22,500.
14 May	ψ	Paid finishing department employees' wages £10,000. Wages were paid to 8 printing employees, each earning the same amount.
14 May	λ	Paid security wages £350. Security wages were paid to one part-time security officer.
16 May		Paid rent, rates and electricity in respect of finishing department, £18,000 in cash. Payment for rent was £9,000, rates £5,000 and electricity £4,000.
28 May	ϖ	Paid finishing department employees' wages £10,000. Wages were paid to the same 8 employees as on 14 May.
28 May	φ	Paid security wages £350. Security wages were paid to the same security officer as on 14 May.
30 May	♥	Employee records show that: 4 finishing department employees worked all month on job 801; 2 finishing department employees worked on job 802; and 2 finishing department employees worked on job 803.
30 May	ξ	It is company policy to allocate production overheads in proportion to labour costs of each job.
30 May	#	Transferred all finished goods to finished goods inventory. There remained no unfinished work-in-progress.
30 May	≈	Riverside Hotel and Mountain Lodge took delivery of their goods. Hydeaway House will take delivery on 10 June.

4   Bridge Builders Ltd undertook a contract to build a pedestrian footbridge for a
     fixed price of £400,000 during the period from May 19X1 to July 19X2. The table
     sets out transactions up to the company's year-end in December, 19X1.

Transactions during 19X1		£000s
May	Materials purchased and delivered to site	91
May	Equipment delivered to site	14
July	Architect's fee	7
June–Dec.	Materials issued from store	73
May–Dec.	Wages paid on site	71
September	Payment to subcontractors	10
May–Dec.	Direct costs	22
December	Head office charges	6
At the end of 19X1		
December	Value of equipment remaining on site	9
December	Value of material remaining on site	15
December	Sales value of work certified	280
December	Amount due to subcontractors	3
December	Direct costs incurred but not yet paid	3

Required

Prepare a statement of contract profit for the year 19X1.

Activity for study groups

As a group, you are planning to establish a partnership supplying examination advice and tuition to school pupils in their homes. Each course of lessons will be regarded as a single 'job'. Courses may vary in length and in target ability level, depending on the requirements of the pupil to be tutored. Divide the group to take on three different roles. One role is that of a tutor who is also a member of the partnership, sharing equally the profits of the business. The second role is that of the accountancy adviser to the partnership. The third role is that of a parent making enquiries about the price charged and the justification for that price.

Each member of the group should take on one of the three roles and separately make a note of:

(a) The expected costs of a job (in terms of types of cost).

(b) How you would justify the costs (if supplying the service).
(c) How you would question the costs (if receiving the service).

Then all members of the group should come together, compare answers, and finally prepare a joint report on the problems of job costing in a service business.

Case studies

Case 4.1

Insulation Ltd has been established to manufacture insulation material for use in houses. At present, one machine is installed for production of insulation material. A further similar machine can be purchased if required.

The first customer is willing to place orders in three different sizes at the following selling prices:

Order size	Selling price per package £
430 packages per day	25.20
880 packages per day	25.00
1,350 packages per day	24.80

The customer will enter into an initial contract of 30 days' duration and will uplift completed packages on a daily basis from the premises of Insulation Ltd.

The following assumptions have been made in respect of Insulation Ltd:

(a) In view of the competitive market the selling prices are not negotiable.
(b) Direct materials will cost £23.75 per package irrespective of the order size.
(c) The output of one machine will be 350 packages per shift.
(d) A maximum of three shifts will be available on a machine within one day. The depreciation charge for a machine will be £100 per day, irrespective of the number of shifts worked.
(e) Labour costs to operate a machine will be £100 for the first shift, £120 for the second shift and £160 for the third shift of the day. If labour is required for a shift, then the full shift must be paid for regardless of the number of packages produced.
(f) The total cost of supervising the employees for each of the first two shifts in any day will be £20 per machine. The supervision cost of the third shift will be £40 per machine.
(g) Other fixed overhead costs will be £280 per day if one machine is used. Buying and using an additional machine would result in a further £100 of fixed costs per day.
(h) Production and sales volume will be equal regardless of order size.
(i) The company does not expect to obtain other work during the term of the initial contract.

Required

Prepare a report for the production director of Insulation Ltd giving:

1 For each order size, details of the overall profitability per day and net profit per package.

2 An explanation of the differing amounts of profit per package.

Case 4.2

Builders Ltd has undertaken to refurbish the Black Swan Hotel. The contract price was agreed at £480,000 based on estimated total costs of £440,000. The contract work began on 1 January 19X8. The accounting year of Builders Ltd ended on 31 August 19X8, at which date the contract was not completed. The following information provides the full contract estimate and the payments up to 31 August:

	Original estimate for full contract £	Actual cash paid up to 31 August £
Subcontractors' costs:		
Substructure	21,910	20,050
Superstructure	140,660	135,200
External works	111,256	95,000
Main contractors' costs:		
Materials:		
Internal finishing	22,800	23,370
Fittings and furnishings	9,300	10,000
Utilities	42,400	31,800
Direct labour and overheads:		
Internal finishing	23,100	17,325
Fittings and furnishings	9,100	6,916
Utilities	39,100	30,107
Administration overhead	20,374	15,402
	440,000	385,170

Further information

(a) The substructure was completed on 31 July but a subcontractor's invoice for £2,500 in respect of the final work done was not paid until 4 September.

(b) The superstructure was also completed on 31 July and subcontractors were paid in full during August.

(c) External works were 80 per cent completed at 31 August. There was a delay in March due to adverse weather affecting the harling, which cost £3,500 to remove and restore.

(d) Cash paid for materials for internal finishing covered the cost of all paint and wallpaper necessary to complete the contract. The actual paint and wallpaper unused at 31 August was valued at £4,000.

(e) All fittings and furnishings required for the contract had been bought and paid for before 31 August. Only 70 per cent by value had been installed by 31 August.

(f) Materials costs of utilities were 80 per cent complete in respect to estimates.

(g) Labour hours worked up to 31 August on internal finishing, fittings and furnishings and services were 70 per cent of the estimated total.

(h) Administration overhead is allocated as a percentage of total sales value.

(i) It is company policy to credit to management profit and loss account not more than 75 per cent of the profit earned in any period.

(j) It is estimated that the main contractor's material and labour costs for the remainder of the contract will be incurred at the same rate as was experienced up to 31 August.

(k) An independent surveyor estimated the contract value of work done up to 31 August at £400,000.

(l) On 31 August the customer paid £380,000 on account of work completed.

Required

Prepare a report for the directors of Builders Ltd containing:

1 The profit on the contract for the accounting year ended 31 August 19X8.

2 An estimate of the actual profit to be achieved on the contract as a whole.

3 Brief comments on the contract outcome.

Chaper 5

Process costing

Learning objectives	After studying this chapter you should be able to:
	1 Explain how process costing differs from job costing.
	2 Apply the idea of an equivalent unit to work-in-progress in a process.
	3 Calculate the costs of joint products and by-products.
	4 Understand the use of process costs for planning and control.
	5 Understand the need for care in using process costs for decision making.

5.1 Introduction

Special costing techniques are required where there is a continuous flow of production of similar units of output. This situation of a continuous process arises in the chemical industry and in other industries such as textiles, paint, food, steel, glass, mining, cement and oil.

As an example of a company where processes are important, exhibit 5.1 contains an extract from the annual report of Courtaulds plc describing the group's products. The products of Courtaulds plc which derive from these chemical processes are many and varied. Viscose rayon, the first cellulose fibre, is a chemical name most readily related to womenswear and furnishing fabrics, but it is also found in clutch linings, insulating material within railway signalling cables, and tea bags. The rayon process is also used to make film for sweet wrappings, baked goods and soft cheeses. In the area of coatings, the company produces marine paint which keeps the hulls of ships and yachts free of barnacles. Another type of paint for the superstructure of ships transforms rust stains into colourless deposits. Other products involving a flow process include the manufacture of specialist film which makes glass shatter-resistant, toothpaste tubes and rigid packaging products such as special housings for asthma inhalers.

Exhibit 5.1:
The products of Courtaulds plc

> Courtaulds is a chemical materials company. Our products are made by chemical processes. But with a few exceptions they are not themselves pure chemicals: they are products made from chemicals. These products are based on two related technical disciplines. The first of these is polymer technology linked with surface science – used to coat, seal or protect a diverse range of surfaces. The second is fibre technology, with particular emphasis on cellulose chemistry.

This is the type of business where individual products are indistinguishable in nature and there are no special needs of customers in relation to individual items of product. What is of interest to management is the cost and performance of the continuous process as a whole.

Definition

Process costing is appropriate to a business or operation where there is a continuous flow of a relatively high volume of similar products during a reporting period.

5.2 The role of management accounting

Management's purposes in a continuous process business are no different from those in any other organisation. There is an overall requirement on the part of management for decision making and judgement. In this context, accounting information is required for management purposes of planning, decision making and control.

Management accounting contributes by:

- directing attention
- keeping the score
- solving problems.

In particular management accounting must be able to show, in relation to a flow process, how much cost has flowed through with the product into finished goods and how much remains with the work-in-progress. That is part of the scorekeeping aspect of management accounting. If the process splits, taking different directions for different output, the management accountant will be expected to contribute information relevant to decision making about the various products. That is an example of the problem-solving aspects of management accounting.

This description of the management accountant's role is not substantially different from a description which could apply in any job-costing situation, however, there are some specific problems in the process industries which require specially designed management accounting techniques. In this chapter we deal with two of these problems, as follows:

1 Individual products cannot be distinguished for costing purposes. Costs cannot be assigned directly to products but must be allocated (spread) using some averaging basis.
2 Joint products and by-products are produced as an unavoidable result of the process of creating the main products. Total costs must therefore be shared across main products and by-products. Joint products each have a significant sales value. By-products usually have relatively low sales value.

5.3 Allocation of costs to products in a process industry

In process costing, items in production flow from one process to the next until they are completed. Each process contributes to the total operation and then passes its output to the next process until the goods are finished and can be stored to await sale. Recording of costs follows the physical flow as closely as possible. Because it is not possible to identify each unit of output on its way through the various processes, the concept of an *equivalent unit* is applied. Each completed item is equivalent to one unit of output, but each incomplete item is equivalent to only a fraction of a unit of output. This concept is particularly important at the end of the reporting period for dealing with items in process which are incomplete.

Definition

An *equivalent unit* of output is the amount of output, expressed in terms of whole units, which is equivalent to the actual amount of partly or fully completed production.

Process costing requires several stages of analysis of the costs. These are:

1 collect the data for the period,
2 prepare a statement of physical flows and equivalent units of output for the period,
3 ascertain the total costs to be accounted for this period,
4 calculate the cost per equivalent unit,
5 apportion the cost between finished output and work-in-progress; and
6 check that all costs are accounted for.

Collecting data requires information on the quantities of materials, labour and other resources put into the process and the quantities of products emerging from the process in any period of time. Because of the continuous nature of any process, it is likely that some products will be partly completed at the beginning and end of the period. Such partly completed work is referred to as *work-in-progress*. Information is also required on the costs of the period, separated into material, labour and production overheads. Sometimes the labour and overhead costs are referred to collectively as *conversion costs* because they convert the input materials into products.

Physical flows into and out of the process have to be identified. There will be *opening work-in-progress* at the beginning of the period which is completed during the period. Some products will be started and finished in the period. Some will be started but will be incomplete at the end and will be described as *closing work-in- progress*. Materials may be introduced at the beginning of the period, while further materials may be introduced part way through the period.

Identifying the *total costs to be accounted for* requires some care. There will be costs incurred during the period but there will also be costs brought forward from the previous period, included in the opening work-in-progress. All these costs must be shared between the products completed during the period and the work-in-progress remaining at the end of the period.

The *cost per equivalent unit* is a particular feature of process costing which takes into account the problem of partly completed units at the beginning and end of the period. If an item is 40 per cent completed, then it represents the equivalent of 40 per cent (or 0.4 as a fraction) of one completed unit. So if there are 3,000 units held, each of which is 40 per cent complete, they can be said to represent the equivalent of 1,200 completed units and would be described as *1,200 equivalent units*.

Apportioning costs between finished output and work-in-progress is relatively straightforward. Once the cost per equivalent unit has been calculated, it is multiplied by the number of equivalent units of finished items to give the cost of finished output and by the number of equivalent units of closing work-in-progress to give the cost of closing work-in-progress.

Finally, it is essential to check that nothing has been gained or lost in the arithmetic process by comparing the total costs of input to the process with the total costs of output in the period. If the totals are the same, then the worst problem that can have occurred is a misallocation between finished goods and work-in-progress. If the totals are not the same, a careful search for errors is required.

These steps in the process costing approach are conveniently illustrated and explained by working through an example and commenting on the main features of interest.

5.3.1 Process costing where there is no opening work-in-progress

Process costing is an exercise which can be complicated. However, to learn the approach it is best to start with a simplified example and work up to the various complications one at a time. Exhibit 5.2 illustrates process costing for the first month of a reporting period where there is no work-in-progress at the start of the month but there is some at the end of the month. Five steps are shown, corresponding to the first five stages of the process described earlier in this section.

Exhibit 5.2
Process costing illustration: No opening work-in-progress

Step 1: Collect data for the period
The following information relates to the assembly department in a company manufacturing shower units for bathrooms. A pack of materials is introduced at the start of the process. The pack contains a plastic shower head, flexible hose and various plumbing items. These are assembled by employees and then passed from the assembly department to the electrical department for con- nection to the electric power unit. At the end of the month there will be some shower units only partly completed. The supervisor of the assembly department has estimated that these units are 40 per cent completed at that date.

Continued overleaf

Exhibit 5.2 continued

Data in respect of month 1

No work-in-progress at start of month.
60,000 units of raw materials introduced for conversion.
40,000 units of output completed during the month.
20,000 units of work-in-progress, 40 per cent completed at end of month.

Costs incurred on material, labour and overheads: £120,000.

*Step 2: Prepare a statement of physical flows and equivalent units of output for
the month*

The physical flow involves 60,000 units entering the process for assembly. Of
these, 40,000 are fully assembled and 20,000 partly assembled at the end of
the period. This physical flow is shown in the left-hand column as a check that
all items are kept under control. For accounting purposes the concept of an
equivalent unit, as explained earlier, is more important. So the final column
contains the equivalent units. For the goods which are finished during the
month, the equivalent units are 100 per cent of the physical units. For the goods
which are still in progress, the equivalent units of 8,000 are calculated as 40 per
cent of the physical amount of 20,000 units of work-in-progress.

	Physical flow (units)	Equivalent units of output
Input:		
Materials introduced	60,000	
	60,000	
Output:		
Goods finished this month	40,000	40,000
Work-in-progress at end (40 per cent completed)	20,000	8,000
Total equivalent units	60,000	48,000

Step 3: Ascertain total costs to be accounted for this period

As there is no work-in-progress at the beginning of the period, the only costs to
be accounted for are the costs of £120,000 incurred during the period.

	£
Opening work-in-progress	none
Incurred this month	120,000
Total to account for	120,000

Step 4: Calculate cost per equivalent unit

Continuing the emphasis on equivalent units (rather than physical units), a unit cost is calculated by dividing the costs of the period, £120,000 as shown in step 3, by the number of equivalent units, 48,000, as shown in step 2. The benefit of having a cost per equivalent unit is that it gives a fair allocation to completed and partly completed units, as shown in step 5.

$$\text{Cost per equivalent unit} = \frac{£120,000}{48,000} = £2.50$$

Step 5: Apportion cost between finished output and work-in-progress

The cost per equivalent unit, which is £2.50, is now applied to the finished output and to the work-in-progress, measuring the quantity of each in equivalent units.

	£
Value of finished output 40,000 × £2.50	100,000
Work-in-progress 8,000 × £2.50	20,000
Total costs accounted for	120,000

Fiona McTaggart has the following comment.

FIONA: *From step 5 of exhibit 5.2 you will see that the total costs accounted for are the same as the costs in step 3 which required allocation. It is always important to check back to the starting data to make sure that nothing has been lost or created inadvertently in the calculation process. There could still be an error within the allocations if the wrong approach has been taken, so a separate check of all calculations is generally useful.*

It is also good practice to explain in words what each calculation is intended to achieve. If you cannot explain it in words, that is an indication that you do not fully understand the calculation and neither will anyone else reading your work. If you can explain with confidence, then it is more likely that you are correct or, if you are incorrect, that the cause of any error will be seen readily by another person.

Activity 5.1

Starting again with the data of exhibit 5.2, close the book and check that you are able to produce the process cost information ending with the value of finished output and the value of work-in-progress. You must understand and be confident about exhibit 5.2 before you read further.

5.3.2 Process costing where there is work-in-progress at the start of the period

The first complication to be introduced is the presence of work-in-progress at the start of the period. Opening work-in-progress introduces a complication because it carries costs from the end of one period to the beginning of the next. The problem faced by the management accountant is to decide between two possible courses of action. The first is to take those costs as being added to (*accumulated* with) the costs incurred in the current period and spread over all equivalent units of output. The second is to regard them as remaining firmly attached to the partly completed products with which they arrived. The first of these possibilities is called the *weighted average method* and the second is called the *first-in-first-out method*. It will be sufficient for the purposes of this textbook to illustrate the weighted average method, which is the more commonly used in practice.

Exhibit 5.3 takes on to month 2 the story which began in exhibit 5.2. Work-in-progress is carried from the end of month 1 to the start of month 2. The weighted average method follows the same five steps as were used in exhibit 5.2. The cost figure calculated at step 3 is the total of the costs brought forward with the opening work-in-progress and the costs incurred in the month. At step 4 the cost per equivalent unit is calculated by dividing all costs by total equivalent output.

Exhibit 5.3
Process costing illustration: opening work-in-progress

Step 1: Collect data for the period

Step 1 starts by bringing forward the work-in-progress of month 1. If you look back to step 1 of exhibit 5.2 you will see that the closing work-in-progress was 20,000 units, each 40 per cent complete. To this is added 30,000 shower head packs for assembly. We are then told that 35,000 units are completed and 15,000 are one-third completed at the end of month 2.

> *Data in respect of month 2*
> 20,000 units work-in-progress at start, 40 per cent complete.
> 30,000 units of raw materials introduced for conversion.
> 35,000 units of output completed during the month.
> 15,000 units of work-in-progress, one-third completed at end of month.
>
> Costs incurred on material, labour and overheads: £120,000.

Step 2: Prepare a statement of physical flows and equivalent units of output for the month

In step 2 the left-hand column is used to keep track of the physical flow of units and the right-hand column shows the equivalent units of output for month 2. For the finished goods the equivalent units are 100 per cent of the finished physical units but for the work-in-progress the equivalent units are one-third of the physical units, as specified in step 1.

	Physical flow (units)	Equivalent units of output
Input:		
Work-in-progress at start	20,000	
Material introduced	30,000	
	50,000	
Output:		
Goods finished this month	35,000	35,000
Work-in-progress at end (33.3 per cent completed)	15,000	5,000
Total equivalent units	50,000	40,000

Step 3: Ascertain total costs to be accounted for during this period

There are two separate elements of cost which together must be allocated to the total equivalent units of output for the period. The first element is the value of work-in-progress at the start of the period. This is a portion of the costs incurred in the first month that has been brought forward to the second month in order to match it with the units completed during the period. The second element is the new cost incurred during the second month.

	£
Opening work-in-progress brought forward	20,000
Incurred this month	120,000
Total to account for	140,000

Step 4: Calculate cost per equivalent unit

Continuing the emphasis on equivalent units, the cost of £140,000 calculated in step 3 is divided by the total number of equivalent units calculated as 40,000 in step 2. The result is a cost of £3.50 per equivalent unit, calculated as follows:

$$\text{Cost per equivalent unit} = \frac{£140,000}{40,000} = £3.50$$

Step 5: Apportion cost between finished output and work-in-progress

The cost of £3.50 per equivalent unit is applied to the equivalent units of finished output and to the equivalent units of work-in-progress. This gives a fair allocation of the total cost of £140,000 between the finished and unfinished goods as follows:

	£
Value of finished output 35,000 × £3.50	122,500
Work-in-progress 5,000 × £3.50	17,500
Total costs accounted for	140,000

Here is Fiona McTaggart to comment.

FIONA: *This method is called the weighted average approach because it averages* all *costs over* all *equivalent output and ignores the fact that some of the production started in the previous period.*

I usually like the weighted average method because it is not too fiddly and allows me to divide all costs of the period by the equivalent units of output without having to worry about what started where. However, some of my clients do not like this approach because, they say, it is mixing some of last month's costs with other costs incurred this month. Instead of spreading all costs over all production, their suggestion is to allocate this month's cost to the items started and finished in the month and to allow opening work-in-progress to carry the costs with which it arrived.

My answer is that it's a good idea, but more time-consuming. I also mention, tactfully, that the approach has already been thought of and is called the first-in-first-out method of process costing. It requires more work by the accountant but generally gives results only marginally different from the weighted average method.

Activity 5.2

> *Pause here to test your confidence of exhibit 5.3. Take a note of the data provided at the start of the example, close the book and write out the steps of the process cost calculations. Write down a brief explanation of each step which you could give to a fellow student who has not read this chapter but would like an idea of what it contains.*

5.3.3 Separate material and conversion costs

The illustrations provided so far have assumed that all materials are introduced at the start of the process. In practice, materials may be added at intervals during the process, so that conversion work can be carried out in stages.

Exhibit 5.4 shows the separate analysis of materials and conversion costs. It relates to a company which introduces materials into the process in two batches, so that work-in-progress might have all its materials added or might contain only half of the total, depending on the stage of production reached at any particular month-end. The conversion work is continuous throughout the month.

Exhibit 5.4
Separate materials and conversion costs

> *Step 1: Collect data for the period*
>
> The business assembles plant propagation boxes. At the start of the process a set of plastic components is introduced, assembled and coated with a weatherproof protective coating. The glass plates are then added and a decorative finish given to the assembled unit. Because there are two points at which materials are introduced (plastic components and then glass plates), some items may be only 50 per cent complete in respect of materials at the end of the reporting period.

Data in respect of the month of April
4,000 units work-in-progress at start, 100 per cent complete in respect
of materials, 25 per cent complete in respect of conversion.
6,000 units of raw materials introduced for conversion.
8,000 units of output completed during the month.
2,000 units of work-in-progress, 50 per cent complete in respect of
materials, 10 per cent complete in respect of conversion.

Cost of opening work-in-progress, £60,000, consisting of £30,000 for
materials and £30,000 for conversion costs.
Costs incurred in the month on materials are £150,000 and on
conversion costs £216,000.

*Step 2: Prepare a statement of physical flows and equivalent units of output for
the month*

As in exhibits 5.2 and 5.3 the physical flow is recorded in the left-hand column.
However, there are now two columns to the right of this, each showing one
component of the equivalent units of output. Using two columns allows different
percentages to be applied to work-in-progress for materials and conversion costs
as follows:

	Physical flow (units)		Equivalent units of output		
			Material		Conversion
Input:					
Work-in-progress at start	4,000				
Material introduced	6,000				
	10,000				
Output:					
Goods finished this month	8,000		8,000		8,000
Work-in-progress at end	2,000	50%	1,000	10%	200
Total equivalent units	10,000		9,000		8,200

Step 3: Identify total costs to be accounted for this period

In step 1 there is information about costs brought forward and costs incurred in
the month. In each case the costs of the components of materials and conversion
are shown separately. This separate classification allows the calculation of a
separate unit cost for each component. The total cost to be accounted for under
each heading are as follows:

	Material £	Conversion £	Total £
Opening work-in-progress brought forward	30,000	30,000	60,000
Incurred this month	150,000	216,000	366,000
Total costs to be accounted for	180,000	246,000	426,000

Continued overleaf

Step 4: Calculate cost per equivalent unit

Two costs per equivalent unit can now be calculated, one relating to materials and one to conversion. The total costs from step 3 are divided by the equivalent units from step 2. Materials have been used in 9,000 equivalent units of output but conversion costs have been applied to only 8,200 equivalent units of output. The calculations are as follows:

	Material	Conversion
Total costs to be accounted for	£180,000	£246,000
Number of equivalent units	9,000	8,200
Cost per equivalent unit	£20	£30

The total cost of an item of completed output is therefore £50 per equivalent unit. Work-in-progress at the end of the period has to be calculated in two separate components, using the figures of £20 per equivalent unit of materials and £30 per equivalent unit of conversion work.

Step 5: Apportion cost between finished output and work-in-progress

The unit costs calculated in step 4 may now be applied to the finished goods and work-in-progress. The finished goods are 100 per cent complete in respect of materials and conversion costs, so it saves calculation time to use the total unit cost of £50 and multiply it by the 8,000 finished units.

For work-in-progress some care is needed. For the materials component, the work-in-progress is equivalent to 1,000 units, but for conversion costs it is equivalent to only 200 units, as shown in step 2. Separate calculations are shown in the table below for each component. The total costs accounted for are £426,000 which is equal to the total costs shown in step 3 above.

	£	£
Value of finished output 8,000 × £50		400,000
Work-in-progress:		
Materials 1,000 × £20	20,000	
Labour 200 × £3	6,000	
		26,000
Total costs accounted for		426,000

Activity 5.3

Go back to the start of exhibit 5.4. Take a note of the data provided and then close the book. Write out all the steps of cost allocation for the process and make sure that you understand each stage. Imagine that you are a manager instructing an employee who will prepare the monthly process cost statements. How would you explain the steps of cost allocation in such a way that the employee could produce reliable data? How would you check the work of such an employee?

5.4 Joint product costs and by-products

A manufacturing process may result in more than one product. If the second item is produced as an unavoidable result of producing the the first, but is of negligible sales value, then it is called a *by-product*. If the second item is produced as an unavoidable result of producing the first, but has a significant sales value in comparison with the first, then it is called a *joint product*. In the case of joint products, it is desirable to know the separate cost of each item. Product costs may be required for valuing of stocks and work-in-progress, calculating product profitability, setting selling prices which cover costs, and deciding whether to vary the mix of products.

The accounting treatment of a by-product is somewhat different. Any proceeds of sale of the by-product are used to offset the cost of the main product, which includes the cost of manufacturing the by-product. In the case of by-products it is not necessary to have a valuation for stock purposes because the item is relatively insignificant. It is more important for management purposes to know that the proceeds of sale of the by-product reduces the effective cost of the main product.

Definition

Joint products are two or more products arising from a process, each of which has a significant sales value.

A *by-product* is a product arising from a process where the sales value is insignificant by comparison with that of the main product or products.

This section looks first at joint costs and then at by-products. There are several methods of allocating cost to joint products, two of which will be explored here. These are: by physical measures; and by relative sales value. The example contained in exhibit 5.5 will be used to compare both approaches.

Exhibit 5.5
Data for use in allocation of joint costs

A chemical process requires input of materials costing £900 per batch. From each batch there are two products, being 1,000 litres of perfume oil base which sells for £2 per litre and 500 litres of oil for artists' paint which sells at £1 per litre.

5.4.1 Joint costs allocated on the basis of physical measures

As stated in exhibit 5.5, the proportions of physical measures are 1,000 : 500, which reduces to 2:1. Allocating the joint costs of £900 on the basis 2:1 gives £600 as the cost of perfume oil and £300 as the cost of artists' paint oil.

A statement of product profit is shown in exhibit 5.6. The calculation of profit on each product is based on subtracting the allocated joint costs from the separate sales figures. In the final line of the exhibit the profit as a percentage of sales is shown.

Exhibit 5.6
Statement of product profit for joint products: physical measures

	Perfume oil base	*Oil for artists' paint*
	£	£
Sales	2,000	500
Joint costs allocated	600	300
Profit	1,400	200
Profit as % of sales	70	40

This is not a particularly good method of allocating costs because it shows one product as being much more profitable, in relation to sales, than the other. That profitability is very much dependent on the allocation method used for the joint costs. Taken out of context, such an allocation might lead the managers of the business into an over-hasty decision to raise the price of the perfume oil base. It would, however, be a mistake to base such a decision on an allocation of costs that could change when a different method is used. Look now at what happens when the joint costs are allocated by reference to the sales value at the point of separation.

5.4.2 Joint costs allocated by relative sales value at the point of separation

A method which is generally thought to be an improvement on allocation by physical measures is that of allocating the joint cost of £900 in relation to the sales value at the point of separation. The sales value proportions are 2,000 : 500 so that the allocation is as follows:

		£
Perfume oil base	2,000/2,500 × £900	720
Oil for artists' paint	500/2,500 × 900	180
		900

A statement of product profit, based on this allocation, would appear as in exhibit 5.7.

Exhibit 5.7
Statement of product profit for joint products: relative sales value

	Perfume oil base	*Oil for artists' paint*
	£	£
Sales	2,000	500
Joint costs allocated	720	180
Profit	1,280	320
Profit as % of sales	64	64

This approach leads to a profit which is 64 per cent of sales for each product. Allocating joint costs in proportion to sales value means that the performance measure, taken as the profit margin on sales, is not distorted by the cost allocation process. The calculation would leave the managers of a business satisfied that they had no problems with either product and would avoid bringing on an ill-considered decision to cease production of one product item.

5.4.3 Further processing costs

Now consider a variation on the previous story. Suppose there are further costs incurred after the separation of the joint products. The information used earlier is now amended somewhat in exhibit 5.8, to introduce and illustrate this variation. The amendments are shown in bold print.

Exhibit 5.8
Joint cost allocation where there are further processing costs

A chemical process requires input of materials costing £900 per batch. From each batch there are two products, being 1,000 litres of perfume oil base which sells for £2 per litre and 500 litres of oil for artists' paint which sells at £1 per litre. **After the two products have been separated, further processing costs are incurred, amounting to £600 per batch in the case of perfume oil base and £100 per batch in the case of oil for artists' paint.**

The recommended approach in this situation is to calculate a notional sales value at the point of separation. That is not as fearsome as it sounds. It requires taking the final sales price of the item and deducting the processing costs incurred after separation. That leaves the notional sales value at the point of separation. Calculations are shown in Exhibit 5.9, and from these calculations it may be seen that the profit as a percentage of sales is no longer the same for each product. That is to be expected, however, because the costs after separation have a relatively different impact on each.

5.4.4 Treatment of by-products

By-products are items of output from a process which have a relatively minor sales value compared with that of the main product.

The accounting treatment of by-products is similar to the accounting treatment of scrap. The proceeds of sale are offset against the cost of the main product. An example of a process which leads to a by-product is set out in exhibit 5.10.

The calculation of the cost of the main product, perfume oil base, and the resulting profit is shown in exhibit 5.11. The joint cost of £900 is reduced by the sales proceeds from the by-product, which are £50. The net cost of £850 becomes the cost of sales of the perfume oil, which is the main product. There would be no useful purpose in allocating cost to the by-product and then calculating a separate figure of profit, because the amounts are insignificant.

Exhibit 5.9
Cost allocation based on notional sales value at the point of separation

(a) *Calculation of notional sales value at the point of separation*

	£	£
Selling price per batch	2,000	500
Costs incurred after separation	600	100
Notional selling price before separation	1,400	400

(b) *Allocation of joint cost based on notional selling price before separation*

		£
Perfume oil base	1,400/1,800 × £900	700
Oil for artists' paint	400/1,800 × 900	200
		900

(c) *Calculation of profit for each joint product*

	Perfume oil base		Oil for artists' paint	
	£	£	£	£
Sales		2,000		500
Joint costs allocated	700		200	
Costs after separation	600		100	
		1,300		300
Profit		700		200
Profit as % of sales		35		40

Exhibit 5.10
Process which creates a by-product

A chemical process requires input of materials costing £900 per batch. From each batch there are two products, being 1,000 litres of perfume oil base which sells for £2 per litre and 500 litres of waste oil which sells at 10 pence per litre.

Exhibit 5.11
Joint cost allocation and profit calculation

	£	£
Sales of perfume oil base, per batch		2,000
Joint costs	900	
less: sales proceeds of waste oil by-product	(50)	
Net cost per batch		850
Profit per batch		1,150

5.4.5 Relevance of allocating joint costs

Is the allocation of joint costs useful? In this chapter we have shown that this type of cost allocation is an exercise where there is a variety of possible outcomes. Sometimes this variety of outcomes is described as an *arbitrary allocation process* because it depends so much on the choice made by the individual manager.

Throughout this management accounting text there is an emphasis on the management purposes of planning, decision making and control. If the purpose of the joint cost exercise is to allocate all costs in the fairest possible manner for purposes of planning and control, then using notional sales value at the point of separation will give a fair allocation in many circumstances. The allocation of full cost may be required for purposes of stock valuation or it may be required for control purposes to make senior managers aware that ultimately they have a responsibility for all costs.

If, however, a decision has to be made such as processing further or changing a selling price, then that decision must be based on *relevant costs* rather than on a full allocation of joint costs.

Definition

Relevant costs are those future costs which will be affected by a decision to be taken. Non-relevant costs will not be affected by the decision. The decision-making process therefore requires careful attention to those costs which are relevant to the decision.

We conclude this chapter by setting out a decision where joint costs are present but the allocation of those costs is not relevant to the decision.

Activity 5.4

Explain to a production manager the joint cost problems raised by the following description of a process producing glass bottles.

A typical mixture might be sand 60 per cent; limestone 17 per cent; soda ash 18 per cent; mineral additives 5 per cent. Up to 25 per cent of the mix can comprise cullet (recycled glass). From one mixture the molten glass would be run off into moulds for narrow bottles (such as wine bottles) and wide-mouth containers (such as jam jars). Bottles which have flaws or chips are broken up and recycled.

5.5 Decisions on joint products: sell or process further

Where there are joint products there may be a decision required at the point where they separate. The decision usually involves the prospect of incurring further costs with the hope of improving revenue thereby. Is it worthwhile to incur the extra cost of adding perfume? The decision should be based on *incremental* costs and revenues, as illustrated in the example shown in exhibit 5.12, which is analysed in exhibit 5.13.

Definition

> *Incremental costs* are the additional costs that arise from an activity of the organisation. To justify incurring incremental costs it is necessary to show they are exceeded by incremental revenue.

Exhibit 5.12
Situation requiring a decision

> In a company manufacturing personal care products, a process requires the input of ingredients costing £400 per batch. Separation of the output from each batch yields 200 litres of hand cream which sells at a price of £1.60 per litre and 200 litres of soap solution which sells at a price of 80 pence per litre. The soap solution in that form is suitable for industrial use, but at a further cost of £50 per batch of 200 litres it could be perfumed and sold for domestic use at £1.20 per litre.

Activity 5.5

> *Write down, with reasons, the action you would recommend for the situation described in exhibit 5.12. Then read the commentary by Fiona McTaggart and check your answer against exhibit 5.13. Did you arrive at the same answer? If not, what was the cause of the difference?*

Fiona McTaggart has given some thought to this problem.

FIONA: *The decision question contained in exhibit 5.12 is, 'Do we make soap for industrial use or do we make it suitable for domestic use?' What is not in question is the production of hand cream and the production of soap solution. This means that the information about hand cream is not relevant to the decision and neither is the information about the costs of ingredients. I have rewritten the information in exhibit 5.12 and highlighted the information relevant to this decision problem, as follows:*

> In a company manufacturing personal care products, a process requires the input of ingredients costing £400 per batch. Separation of the output from each batch yields 200 litres of hand cream which sells at a price of £1.60 per litre and **200 litres of soap solution which sells at a price of 80 pence per litre.** The soap solution in that form is suitable for industrial use, but at a **further cost of £50 per batch of 200 litres it could be perfumed and sold for domestic use at £1.20 per litre.**

My calculation of the incremental revenue and costs is shown in exhibit 5.13. It shows that there is an extra profit of £30 per batch if the soap solution is perfumed for domestic use. So the decision should be to go ahead.

Exhibit 5.13
Statement of incremental costs and revenues

		£
Extra revenue	200 litres × (£1.20 − 0.80)	80
Extra cost		50
Extra profit per batch		30

In relation to the decision, allocation of the joint cost of £400 is *not* relevant because it is a cost which is incurred regardless of whether the perfume is added. In a similar vein, pricing decisions should have regard to the need to cover total costs but should not be based on arbitrary allocations of costs across products.

5.6 Summary

This chapter has explored some of the cost recording problems faced in process industries. The chapter began by examining the allocation of cost where there are finished units and work-in-progress at the start and end of the reporting period. The idea of an *equivalent unit* of output was introduced. The illustration was expanded to deal with separate costs of materials and conversion costs because materials may be introduced at definite stages in a process while conversion costs occur continuously. Finally, the chapter examined the problems of allocating costs to joint products and by-products. That section also illustrated the need to consider whether costs are being used for decision making rather than for planning and control purposes. In such decision-making situations, it is the incremental costs and revenues which are important.

Further reading

Drury, C. (1994), *Management and Cost Accounting*, 3rd edn, Chapman & Hall.

Horngren, C. T., Foster, G. and Datar, S. (1993), *Cost Accounting: A Managerial Emphasis*, Prentice Hall.

Morse, W. J. and Roth, H. P. (1986), *Cost Accounting: Processing, Evaluating and Using Cost Data*, Addison-Wesley.

Self-testing on the chapter

1   Which industries might need to use the techniques of process costing?

2   What is meant by the term *equivalent unit*?

3   What are the steps to follow in calculating the cost of finished goods and the value of closing work-in-progress in respect of a reporting period?

4 Where there is work-in-progress at the start of any reporting period, how is this accounted for using the weighted average approach?

5 Why may it be necessary to account for materials and conversion costs separately?

6 What is the difference between a joint product and a by-product?

7 How may joint costs be allocated to joint products using a basis of physical measures?

8 How may joint costs be allocated to joint products using a basis of relative sales value?

9 How is relative sales value at the point of separation determined when there are further processing costs of each joint product after the separation point?

10 What is the accounting treatment of cash collected from the sale of a by-product?

11 Why should care be taken when using process costing information for decision making in respect of joint products?

12 Work-in-progress at the end of the month amounts to 2,000 physical units. They are all 40 per cent complete. What are the equivalent units of production? The cost of production is £3 per equivalent unit. What is the value of work-in-progress?

13 In process X there are 12,000 units completely finished during the month and 3,000 units of work-in-progress. The work-in-progress is 60 per cent complete for materials and 20 per cent complete for conversion costs (labour and overhead). What are the equivalent units of production for the work-in-progress?

14 XYZ Ltd processes and purifies a basic chemical which is then broken down by reaction to give three separate products. Explain the approaches to joint cost allocation using the following information:

Product	Units produced	Final market value per unit (£)	Costs beyond split-off point (£)
A	3,000	5.00	4,000
B	1,000	4.00	1,800
C	2,000	3.00	2,400

Joint costs incurred up to the split-off point are £2,000.

15 In a continuous flow process, the following information was collected in relation to production during the month of May:

	Units
Work-in-progress at start of month (60 per cent complete)	50,000
New units introduced for processing	80,000
Completed units transferred to store	100,000
Work-in-progress at end of month (20 per cent complete)	30,000

Opening work-in-progress was valued at cost of £42,000. Costs incurred during the month were £140,000.

Required

Calculate the value of finished output and work-in-progress using the weighted average method.

16 Clay Products Ltd produces handmade decorative vases. A process costing system is used. All materials are introduced at the start of the process. Labour costs are incurred uniformly throughout the production process.

The following information is available for the month of July:

Work-in-progress at 1 July (60 per cent complete) 2,000 units
Work-in-progress at 31 July (30 per cent complete) 1,200 units

The value of work-in-progress at 1 July is as follows:

	£
Direct materials cost	1,700
Direct labour costs	1,900
	3,600

During the month of July, 7,000 vases were transferred to finished goods stock. Materials introduced cost £14,700. Labour costs incurred were £12,820.

Required

Using the method of weighted averages, prepare a process cost statement for the month of July showing unit costs, the value of finished goods and the value of work-in-progress at the end of the month.

Activity for study groups

Obtain the annual report of a large public company which operates in a process industry and read the description of the operations of the business. Divide into two subgroups, one representing the finance team and the other representing the production team.

The finance team should prepare a briefing note for the production team on the management accounting problems which may arise because of the nature of the business. The briefing note should include explanations of how management accounting may address these problems.

The production team should prepare a briefing note for the finance team describing the process (or processes). The briefing note should include the team's views on the type of information they would like to receive from the finance team in respect of the costs of the process.

The teams should exchange briefing notes and then come together for a group evaluation of the similarities and differences in the approach taken by each team.

Case studies

Case 5.1

Refinery Ltd buys crude oil which is refined, producing liquefied gas, oil and grease. The cost of crude oil refined in the past year was £105,000 and the refining department incurred processing costs of £45,000. The output and sales for the three products during that year were as follows:

Product	Units of output	Sales value £	Additional processing costs £
Liquefied gas	10,000	20,000	12,000
Oil	500,000	230,000	60,000
Grease	5,000	8,000	–

The company could have sold the products at the split-off point directly to other processors at a unit selling price of 50p, 35p and £1.60 respectively.

Required

1 Compute the net profit earned for each product using two suitable methods of joint cost allocations.

2 Determine whether it would have been more or less profitable for the company to have sold certain products at split-off without further processing.

Case 5.2

A product is manufactured in a continuous process carried on successively in two departments, Assembly and Finishing. In the production process, materials are added to the product in each department without increasing the number of units produced. For July 19X2 the production records contain the following information for each department:

	Assembly	Finishing
Units in process at 1 July	0	0
Units commenced in Assembly	80,000	–
Units completed and transferred out	60,000	50,000
Units in process at 31 July	20,000	10,000
Cost of materials (£)	240,000	88,500
Cost of labour (£)	140,000	141,500
Cost of production overhead (£)	65,000	56,600
Percentage completion of units in process:		
Materials	100%	100%
Labour and overhead	50%	70%

Required

Determine the cost per equivalent unit for each department.

Case 5.3

Chemicals Ltd owns a supply of North Sea gas liquids, and is developing its downstream activities. It is producing two main products, propane and butane, and there is a by-product, arcone. There are four manufacturing processes involved where the gas passes through Modules 1, 2, 3, and 4.

Production information for April 19X2 is as follows:

1,000 tons of liquid A and 600 tons of liquid B were issued to Module 1.
Liquid C is issued to Module 2 at the rate of 1 ton per 4 tons of production
  from Module 1.
Liquid D is added to Module 4 at the rate of 1 ton per 3 tons of output
  from Module 2.

Arcone arises in Module 1 and represents 25 per cent of the good output of that process. The remaining output of Module 1 passes to Module 2. Of the Module 2 output 75 per cent passes to Module 3 and 25 per cent passes to Module 4. The output of Module 3 is propane and the output of Module 4 is butane.

Materials costs are:

	£
Liquid A	60 per ton
Liquid B	40 per ton
Liquid C	75 per ton
Liquid D	120 per ton

The labour and overhead costs during the month were:

	£
Module 1	22,400
Module 2	38,750
Module 3	12,000
Module 4	10,000

The company is considering selling the products at the undernoted price:

	£
Propane	130 per ton
Butane	150 per ton
Arcone	100 per ton

Required

1   Draw a diagram of the various processes described.

2   Ascertain the percentage profit on selling price per ton of each of these products.

Part 3

Planning and controlling

Chapter 6

Preparing a budget

<table>
<tr><td>

Learning objectives
</td><td>

After studying this chapter you should be able to:
1 Explain the need for, and process of, long-range planning.
2 Explain the need for, and process of, setting a strategy.
3 Explain the need for, and process of, preparing operational budgets.
4 Explain how the budget process is administered.
5 Understand the potential benefits of budgeting.
6 Understand and evaluate the potential problems of budgeting.
7 Prepare a master budget.
</td></tr>
</table>

6.1 Purpose and nature of a budget system

The purpose of a budget system is to serve the needs of management in respect of the judgements and decisions it is required to make and to provide a basis for the management functions of planning and control, described in Chapter 1. That chapter also refers to the importance of communication and motivation as an aspect of management to which management accounting should contribute.

In this chapter we will consider the purpose and nature of the budgetary process and will explain the method of preparation of budgets, with particular emphasis on the planning process. The use of budgets for control is touched upon in this chapter but elaborated in more detail in Chapter 7.

In exhibit 1.2 there is an illustration of the interrelationships of these management functions in respect of the process by which a chain of shops supplying motor cycles might go about the business of planning to open a new shop in the suburbs of a city. Where this type of planning is taking place, management accounting assists through a budget system by providing quantification of each stage of the planning process. That example of the motor-cycle shop related to a long-range planning situation but a more complex example would show the way in which the long-range planning leads on to successively more detailed developments, finishing with a collection of short-term operational budgets covering a period such as a year, six months or perhaps no more than one month ahead.

6.1.1 Long-range planning

In long-range planning, the senior managers of a business will begin by specifying a mission statement which sets out in the broadest terms their vision of the future direction of the organisation. Based on this mission statement the senior managers will then prepare a list of objectives which will specify the intended future growth and development of the business. For example, a company might state its mission and its long-range corporate objectives, for a five-year period ahead, in the terms shown in exhibit 6.1.

Exhibit 6.1
Company's mission statement and long-range corporate objectives

---

Mission
The company intends to maintain its position as the market leader in the electrical repair industry, having regard to providing investors with an adequate rate of growth of their investment in the business.

Corporate objectives

- The company intends to increase the value of the investment by its shareholders at a minimum rate of 4 per cent per annum, in real terms.
- The company intends to remain in the electrical goods repair business and to concentrate on this as the core business.
- The company will provide service in the home and at its main repair centres.
- The company will continue to maintain its geographical focus on the high-earning suburban areas around the three largest cities.
- The company seeks to enlarge its market share in those geographical areas to 20 per cent of the total market.
- The company has a profit objective of 30 per cent gross profit on turnover.

The corporate objectives shown in exhibit 6.1 relate to the business as a whole. They will then be taken down to another level of detail to create objectives for each division of the business. Within divisions, they will be translated into departmental objectives.

6.1.2 Strategy

Having a mission statement and corporate objectives is an essential first step, but the organisation must then decide exactly how it will achieve those objectives. The term *strategy* is used to describe the courses of action to be taken in achieving the objectives set.

Setting out the strategy will involve senior management from the various functions such as marketing, customer service, production, personnel and finance. These functions are separate but must work together in the interests of the company as a whole. Each functional manager has to understand how the plans made by that function will affect other functions and the company as a whole. This requires communication and co-ordination with the assistance of a management accountant.

For purposes of quantifying the strategy of the business, management accounting has developed specialist techniques under the global heading of *budgetary planning and control*. The rest of this chapter explains the processes involved.

6.1.3 Budgets

Definition

> A *budget* is a detailed plan which sets out, in money terms, the plans for income and expenditure in respect of a future period of time. It is prepared in advance of that time period and is based on the agreed objectives for that period of time, together with the strategy planned to achieve those objectives.

Each separate function of the organisation will have its own budget. Exhibit 6.2 shows a typical scheme of budget structure within an organisation. It shows how the organisation moves from setting objectives, through the strategy stage and into the preparation of budgets. The long-term objectives are set first. It is important to note at that stage any key assumptions which might have a critical effect on future implementation of those objectives. The implementation of those long-term objectives is then formed into a strategy which results in some intermediate objectives for the short term. Again it is important to note any key assumptions which might later cause the organisation to question the objectives. In many businesses the critical factor determining all other budgets is the sales forecast. The business exists primarily to make sales and hence generate profit, so each separate function will be working towards that major target. Each function of the business then prepares its own budget as a statement of its operational plan for achieving the targets that have been set.

In practice these budgets would be prepared at the same time with a great deal of interaction among the managers of the various functions. That is difficult to show in a diagram. Exhibit 6.2 shows only the main budget relationships, moving from the sales forecast to the production plan and the resulting working capital needs (stock, debtors and trade creditors) and capital investment in fixed assets. The various detailed budgets are brought together within a finance plan and then formed into conventional accounting statements such as budgeted profit and loss account, cash flow statement and balance sheet. This package is sometimes referred to as the *master budget*. The process leading to the preparation of the master budget, as outlined in exhibit 6.2, will be used in the next section of this chapter as a basis for explaining the administration of the budgeting process.

Activity 6.1

> *Imagine you are the managing director of a large company about to embark on budget preparation for the following year. How would you manage the various people you would need to meet in order to make operational the budget relationships shown in exhibit 6.2? Would you meet them all together or have separate meetings? Would you take sole charge or would you establish teams? Write down your thoughts on this before you read the next section and then check it against your ideas.*

Exhibit 6.2
Budget planning and relationships

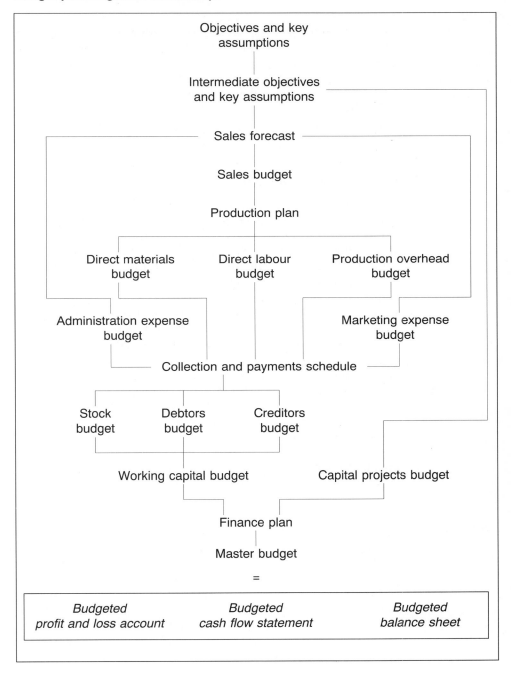

6.2 Administration of the budgeting process

The budgeting process has to be administered effectively in terms of initial planning, final approval and subsequent monitoring of implementation. A budget committee is essential for the significant aspects of each stage of administration. The accounting staff will have a close involvement. The budget will need to be set out in written form in a manual which is available to all participants. A continuing cycle evolves in which initial budgets are prepared, negotiations take place with line managers, the initial budgets are revised, the final budget is accepted and a review follows which starts the cycle over again.

6.2.1 The budget committee

To implement the strategy decisions, a budget committee will be formed, comprising the senior managers who are responsible for designing the strategy. The budget committee receives the initial budgets from each functional manager. If the initial budget is based on unrealistic targets, then the functional manager will be asked to modify the budget within the organisation's overall targets. There is a motivational aspect of budget preparation, so it is important that the functional manager understands the need for revising the budget within the organisation's strategy. Budget negotiation can be quite a delicate process.

Fiona McTaggart describes her experiences of the initial budget formation in a conglomerate company having a stock exchange listing:

FIONA: *There are four divisions whose activities are quite dissimilar but the linking theme is their ability to generate cash for the group which, in turn, is translated into dividends for the shareholders and capital investment for the divisions. The budget committee is formed from the board of directors of the holding company. Budget negotiations start each year when each divisional manager sets targets in six critical areas: capital expenditure, turnover, gross and net profit margins, cash flow and working capital requirements.*

The budget committee knows over the years that the transport division manager is always too enthusiastic for capital expenditure and has to be persuaded to be more cautious in replacing and expanding the fleet.

The musical instrument division is on a steady-state pattern without much growth, but is regarded as a steady source of cash flow, so is not encouraged to be more ambitious.

The knitwear division has some problems associated with fashion goods and tends to be too conservative in its planning. A measure of risk taking is encouraged and almost every year that division has to be asked to revise its initial turnover targets upwards.

The fourth division is stationery supplies and their problem is profit targets in a competitive sector. Little can be done about gross profit, but there is plenty of scope for cost efficiencies to improve the contribution of net profit to cash flow.

6.2.2 The accounting department

The staff of the accounting department do not initiate the preparation of budgets but will be assisting in the practical aspects of budget preparation. They should have the knowledge and experience to provide advice to line managers on the preparation of budgets. The accounting department will have the computer facilities to prepare and co-ordinate the budget preparation process.

6.2.3 Sequence of the budgeting process

Exhibit 6.2 shows the relationships among the various budgets but does not portray the time sequence of the budgeting process. The principal stages of this sequence are:

1 communicate the details of objectives and strategy to those responsible for preparation of budgets;
2 communicate the details of budget preparation procedures to those responsible for preparation of budgets;
3 determine the limiting factor which restricts overall budget flexibility and forms the focus of the budget cascade;
4 prepare initial set of budgets;
5 negotiate budgets with line managers;
6 co-ordinate and review budgets;
7 accept budgets in final form;
8 carry out ongoing review of budgets as they are implemented.

Communicate objectives and strategy

The long-range plan should be contained in a strategy document which is circulated within the organisation at intervals throughout the year. Regular circulation, with invitations to comment and a visible process of revision to accommodate changing circumstances, means that those responsible for preparation of budgets have the fullest understanding of the basis for the budget process. The strategy document should contain clear narrative descriptions of the objectives of the organisation, supplemented by quantified illustrations of the impact on the organisation as a whole and on major divisions. The objectives may initially be expressed in non-financial terms such as production or sales targets by volume, or workforce targets by quantity and quality. Ultimately, all these non-financial targets will have a financial implication.

Communicate procedures

For communication of budget preparation procedures within the organisation there must be a budget manual. This will set out the timetable for budget preparation, formats to be used, circulation lists for drafts, and arbitration procedures where conflicts begin to show themselves.

Determine the limiting factor

For many organisations, sales are the limiting factor. There is no point in producing goods and services which do not sell. There may be occasions when the demand is not a problem but the supply of materials or labour resources is restricted. (Such restrictions on production factors should be temporary in a competitive market because materials will eventually be found at a higher price, while labour will move from one geographical area to another or will train to develop new skills within the area.) Whatever the limiting factor, it must determine the starting point of the budgeting process. For this chapter it will be assumed that sales are the limiting factor. That assumption is the basis of the chart of budget relationships shown in exhibit 6.2 where the cascade flows down from the top to the foot of the page.

Preparing an initial set of budgets

The *sales budget* is a representation of the volume of sales planned for the budget period, multiplied by the expected selling price of each item. For most organisations, sales volume is the major unknown item because it depends on customers whose choices may be difficult to predict. In practice an organisation will carry out some form of market research, ranging from very sophisticated market research surveys to some simple but effective techniques such as contacting past customers and asking them about their intentions for the period ahead. Sales representatives will, as part of their work, form continuous estimates of demand in their region of responsibility. Past performance in sales may usefully be analysed to identify trends which may be an indicator of future success in sales.

From the sales plan flow the *operational budgets*. Exhibit 6.2 shows the subsequent pattern of budget development once the sales budget has been determined. The *production plan*, setting out quantities of resource inputs required, leads into operational budgets for direct labour, direct materials and manufacturing overhead which combine resource quantities with expected price per unit. At the same time budgets for administration and marketing are being prepared based on quantities and prices of resources needed for production and sales.

That information provides the basis for a profit and loss account matching sales and expenses. A cash flow estimate is also required based upon working capital needs and fixed asset needs. Working capital depends on the mix of stock, debtors and creditors planned to support the sales and production levels expected. Fixed asset needs derive from the capital projects budgeted as a result of the objectives of the organisation.

This all feeds into a *finance plan* from which the *master budget* emerges containing the budgeted profit and loss account, the budgeted cash flow statement and the budgeted balance sheet.

Negotiate budgets with line managers

The success of the budgetary process is widely held to depend on the extent to which all participants are involved in the budget preparation process. The budgets will be initiated in each of the departments or areas responsible but each budget may have an impact on other line managers. There may be a problem of restricted resources which requires all budgets to be cut back from initial expectations. There may be an expansionary programme which has not been taken sufficiently into account by those preparing the budgets. Whatever the particular circumstances, a negotiation stage will be required which will usually involve the budget committee in discussions with various line managers. At the very least this will be a communications exercise so that each participant understands the overall position. More often it will be an opportunity for fine-tuning the plans so that the benefit to the organisation as a whole is maximised.

Although exhibit 6.2 is presented as a downward-flowing cascade because of the increasing level of detail involved, it does not adequately represent the negotiation processes involved. Exhibit 6.3 is a different way of showing the budgetary process outlined in exhibit 6.2. It emphasises people rather than the documentation resulting from the process, and also shows the combination of what is sometimes described as the 'bottom-up' preparation of budgets with the 'top-down' approval by senior management. In exhibit 6.3, dotted lines show some of the interactions which might take place in the negotiation stage, distinguishing negotiations among the line managers and negotiations between the line managers and the budget committee Quite deliberately, the lines are shown without directional arrows because the negotiation process is two-way. Even then a two-dimensional diagram cannot do justice to the time span and the sequence of negotiations over a relatively short space of time.

Accept the budgets in final form

At the end of the negotiation period it will be necessary for the budget committee to approve and accept a definitive set of budgets which will set out the organisation's plan for the period ahead. It is possible that, as a result of the negotiation stage, some managers will feel more satisfied than others. A good system of budget setting will by this stage have ensured that all managers, whether disappointed or not, understand the reasoning and understand what is expected in their area of responsibility.

Carry out ongoing review

The budget process is not an end in itself. It is a formal process of planning which guides subsequent action. Monitoring that subsequent action against the budget plan is therefore an essential follow-up to the budget process. An organisation might decide that monthly monitoring of progress against budget is adequate for control purposes and for contributing to future planning.

Within the control function, monthly monitoring of the actual outcome against the budget will allow corrective action to be taken at the earliest opportunity, although care is required in this respect. It could be that conditions have changed since the budget was set and the actual outcome is a better representation than the budget. In such a case it might even be appropriate to revise the budget in line with the changed conditions.

Budgeting is a continuous process which requires adaptation of existing

Exhibit 6.3
The negotiating aspects of budget planning

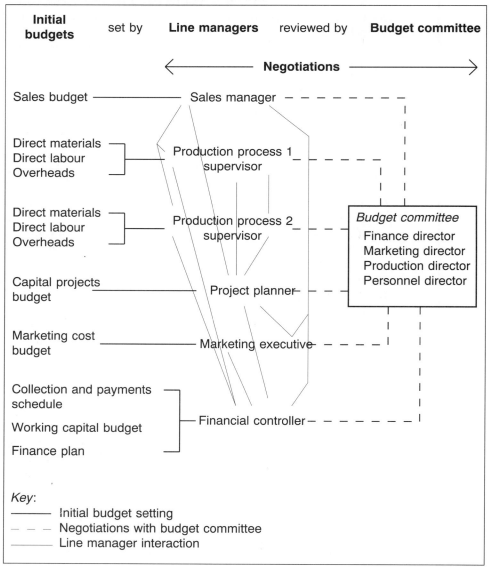

budgets where a need for change is indicated, and the consideration of performance against past budgets when the next round of budget preparation begins. The budget committee is therefore active the whole year around.

Activity 6.2

Write down five ways in which budgets appear to benefit an organisation. Then read the next section. How does your list compare with the text? Have you identified benefits additional to those described? Have you used different words to describe a benefit which is in the text?

6.3 The benefits of budgeting

The budgetary process contributes to effective management in the following areas: planning; control; communication and co-ordination; and performance evaluation. Each of these areas is now considered in turn.

6.3.1 Planning

The preparation of budgets forces management to carry out a formal planning exercise which identifies every part of the organisation and brings the separate parts together on a quantified basis. Major planning decisions are made as part of the long-term planning process, and these are then refined into progressively greater detail as management turn them into short-term operational plans. A formal planning process encourages all parts of the organisation to contribute on a regular basis to the formation of the overall plan and to identify potential difficulties at an early stage. Here is Fiona McTaggart to describe the budget planning process in a major multinational company.

FIONA: *I once participated in the planning process within a major international oil company. The financial year ran from January to December. The company's head office was in Brussels, with operational centres around the world. I was working in one of the UK operational centres, seeing the process from part way along the chain. A company strategy group, comprising the senior management from head office and the operational centres, would form a rolling five-year statement of objectives. Having a rolling plan means that the company always looks to the next five years, but each January the rolling plan is reviewed, the current year is deleted and year 5 is added.*

The effect is that the rolling five-year plan is updated every January in respect of the five-year period starting the following January. That means the company has twelve months in which to prepare its operational budgets for the one year starting in the following January. Preparation of the five-year plan is described as Stage A. Each operational centre around the world then has two months to come back to head office with the results of its one-year budgeting, described as Stage B.

Stage B involves each operational centre specifying how the implementation of the five-year plan will be carried out for one year ahead within the operational centre, bringing out a master budget of quarterly cash flows and profit. At that stage they don't produce the detailed operational budgets within the operational centre, but each centre will have consulted with its various managers as to the way in which their departmental objectives for one year ahead will mesh with the five-year plan from head office and from the operational centre.

Stage C lasts one month and allows some fine-tuning of the five-year plan, by the head office, in the light of the reaction from the operational centres. That takes matters up to the end of June, and after that point there is little further opportunity for change in the five-year plan, or in the one-year targets of each operational centre, short of a major change in circumstances in the company or in the industry.

Stage D lasts four months and involves detailed budget planning within each operational centre. That will be an iterative process, where each manager of an operational unit produces a draft budget covering a twelve-month period, the draft budgets are collected together, an overall view is taken, and the draft budgets go back to the managers for revision.

Everything is tidied up by the end of October and then there are two months left to put the documentation together so that budgets are ready for implementation from the start of the next year in January.

Meanwhile, the senior managers in Brussels will have started, in October, their deliberations with a view to revising the rolling five-year plan in the following January. Then the whole process starts over again!

6.3.2 Control

Once the budget is in place, implementation of the organisation's plans takes place and the actual outcome may be compared against the budget. Some revenues and costs will behave according to expectations, but some will not. Attention needs to be given to the items which are not meeting expectations. Having a budget as a basis for comparison allows management to identify the exceptions which require attention. Identifying such matters at an early stage allows corrective action to be taken to remedy the problem.

Here is Fiona to continue her story.

FIONA: *I've told you how the oil company produces its budgets for the year ahead. From January of each year the actual out-turn of the operations has to be compared against the budget. That is where the problems really start, because the oil industry is at the high end of the uncertainty spectrum. The price of oil is controlled in world markets and influenced by world events well beyond the power of any company. A threat of war in some far-away country which borders on the main shipping lanes will send the price of oil up but threaten supplies for individual production companies seeking to take advantage of the price rise. Recession in developed countries will lower the demand and hence lower the price, so that companies have oil in the ground but may as well leave it there if demand has disappeared. These major changes occur on a short-term basis and may cause the short-term plans to require urgent change.*

It would not be feasible to return to the five-year plan every month because of a crisis, so the operational centres have to adapt to change. A few years ago, the operational centres did nothing to amend the budgets after they had been finalised. The consequence was that the budgets grew increasingly irrelevant to reality as the year progressed. As a result, the operational managers largely ignored the budgets and set their own unofficial targets in operational terms without having regard to the precise financial implications.

Senior management realised that this by-passing of the management accounting budgets was linked to a lack of awareness of cost control, vital to a business which has little control over its selling prices. So a quarterly revision process was devised whereby the operational centre is allowed to revise the budgets to keep them relevant to changing circumstances. This may lead to a deviation from the five-year plan set at the start of the year, but the view is that the increased relevance to operational practice is more important than the deviation from the plan. Of course, information about the revision is fed back to head office as input to the next round of five-year planning.

It seems to be working, and the managers at the operational level, such as platform supervisors and supply service managers, now use their quarterly budgets as a basis for explaining how they control costs for which they are responsible. There is also a benefit to the five-year planning exercise because indications of change are fed in during the year and the long-term exercise itself is becoming smoother.

6.3.3 Communication and co-ordination

In Chapter 1 there is an organisation chart (exhibit 1.1) which shows line relationships and horizontal relationships where effective communications are essential. Lines of communication ensure that all parts of the organisation are kept fully informed of the plans and of the policies and constraints within which those plans are formed.

Fiona continues with her experiences in an oil company.

FIONA: *One of the major problems of any large organisation is to encourage communication and co-ordination within the separate parts of the entity. The oil company is organised into divisions based on the six different exploration fields. Sometimes those different fields appear to regard themselves as self-contained units with no other relationships. It is important to overcome this insularity by skilful use of communication and co-ordination. The process of communication and co-ordination starts with the early stages of the budget planning process when each divisional head is required to review the plans for the division in the context of the other five divisions. Targets set within the budget are comparable across the divisions, but there is an allowance for the relative exploration difficulty. That first stage of review may encourage a self-centred attitude of protecting the division's interests, but it does at least encourage a wider awareness of global targets.*

The communication process continues when detailed budget plans are prepared. Divisional heads attend monthly meetings when the budget planning team sets out the main features of the budgets. That allows one-to-one communication and creates an awareness of the possibilities of mutual savings by co-ordination. As one small example, a helicopter might be leaving the airport to take supplies out to a rig. The return trip could usefully be turned into a full payload by calling at a rig on a nearby field on the way back. That requires some co-ordination but could halve the overall flight cost for each field.

The control stage encourages further awareness of the need for co-ordination when the actual costs are compared with the budget. Each divisional head receives an exception report showing costs which are running over budget, and there is a system of marking cost headings where co-ordination could reduce overall costs. A commentary section attached to the exception report gives the divisional head guidance as to where co-ordination might usefully be applied.

6.3.4 Basis for performance evaluation

Performance evaluation within organisations must sooner or later be taken to the stage of detail which requires evaluation of the performance of individuals working within the organisation. In some situations there will be a monetary reward for high performance standards, in terms of bonus payments and possibly promotion. There may be penalties for underperforming, the most drastic of which is to be dismissed from the post. Apart from the organisation's needs to evaluate the performance of those working within the organisation, there is also an individual's need for self-assessment. Whatever the type of performance evaluation of the individual or group of individuals, targets must be set in advance which are known to, and understood by, all participants. The budgetary process forms a systematic basis for setting performance targets in financial terms.

The financial targets may then have to be translated into non-financial targets (such as number of items produced per week, or frequency of corrective work, or number of administrative tasks undertaken) because the person concerned will identify more readily with the non-financial performance measure. The subject of non-financial performance measures is explored further in Chapter 8.

<table><tr><td>Activity 6.3</td><td>*Write down five ways in which budgeting may cause problems for an organisation. Then read the next section and compare your list with the text. Have you found additional problems? Are the problems you have identified more serious or less serious than those described in the text?*</td></tr></table>

6.4 Problems of budgeting

So far this chapter has presented what is largely conventional wisdom as to the desirability of, and systematic approach to, the setting of budgets. In real life, things are not always so simple. You now move on to look at two potential problems, namely, the behavioural aspects of budgeting and the limitations of line item budgets.

6.4.1 Behavioural aspects of budgeting

The earlier description of the technical process of setting a budget emphasised the need for involvement at all stages of the process. In an ideal world that would produce the best solution, but the world is not ideal and not everyone can be allowed to do exactly as he or she would wish at the first instance. So potential conflicts arise and those involved in the budgetary process need to be aware of the behavioural aspects in order to maximise the good points and minimise the problems.

The behavioural aspects may conveniently be summarised as relating to motivation, participation, feedback, group effects, budget slack and the politics of the organisation. In each of these areas there has been research into the effects, sometimes with inconclusive results. This chapter does not seek to give detailed reference to the research work, but rather to bring out some of the findings as points to consider in relation to the technical process.

Motivation

It was suggested earlier in this chapter that budgets should help in performance evaluation because they provide formal targets against which to measure performance. If the targets are set with care, there should be motivation for the individual to achieve those targets. The question then arises as to what type of targets should be set. Relatively easy targets will be achieved by all, but they will know the targets were easy and will not feel fully motivated by that level of evaluation of performance. If the targets are moderately difficult there will be a stronger motivation for some individuals to achieve those targets, with a sense of personal satisfaction in doing so. Others will fail and will become despondent. They may decide not to put any further effort in because the targets are too difficult.

The literature on goal setting suggests that it is important that the budget targets are accepted by the individuals involved. In that context, budget targets should be at the 'difficult' end of the range, by way of creating a challenge, but should be seen as being attainable. If budget targets are unrealistic there may be a negative reaction where the individual does not even attempt a reasonable level of performance. Communication between levels in the organisation is also important, so that the individual knows that achievement of targets is reported at a higher level and recognised in some form. Within all these considerations of positive factors of motivation, there may be personality problems which invalidate approaches which would otherwise be successful.

Participation

A full understanding of the behavioural aspects of the budgetary process requires an understanding of psychology. Research into behavioural aspects of budgeting has therefore included psychological studies of the individuals participating in the budgetary process. It is argued that individuals have needs for a sense of belonging, a sense of self-esteem and a sense of personal fulfilment. These needs do not necessarily have to be provided through remunerated employment or self-employment. They could be achieved through charitable work or dedication to a particular way of life. To the extent that people do spend a considerable part of their lives in paid employment, these needs may most readily be satisfied by that work.

Participation is one way of meeting those needs, and therefore participation in the budgetary process is a significant aspect of meeting human needs. Those individuals who participate in the budgetary process will gain a sense of ownership of the process, or belonging to the process. They will experience an increase in self-esteem through having a defined role in the process and will achieve a sense of personal fulfilment through successful implementation of the budget plans.

Feedback

Feedback on actual performance, as compared with the budget, is an essential part of the control process which follows from the setting of the budgets. Feedback is only effective if it is provided in a short time-frame. Good news is preferred to bad news; individuals may thus concentrate on the positive feedback and hope that the negative feedback will disappear. The information on negative feedback may have to be presented in a constructive manner if it is to result in action. For example, 'Sales this month were 10 per cent down' may be seen as a negative aspect about which little can be done after the event, but a statement such as 'Next month's sales effort must take account of the cause of last month's 10 per cent decrease' requires positive action in identifying and seeking to remedy the cause of the decrease.

Feedback must relate closely to the responsibility level of the individual if it is to encourage remedial action. There may be a personality problem here, as elsewhere, if individuals see the feedback as criticism of their work. That adverse reaction to criticism could be a function of age or insecurity. Negative aspects of feedback may need a different form of communication from that needed for positive aspects.

Group effects

The impact of the budgetary process on a group of persons may be quite different from the impact on the individual within the group. Participation by individuals will lead to greater group interaction, which will be a good thing if the individuals value their membership of the group and see the goals of the group as being collective targets that they all regard as desirable. Such a group will show cohesion, which will be increased by participation in the budget process.

Where a group does not have such cohesion, or the majority pressure is towards lower targets, the performance of the individual may be reduced by participation within the group. It may therefore be important for senior management, wishing to make effective use of the budgetary process, to have careful regard for the composition of groups within the organisation.

Budget slack

Where budgets are used to measure performance, the managers who set those budgets may be tempted to build in some element of spare resources that allows a lapse from actual high levels of performance without deviating from budget targets. The element of spare resources could involve overestimating the time required for any particular task, or using the highest price of input materials available in the price list, or asking for more equipment than is strictly necessary. Quite apart from such deliberate creation of slack there could also be unintentional errors such as planning activity for 52 weeks in the year when the premises are only open for 50 weeks.

The use of such bias at a lower level of budget preparation may be countered by a correspondingly strict attitude at a higher level to compensate for the built-in slack. That could be unfortunate for the lower level manager who does not build in slack but is penalised along with the rest. The answer to this problem is that the process of budget setting should be specific as to input information so that built-in slack is identified at the earliest possible stage. Flexibility in budgeting is also important to ensure that where slack does become evident it is dealt with by budget revision.

Politics of the organisation

Irrespective of the type of entity, it is almost inevitable that there will be a political aspect to its management structure. The word 'politics' here refers to the power struggle within the organisation. It might be a power struggle in which labour unions seek to impose their will on management. It might be a power struggle within the board of directors or between divisions of the enterprise. Whatever its nature, such a power struggle is evidenced in the budget process where various units of the enterprise are engaged in rivalry over the formulation of the budget. Thus the budgetary process may be more important as a manifestation of the political struggle than as an item of financial planning.

There may be two aspects to budgeting: the public image of resource allocation, and the private image of resolving conflict. For the purposes of this textbook we will concentrate on the technicalities of providing information for resource allocation, but the other potential aspects should not be ignored entirely. They form a significant element of more advanced study in management accounting.

6.5 Limitations of line item budgets

The budgetary process described in this chapter has focused on the separate items which contribute to the overall budget. There will be a line for each item, such as direct materials, direct labour, various kinds of production overhead, various categories of administration, and selling and distribution costs. That type of budget is called a *line item* budget. The line item budget concentrates on the inputs to the process.

It would be equally valid to approach the budgetary process from a totally different direction and concentrate on *outputs* from the process. An output-based approach could be taken by any organisation, but the greatest extent of its practical application has been observed in the non-profit-making organisations, where their activity output is the most important focus of their work.

An output-based approach to budgeting requires starting with an estimate of the quantity and quality of service to be provided. For the non-profit-making organisation the service output takes the place of sales for the profit-seeking organisation. Having defined the desired output the organisation then budgets to determine what will be required to achieve that output. If the organisation is a charity, it will then set about fund-raising. If it is central or local government, it will levy taxes. If the charitable funds available, or the tax revenue to be generated, does not meet all the requirements, then the output activities may be curtailed.

Such an output-based approach focuses on programmes of action. Various budgeting techniques have been suggested for dealing with output-based budget. Two such techniques are planning, programming budgeting systems (PPBS) and zero-base budgeting (ZBB).

6.5.1 Planning, programming budgeting systems

Planning, programming budgeting systems (PPBS) is an approach that seeks to separate the policy planning aspects of budgeting from the short-term financial planning process. From the overall objectives, the organisation moves on to identify the programmes which will achieve those objectives. The costs and benefits of each programme are then identified so that the programmes may be given relative priorities. Subjective judgement is required to select the most suitable programmes for implementation and the resources required are then allocated to those programmes.

The techniques of PPBS were advocated with enthusiasm in the USA for government budgeting in the 1970s, but by the 1980s had disappeared from favour. The reason was that although the system sounds ideal, it is very difficult to administer because government departments are not organised by outcomes. They are organised on an input basis.

Take as an example a programme to integrate into the community patients who have suffered mental illness. The programme will require the establishment of houses where the former patients may enjoy a degree of independence but will have access to help should it be required. That will involve a social welfare aspect and will increase the burden on the budget of the social services. The hospitals will have fewer long-stay mental patients and so will be able to close psychiatric wards. The health service will regard the corresponding funding as being released for other health service purposes such as acute medical care. Thus a programme which might be seen as having a positive social outcome may not result in a mutually amicable budgetary process where the two input departments are not under any constraint to work in harmony on achieving the overall objective.

The fact that PPBS has not worked effectively in a government budgeting context may be due more to the organisation of government departments than to any intrinsic weakness in the concept. If the organisation's objectives are set in terms of programmes, then the organisational structure needs to reflect those programmes or it risks being ineffective if employees relate more closely to their input function than to the defined outputs.

6.5.2 Zero-base budgeting

Zero-base budgeting (ZBB) was devised as a reaction to the traditional incremental approach to budgeting. That traditional approach favoured starting with the previous year's expenditure budget, adding a percentage to cover inflation and making adjustment for any unusual factors or incremental changes. The success of the incremental approach depended critically on the suitability of the previous year's figures. Any errors in estimation would continue indefinitely.

Zero-base budgeting requires a completely clean sheet of paper every year. Each part of the organisation has to justify over again the budget it requires. Some thought-provoking questions may need to be answered, such as:

- What is the need for this activity?
- How much of it is needed?
- Is there a more cost effective way of carrying it out?
- What is the optimal cost?

The approach is particularly useful for the output-driven approach to budgeting because it forces questions to be asked about the programmes planned and the cost-benefit aspects of the plans. On the negative side, it is a time-consuming activity and is perhaps most usefully applied on a selective basis where the questioning approach is most useful. Some activities of an organisation carry an element of discretion and it is worthwhile reappraising them on occasions. Others form an essential core, so that it might be less appropriate to take a zero-based approach.

Activity 6.4

Write down your personal budget for (a) the week ahead, and (b) the month ahead. Show money coming in and money going out. How difficult is it to prepare a budget? What problems did you encounter? To what extent is uncertainty about the future a problem? In the example which follows there is no uncertainty – it assumes the future may be forecast precisely. Work through the example and then consider how much such an exercise would be affected by uncertainty in the real world.

6.6 Practical example

This practical example is based on the operational budgeting in the company called DressSense Partnership. There are two working partners who have built up, over ten years, a small but successful business which makes a range of ladies' dresses sold through boutiques and selected regional department stores. The image of an exclusive label is maintained by not selling through national department stores. The example sets out the mission statement and objectives of the company. It then sets out the budget details for 19X5, as agreed by line managers after negotiations in the later months of 19X4, together with the balance sheet expected at 31 December 19X4 as a starting point to the budget preparation for 19X5.

To help the reader follow the trail through the practical example, each table of information has a reference of the type **(T 1)** at the top left-hand corner. This reference is used in later tables to give a cross-reference to the source of data used in calculation. It is always good practice, in working practical examples, to give plenty of cross-referencing and to show full workings so that the reader can follow the sequence.

6.6.1 Mission statement and objectives

DressSense Partnership

Mission statement
The company intends to maintain its position in a niche market in supplying fashionable designer dresses at affordable prices for the discerning buyer. The relatively small scale of the operation will be maintained as part of the attraction of the product.

The two working partners, who together own the business, are committed to maintaining a close relationship with customers and staff so that quality of service remains uppermost at all times.

Objectives

- The company intends to recruit high-quality staff.
- The company will continue its no-quibble money-back-within-30-days policy.
- The company has a target gross profit of at least 35 per cent on total sales.

6.6.2 Budget details for 19X5 as agreed by line managers after negotiations

The information presented in tables T 1 to T 5 has been agreed by the line managers as a basis for preparation of the master budget and its component parts for the year 19X5.

Sales and production volumes and direct costs

(T 1)

	Evening dress	Costume dress	Daywear
Unit sales for year	900	1,200	1,500
	£	£	£
Unit selling price	510	210	150
Unit variable cost:			
Direct material	100	80	70
Direct labour	80	70	65

Direct labour costs are based on an average cost of £16,000 per person per year.

Other costs
(T 2)

Production heat and light	£7,000 for the year
Production business rates	£5,000 for the year
Partners' salaries	£60,000 for the year
Rent of premises	£10,000 for the year
Office staff salaries	£56,250 for the year
Marketing and distribution	20 per cent of sales

Working capital targets
(T 3)

Debtors at end of year	One-and-a-half months' sales.
Trade creditors for material	One month's purchases.
Stock of raw materials	Enough for 80 per cent of next month's production.
Stock of finished goods	No stock held, as goods are made to order and delivered to the customer when completed.

Sales and purchases are planned to be spread evenly over the year.

Capital budget plans
(T 4)

Purchase one new cutting and sewing machine at £80,000, at the start of the year. Depreciate all machinery for full year at 15 per cent per annum on a straight line basis.

Balance sheet at 31 December 19X4
(T 5)

	£	£
Equipment at cost		100,000
Accumulated depreciation		30,000
Net book value		70,000
Stock of raw materials:		
For 56 evening dresses @ £100 each	5,600	
For 85 costume dresses @ £80 each	6,800	
For 80 daywear @ £70 each	5,600	
Trade debtors	83,000	
Cash	3,000	
	104,000	
Trade creditors	23,000	
Net current assets		81,000
Total assets less current liabilities		151,000
Partners' capital		151,000

6.6.3 Preparation of individual budgets

From the information presented in tables T 1 to T 5 the various detailed budgets are prepared as shown in tables T 6 to T 18. These lead to the master budget set out in tables T 19 to T 21.

Sales budget: sales and debtors

The sales budget sets out the volume of sales expected for each product, multiplied by the expected selling price, to obtain the total sales by value expected for each product. The total sales for the year ahead may then be calculated, shown in bold print in the sales budget.

(T 6)

Sales budget	Ref.	Evening dress	Costume dress	Daywear	Total for year
Unit sales for year	T 1	900	1,200	1,500	
		£	£	£	£
Unit selling price	T 1	510	210	150	
Total sales		459,000	252,000	225,000	**£936,000**

The year-end debtors are calculated as one and a half months' sales (one-eighth of the total year's sales if these are spread evenly throughout the year)

(T 7)

Debtors budget	Ref.	Evening dress £	Costume dress £	Daywear £	Total for year £
Total sales	T 6	459,000	252,000	225,000	936,000
		divide by 8	divide by 8	divide by 8	
Debtors at year end		57,375	31,500	28,125	**117,000**

Production plan

The production plan starts with the volume of output, calculated by taking the planned sales volume and adjusting this for planned levels of opening and closing stock of finished goods. If it is planned to have a level of closing stock, then this will require additional production. To the extent that there exists stock at the start of the period, that will reduce the need for current production. From T 3 it may be noted that the business plans to have no amounts of opening or closing stock because all units are made to specific order. That is a simplification introduced to keep the length of this exercise reasonable, but it is somewhat unusual because most businesses will hold stock of finished goods ready for unexpected demand. As a reminder that stock plans should be taken into account, the production plans in T 8 are shown with lines for opening and closing stock of finished goods.

(T 8)

Production plan in units	Ref.	Evening dress	Costume dress	Daywear
Planned sales volume	T 1	900	1,200	1,500
add: Planned closing stock of finished goods	T 3	–	–	–
less: Opening stock of finished goods	T 3	–	–	–
Planned unit production for year		900	1,200	1,500

Direct materials budget: purchases, stock and trade creditors

Once the production plan has been decided, the costs of the various inputs to production may be calculated. Direct materials must be purchased to satisfy the production plans, but the purchases budget must also take into account the need to hold stock of raw materials. After the purchases budget has been quantified in terms of cost, the impact on trade creditors may also be established.

The *purchases budget* is based on the units of raw material required for production in the period, making allowance for the opening and closing stock of raw materials. The plan is to hold sufficient stock at the end of the period to meet 80 per cent of the following month's production (see T 3). The number of units to be purchased will equal the number of units expected to be used in the period, plus the planned stock of raw materials at the end of the period minus the planned stock of raw materials at the end of the period (calculated in T 9).

(T 9)

Purchases budget in units	Ref.	Evening dress	Costume dress	Daywear
Production volume	T 8	900	1,200	1,500
add: Raw materials stock planned for end of period	T 3	60 (80% of 900/12)	80 (80% of 1,200/12)	100 (80% of 1,500/12)
less: Raw materials stock held at start of period	T 5	56	85	80
Purchases of raw materials planned		904	1,195	1,520

(T 10)

Purchases budget in £s	Ref.	Evening dress	Costume dress	Daywear	Total for year
Volume of purchases (units)	T 9	904	1,195	1,520	
		£	£	£	£
Cost per unit	T 1	100	80	70	
Total purchase cost		90,400	95,600	106,400	**292,400**

Trade creditors are calculated as one month's purchases, a relatively uncomplicated procedure in this instance because the purchases remain constant from month to month.

(T 11)

One month's purchases 292,400/12	**£24,367**

The direct materials to be included in the cost of goods sold must also be calculated at this point, for use in the budgeted profit and loss statement. The direct materials to be included in the cost of goods sold are based on the materials used in production of the period (which in this example is all sold during the period).

(T 12)

Direct materials cost of goods sold	Ref.	Evening dress	Costume dress	Daywear	Total for year
Production (units)	T 8	900	1,200	1,500	
		£	£	£	£
Materials cost per unit	T 1	100	80	70	
Total cost of goods to be sold		90,000	96,000	105,000	**291,000**

Direct labour budget

The direct labour budget takes the volume of production in units and multiplies that by the expected labour cost per unit to give a labour cost for each separate item of product and a total for the year, shown in bold print.

(T 13)

Direct labour budget	Ref.	Evening dress	Costume dress	Daywear	Total for year
Production (units)	T 8	900	1,200	1,500	
		£	£	£	£
Labour cost per unit	T 1	80	70	65	
Total cost		72,000	84,000	97,500	**253,500**

It is also useful to check on the total resource requirement which corresponds to this total labour cost, since it takes time to plan increases or decreases in labour resources. The average direct labour cost was given in T 1 as £16,000 per person per year. The following calculation assumes that the employees can work equally efficiently on any of the three product lines.

(T 14)

> *Resource requirement:*
> Based on an average cost of £16,000 per person per year, the total labour cost of £253,500 would require 15.8 full-time equivalent dressmakers.

Production overhead budget

Production overheads include all those overhead items which relate to the production activity. In this example it includes heat and light, business rates and depreciation. Depreciation is calculated at a rate of 15 per cent on the total cost of equipment held during the year (£100,000 at the start, as shown in T 5, plus an additional £80,000 noted in T 4).

(T 15)

Production overhead budget	Ref.	£
Heat and light	T 2	7,000
Business rates	T 2	5,000
Depreciation	T 4	27,000
Total		**39,000**

Total production cost budget

Total production cost comprises the cost of direct materials, direct labour and production overhead.

(T 16)

Production cost budget	Ref.	£
Direct materials	T 12	291,000
Direct labour	T 13	253,500
Production overhead	T 15	39,000
Total		**583,500**

Administration expense budget

The administration expense budget includes the partners' salaries because they are working partners and their labour cost represents a management cost of the operations. The fact that the managerial role is carried out by the partners, who are also the owners of the business, is not relevant to the purposes of management accounting. What is important is to record a realistic cost of managing the business. Other administration costs in this example are rent of premises and the salaries of office staff (as shown in T 2).

(T 17)

Administration budget	Ref.	£
Partners' salaries (drawn monthly in cash)	T 2	60,000
Rent of premises	T 2	10,000
Office staff	T 2	56,250
Total		**126,250**

Marketing expense budget

The marketing expense budget relates to all aspects of the costs of advertising and selling the product. The information in T 2 specifies a marketing cost which is dependent on sales, being estimated as 20 per cent of sales value.

(T 18)

Marketing expense budget	Ref.	£
20 per cent of £936,000	T 2 & T 6	187,200

6.6.4 Master budget

The master budget has three components: the budgeted profit and loss account for the year, the budgeted cash flow statement and the budgeted balance sheet. These are now set out using the foregoing separate budgets. Where the derivation of figures in the master budget should be evident from the earlier budgets, no explanation is given, but where further calculations have been performed these are shown as working notes.

Budgeted profit and loss account

(T 19) Budgeted profit and loss account for the year ended 31 December 19X5

	Ref.	Evening dress £	Costume dress £	Daywear £	Total for year £
Total sales	T 6	459,000	252,000	225,000	**936,000**
Materials cost	T 12	90,000	96,000	105,000	**291,000**
Labour cost	T 13	72,000	84,000	97,500	**253,500**
Total variable cost		162,000	180,000	202,500	**544,500**
Contribution		297,000	72,000	22,500	**391,500**
% on sales		64.7%	28.6%	10.0%	37.7%
Production overhead	T 15				**39,000**
Gross profit					**352,500**
Administration cost	T 17				**126,250**
Marketing cost	T 18				**187,200**
Net profit					**39,050**

Budgeted cash flow statement

Where expenses are paid for as soon as they are incurred, the cash outflow equals the expense as shown in the budgeted profit and loss account. In the case of cash collected from customers, debtors at the start and end of the period must be taken into the calculation. In the case of cash paid to suppliers the creditors at the start and end of the period must be taken into account. The cash flow statement contains references to working notes which follow the statement and set out the necessary detail.

(T 20) Budgeted cash flow statement for the year ended 31 December 19X5

	Note	£	£
Cash to be collected from customers	1		902,000
Cash to be paid to suppliers	2	291,033	
Direct labour	3	253,500	
Heat and light	3	7,000	
Business rates	3	5,000	
Partners' salaries	3	60,000	
Rent of premises	3	10,000	
Office staff costs	3	56,250	
Marketing costs	3	187,200	
			869,983
Net cash inflow from operations			32,017
New equipment to be purchased			80,000
Net cash outflow			(47,983)
Cash balance at beginning			3,000
Cash balance at end			(44,983)

Note 1: Cash to be collected from customers

	Ref.	£
Sales during the period	T 6	936,000
less: Credit sales which remain as debtors at the end of the year	T 7	117,000
		819,000
add: Cash collected from debtors at the start of the year	T 5	83,000
Cash to be collected from customers		902,000

Note 2: Cash to be paid to suppliers

	Ref.	£
Purchases during the period	T 10	292,400
less: Credit purchases which remain as creditors at the end of the year	T 11	24,367
		268,033
add: Cash paid to creditors at the start of the year	T 5	23,000
Cash to be paid to suppliers		291,033

Note 3: Other cash payments
It has been assumed, for the convenience of this illustration, that all other expense items are paid for as they are incurred. In reality, this would be unlikely and there would be further calculations of the type shown in Note 2, making allowance for creditors at the start and end of the period.

Budgeted balance sheet

(T 21) Budgeted balance sheet at 31 December 19X5

	Note	£	£
Equipment at cost	1		180,000
Accumulated depreciation	2		57,000
Net book value			123,000
Stock of raw materials	3	19,400	
Trade debtors (T 7)		117,000	
		136,400	
Bank borrowing (T 20)		44,983	
Trade creditors (T 11)		24,367	
		69,350	
Net current assets			67,050
Total assets less current liabilities			190,050
Partners' capital	4		190,050

Note 1

		£
Equipment at cost = £100,000 + £80,000	=	180,000

Note 2

Accumulated depreciation = £30,000 + £27,000	=	57,000

Note 3

Stock of raw material:

For 60 evening dresses @ £100 each	6,000
For 80 costume dresses @ £80 each	6,400
For 100 daywear @ £70 each	7,000
	19,400

Note 4

Partners' capital = £151,000 + £39,050	=	190,050

6.6.5 Interpretation of the practical example

Fiona McTaggart has reviewed the budget illustrated here and now offers some comments.

FIONA: *This illustration shows how much detail has to go into even the simplest of budgeting exercises. Comparing the budget with the statement of objectives, I was a little surprised to find no provision in the budgeted profit and loss account in relation to the money-back promise. If I were involved in this exercise I would include a provision based on past experience of the level of returns. That wouldn't affect the cash flow of course because provisions are accounting allocations with no cash flow implications.*

The target gross profit percentage will be achieved overall (gross profit shown in the master budget is 37.7 per cent of total sales) but is heavily dependent on the high margin on evening dresses. I hope there is plenty of market research to back up those sales projections. The overall net profit budgeted is 4.2 per cent of total sales, which means there is little scope for error before the budgeted profit turns to a budgeted loss.

The budgeted cash flow statement shows an overall surplus on operations of the year, turning to a cash deficit when the effect of buying the new equipment is brought into the calculation, but that does not tell the whole story. The £80,000 cash outlay for the new equipment is needed at the start of the year whereas the cash inflows will be spread over the year, so the company will need to borrow early in the year to pay for the equipment. There will have to be a monthly statement of cash flows to show the bank how the cash will flow out and in over the year as a whole. The borrowing could perhaps be short-term borrowing in view of the overall surplus, but there are other potential cash flows which are not dealt with here. The partners are working partners and are taking salaries in cash but they may also need to draw out more cash to pay their tax bills.

It is interesting to compare these management accounts with the way in which external reporting for financial purposes might appear. The textbooks always suggest that partners' salaries are an appropriation of profit for financial reporting purposes and should appear as such in the partners' capital accounts with a matching entry for drawings.

That's all far too elaborate for management accounting purposes. What matters here is that these are working partners and if they did not do the work, someone else would have to. Provided the salary is a reasonable representation of a reward for the work done, it is far more sensible to show the expense in the profit and loss account.

6.7 Summary

In this chapter you met the definition of a budget as a detailed plan that sets out, in money terms, the plans for income and expenditure in respect of a future period of time. It is prepared in advance of that time period and is based on the agreed objectives for that period of time, together with the strategy planned to achieve those objectives.

The short-term budgetary process has been set in the context of long-range planning. Preparing a master budget has been set out in diagrammatic form in exhibit 6.2. The administration of the budgeting process has been described and the benefits of budgeting have been put forward in terms of planning and control. The budgetary process is a powerful tool of management accounting but also carries potential problems of adverse behavioural reactions if handled badly. The behavioural aspects have been outlined here as an introduction to a major area of study which will be encountered in subsequent study of the subject. Finally, the chapter has developed in detail a practical example of the preparation of a master budget.

Budgets are also important for control, where the actual results of a period may be compared with the expectations when the budget was set. The use of budgets for control purposes has been touched upon in this chapter but is dealt with in more detail in Chapter 7.

Further reading

Drury, C. (1992), *Management and Cost Accounting*, Chapman & Hall.

Horngren, C. T., Foster, G. and Datar, S. (1993), *Cost Accounting: A Managerial Emphasis*, Prentice Hall.

Pendlebury, M. (1991), *Management Accounting in the Public Sector*, Butterworth-Heinemann, London.

Wilson, R. M. S. and Chua, W. F. (1992), *Managerial Accounting: Method and Meaning*, Chapman & Hall.

Self-testing on the chapter

1　Explain the purpose of long-range planning.

2　Explain the purpose of setting a strategy.

3　Define the term 'budget'.

4　Explain the budget planning process and the main relationships within that process.

5　What is the role of the budget committee?

6　What are the main steps in the budgeting process?

7　How does budgeting help the management function of planning?

8　How does budgeting help the management function of control?

9　How does budgeting help the management function of communication and co-ordination?

10　What are the behavioural aspects of budgeting which may give rise to problems?

11　How may these behavioural problems be avoided or minimised?

12　What are the limitations of line budgets?

13　Explain the nature and purpose of planning, programming budgeting systems (PPBS).

14　Explain the nature and purpose of zero-base budgeting (ZBB).

15　A company has 1,000 units of finished goods held in store at the start of the month. It produces a further 4,000 units during the month and sells 4,200. How many units are in store at the end of the month?

16　The sales budget for the BeeSee Company for the first six months of the year is:

	£
January	12,000
February	13,000

	£
March	14,000
April	13,500
May	12,600
June	11,100

There are no debtors at the start of January. One month's credit is allowed to customers. What is the budgeted cash received in each month?

17 Trade creditors at the start of January are £12,500. They are all paid during January. During the month, goods costing £18,000 are purchased, and at the end of January there is an amount of £13,600 owing to trade creditors. State the amount of cash paid to trade creditors during January.

18 The cost of indirect materials in any month is 40 per cent variable (varying with direct labour hours) and 60 per cent fixed. The total cost of indirect materials during the month of March was budgeted at £500. During the month of April it is expected that the direct labour hours will be 20 per cent higher than during March. What should be budgeted for the cost of indirect materials in April?

19 Newtrend Ltd is a new business which has been formed to buy standard radio units and modify them to the specific needs of customers.

The business will acquire fixed assets costing £200,000 and a stock of 1,000 standard radio units on the first day of business. The fixed assets are expected to have a five-year life with no residual value at the end of that time.

Sales are forecast as follows:

	Year 1				Year 2
	Quarter 1	Quarter 2	Quarter 3	Quarter 4	Quarter 1
Modified radio units	8,100	8,400	8,700	7,800	8,100

The selling price of each unit will be £90.
The cost of production of each unit is specified as follows:

	£
Cost of standard unit purchased	30
Direct labour	33
Fixed overhead	12
	75

The fixed overhead per unit includes an allocation of depreciation. The annual depreciation is calculated on a straight line basis and is allocated on the basis of a cost per unit to be produced during the year.

Suppliers of standard radio units will allow one month's credit. Customers are expected to take two months' credit.

Wages will be paid as they are incurred in production. Fixed overhead costs will be paid as they are incurred.

The stock of finished goods at the end of each quarter will be sufficient to satisfy 20 per cent of the planned sales of the following quarter. The stock of standard radio units will be held constant at 1,000 units.

It may be assumed that the year is divided into quarters of equal length and that sales, production and purchases are spread evenly throughout any quarter.

Required

Produce, for each quarter of the first year of trading:

(a) the sales budget;
(b) the production budget; and
(c) the cash budget.

20 Tools Ltd is a new business which has been formed to buy standard machine tool units and adapt them to the specific needs of customers.

The business will acquire fixed assets costing £100,000 and a stock of 500 standard tool units on the first day of business. The fixed assets are expected to have a five-year life with no residual value at the end of that time.

Sales are forecast as follows:

	Year 1				Year 2
	Quarter 1	Quarter 2	Quarter 3	Quarter 4	Quarter 1
Modified tool units	4,050	4,200	4,350	3,900	4,050

The selling price of each unit will be £90.

The cost of production of each unit is specified as follows:

	£
Cost of standard unit purchased	24
Direct labour	30
Fixed overhead	10
	64

The fixed overhead per unit includes an allocation of depreciation. The annual depreciation is calculated on a straight line basis and is allocated on the basis of a cost per unit to be produced during the year.

Suppliers of standard tool units will allow one month's credit. Customers are expected to take two months' credit.

Wages will be paid as they are incurred in production. Fixed overhead costs will be paid as they are incurred.

The stock of finished goods at the end of each quarter will be sufficient to satisfy 10 per cent of the planned sales of the following quarter. The stock of standard tool units will be held constant at 500 units.

It may be assumed that the year is divided into quarters of equal length and that sales, production and purchases are spread evenly throughout any quarter.

Required

Produce, for each quarter of the first year of trading:

(a) the sales budget;

(b) the production budget; and

(c) the cash budget.

21 Bright Papers Ltd has established a new subsidiary company to produce extra-large rolls of wall covering. Management forecasts for the first four years of trading are as follows:

	Year 1	Year 2	Year 3	Year 4
Sales (in units)	800,000	950,000	1,200,000	1,500,000
Production (in units)	850,000	1,000,000	1,300,000	1,600,000
	£	£	£	£
Selling price per unit	10.20	10.56	11.04	12.00
Costs per unit:				
Direct materials	2.04	2.28	2.64	3.00
Direct labour	0.60	0.75	0.90	0.90
Variable overhead	0.40	0.50	0.60	0.60
Fixed overhead	£5,000,000	£5,100,000	£5,200,000	£5,300,000
Average credit period given to customers	1 month	1 month	1.5 months	2 months
Average credit period taken from suppliers of materials	2 months	1.5 months	1.5 months	1 month

Further information:

(a) Estimates for the average credit period given and taken are based on balances at the end of each year.

(b) Costs other than direct materials are to be paid for in the month they are incurred.

(c) The company will adopt the FIFO assumption in relation to cost of goods sold.

(d) No increases in production capacity will be required during the first four years of business.

(e) Fixed overhead costs include depreciation of £1,500,000 per annum.

(f) No stock of direct materials will be held. The supplier will deliver goods daily, as required. No work-in-progress will exist at the end of any year.

Required

Prepare annual cash budgets for the new subsidiary for each of the first four years of trading.

Activity for study groups

Today's task is to review the first stage of budget preparation in a major hospital dealing with a wide range of medical conditions, including accident and emergency services. (There are indications within the case study of how to allocate the time on the presumption that one hour is available in total, but the times may be adjusted proportionately for a different overall length.)

Before the activity starts obtain and look through the annual report and accounts of a hospital trust and a regional health authority, looking for discussion of the budgetary process and the way in which budgets are presented in the annual report.

Half of the group should form the budget committee, deciding among themselves the role of each individual within the hospital but having regard for the need to keep a balance between medical services, medical support staff and administration. The other half of the group should take the role of specialty team leaders presenting their budgets (specialty being the term used to describe one particular specialist aspect of hospital treatment, e.g. children's specialisms (paediatrics) women's conditions (obstetrics and gynaecology), or dealing with older persons (geriatrics)).

Initially the group should work together for 20 minutes to write a mission statement and set of corporate objectives. The budget committee should then hold a separate meeting lasting 10 minutes to decide (a) what questions they will ask of the specialty team leaders when they present their budget plans, and (b) where the sources of conflict are most likely to be found. In the meantime each specialty team leader should set out a brief statement of objectives for that specialty team and a note of the main line items which would appear in the budget, indicating where conflict with other teams within the hospital is most likely to arise as a result of the budgeting process.

The budget committee should then interview each specialty manager (5 minutes each), with the other specialty managers attending as observers. After all interviews have been held, the budget committee should prepare a brief report dealing with the effectiveness and limitations of the budgetary process as experienced in the exercise. The specialty managers should work together to produce a report on their perceptions of the effectiveness and limitations of the budgetary process (15 minutes).

Case studies

Case 6.1

The Garden Ornament Company manufactures two types of garden ornament: a duck and a heron. The information presented in tables T 1 to T 5 has been prepared, as a result of discussions by line managers, for the purposes of preparing a master budget for 19X6.

Sales and production volumes and direct costs

(T 1)

	Ducks	Herons
Unit sales for the year	8,000	15,000
	£	£
Unit selling price	30	45
Unit variable cost:		
Direct material	14	16
Direct labour	12	13

Direct labour costs are based on an average cost of £15,000 per person per year.

Other costs

(T 2)

Production heat and light	£8,000 for the year
Production fixed overheads	£4,000 for the year
Partners' salaries	£55,000 for the year
Rent of premises	£11,000 for the year
Office staff salaries	£48,450 for the year
Marketing and distribution	18 per cent of sales

Working capital targets

(T 3)

Debtors at end of year	Half of one month's sales.
Trade creditors for materials	One month's purchases.
Stock of raw materials	Enough for 60 per cent of next month's production.
Stock of finished goods	No stock held, as goods are made to order and delivered to the customer on completion.

Sales and purchases are planned to be spread evenly over the year.

Capital budget plans

(T 4)

Purchase one new moulding machine at £70,000, at the start of the year.
Depreciate all machinery for a full year at 20 per cent per annum on a straight line basis.

Balance sheet at 31 December 19X5

(T 5)

	£	£
Equipment at cost		190,000
Accumulated depreciation		40,000
Net book value		150,000
Stock of raw materials:		
For 400 ducks @ £14 each	5,600	
For 750 herons @ £16 each	12,000	
Trade debtors	32,000	
Cash	2,500	
	52,100	
Trade creditors	30,000	
		22,100
		172,100
Partners' capital		172,100

Required

Prepare a master budget and all supporting budgets.

Case 6.2

The following budgeted accounting statements were submitted to the board of directors of Alpha Ltd on 1 October 19X4:

Budgeted profit and loss account for the year to 30 September 19X5

	£	£
Sales		15,600,000
Cost of sales		10,452,000
Gross profit		5,148,000
Fixed overheads:		
Selling and advertising	1,500,000	
General administration	1,094,500	
		2,594,500
Operating profit		2,553,500
Interest payable on medium-term loan	135,000	
Royalties payable on sales	780,000	
		915,000
Net profit		1,638,500

Budgeted balance sheet at 30 September 19X5,
with comparative figures at 1 October 19X4

	30 September 19X5	1 October 19X4
	£	£
Fixed assets at cost	2,300,000	1,800,000
less: accumulated depreciation	585,000	450,000
	1,715,000	1,350,000
Trading stock	3,200,000	4,000,000
Trade debtors	2,600,000	2,200,000
Cash in bank	1,854,750	–
Total assets	9,369,750	7,550,000
Share capital	4,400,000	4,400,000
Retained earnings	3,313,500	1,675,000
	7,713,500	6,075,000
Medium-term loan	1,000,000	1,000,000
Trade creditors	656,250	475,000
	9,369,750	7,550,000

At 31 March 19X5 the following information was available in respect of the first six months of the trading year:

(a) Sales were 20 per cent below the budgeted level, assuming an even spread of sales throughout the year.

(b) The gross profit percentage was two percentage points below the budgeted percentage.

(c) Actual advertising expenditure of £100,000 was 50 per cent below the budgeted amount. All other selling expenses were in line with the budget.

(d) General administration costs were 10 per cent below the budgeted level.

(e) Trading stock at 31 March was £200,000 higher than the budgeted level. It was assumed in the budget that stock would decrease at a uniform rate throughout the year.

(f) Trade debtors at 31 March were equivalent to two months' actual sales, assuming sales were spread evenly throughout the six months.

(g) Trade creditors at 31 March were equivalent to one month's actual cost of goods sold, assuming costs were spread evenly throughout the six months.

(h) On 1 January 19X5 the rate of interest charged on the medium-term loan was increased to 16 per cent per annum.

The budget for the second six months was revised to take account of the following predictions:

(a) Revenue during the second six months would continue at the level achieved during the first six months.

(b) Cost control measures would be implemented to restore the gross profit percentage to the budgeted level.

(c) Advertising, selling and general administration costs would be maintained at the levels achieved in the first six months.

(d) Trading stocks would be reduced to the level originally budgeted at 30 September.

(e) Trade debtors would be reduced to the equivalent of one month's sales.

(f) Trade creditors would be maintained at the equivalent of one month's cost of goods sold.

(g) Interest on the medium-term loan would remain at 16 per cent per annum.

The directors of the company wish to know what change in the cash in bank will arise when the revised budget for the second six months is compared with the consequences of continuing the pattern in the first six months.

Taxation has been ignored.

Required

1 Prepare an accounting statement for the six months to 31 March 19X5 comparing the actual results with the original budget.

2 Prepare a revised budget for the second six months and compare this with the actual results which would have been achieved if the pattern of the first six months had continued.

Case 6.3

You have been appointed finance director of Constructabus plc, a coach building company, which specialises in two types of bus, a standard double-deck vehicle and a luxury coach model. The chassis and engine are bought in and the framework of each bus is built on the assembly floor. All the fixtures and fittings are added in the finishing shed to meet customers' specifications.

The head of the accounts department has provided you with the following information for the year ended 31 August 19X8:

	Standard bus	*Luxury coach*
Sales in units	100	120
Total sales value	£3,075,000	£4,020,000
Production in units	90	80
Stock of finished units at 31 August 19X8	20	30
Labour hours per unit:		
Assembly floor	2,000	1,000
Finishing shed	1,000	1,500
Direct materials cost per unit	£4,000	£4,000
Total variable selling	£150,000	£144,000

Departmental costs

	Assembly floor £	Finishing shed £
Labour	1,300,000	1,260,000
Variable overhead	520,000	210,000
Fixed overhead	200,000	180,000

Further information

(a) Stocks are valued at variable cost of production for management accounting purposes. Work-in-progress may be ignored. At 1 September 19X7, stock values were £25,000 per standard bus and £21,500 per luxury coach.

(b) The assembly floor has achieved full working capacity during the year but the finishing shed was 25 per cent underutilised.

The head of the accounts department has prepared the following budget for the year ending 31 August 19X9:

	Standard bus	Luxury coach
Sales in units	60	150
Total sales value	£1,845,000	£5,475,000
Production in units	60	145
Direct materials costs	£240,000	£725,000
Total variable selling costs	£105,000	£180,000

Departmental costs

	Assembly floor £	Finishing shed £
Labour	1,590,000	1,665,000
Variable overhead	795,000	277,500
Fixed overhead	200,000	220,000

Further information

(a) Labour hours per unit are assumed to be the same as for the year ended 31 August 19X8.

(b) Due to changing patterns in public transport, the budget has recognised that demand for standard buses has fallen by 40 per cent but that sales of the luxury coaches will expand by 25 per cent.

Required

Prepare a report for the board which provides:

1 A statement of budgeted profit for each product for the year ending 31 August 19X9.

2 A comparison of this budget with the actual results for each product for the year ended 31 August 19X8.

3 Comments on your analysis.

Case 6.4

Holyrood Products Ltd makes cassette recorders. The management accountant has produced the following summary of the company's trading in the year ended 30 June 19X3:

	£	£
Sales: 30,000 recorders.....................................		375,000
add: Increase in finished goods stock...............		16,000
....		391,000
Deduct:		
Direct materials	128,000	
Direct labour..	96,000	
Works and administration overhead	50,000	
Selling overhead..	20,000	
....		294,000
Trading profit...		97,000

The following additional information is available:

(a) Works and administration overhead was 64 per cent variable and 36 per cent fixed, the latter including £2,500 for depreciation of plant surplus to current requirements.
(b) Selling overhead was 75 per cent variable and 25 per cent fixed.
(c) For management accounting purposes, finished goods stock is valued at variable cost excluding selling overhead.
(d) There was an increase of 2,000 units in finished goods stock over the year .

The production manager has made the following estimates for the year to 30 June 19X4 which show that:

(a) The excess plant will be utilised for the production of a radio and a watch in quantities of 5,000 and 10,000 respectively. The variable costs are:

	Radio £	Watch £
Direct materials	15,000	10,000
Direct labour	10,000	25,000
Works and administration overhead	2,500	15,000
Selling overhead	4,500	2,250

(b) Finished goods stock of cassette recorders will remain unchanged and stocks of radios and watches will be built up to 10 per cent of production.

(c) Production of cassette recorders will be at the same level as that achieved in the year to 30 June 19X3.

(d) Fixed overhead:

	Cassette recorder	Radio £	Watch £
Works and administration	No change	8,000*	13,500*
Selling	60% increase	2,250	6,750

Note: *excluding depreciation.

(e) Materials costs for cassette recorders will be increased by £1 per unit. Other variable costs will be held at the level attained in the year ended 30 June 19X3.

The marketing director has advised that each product should be priced so as to achieve a 20 per cent profit on total cost.

Required

Prepare a statement of budgeted profit for the year ended 30 June 19X4.

Standard costs

After studying this chapter you should be able to:

1 Explain why standard costs are a useful tool of management accounting.

2 Understand the method of calculating standard costs.

3 Apply standard costs and understand the results.

4 Evaluate the benefits and limitations of using standard costs.

7.1 Introduction

Chapter 6 has explained the budgetary process and illustrated in detail a method of preparing budgets for planning purposes. The use of budgets for control purposes was explained in that chapter in terms of comparing the actual outcome with the expected results as shown by the budget.

When actual costs are compared with budgeted costs, the comparison is of the total cost for the line item under consideration (e.g. cost of various types of materials, cost of various categories of labour, or cost of a range of categories of overheads). Where there is a significant difference between the budget and the actual outcome, that difference may be investigated. (It has to be remembered, however, that the investigation will itself have a cost and that cost may be minimised by first trying to narrow down the causes of the difference.)

To analyse the difference between what was expected and what actually happened, it is useful to make comparisons in terms of *cost per unit* rather than total cost of a line item in the budget. Such costs per unit may be estimated in advance and used as a standard against which to compare the actual costs incurred. The cost per unit, measured in advance of the operations to be undertaken, is called a *standard cost*.

Definition

Standard costs are target costs which should be attained under specified operating conditions. They are expressed as a cost per unit.

Once the standard cost has been decided, the actual cost may be compared with the standard. If it equals the standard then the actual outcome has matched expectations. If the actual cost is greater than, or less than, the standard cost allowed, then there will be a variance to be investigated. This chapter explains how the standard costs may be determined and how the variances may be quantified.

Definition

A *variance* arises when an actual cost per unit differs from the standard cost for that unit.

7.2 Purpose of creating standard costs

It has already been shown (in Chapter 2) that calculation of the cost of an item of input or output may be analysed in terms of two measurements:

1 a physical quantity measurement

multiplied by

2 a price measurement.

Actual costs are measured after the event by reference to the quantity of the resource used and its price. When the actual cost is measured there is no doubt as to the quantity and price.

Standard costs are measured in advance of the period of time to which they relate, so that estimation is necessary. This requires estimation of physical inputs and outputs, and monetary estimates of prices of inputs and outputs. In order to determine useful standards it is necessary first of all to consider the purpose for which the standards will be used. The purpose could cover any or all of the following:

1 to provide product costs for stock evaluation;
2 to increase control within a budgeting system;
3 to gauge performance of a business unit by use of variance analysis;
4 to integrate costs in the planning and pricing structure of a business;
5 to reduce record-keeping costs when transactions take place at different prices.

This chapter will concentrate on items (2), (3) and (4) of the foregoing list, showing how variance analysis may be used for purposes of control, performance evaluation and planning. First, the standard cost is explained. The control process is then outlined by means of a flow diagram. Most of the chapter deals with the calculation and interpretation of variances in the cost of direct materials, direct labour and production overhead. That provides information to management for use in making judgements and carrying out performance evaluations. The final section discusses the usefulness of variance analysis based on standard costing in planning the efficient operation of the business.

7.3 The level of output to be used in setting standards

Calculation of the standard cost requires a view to be taken on the most appropriate physical measurement to incorporate in the cost calculation. Three approaches are instanced here. The first uses a basic level of output, the second looks to an ideal level of output, and the third uses a currently attainable level of output.

The *basic standard* is one which never changes and consequently remains a permanent basis for comparison. This gives a base line against which to make long-term comparisons. It has the disadvantage of becoming increasingly unrealistic as circumstances change.

The *ideal standard* is one which applies in dream conditions where nothing ever goes wrong. It represents the cost incurred under the most efficient operating conditions. It is an almost unattainable target towards which an organisation may constantly aim, but it may also cause a lowering of morale in the organisation if staff can never reach the target.

Currently attainable standards lie between these two extremes, defined as standards which should normally equal expectations under 'normally efficient operating conditions'. They may represent quite stiff targets to reach, but they are not beyond possibility. Currently attainable standards are the most frequently used because they give a fair base for comparisons, they set a standard which ought to be achieved and they give staff a sense of achievement when the attainable target is reached. Thus they contribute to all the management functions of planning and control which were explained in Chapter 1.

Although the standard cost may be quantified as a single figure, it may in practice represent a whole range of possible figures because it is an estimate from a range of possible outcomes. This chapter will apply a single figure standard in illustrative case studies, without questioning further the basis on which the standard was created.

Activity 7.1	*These first three sections of the chapter have explained the meaning of a standard and the various different approaches to creation of a standard. Read the sections again and satisfy yourself that you are aware of the differences. That awareness will help you in thinking about the interpretation of variances.*

We now turn to an explanation of how standards are used in the control process.

7.4 The control process

Exhibit 7.1 shows the process of calculating and using standard costs for control purposes. The calculation of standards involves asking technical specialists, who are probably not management accountants, to specify the standard inputs of resources. The management accountant takes this information and prepares a standard cost specification, usually converting that to a cost per unit of input or output. Actual costs are then measured and compared with the standard. Variances which emerge are quantified, analysed and reported. This may lead to control actions in relation to eliminating variances. It may also lead to revision of the standard costs if they are no longer relevant.

Exhibit 7.1
Use of standards in the control process

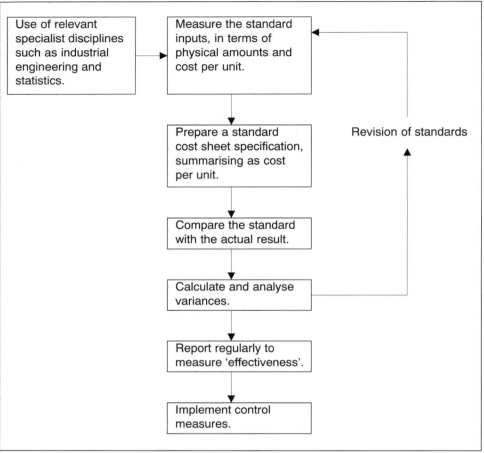

The presence of a standard cost provides a benchmark against which to evaluate the actual cost. The technical term for this process is *variance analysis*. Cost variances may described as *adverse* or *favourable*, depending on how the standard and the actual costs compare. If the actual cost is greater than the standard expected, then the variance is said to be 'adverse'. If the actual cost is less than the standard expected, then the variance is said to be 'favourable'. The existence of either type of variance could lead to investigation of the cause. The component costs must be investigated separately so that they may be separately analysed and interpreted. We now move on to give more detail on the process of calculating and analysing variances for direct materials cost and direct labour cost.

Definitions   An *adverse variance* arises when the actual cost is greater than the standard cost.
A *favourable variance* arises when the actual cost is less than the standard cost.

Activity 7.2

> *Suggest three situations in which a business organisation might decide to revise standards, as indicated in exhibit 7.1, following calculation and analysis of variances. Is revision equally likely for adverse and for favourable variances? Make sure that you know the definitions of adverse and favourable variances. They will appear frequently in the following sections.*

7.5 Direct materials cost variance

Take as a starting point one of the ingredients of prime cost: direct materials. If the actual cost differs from the standard cost, then the cause may lie in the materials usage, or in the price of the materials, or in a mixture of both. An adverse cost variance could indicate that the price paid was higher than expected when the standard was set, or it could indicate that the amount of materials used was greater than that expected.

In diagrammatic form:

Direct materials cost variance

equals

Price variance	Usage variance

Exhibit 7.2 sets out in words the calculation of variances. Alongside there are abbreviated symbols for those who are comfortable with an algebraic representation.

At this point in learning about variance analysis, some students will ask: 'Why are the formulae in this form? I can see other combinations of symbols which could break the cost variance down into two components.' The answer is that there are other combinations but one of the aims of management accounting is to present relevant information. In the form given in the exhibit, these variances produce relevant information.

To understand the relevance of the variances, it may help to think of the standard cost as a rectangle whose area is measured by multiplying the standard price of materials by the actual quantity of materials used (exhibit 7.3).

Now imagine that the actual cost is greater than standard cost so that a rectangle representing actual cost will fit around the outside of the standard cost rectangle. Exhibit 7.4 shows the two rectangles together. The total cost variance is represented by the shaded 'inverted L' shaped area to the top and the right-hand side of the diagram. The top part of the shaded area represents variance caused by actual price being greater than standard price. The right-hand side represents variance caused by actual quantity used being greater than the standard quantity allowed. In terms of management responsibility, the price variance will be in the hands of the purchasing department, while the usage variance will be in the hands of the production department. But who should be

169

Exhibit 7.2
Calculation and formulae for direct materials variances

Variance	Calculation	Formula
Total cost variance	Standard cost of materials (SC) minus actual cost of materials (AC)

This may be shown in more detail as:

Standard cost (SC) = standard price per unit (SP) multiplied by standard quantity allowed (SQ)

minus

Actual cost (AC) = actual price per unit (AP) multiplied by actual quantity used (AQ) | $SC - AC$

$SC = (SP \times SQ)$

minus

$AC = (AP \times AQ)$ |
| Direct materials price variance | Actual quantity used (AQ), multiplied by the difference between the standard price per unit (SP) and the actual price per unit (AP) | $AQ (SP - AP)$ |
| Direct materials usage variance | Standard price per unit of materials (SP) multiplied by the difference between the standard quantity (SQ) allowed and the actual quantity used (AQ) | $SP (SQ - AQ)$ |

Exhibit 7.3
Representing standard cost as a rectangular area

SP
Standard cost
SQ

Exhibit 7.4
Representing actual cost and standard cost as two areas superimposed

held accountable for the top right-hand corner where a question mark appears? This is a mixture of price variation and usage variation. The production manager will disclaim any responsibility for the price aspect and the buying department will say it has no control over quantity.

Management accounting is full of hard decisions and as far as possible tries to be fair. For the top right-hand corner of the diagram, that is almost impossible, however there is a view that usage is within the organisation's control to a greater extent than the price of inputs taken from an external supplier. Management accounting therefore takes the view that the production manager's responsibility for usage should be limited in order to leave out the area containing the question mark. By default, therefore, that area at the top right-hand corner is allowed to fall entirely into the price variance.

Activity 7.3	*Read this section again to ensure that you understand fully the method of calculating direct materials cost variance. Compare the formulae in exhibit 7.2 and the diagram in exhibit 7.4. If there is any step which you do not understand, seek help at this stage from your tutor or a fellow student. The method of calculation is applied later in a case study.*

7.6 Direct labour cost variance

The starting point in analysis of direct labour cost variances resembles closely that used for direct materials, except that the price variance changes its name to labour rate variance and the usage variance changes to labour efficiency variance.

Direct labour cost variance	

equals

Rate variance	Efficiency variance

The formulae for calculating direct labour variances are similar to those used for direct materials. They are shown in exhibit 7.5.

If you try to draw a diagram for direct labour variances, superimposing the actual cost on the standard cost as shown for direct materials in exhibit 7.4, you will find that the area labelled with a question mark in exhibit 7.4 has all been allocated to the rate variance. It is argued in management accounting that the organisation is more likely to have control over efficiency than it is over labour rate, which may well be determined by the labour market in general. The efficiency variance should therefore not include any element of variation in labour rate, and the top right-hand corner of the diagram is all taken into the rate variance.

Exhibit 7.5
Calculation and formulae for direct labour variances

Variance	Calculation	Formula
Total cost variance	Standard cost of labour (SC) minus actual cost of labour (AC)	SC – AC
	This may be shown in more detail as:	
	Standard cost (SC) = standard labour rate (SR) multiplied by standard hours allowed (SH)	SC = (SR × SH)
	minus	minus
	Actual cost (AC) = actual labour rate (AR) multiplied by actual hours worked (AH)	AC = (AR × AH)
Direct labour rate variance	Actual hours worked (AH), multiplied by the difference between the standard labour rate (SR) and the actual labour rate (AR)	AH (SR – AR)
Direct labour efficiency variance	Standard labour rate (SR) multiplied by the difference between the standard hours allowed (SH) and the actual hours worked (AH)	SR (SH – AH)

Activity 7.4

Read this section again to make sure that you understand fully the formulae in exhibit 7.5. Try to produce a diagram similar to that drawn in exhibit 7.4 for direct materials. Note down the similarities and the differences between the formulae for direct materials variances and the formulae for direct labour variances.

7.7 Variable overhead cost variance

It was explained in Chapter 2 that the most effective method of calculating an overhead cost rate is to calculate the overhead cost per direct labour hour. This is because labour working usually causes most of the overhead costs to be incurred (unless the business is highly machine-intensive). It will be assumed throughout this chapter that a standard cost of variable overheads can be expressed as a cost per direct labour hour. As well as being the preferred choice from Chapter 2, it also makes the calculation of variable overhead variances look very similar to the calculation of direct labour variances.

Variable overhead cost variance

equals

Rate variance	Efficiency variance

The variances are expressed in words and formulae in exhibit 7.6.

Exhibit 7.6
Calculations and formulae for variable overhead variances

Variance	Calculation	Formula
Total cost variance	Standard cost of variable overhead (SC) minus actual cost of variable overhead (AC)	SC – AC
	This may be shown in more detail as:	
	Standard cost (SC) = standard variable overhead rate (SR) multiplied by standard hours allowed (SH)	SC = (SR × SH)
	minus	minus
	Actual cost (AC) = actual variable overhead rate (AR) multiplied by actual hours worked (AH)	AC = (AR × AH)
Variable overhead rate variance	Actual hours worked (AH), multiplied by the difference between the standard variable overhead cost rate (SR) and the actual overhead cost rate (AR)	AH (SR – AR)
Variable overhead efficiency variance	Standard variable overhead cost rate (SR) multiplied by the difference between the standard hours allowed (SH) and the actual hours worked (AH)	SR (SH – AH)

Activity 7.5

Read this section again and make sure that you understand fully the formulae for calculating variable overhead cost variances. Compare these formulae with those used for direct labour cost variances. What are the points of similarity? What are the points of difference? Can you see consistent patterns in the variances for direct materials costs, direct labour costs and variable overhead costs?

7.8 Fixed overhead expenditure variance

Although a fixed overhead cost per unit may be calculated for purposes of valuing stock, it leads to all manner of problems because, by definition, fixed overhead costs do not vary with volume. For the purposes of control, it is more important to know whether the total amount of actual expenditure equals or exceeds the budgeted amount. Thus no attempt will be made here to deal with fixed overhead cost variances on the basis of a standard cost per unit. The variance which is most important is the *fixed overhead expenditure variance*, found by subtracting the actual fixed overhead incurred from the amount of fixed overhead budgeted (*see* exhibit 7.7). If the actual fixed overhead is greater than the budget, there is an adverse variance. If the actual fixed overhead is less than the budget, there is a favourable variance.

Exhibit 7.7
Calculation and formula for fixed overhead variance

Fixed overhead expenditure variance = Budgeted fixed overhead (BFO) minus actual fixed overhead (AFO)

Activity 7.6

As a final check, go back to the start of the chapter and satisfy yourself that you understand everything presented up to this point. The rest of the chapter introduces no new technical material but it applies the formulae to a full example.

7.9 Case study: Allerdale Ltd

The chapter now moves into a case study as a means of providing an illustration of the calculation and interpretation of variances. Allerdale Ltd uses a manufacturing process which involves fastening laminated surfaces onto work-benches. The material for the laminated plastic surface is purchased in large sheets and cut to size at the start of the process. The sheets of laminated plastic represent the direct materials cost of the process. Employees work on cutting and fastening the laminated surfaces and trimming them to fit. This work is classed as direct labour cost. Overhead costs are incurred in using indirect materials such as glues and staples, indirect labour such as cleaners for the production area, and the costs of heating, lighting and maintaining the factory premises. The overheads are partly variable (such as the indirect materials and power) and partly fixed (such as insurance, rent and business rates).

The variances in respect of direct materials, direct labour, variable overhead and fixed overhead are now explained in turn, using data provided by the accounting records.

7.9.1 Direct materials variances

> *Data for direct materials*
> The standard amount of laminated material allowed is two square metres per workbench. The standard price of the material is £0.90 per square metre. During the month of June, 200 workbenches were laminated. The amount of material used was 430 square metres and the price paid was £0.95 per square metre.

Calculations of direct materials variances are shown in exhibits 7.8 and 7.9, using the formulae set out in exhibit 7.2.

Exhibit 7.8
Calculation of direct materials total variance

> The standard allowance is 2 square metres each for 200 workbenches, which is 400 square metres standard quantity (SQ) in total. Standard price per unit (SP) is £0.90 per square metre. Actual quantity used (AQ) is 430 square metres and actual price per unit (AP) is £0.95 per square metre.
>
> Total cost variance = standard cost minus actual cost (SC − AC)
>   = (SQ × SP) minus (AQ × AP)
>   = (400 sq metres × £0.90) minus (430 sq metres × £0.95)
>   = £360 minus £408.50
>   = £48.50 adverse variance

In exhibit 7.8, the variance is *adverse* because the actual cost is greater than the standard cost set for the direct materials to be used. The total variance may be subdivided into direct materials price and usage variances, using the formulae from exhibit 7.2 to give the analysis shown in exhibit 7.9. The data for this calculation has already been set out in words and in symbols at the start of exhibit 7.8. The same symbols and figures are used in exhibit 7.9.

Exhibit 7.9
Calculation of direct materials price and usage variances

Price variance	Usage variance
= AQ (SP − AP)	= SP (SQ − AQ)
= 430 sq metres (£0.90 − £0.95)	= £0.90 (400 − 430)
= £21.50 adverse variance	= £27.00 adverse variance

You will see that the actual price per unit of materials is 95 pence, which is greater than the 90 pence per unit set as a standard cost. The price variance of £21.50 is therefore adverse. The actual amount of direct materials used is 430 square metres, which is greater than the 400 square metres set as a standard. The usage variance is therefore also adverse. The two variances, added together, equal the total adverse variance of £48.50 calculated in exhibit 7.8. We now know that the overall variance is caused by both price and usage effects but that the usage problem is the greater of the two.

7.9.2 Adverse or favourable variances?

If you have followed these calculations yourself you will have obtained negative signs in each calculation. The negative sign corresponds to an adverse variance because in each case the actual outcome is worse than the predetermined standard. However, it is risky to rely on plus and minus signs, because it is easy to make careless errors in calculations and to turn the formula round accidentally. It is always safer to look at each calculation on a common-sense basis. The total cost variance will be adverse where the actual outcome is worse than the standard cost allowed. The price variance will be adverse where the actual unit price is greater than the standard price allowed. The usage variance will be adverse where the actual quantity used is greater than the standard quantity allowed.

7.9.3 What caused the variance?

It is often impossible to be definite about the cause of a particular variance but suggestions may be made as a basis for further investigation. A variance in the *price* of materials indicates that the actual price paid per unit differs from that expected when the standard was set. That could be because the price has changed, in which case the standard should be revised. The variance could be due to purchasing a more expensive quality of material, in which case there will need to be an investigation as to whether this was due to the production department requesting a higher quality than that permitted when the standard was set, or whether it was a procedural error in the buying department. Perhaps the higher quality was found to be necessary because the previous quality of materials was causing too much labour time to be wasted on substandard products. Variances may interact, which means it is important to look at the cost control picture as a whole.

A variance in the *usage* of materials may be an indication that lack of quality in the materials is causing too much wastage. It may be that employees have not received sufficient training in the best way of using the material. Perhaps a new machine has been installed which operates much faster to meet expanding demand levels but has a naturally higher wastage rate.

Once the calculation of two variances has been mastered, the mathematically minded student soon realises that the subdivisions could be taken further. The usage variance may be split into a yield variance, comparing what goes in with what comes out of the process, and a mix variance, looking at the effect of having a different mix of input materials than was planned when the standard was set. That level of detailed analysis will not be taken further here, but you should be aware that there is a world of detail, to explore at another time, in relation to variance analysis.

Some of the foregoing causes of variance may lead to remedial action. Others may lead to a decision that it is in the interests of the organisation to accept the difference and revise the standard accordingly. Fiona McTaggart gives her views.

FIONA: *I see my job as reporting the variances accurately and in good time. The decisions on how to use those variances are for those who manage the operations of the business. If they tell me that a variance has become an accepted part of the operation, I will discuss with them whether the new data should be incorporated in a revised standard, or whether there is a continuing control aspect of identifying that variance to ensure that it stays within acceptable limits.*

The case study now continues to illustrate the calculation of direct labour cost variances.

7.9.4 Direct labour variances

> *Data for direct labour*
> Allerdale Ltd has set a standard labour rate of £4 per direct labour hour. Actual hours worked in June were 9,820 at an actual cost of £37,316. The standard allowance of direct labour hours, for the output achieved, was 10,000 hours.

Calculations of variances are shown in exhibits 7.10 and 7.11, using the formulae set out in exhibit 7.5. In exhibit 7.10, the variance is favourable because the actual cost is less than the standard cost set for the direct labour to be used. The total variance may be subdivided into direct labour rate and efficiency variances, using the formulae from exhibit 7.5, to give the analysis shown in exhibit 7.11. The symbols and the relevant figures needed for these variances are set out at the start of exhibit 7.10.

Exhibit 7.10
Calculation of direct labour total variance

> The standard allowance of direct labour time is 10,000 standard hours (SH). The standard labour rate set (SR) is £4 per hour. Actual hours worked (AH) are stated to be 9,820. The actual labour rate (AR) is not stated but can be calculated by dividing the actual cost (AC) of £37,316 by the actual hours of 9,820, to give £3.80 per hour.
>
> Total cost variance = standard cost minus actual cost (SC − AC)
>   = (SR × SH) minus (AR × AH)
>   = (£4 × 10,000) minus (£3.80 × 9,820)
>   = £40,000 minus £37,316
>   = £2,684 favourable variance

Exhibit 7.11
Calculation of direct labour rate and efficiency variances

Rate variance	Efficiency variance
= AH (SR − AR)	= SR (SH − AH)
= 9,820 hours (£4.00 − £3.80)	= £4.00 (10,000 − 9,820)
= £1,964 favourable variance	= £720 favourable variance

The actual rate of pay per hour is less than the standard rate and the rate variance is therefore favourable. The actual hours worked are less than the standard hours allowed which means that the efficiency variance is also favourable. The total favourable variance of £2,684 has, therefore, two components of which the rate variance of £1,964 is the more important.

7.9.5 What caused the variance?

With direct labour, as with direct materials, it is easier to apply conjecture than to find sure and certain explanations. A favourable variance in the *labour rate* is an indication that the actual wage rate per employee was lower than that which was expected when the standard was set. That could be due to an anticipated pay increase having failed to materialise. Alternatively, it could suggest that the mix of employees is different from that intended when the standard was set, so that the average wage paid is lower than planned. A variance in *labour efficiency* means that fewer hours were worked than were expected when the standard was set. This could be due to a new training scheme, or less than the expected amount of enforced idle time when machinery is not operating. Perhaps better quality material was purchased, giving a higher purchase price, but this caused less wastage and allowed employees to work more efficiently in producing the finished goods.

As with direct materials, there is no particular reason to stop with analysing only two variances. A change in the mix of employees could be a cause for variance within the overall efficiency variance. The number of subdivisions depends only on the ingenuity of those devising the variance analysis. This textbook will, however, be content with analysing only two causes of direct labour cost variance.

Fiona McTaggart has discovered that often there are interlocking effects in variances on direct materials and direct labour. She was recently in discussion with the plant manager:

FIONA: *It is the management accountant's job to produce the variance report and it is the plant manager's job to interpret the result, but naturally I am always interested in the explanation. Last month we had a favourable variance on direct materials price but unexpected adverse variances on direct materials usage and direct labour efficiency. On investigation, it was found that the buying department had seen a special offer on metal sheeting which dramatically cut the unit cost of material, so they bought six months' supply. What they didn't know was that the machinery on the factory floor can't deal with that particular type of metal sheeting because it slips intermittently in the rollers. The result was far more wastage of materials than expected, labour time lost through*

having to process materials twice, and some very irate operatives who lost bonuses because so much time was wasted. The problem was so bad that after one month the remaining unused material was sold for scrap and the correct specification was purchased. It was a very expensive lesson in the need for interdepartmental communication.

7.9.6 Variable overhead cost variance

> *Data for variable overhead*
> Allerdale Ltd has set a standard variable overhead cost rate of £2 per direct labour hour. Actual hours worked in June were 9,820 and the actual variable overhead cost incurred was £22,586. The standard allowance of direct labour hours, for the output achieved, was 10,000 hours.

Calculations of variances are set out in exhibits 7.12 and 7.13, using the formulae set out in exhibit 7.6. The standard allowance of direct labour time is 10,000 standard hours (SH). The standard variable overhead cost rate set is £2 per direct labour hour. The actual variable overhead cost rate (AR) is not stated but can be calculated by dividing the actual cost (AC) of £22,586 by the actual direct labour hours of 9,820, to give £2.30 per direct labour hour.

Exhibit 7.12
Calculation of variable overhead cost variance

Total cost variance	= standard cost minus actual cost (SC − AC)
	= (SR × SH) minus (AR × AH)
	= (£2 × 10,000) minus (£2.30 × 9,820)
	= £20,000 minus £22,586
	= £2,586 adverse variance

Exhibit 7.13
Calculation of variable overhead rate and efficiency variances

Rate variance	Efficiency variance
= AH (SR − AR)	= SR (SH − AH)
= 9,820 hours (£2.00 − £2.30)	= £2.00 (10,000 − 9,820)
= £2,946 adverse variance	= £360 favourable variance

The symbols and the relevant figures needed in order to calculate the variable overhead rate and efficiency variances are set out at the start of exhibit 7.12. The actual variable overhead cost rate of £2.30 per direct labour hour is greater than the standard rate of £2 and there is an adverse variance of £2,946. This is offset to some extent by a favourable efficiency variance due to the actual hours worked being less than the standard allowed, but this gives a favourable variance of only £360 so that the combination of the two explains the overall adverse variance of £2,586.

7.9.7 What caused the variance?

The adverse rate variance means that some item of variable overhead has cost more than expected. There is not sufficient detail available here for an answer to emerge but in practice the management accountant would now look at the unit cost of each item, such as glues, staples, paint, cleaning costs and any other variable cost items, to find which had risen above the standard set. The favourable efficiency variance is directly due to labour hours being less than expected when the standard was set. The explanation will be the same as that given for the favourable efficiency variance on direct labour.

7.9.8 Fixed overhead expenditure variance

> *Data for fixed overhead*
> Allerdale Ltd budgeted fixed overhead expenditure at £10,000 for the month of June. The actual amount of fixed overhead expenditure was £11,000.

The most important question to answer here is, 'Why did we spend more than expected?' This is quantified in the fixed overhead expenditure variance, calculated as budgeted fixed overhead minus actual fixed overhead. In this example, the result is an adverse variance of £1,000. Causes could include an increase in the cost of fixed overhead or an extra category of fixed overhead, neither of which was expected when the budget was set.

Activity 7.7

> *Copy out the data for the case study, then close the book and test yourself by producing the calculations and analyses. That exercise will establish your confidence in knowing the technical material of the chapter.*

7.10 Investigating variances

Once the variances have been calculated, those who manage the business have to decide which variances should be investigated. Should every adverse variance be investigated? Such an investigation takes time and so itself involves a further cost in searching for a cause. Is it worth incurring this further cost to find out what happened to the costs under investigation? Such an investigation might unearth some unwelcome facts about the world beyond accounting. It has been suggested that the accountant feels 'safe' in a separate accountant's world. Perhaps no one, other than the management accountant, believes in the system in any event. These radical thoughts have been expressed in various parts of the academic literature. One extreme conclusion which might be drawn is that it is safer to avoid any type of investigation.

It is fairly obvious that a reasonable answer lies between the two extremes of investigating everything and investigating nothing. Nevertheless, it may be useful to think about the extreme cases in order to justify the middle ground. Many who take a traditional approach prefer to use judgement in deciding which variance to investigate. Such persons would run their eye down the variance report, item by item, using their knowledge and experience to identify variances for further investigation. That approach is called 'intuition' and is fine for the experienced manager but risky when applied by a trainee manager or someone not familiar with the operational factors behind the variances. It is also difficult to write a computer program for the intuitive approach. If the accounting information is being processed by computer, it is often convenient to let the computer do the work of highlighting the variances for investigation. So some systematic approach is needed.

This may be achieved by setting a *filter rule* which filters out the unimportant but draws attention to the matters regarded as significant. This might be 'Investigate all variances which are more than 10 per cent of the total standard cost of this cost centre'. It might be 'Investigate all variances which are more than £10,000 in amount each month'. Establishing filters is a matter of experience and judgement in order to ensure that no significant difference by amount is overlooked.

Using filters may not always be the perfect approach. The choice of what is important may vary depending on the nature of the variance or the nature of the cost item. Using the filter does not take into accounts the costs and benefits of variance investigation. It does not incorporate the past history of performance in that item, where inefficiencies are persisting through lack of remedial action. The item may be one where the variance has suddenly worsened dramatically but still falls within the filter limits (e.g. where a cost item has habitually shown a variance within 2 per cent of standard cost but then suddenly increases to 15 per cent, that could be highly significant even though the predetermined filter is set at 20 per cent).

The selection of variances for investigation is therefore very much dependent on circumstances and on the person making the selection. Fiona McTaggart gives her description of the management accountant's role in deciding on which variances to investigate.

FIONA: *In my work I keep in close contact with each of the production supervisors. We have informal meetings once each month to look at the specifications for the standards. They give me their views on the type and level of variance which they regard as significant to their part of the business. From that list I create a set of filters which I apply to the monthly report on how actual costs measure up against standards. I also add some filters based on company policy as to what is material to the overall production operations. My choice of filters has regard to existing pricing policy and a need for management of working capital. These filters produce a variance exception report. The production supervisors are expected to make a comment to the production director on the action to be taken in respect of the variances highlighted by the filter process. Every six months I meet with the production director to review the effectiveness of the filters being applied.*

We now move on to consider the practical problems of calculating variances when the level of output is different from that expected at the time the budget was set.

7.11 Flexible budgets and variance analysis

One of the most commonly occurring problems in variance analysis is deciding which benchmark to use as a basis for comparison. When the standard costs are set at the beginning of a reporting period, they will be presented in the form of a budget based on activity levels expected at that point. Suppose activity levels subsequently fall because of a downturn in demand? Is it preferable to base the variance analysis on the standard set for the original level of output, or to introduce some flexibility and compare actual outcome with the standard expected for the new lower level of activity? Putting the question in that form leads to an almost inescapable conclusion that flexibility is required, but it is surprising how that obvious need for flexibility may be overlooked when a table of figures appears on a page. A case study is now used to show the application of a flexible budget.

7.12 Case study: Brackendale Ltd

Case study description
When the standards for the year ahead were set, it was expected that monthly output of units manufactured would be 10,000 units. By the time July was reached, output had fallen to 8,000 units per month because of a fall in market share of sales. Exhibit 7.14 reports the original budget and the actual outcome for the month of July.

The original budget is based on a standard direct material cost of £4 per kg of raw material, a standard direct labour cost of £5 per hour and a standard variable cost rate of £3 per direct labour hour. Each unit of output requires 0.5 kg of raw materials and 12 minutes of labour time. The actual cost of direct materials was found to be £4.40 per kg, the actual cost of direct labour was found to be £5.50 per hour and the actual variable overhead cost rate was £2.80 per direct labour hour. 3,800 kg of materials were used and the actual labour hours worked were 2,000.

Data relevant to the month of July is set out in exhibit 7.14, as follows:

Exhibit 7.14
Original budget and actual costs for July

	Original budget	Actual for July
Units manufactured	10,000	8,000
	£	£
Direct material	20,000	16,720
Direct labour	10,000	11,000
Variable overhead	4,800	5,600
Fixed overhead	7,000	7,500
Total direct costs	41,800	40,820

Fiona McTaggart now talks through the problem.

FIONA: *It is quite tempting to compare these two columns of figures directly and call the difference the cost variance. But that would be totally misleading because the budget is based on 10,000 units of output and the actual output was down to 8,000 units. Direct materials, direct labour and variable overhead are all variable costs which depend on the level of output. The first step I would take is to introduce a new column headed 'flexible budget' which shows the expected cost of all variable costs if the standard costs per unit are applied to the new output level. Then I would prepare a data analysis sheet so that I am clear in my own mind what the materials and labour quantities are for the new output level. From there, I would analyse the direct materials cost variance into a price variance and a usage variance based on the new output level. Similarly I would analyse both direct labour cost and variable overhead cost variance into rate variance and efficiency variance based on the new output level. Fixed overhead would be analysed in terms of an expenditure variance only. Finally I would write a brief report setting out some guide to the figures so that the production supervisor can give some thought to possible causes.*

Fiona's working notes are now set out in detail. Italics are used in each figure to show where she has calculated a new figure using the data already provided. You should follow her workings through the exhibits and check that you understand how the figures in italics have been calculated.

7.12.1 Summary statement of variances

The summary statement of variances (*see* exhibit 7.15) takes the information for original budget and actual costs contained in the case study description. The flexible budget is created by taking 8/10 of the original budget costs (because the units manufactured are 8/10 of the volume originally budgeted). The variances are then calculated by deducting the actual costs from the flexible budget figures. Italics are used to show the flexible budget figures which have been calculated as 8/10 of the original budget. The only exception is fixed overhead cost, where it would not be expected that the cost was variable. Accordingly there is no flexibility with regard to fixed overhead.

Exhibit 7.15
Calculation of variances using a flexible budget: summary statement of variances

	Original budget (1)	Flexible budget (2)	Actual for July (3)	Variance (2) – (3)	
Units manufactured	10,000	8,000	8,000		
	£	£	£	£	
Direct material	20,000	16,000	16,720	720	(A)
Direct labour	10,000	8,000	11,000	3,000	(A)
Variable overhead	6,000	4,800	5,600	800	(A)
Fixed overhead	7,000	7,000	7,500	500	(A)
Total direct costs	43,000	35,800	40,820	5,020	(A)

7.12.2 Data analysis sheet

The data analysis sheet (*see* exhibit 7.16) uses the information contained in the case study description or in exhibit 7.14 and fills in the gaps by calculation. Italics show the calculated figures in exhibit 7.16, and the workings are at the foot of the tables (a) and (b). Note that fixed overheads are not flexible and are therefore excluded from tables (a) and (b). The output level for the period is 8,000 units.

7.12.3 Direct materials variance

Total cost variance = standard cost minus actual cost (all based on the new output level)
= £16,000 minus £16,720
= £720 adverse variance

The variance is adverse because the actual cost is greater than the standard allowed by the flexible budget for the output of 8,000 units.

Price variance	Usage variance
= AQ (SP – AP)	= SP (SQ – AQ)
= 3,800 kg (£4.00 – £4.40)	= £4.00 (4,000 – 3,800)
= £1,520 adverse variance	= £800 favourable variance

The price variance is adverse because the actual price per kg is greater than the standard price per kg. The usage variance is favourable because the actual quantity used, 3,800 kg, is less than the standard allowed, 4,000 kg, for the actual level of output.

Exhibit 7.16
Calculation of variances using a flexible budget: data analysis sheet

(a) Analysis of standard cost

Item	Standard cost of item £	Standard amount of item per unit of output	Standard quantity for output level 8,000 units[1]	Standard cost for output level 8,000 units[2] £
Direct material	4.00 per kg	0.5 kg	4,000 kg	16,000
Direct labour	5.00 per hour	12 mins	1,600 hours	8,000
Variable overhead	3.00 per dlh[3]	12 mins dlh	1,600 dlh	4,800

Notes: [1] [8,000 × 0.5 kg = 4,000 kg] and [8,000 × 12 mins = 1,600 hours].
[2] [4,000 kg × £4 = £16,000]; [1,600 hours × £5 = £8,000]; [1,600 hours × £3 = £4,800].
[3] dlh = direct labour hours.

(b) Analysis of actual cost

Item	Actual cost of item £	Actual amount of item per unit of output[1]	Actual quantity for output level 8,000 units	Actual cost for output level 8,000 units £
Direct material	4.40 per kg	0.475 kg	3,800 kg	16,720
Direct labour	5.50 per hour	15 mins	2,000 hours	11,000
Variable overhead	2.80 per dlh	15 mins	2,000 hours	5,600

Note: [1] [3,800 kg / 8,000 = 0.475 kg] and [2,000 hours / 8,000 = 15 mins].

7.12.4 Direct labour variance

Total cost variance = standard cost minus actual cost
= £8,000 minus £11,000
= £3,000 adverse variance

The variance is adverse because the actual cost is greater than the standard allowed by the flexible budget for the output of 8,000 units.

Rate variance	Efficiency variance
= AH (SR − AR) = 2,000 hours (£5.00 − £5.50) = £1,000 adverse variance	= SR (SH − AH) = £5.00 (1,600 − 2,000) = £2,000 adverse variance

The direct labour rate variance is adverse because the actual rate is higher than the standard rate per hour. The direct labour efficiency variance is adverse because the actual hours worked (2,000) were greater than the standard allowed (1,600) for the output achieved.

7.12.5 Variable overhead variance

Total cost variance	= standard cost minus actual cost
	= £4,800 minus £5,600
	= £800 adverse variance

The variance is adverse because the actual cost is greater than the standard allowed by the flexible budget for the output of 8,000 units.

Rate variance	Efficiency variance
= AH (SR − AR)	= SR (SH − AH)
= 2,000 hours (£3.00 − £2.80)	= £3.00 (1,600 − 2,000)
= £400 favourable variance	= £1,200 adverse variance

The variable overhead rate variance is favourable because the actual rate is less than the standard rate per hour. The variable overhead efficiency variance is adverse because the actual hours worked (2,000) were greater than the standard allowed (1,600) for the output achieved.

7.12.6 Fixed overhead variance

The fixed overhead expenditure variance is equal to the budgeted fixed overhead minus the actual fixed overhead. That has already been shown to be £1,000 adverse due to overspending compared with the budget.

7.12.7 Variance report

From the foregoing calculations a variance report may be prepared. This brings to the attention of the production manager the main items highlighted by the process of variance analysis, as shown in exhibit 7.17.

Activity 7.8

Copy out the data for the foregoing case study, close the book and attempt the variance analysis yourself. This will test your understanding of the technical material. Make a note of any problems or difficulties and consult your tutor about these.

Exhibit 7.17
Brackendale Ltd: variance report

BRACKENDALE LTD

Variance report

To: Production manager
From: Management accountant

Subject: **Variance report for July**

During the month of July there were 8,000 units manufactured, as compared with 10,000 expected when the budget was set. Allowing flexibility for the lower level of output, there was nevertheless an adverse variance of £5,020 for the month, of which £720 related to direct material, £3,000 related to direct labour, £800 related to variable overhead and £500 to related to fixed overhead.

The most serious of these is clearly the direct labour variance, where adverse changes in labour rate contributed £1,000 and less efficient working contributed £2,000 to the total £3,000. The direct materials cost variance of £720 looks worse when decomposed into an adverse price variance of £1,520 offset partially by a favourable usage variance of £800. The variable overhead cost variance of £800 adverse also looks worse when decomposed into an adverse efficiency variance of £1,200, partly offset by a favourable rate variance of £400. Overspending on fixed overheads was £1,000 for the month.

While the investigation of these problems is a matter for yourself, I might venture to suggest that from past experience we have noticed that a favourable materials usage variance may arise when employees are instructed to work more carefully and, as a consequence, take longer time, which leads to an adverse labour efficiency variance. If that is the case, then the more careful working has had an overall negative effect because the £800 favourable materials usage variance must be compared with the £2,000 adverse labour efficiency variance and the £1,200 adverse variable overhead efficiency variance.

The variance in materials price is almost certainly due to the recent increase in the price of goods supplied. That is not a matter we can control from within the company and the standard cost will be revised next month.

The variance in labour rate is due partly to a recent pay award not included in the original budget, but it is also due to employees being paid at overtime rates because of the extra time spent on working more carefully with materials. There may need to be a major review of how this part of the business is operating, with a view to minimising total variance rather than taking items piecemeal.

Although the variable overhead rate variance is favourable, the categories of variable overhead will be reviewed to see whether any of the standard costs are out of date. Overspending on fixed overhead was due to a change in the depreciation rate of equipment due to revised asset lives. The budget will be revised at the half-yearly review which is coming up next month.

7.13   Is variance analysis, based on standard costs, a useful exercise?

Academic opinion is divided on the usefulness of variance analysis. Solomons has claimed that standard costing probably represents the greatest advance in accounting since the development of bookkeeping. There is another view that perhaps this historical leap forward has given standard costing more importance than it deserves. In this chapter the standard has been portrayed as a single figure, but it is actually an estimate based on the best expectations of the future conditions envisaged in the organisation. If the organisation has a stable technology and works within safely attainable levels of productivity, then there is relatively little likelihood of finding that the expected cost is far away from the true cost. But if the organisation is much riskier in the nature of its operations, perhaps using a less stable technology and working at the upper limits of productivity, then the expected standard cost may be an average measure of a wide range of possible outcomes.

Anthony has questioned whether any scientific enquiry into variance analysis is in reality carried out and has questioned further whether such enquiry is worth doing in any event. He has identified, in practice, a strong intuitive approach to variance analysis.

It may be that accountants tend to overemphasise their own importance. The causes and control of variances lie with those managing and operating the technical aspects of the business. Management accountants only present the information which, if in a relevant and useful form, may help in identifying cause and establishing better control. Setting standards is first and foremost an industrial engineering problem. It might be safer to leave the variance analysis to the engineers and forget about the cost aspects.

Chapter 1 instanced the management functions of planning and control, and the importance of communication and motivation. Well-planned variance reports, based on up-to-date and realistic standards, will provide information for the planning process, encourage control, and communicate the effects of operational actions on the costs of the organisation. Motivation will be enhanced if the variance report is seen to be specific to the information needs of each level of management and if the standard costs are seen to be a fair measure of expected achievement. Motivation could be reduced by a badly designed or carelessly implemented variance report.

Chapter 1 listed three management accounting functions of directing attention, keeping the score and solving problems. Standard costs contribute to all three, when used in conjunction with variance analysis. The variance report, by using predetermined filters, may direct attention to areas of significance. The preparation of the report, on a regular basis, is a vital part of the score-keeping operation. Analysis of the variances, to which the management accountant will make a contribution in deciding on the level of detail, will be a problem-solving exercise requiring logical and systematic analysis of the problem represented by the accounting figures.

7.14 A broader view of applications of variance analysis

At the start of the chapter a list was set out of five ways in which standard costs may be used by an organisation:

1 to provide product costs for stock valuation;
2 to bring an element of control within a budgeting system;
3 to gauge performance of a business by use of variance analysis;
4 to integrate costs in the planning and pricing structure of a business;
5 to reduce record-keeping costs when transactions take place at different prices.

Are these purposes useful? Is it worthwhile to make the effort of developing standard costs? Some brief answers are now provided.

(a) The objective of providing product costs for purposes such as stock valuation falls within the general heading of 'What should it cost?', a question which in turn leads to more questions about the effective use of resources. It is as important to ask questions about the cost of goods not sold as it is to look at the variance in cost of the goods which have been sold. If stock is valued at actual cost, it will carry with it a share of the problems which led to a cost variance and will burden the next reporting period with those problems. If the stock is valued at standard cost, all variances in price are dealt with in the period when they arose.

(b) A budgeting system may be based on actual costs, but it will have greater usefulness if it is based on standard costs as a measure of the predetermined targets for a period. A budget relates to an activity or operation as a whole, while a standard cost is a cost per unit which gives a very precise focus to the budgetary planning process. Budgets do not necessarily need to be based on standard cost, but the standard costs bring additional benefits in allowing the organisation to examine more precisely how the budget compares with the actual outcome.

(c) Performance is gauged by comparing actual costs with standard costs and analysing the differences. The resulting variance may indicate where, in the control of the organisation, future action is required. Performance may be related to responsibility so that the management accounting information is matched to the management aims of the organisation.

(d) Planning and pricing are aspects of long-term decision making which require a strategic outlook on business problems. Pricing will usually be a forward-looking activity based on estimated costs and out-turns. Standard costs provide a benchmark against which to plan pricing and, in retrospect, to evaluate the success of a pricing policy in terms of recovering costs incurred.

(e) If all costs are recorded on a standard basis, then the variations in quantity may be separated analytically from the variations in price. In practice the price variations are isolated as soon as the goods are purchased. Thereafter, the progress of costs, in moving through to finished goods and to output in the form of sales, is all monitored at standard cost so that the emphasis is on quantity and variations in quantity. That reflects the control process in that, once the goods have been purchased, or services paid for, there is no further opportunity to take action over price. Success in cost control thereafter depends entirely on control of usage, which is in the hands of those controlling and carrying out operations.

7.15 Summary

In this chapter we have shown how control through the use of standard costs per unit leads to a more specific analysis than is available where control is through the use of budgets. Budgets give only the total cost of each line item. Standard costing allows decomposition into cost per unit and quantity of units.

Variances have been defined and illustrated for:

- direct materials (total cost variance, analysed into price and usage variances)
- direct labour (total cost variance, analysed into rate and efficiency variances)
- variable overhead (total cost variance, analysed into rate and efficiency variances)
- fixed overhead (expenditure variance only).

Flexible budgeting has also been explained, showing that where the level of output is different from that expected when the budget was prepared, the standard costs should be used to prepare a new flexible budget for the new level of output. All variable costs should be recalculated to reflect the change in output. Fixed overhead costs are independent of activity level and therefore have no flexibility.

The chapter has also given some flavour of the debate on the importance and usefulness of standard costs. They are widely used but, to be effective, must be chosen with care to meet the needs of the business and of the management purposes of planning and control.

Further reading

Anthony, R. N. and Dearden, J. (1980), *Management Control Systems*, Irwin.

Drury, C. (1992), *Management and Cost Accounting*, Chapman & Hall.

Hopwood, A. (1974), *Accounting and Human Behaviour*, Haymarket, London.

Horngren, C. T., Foster, G. and Datar, S. (1993), *Cost Accounting: A Managerial Emphasis*, Prentice Hall.

Kaplan, R. S. (1982), *Advanced Management Accounting*, Prentice Hall.

Puxty, A. G. and Lyall, D. (1989), *Cost Control into the 1990s: A Survey of Standard Costing and Budgeting Practices in the UK*, Chartered Institute of Management Accounting, London.

Solomons, D. (1972), 'Flexible budgets and the analysis of overhead variances', in H. R. Anton and P. A. Firmin (eds), *Contemporary Issues in Cost Accounting*, Houghton Mifflin.

Wilson, R. M. S. and Chua, W. F. (1992), *Managerial Accounting: Method and Meaning*, Chapman & Hall.

Self-testing on the chapter

1 What is a standard cost?

2 Why are standard costs useful?

3 How are standard costs measured?

4 How are standard costs used in the planning process?

5 How are standard costs used in the control process?

6 How are direct materials price and usage variances calculated?

7 Give three possible causes of an adverse direct materials price variance.

8 Give three possible causes of a favourable direct materials usage variance.

9 How are direct labour rate and efficiency variances calculated?

10 Give three possible causes of a favourable direct labour rate variance.

11 Give three possible causes of an adverse direct labour efficiency variance.

12 Explain how you would identify which variances to investigate.

13 Explain the importance of using a flexible budget with variance analysis.

14 Give three reasons for regarding variance reports as a useful tool of management.

15 It was budgeted that to produce 20,000 concrete building blocks in one month would require 100,000 kg of material. In the month of May, only 16,000 blocks were produced, using 80,080 kg of material. Materials costs £3 per kg. What is the materials usage variance?

16 The standard cost of direct labour in the month of August is £36,000. There is a direct labour rate variance of £6,000 adverse and a direct labour efficiency variance of £2,500 favourable. What is the actual cost of direct labour in the month?

17 Fixed overhead for the month of October has been budgeted at £16,000 with an expectation of 8,000 units of production. The actual fixed overhead cost is £17,500 and the actual production is 7,000 units. What is the variance?

18 The monthly budget of Plastics Ltd, manufacturers of specialist containers, was prepared on the following specification:

Production and sales	30,000 units
Selling price	£70 per unit
Direct materials input	5 kg per unit at a cost of £1.20 per kg
Direct labour input	2 hours per unit at a rate of £4 per hour
Variable overhead	£2 per direct labour hour
Fixed overhead	£90,000 per month

The following actual results were recorded for the month of May 19X8:

Stock of finished goods at start of month	8,000 units
Sales	40,000 units
Production	42,800 units
Stock of finished goods at end of month	10,800 units

Actual costs incurred were:

	£	
Direct material	267,220	(213,776 kg at £1.25 per kg)
Direct labour	356,577	
Variable overhead	165,243	
Fixed overhead	95,000	

Further information

(a) Throughout May the price paid for direct materials was £1.25 per kg. Direct material is used as soon as it arrives on site. No stocks of materials were held at the start or end of May.
(b) The labour rate paid throughout the month was £4.10 per hour.
(c) The selling price of finished goods was £70 per unit throughout the month.
(d) Stocks of finished goods are valued at standard cost of production.

Required

(a) Calculate the budgeted profit for May 19X8, based on the actual sales volume achieved.
(b) Calculate the cost variances for the month of May.
(c) Explain how cost variances may be used to identify responsibility for cost control within the company

19 The upholstery department of a furniture manufacturing business prepared the following statement of standard costs at the start of the calendar year:

Standard cost per unit

	£
Direct material	250
Direct labour	150
Fixed manufacturing overhead	100
	500

In preparing the statement, it was budgeted that 100 units would be completed each month.

During the month of May the following results were reported:

	£
Direct materials cost	31,200
Direct labour cost	16,800
Fixed manufacturing overhead	9,600
	57,600

The actual level of production achieved in May was 120 units.

The budget for direct materials was based on an allowance of 10 kg materials per unit produced. The budgeted cost of materials was £25 per kg. Actual materials used during May amounted to 1,300 kg.

The budget for direct labour was based on an allowance of 15 hours per unit, at a labour rate of £10 per hour. At the start of May, an agreed incentive scheme increased the labour rate to £12 per hour. All employees receive the same rate of pay.

Stocks of finished goods are valued at full standard cost of manufacture.

Required

(a) Prepare an accounting statement reconciling the budgeted costs for the month of May with the actual costs incurred, including in your answer relevant cost variances.
(b) Suggest possible causes for the variances you have calculated.

20 The following report has been prepared for the production department of Cabinets Ltd in respect of the month of May 19X4:

	Actual costs or quantities recorded	Variance £
Direct materials price	£2.80 per kg	2,240 favourable
Direct materials usage	11,200 kg	4,800 adverse
Direct labour rate	£9 per hour	5,600 adverse
Direct labour efficiency	3.5 hours per unit	6,400 adverse
Fixed overhead expenditure	£39,000	3,000 adverse

The department manufactures storage cabinets. When the budget was prepared, it was expected that 1,800 units would be produced in the month but, due to a machine breakdown, only 1,600 units were produced.

Required

(a) Reconstruct the original budget, giving as much information as may be derived from the data presented above.
(b) Provide an interpretation of the performance of the production department during the month of May 19X4.

21 Fixit Ltd is a manufacturing company which produces a fixed budget for planning purposes. Set out below is the fixed monthly budget of production costs, together with the actual results observed for the month of July 19X7.

	Budget	Actual
Units produced	5,000	5,500
	£	£
Costs:		
Direct materials	20,000	22,764
Direct labour	60,000	75,900
Variable production overhead	14,000	14,950
Fixed production overhead	10,000	9,000
Depreciation	4,000	4,000

In preparing the fixed budget, the following standards were adopted:

Direct material	10 kg of materials per unit produced.
Direct labour	2 hours per unit produced.
Variable production overhead	A cost rate per direct labour hour was calculated.
Fixed production overhead	A cost rate per unit was calculated.
Depreciation	Straight line method is used for all assets.

The following additional information is available concerning the actual output:

(a) the actual usage of materials in July was 54,200 kg; and
(b) the nationally agreed wage rate increased to £6.60 per hour at the start of July.

Required

(a) Prepare a flexible budget in respect of Fixit Ltd for the month of July 19X7.
(b) Analyse and comment on cost variances.

Activities for study groups

1 In groups of three persons, prepare a standard cost specification for direct labour costs in operating a campus bus service. One person should take the role of the transport planner, one should be the personnel manager and one should act as the management accountant. Give a five-minute presentation to the rest of the class explaining how you prepared the standard cost.

2 In groups of three persons, prepare a standard cost specification for direct materials costs in publishing a study guide for sale to students on a course where 500 are expected to enrol. One person should take the role of the editor, one should take the role of the publications manager and one should act as the management accountant. Give a five-minute presentation to the rest of the class explaining how you prepared the standard cost.

Case studies

Case 7.1

Concrete Products Ltd manufactures heavy paving slabs for sale to local authorities and garden paving slabs for domestic use.

The board of directors meets early in each month to review the company's performance during the previous month. In advance of each meeting, the directors are presented with a computer print-out summarising the activity of the previous month. The computer print-out in respect of the month of December 19X8 is set out below:

| | Heavy paving | | Garden paving | |
	Actual tonnes	Budget tonnes	Actual tonnes	Budget tonnes
Sales volume	29,000	27,500	10,500	8,500
Production volume	29,000	27,500	10,500	8,500
	£000s	£000s	£000s	£000s
Revenue	720	690	430	300
Variable cost of sales	280	270	170	127
Contribution	440	420	260	173

Further information

(a) The actual fixed costs incurred during the month equalled the budgeted fixed costs of £310,000.

(b) Stocks are valued at standard cost.

You have recently been appointed a director of Concrete Products Ltd. At an earlier meeting with the finance director you received an explanation of the basis for the company's monthly budget and you are satisfied that the budget has been prepared on a realistic basis.

Required

1 Prepare, from the information contained in the computer print-out, your analysis and comments on the company's performance during the month of December 19X8, as background for the board meeting.

2 List, with reasons, three questions you would ask at the meeting in order to give you a fuller understanding of the company's performance during the month.

Case 7.2

Nu-Line Ltd purchases manufactured machine tools for conversion to specialist use. The converted tools are sold to the textile industry. The following information relates to the month of July 19X3:

	Budget (units)	Actual (units)
Purchases of machine tools	180	180
Completed production	180	140
Sales	130	150
Stock of finished goods at 1 July 19X3	15	15
Stock of finished goods at 31 July 19X3	65	5

There was no stock of purchased machine tools or work-in-progress at either the start or end of the month.

Finished goods are valued at full standard cost of production. The standard cost of one completed production unit is:

	£
Purchased machine tool	600
Direct labour	300
Fixed production overhead	200
Variable production overhead	100
	1,200

The fixed production overhead per unit was determined by reference to the budgeted volume of production per month.

A standard selling price of £2,000 per completed unit was specified in the budget and was achieved in practice.

Actual costs incurred during the month were as follows:

	£
Invoiced price of machine tools purchased	86,800
Direct wages paid	47,500
Fixed production overhead	35,000
Variable production overhead	13,000

Required

1 Prepare a statement of the budgeted profit and the actual profit for the month of July.

2 Using variances, reconcile the budgeted profit with the actual profit.

Case 7.3

Carrypack Ltd manufactures and sells plastic cases for portable computers. Production each month equals sales orders received.

The following monthly budget was prepared at the start of 19X6, to apply throughout the year:

	Units	£	£
Sales (@ £50 per unit):	12,000		600,000
Production:	12,000		
Production costs:			
Direct materials		132,000	
Direct labour		108,000	
Variable overheads		72,000	
Fixed overheads		48,000	
			360,000
Budgeted profit			240,000

Further information

(a) Budgeted direct materials used per month were set at 26,400 kg.
(b) Budgeted direct labour hours per month were set at 36,000 hours.

The following actual report was produced for the month of April 19X6:

	Units	£	£
Sales (@ £50 per unit):	12,300		615,000
Production:	12,300		
Production costs:			
Direct materials		136,220	
Direct labour		129,200	
Variable overheads		72,200	
Fixed overheads		49,400	
			387,020
Actual profit			227,980

Further information

(a) Actual direct materials used during April were 27,800 kg.
(b) Actual direct labour hours worked during April were 38,000 hours.

Required

1 Prepare an explanation, using variances, of the difference between the budgeted profit and the actual profit for the month of April.

2 Comment on possible causes for the variances you have calculated.

Case 7.4

DEF Products Ltd manufactures and assembles one type of furniture unit. The following information is available for the year ended 31 August 18X7.

The budgeted costs and the actual costs incurred during the year were as follows:

Cost	Budgeted production overhead cost £000s	Actual production overhead cost £000s	Nature of cost
Supervision	100	85	Fixed
Machine power	30	22	Varies with machine hours
Heat and light	30	27	Varies with direct labour hours
Rates and insurance	220	203	Fixed
Lubricants	60	45	Varies with machine hours
Indirect materials	50	38	Varies with units of output
Machine depreciation	180	180	Fixed
Maintenance and repairs	80	60	Varies with machine hours
	750	660	

The budgeted and actual activity for the year was as follows:

	Machine hours	Direct labour hours	Units of output
Budget	255,000	500,000	100,000
Actual	180,000	440,000	80,000

At the end of the year, the production director made the following report to his colleagues on the board of directors: 'We budgeted for £750,000 overhead cost based on 500,000 direct labour hours. We incurred £660,000 actual cost but only worked 440,000 hours. This appears to me to be a satisfactory proportionate reduction in costs and there are consequently no adverse variances from budget to be explained.'

The other directors felt this comment ignored the distinction between fixed overhead cost and variable overhead cost. They were also concerned that the production director referred only to the fall in direct labour hours worked, when it was known that some overheads depended on the number of machine hours worked. They asked for a more detailed analysis of the expected level of overhead costs in relation to the activity levels achieved.

Required

Prepare a memorandum to the production director:

1 proposing, with reasons, a suitable method for calculating overhead cost rates;

2 setting out a variance analysis which distinguishes fixed overheads from variable overheads.

Chapter 8

Performance evaluation and feedback reporting

After studying this chapter you should be able to:

1 **Distinguish feed forward control from feedback control.**

2 **Explain the essential features of a management accounting report.**

3 **Explain the use of variance analysis in performance reporting.**

4 **Explain what is meant by divisionalisation of a business.**

5 **Define and explain return on investment as a measure of divisional performance.**

6 **Define and explain residual income as a measure of divisional performance.**

7 **Evaluate the relative merits of return on investment and residual income.**

8 **Understand the importance of non-financial performance measures.**

8.1 Introduction

This management accounting text has been based throughout on the view that those who manage a business have a need and a desire to make informed judgements and decisions. In a continuing cycle of management action, there will be a judgement, from which a decision will be formed, followed by evaluation of that decision and a new judgement based on that evaluation. The stage at which the decision is evaluated requires management accounting to exercise its score-keeping function by devising quantitative measures of performance. It also calls on management accounting to direct attention to those areas most urgently requiring a judgement and a further decision. Management functions have been described in Chapter 1 in terms of planning, decision making and control.

Earlier chapters have dealt with planning. In the more advanced textbooks this is sometimes referred to as *feed forward control*. This means making predictions of outputs expected at some future time and then quantifying those predictions, in management accounting terms. The budgetary process (Chapter 6) and setting standards (Chapter 7) are examples of management accounting approaches which have a feed forward (or planning) aspect. Feed forward control systems are very effective, if carried out well, because they anticipate problems rather than wait for them to happen.

Chapter 7 has also dealt with variance analysis as a technique for control in comparing the actual outcome with the standard expected. In the advanced textbooks this is referred to as *feedback controls*. These are useful for looking back at what went wrong (or what went well) and for taking corrective action to ensure that a problem does not continue.

In this chapter we consider in more depth *feedback control*, which involves comparing outputs achieved against outputs desired and taking corrective action if necessary. To provide this type of control it is essential to identify the responsibility for the costs and for taking whatever action is required. The term *responsibility centre* is used to identify the unit to which a feedback report is to be made. A responsibility centre could be a cost centre where the individual manager has responsibility only for costs, a profit centre where the individual manager has responsibility for costs and revenues, or an investment centre where the individual manager has responsibility for costs, revenues and investment in assets. (Cost centre, profit centre and investment centre are defined in Chapter 2.)

Definitions

> *Feed forward control* means making predictions of outputs expected at some future time and then quantifying those predictions, in management accounting terms.
>
> *Feedback control* involves comparing outputs achieved against outputs desired and taking corrective action if necessary.
>
> A *responsibility centre* is an area of responsibility which is controlled by an individual. It might be a cost centre, a profit centre or an investment centre.

In any control process, feed forward or feedback, there are three essential elements:

1 there must be objectives which state the aim or purpose of the control;
2 there must be a model which can be used to predict an expected outcome;
3 there must be power to act in order to take corrective action.

In addition, for feedback control there must be the ability to measure the actual outcome on the same basis as the predicted outcome.

For a feedback control system to be effective, the following basic principles should be observed:

(a) the benefits from the system should exceed the costs of implementing it;
(b) the performance criteria being measured should be reported promptly so that rapid action may be taken;
(c) reports should be as simple as possible and readily understood;
(d) reports should highlight the significant factors requiring management attention;
(e) the reporting framework should be integrated with the organisational structure so that responsibility is identified correctly.

The operation of feedback control will be explored in this chapter in relation to short-term decision making and divisionalisation. (Feedback in long-term decision making will be covered in Chapter 10 under the heading of 'Post-completion audit'.) First, in this chapter we discuss the nature of the report to be written for performance measurement purposes.

8.2 Preparing performance reports

There are three basic questions in relation to report preparation:

1 To whom should the report be addressed?
2 What should be reported?
3 How frequently should the report be presented?

8.2.1 To whom should the report be addressed?

In the context of the management of responsibility centres, the report should be addressed to the manager in charge of the responsibility centre. That could be a cost centre, a profit centre or an investment centre. If the report is to have meaning for the manager concerned, it must include only those costs which may be controlled by the manager of the responsibility centre.

The level of detail in the report will be influenced by the managerial position of the person to whom it is addressed. Reports to senior management will be condensed so that those managers can see the broader picture. They will of course also have access to the more detailed reports, should they so wish.

8.2.2 What should be reported?

The report should be designed to identify clearly those items that are controlled by the manager of the particular responsibility centre. If the responsibility centre controls the price and quantity of an item, then both should be reported and the combined effect quantified. If the responsibility centre controls quantity but not the price of an item, then the report should be designed to emphasise the quantity aspects of transactions in the reporting period.

It could be that, despite a lack of direct responsibility, it would be helpful for the manager of the responsibility centre to be aware of all the costs incurred as a result of the activity of the centre. If that information is felt to be useful, then it could be included in the report, but subheadings would be required to make clear the distinction between controllable and non-controllable costs.

The design of the report is extremely important because the manager of the cost centre, profit centre or investment centre will not use the report effectively if it does not provide useful information in a helpful manner. Managers should be consulted on design of reports, and there should be trial periods of experimentation with a new design of report before it comes into routine use. Graphs, bar charts and pie diagrams may be ways of communicating more effectively than through tables of figures alone.

8.2.3 How frequently should the report be presented?

The frequency of reporting should be related to management's information needs. There may be a need for information on a daily basis. Computers provide on-screen access to information so that the traditional concept of a reporting period, with a printed report at the end of each period, may no longer be appropriate in all circumstances. There is, however, a danger in reporting all items too frequently. Reports have to be read and acted upon, and reporting which occurs too frequently could result in too much time being spent on the review activities.

The question of frequency of reporting is perhaps best answered in terms of the frequency of the cycle of review and corrective action. If daily action is required in an operation, then daily provision of information about the activity will allow corrective action at the earliest possible opportunity. If a monthly review cycle is more appropriate, then the reporting system should be designed to provide monthly summaries. It is vitally important that, whatever the frequency chosen, the reports are produced in a timely manner.

If a computer is in use to record costs and quantities, then the program should be such that the reports required are generated as part of the process so that there is no delay in transferring information for reporting purposes.

Activity 8.1	*Look back to the variance report on Brackendale presented in Chapter 7. Comment on the good and weak points of that report, in the light of the first two sections of this chapter, and suggest ways in which the report could be improved.*

8.3 Performance evaluation

Performance evaluation will be examined in the context of two practical situations, namely:

1 measurement of short-term performance against budget;
2 divisionalised companies.

These two aspects are dealt with in detail in the following sections, but first a basic framework is outlined.

8.3.1 What to measure

Performance evaluation requires the management accountant to carry out the following process:

- Decide on what to measure
- Plan how to report
- Consider the behavioural aspects.

In looking at *what to measure*, we will draw on the material of previous chapters, selecting aspects of management accounting which lead to a measure of performance. Because each management accounting technique serves a different purpose, the decision on what to measure will also depend on the intended purpose and will be discussed in the context of specific applications.

In planning *how to report*, the general principles applied will be those of responsibility and the separation of *controllable and non-controllable costs*. All costs are controllable at some level of management but they may not be controllable at a lower level. Breaking down cost into the separate elements of quantity and price, the extent of control may vary for each element. There will be those in the organisation who have authority to acquire resources, thus controlling quantity and price. There will be others whose job it is to make use of the resources acquired, in which case they will control only the quantity element of cost. There will be others again whose job is to find the best price for resources. They will control only the price element of cost.

It is important to distinguish controllable from non-controllable costs when seeking to establish responsibility for costs. Frequently, the responsibility will be shared, and it is important that the sharing is correctly identified.

Definition

A *controllable cost* is a cost which is capable of being regulated by a manager within a defined boundary of responsibility.

A *non-controllable cost* is one which is not capable of being regulated by a manager within a defined boundary of responsibility, although it may be a cost incurred so that the responsibility may be exercised.

Performance reporting is partly concerned with planning and control, so the idea of controllable and non-controllable costs is important. However, it is also applied in decision making, and further classifications into relevant/non-relevant and avoidable/unavoidable costs may therefore also be used within the same report.

When a decision is taken there is usually more than one option available. Avoidable costs are those costs that may be saved by not taking a particular option. Unavoidable costs will not be saved by such an action.

Definition

An *avoidable cost* is one which may be eliminated by not taking a particular option.

An *unavoidable cost* will not be eliminated by taking a particular action.

Performance evaluation has behavioural aspects because measurement of performance has a direct impact on the organisation's perceptions of how its staff are performing and on the individual staff member's perception of his or her relative performance. As a general guide, favourable reactions to performance reporting are likely to be maximised if staff are made aware in advance of how the performance measures will be calculated and how the responsibility for costs will be allocated. If the individual has control over quantities and prices, then that person should be regarded as having control over, and responsibility for, that item. If the individual has control over quantities but not prices, then it may be appropriate to report the cost to that individual but only regard responsibility as extending to the quantity aspects. If the individual has no control over quantity or price, then no responsibility for the cost of that item can be identified, although there may be a separate question of whether that item should be reported to the individual in order to heighten awareness of the impact of non-controllable costs.

Activity 8.2

> *You are the team leader for a group of social workers who specialise in dealing with the needs of elderly persons in their homes. You have been told by your line manager that your team's budgeted spending limit will be exceeded by the end of the year if you continue with the present level of activity. The major items of cost are: team members' salaries; travel to clients' homes for visits; and a charge from the local authority for the provision of office facilities. Salaries have increased because of a national pay award not allowed for in the budget. Travel costs have increased over budget because of fuel price increases. The local authority has kept the charge for office facilities within the budget. Your line manager has some discretion to make savings under one expense heading to match overspending under another. How will your team explain its performance in the end-of-year report?*

8.4 Measurement of performance against budget

In Chapter 6 the budgetary process was described in detail. Passing reference was made to the use of budgets as a basis for performance evaluation. The budgetary process allows performance targets to be set in financial terms and then compared with the eventual output as it occurs. In Chapter 6 there was reference also to the evaluation of the performance of individuals working within the organisation. There may be financial rewards for high performance and there may be penalties for underperformance. It is therefore important to ensure that the measurement of performance against budget is as fair as possible. A major principle applied in management accounting in this context is the use of flexible budgeting.

When performance is being evaluated, it is important to distinguish costs which vary with activity level from those which are fixed irrespective of activity level. If the cost of materials for teaching 20 hours of craft classes is estimated at £1,000 but, in the event, the number of hours is increased, because of increased demand, to 25, then clearly it would be unfair to attribute any performance failure to the teacher when it is found that the cost of materials has risen to £1,250. The idea of flexible budgeting would be applied to report this information as shown in exhibit 8.1.

The technical aspects of flexible budget preparation were covered in some detail in Chapter 7. That chapter contained the warning that some costs will be partly fixed and partly variable, so that some care may be needed in constructing the formulae to be applied in the flexible budget.

Exhibit 8.1
Presentation of a flexible budget statement

	Original budget	*Flexible budget*	*Actual outcome*	*Variance*
Activity level	20 hours of classes	25 hours of classes	25 hours of classes	
Cost of materials	£1,000	£1,250	£1,250	nil

8.4.1 How to report

In the example in exhibit 8.1, it was reasonably obvious that the number of hours taught should be the basis of the flexible budget calculation. In real life situations the basis of flexibility may not always be so obvious. Activity is measured by output, where the output could be quantified in number of units of product in a manufacturing business, number of hours of service in a service-based business, or number of times a service activity of a standard type is performed. On the other hand, variable costs vary with input. That is no problem if all input leads to output, but in practice it may be found that some input is lost through wastage, inefficiency or unavoidable problems. Performance reporting has to be related to output, but some care has to be taken in deciding how to report the effects of input which is lost, for whatever reason.

Measures of output could be any of the following:

- physical units of output
- standard number of hours of labour allowed for each unit of output
- standard number of machine hours allowed for each unit of output.

A standard hour is the amount of time allowed as standard for each unit of output. If the actual hours of input equal the standard hours allowed for the output, then there is no problem. If the actual hours of input are greater than the standard hours allowed for the output, then there is evidence of inefficiency. If the actual hours of input are less than the standard hours allowed, then there would appear to have been efficiency savings.

Once the activity level has been decided upon, the report design must also be considered. It will be addressed to a named manager of a responsibility centre and will focus on the items which are controllable by that manager. The content must emphasise the costs controllable by the person receiving the report, but should also make the recipient aware of the wider context within which the responsibility centre operates.

Reporting on a monthly basis might be appropriate. A month is sufficiently long to smooth out the daily fluctuations of activity, but also sufficiently short to bring out the regular pattern of activity and the potential impact of seasonal factors.

8.4.2 Behavioural aspects

Chapter 7 concentrated on the technical aspects of cost control by way of variance analysis. There also needs to be a concern with the human implications of variance analysis. It may be that the variance analysis approach is seen as a means of managerial review of subordinates, in which favourable variances receive praise and adverse variances are seen as a cause for corrective action to be taken. That approach may have undesirable consequences for a number of reasons:

1 Employees may reject standards because they were not adequately consulted in setting them.

2 Those under review may divert their efforts into minimising the adverse variances rather than making positive steps towards overall performance improvement.

3 Negative feedback may reduce motivation, leading to reduced effort and lower performance levels.

Those who are concerned at these negative aspects of traditional variance analysis have suggested that there may be a need for accounting systems which are less evaluative in approach. The emphasis should perhaps move to learning and improvement rather than stressing personal responsibility, accountability and past achievement. Later in this chapter there are some ideas about performance measurement using non-financial measures which may be more relevant than financial measures at the individual manager level. First, however, a case study is used to illustrate the traditional variance analysis approach to performance evaluation and control.

Activity 8.3	*You are the financial manager of a school where some teaching departments are spending more than their budget allowance on materials and others are being frugal and spending less. It is six months into the financial year and you would like to give a warning to the overspenders, but also find out why there are underspenders. Suggest two ways of dealing with this problem, of which one way would probably create friction between yourself and the teachers, while the other would encourage the teachers to work with you in controlling the overall budget for the school.*

8.4.3 Case study: performance reports using variance analysis

Fiona McTaggart now explains a situation where she prepared performance reports using flexible budgets and also shows how the performance report appeared in each case.

FIONA: *My client was in a manufacturing business which produced hand-crafted cane furniture. I was asked to devise a monthly performance reporting system which would provide performance measurement of the manufacturing activity. Three levels of reporting were required. The managing director required a brief summary of any matter requiring executive action but did not want all the details each month. The furniture supervisor needed a much more specific analysis of the performance of the activity as a whole and the relative performance of each employee. There was also a proposal to give each employee a personal performance statement that showed some indication of the average performance of the activity as a whole, without giving individuals access to information which was best kept personal to each employee.*

The budget was set at the start of the year based on average monthly output of 300 chairs and 80 tables. In practice the actual monthly output varied around this average. I recommended a three-column form of report which would show the original budget for one month's output, the flexible budget showing the costs expected for the actual level of output achieved, and the actual costs incurred.

I made a list of all the costs incurred in making cane furniture. The main direct costs were materials and skilled labour. Although the employees were employed on full-time contracts, it was useful to identify separately the time they spent in productive activity making the furniture, which I classed as a direct cost, and the time they spent in non-productive activity, which I classed as an indirect cost.

I then listed all the indirect costs and subdivided them according to various levels of responsibility. Each employee was responsible for a portion of indirect materials used in fastening the cane together and was also responsible for a portion of equipment maintenance and depreciation. This indirect cost was allocated in proportion to the output produced. It might sound rather hard that the employee's responsibility for cost increased as the output increased, but it was decided in discussion that staff needed to be aware of the costs incurred when productive output takes place. Individual employees would not be regarded as being responsible for unproductive time unless they were the direct cause as a result of their individual actions.

The furniture supervisor was responsible for control of the total costs allocated to the individual operative staff, plus the cost of non-productive time (to the extent this was in the control of the supervisor), and the overhead costs of heating and lighting the workshop area.

The managing director had ultimate responsibility for all costs, including the cost of administration, providing adequate working conditions, the employer's share of employment costs and any non-productive work due to causes beyond the control of the furniture supervisor.

Exhibit 8.2 shows how the performance report was designed. There were three separate parts to the report. The first was for individual members of staff. The second was for the furniture supervisor, who also had access to the individual staff reports, and the third was for the managing director, who had access to the more detailed reports if these were required.

Each report set out the variances from flexible budget for each element of cost. At the foot of the report was a section for highlighting matters for attention and a space below for the person receiving the report to write a comment. In the case of individual employees, a comment was expected on any action planned in response to matters noted. This action plan would be discussed and agreed with the supervisor. In the case of the report to the supervisor, the comment was expected to show the action planned for the production activity as a whole, or for individual employees where there was a particular problem. In the case of the report to the managing director, the comment was expected to confirm discussions with the supervisor but also to note any action on indirect costs regarded as the managing director's responsibility.

We had a trial run of this reporting format for three months, to iron out any wrinkles, and during that time there were some difficulties in getting the overhead responsibility allocation right. Everyone denies responsibility for indirect costs but, at the end of the day, they have to be incurred and are an unavoidable consequence of business activity. It was eventually agreed that the direct cost allocation would remain, but that, for employees and the supervisor, the emphasis would be on responsibility for the volume aspects of the allocation, with any external price increases being regarded as non-controllable or else a matter for discussion with the purchasing section.

Exhibit 8.2
Monthly performance report: (a) employee report; (b) supervisor's report;
(c) managing director's report

Part A: Employee report	Name..........*Employee X*..........			
Date of statement	....			
	Budget	Flexible budget	Actual	Variance
Output: target/actual	100 chairs 20 tables	110 chairs 18 tables	110 chairs 18 tables	
Direct materials	...	...	...	...
Direct labour	...	...	...	...
Controllable indirect costs	...	...	...	...
Indirect materials	...	...	...	...
Total controllable costs for employee X	...	...	...	...
Cumulative controllable costs for year to date	...	...	...	...
Maintenance	...	...	...	...
Depreciation	...	...	...	...
Total for exployee X	...	...	...	...
Cumulative for year to date	...	...	...	...
Matters for attention				
Action planned				

8.4.4 Comment

Fiona's description has concentrated very much on the two questions of what to measure and how to report. Since she is describing the early stages of designing and implementing a new system, there is no information on the behavioural aspects of how the reporting system operated in practice. There is a description of the trial run and the extent to which the views of participants were taken into

Exhibit 8.2 (continued)

Part B: Supervisor's report	Name...			
Date of statement	....			
	Budget	Flexible budget	Actual	Variance
Output: target/actual	300 chairs 80 tables	320 chairs 76 tables	320 chairs 76 tables	
From Part A Controllable costs for each employee				
Costs of employee X	...	...	...	...
Costs of employee Y	...	...	...	...
Costs of employee Z	...	...	...	...
Total controllable costs				
Overheads				
Controllable indirect costs	...	...	...	...
Non-productive time	...	...	...	...
Heating & lighting	...	...	...	...
Matters for attention				
Action planned				

(In practice this report would also include cumulative totals for the year to date, as shown on Part A, but they are omitted here so that the main features are more readily seen.)

Continued overleaf

account in the design of the final report. The case study would need to be followed up after a period of, say, three months of operation, to find out how effectively the new system was achieving satisfactory control.

Activity 8.4

Read the case study again and identify the points at which Fiona McTaggart's actions match the principles of reporting set out in this chapter.

Exhibit 8.2 (continued)

Part C: Managing director's report		Subject: *Cane furniture production*		
Date of statement	....			
	Budget	Flexible budget	Actual	Variance
Output: target/actual	300 chairs 80 tables	320 chairs 76 tables	320 chairs 76 tables	
From Part B				
Total employee controllable costs	...	...	...	...
Total indirect costs for which supervisor is responsible	...	...	...	...
Other overheads				
Administration	...	...	...	...
Employment costs	...	...	...	...
Abnormal non-productive time	...	...	...	...
Total				
Matters for attention Action discussed with supervisor				

(In practice this report would also include cumulative totals for the year to date, as shown on Part A, but they are omitted here so that the main features are more readily seen.)

8.5 Divisionalised companies

Large organisations have a variety of activities which they carry out in different locations. In order to manage such an organisation effectively, it may be subdivided into separate units, each of which is responsible for planning and control of its own activities and for some aspects of decision making. Each of the separate units is called a *division* of the company. The benefit of creating a divisional structure is that those managing and working in each division have a sense of responsibility for their own area of operations. The risk lies in the divisional management taking actions which may appear to be beneficial to the division but which are not good for the organisation as a whole.

Definition

> A *division* is a part of the organisation where the manager has responsibility for generating revenues, controlling costs and producing a satisfactory return on capital invested in the division.

It was explained in Chapter 1 that the management accounting approach to any situation will depend on the nature of the organisation. The size of a department may vary from one organisation to the next and the nature of a department will merge with that of a division as the department becomes larger. In some cases, the words may be used interchangeably. For the purposes of this text, a *division* will have responsibility for its costs, profits and return on investment in assets, whereas a *department* would be responsible only for its costs, or possibly for costs and profits.

8.5.1 Advantages of divisionalisation

Where divisions exist and managers have decision making power, their decisions about the business may be made more readily and with greater regard for the nature of the division. If all decisions are taken at a remote head office, the process may be delayed and may not have sufficient regard for any special circumstances of the division.

The freedom to make decisions also creates a challenge for those who manage the division and may make them feel more highly motivated towards achieving success for the division. They will have responsibility for investment in assets and investment in employees, which gives a sense of controlling an entire business operation rather than being sandwiched between those who make the decisions and those who are required to implement them.

The existence of the division may also give employees a greater sense of identity with the operation of the division, particularly if it is in a separate geographical area or carries out a different operation from the rest of the organisation.

8.5.2 Disadvantages of divisionalisation

Managers of divisions may forget that they also have a responsibility towards the organisation as a whole and may make decisions which have adverse consequences elsewhere in the organisation. Take the case of a company where one division was producing flour in a flour mill and was selling it to another division which was a bakery. The manager of the flour mill decided to attempt to increase profit by increasing the price charged for the flour, whereupon the manager of the bakery decided it was cheaper to buy flour from a rival organisation and did so. The result was that, although the bakery kept its costs under control, the flour mill went out of business and there was a substantial loss to the organisation as a whole. That loss could have been avoided if there had been a mechanism within the organisation to reconcile the separate objectives of the managers of the flour mill and the bakery.

Divisional organisation may also mean that some of the economies of central organisation are lost. Purchasing goods for all divisions from a central location may allow quantity discounts to be negotiated which would not be available to the separate divisions.

Placing too much emphasis on the divisional structure may cause those in each division to fail to identify with the total organisation and may cause the senior management of the total organisation to be remote from the day-to-day activities of the separate parts of the overall business. Communication and motivation may become more significant in achieving effective management in such circumstances.

8.5.3 Management accounting approach

Management accounting techniques required in dealing with a division need to cover the entire range of directing attention, keeping the score and solving problems. In relation to the classification of costs, the division may be regarded as an investment centre. In Chapter 2, an investment centre was defined as a unit of the organisation in respect of which a manager is responsible for capital investment decisions as well as revenue and costs. One very important aspect of management accounting is to measure the performance of the divisional manager in relation to capital investment, revenue and costs.

8.5.4 Profit as a measure of divisional performance

The statement of profit for a division will contain many of the management accounting features explained in earlier chapters. Exhibit 8.3 shows the main components of divisional profit and uses italics to highlight three possible measures of profit performance.

Of the three profit measures highlighted, *contribution* may be useful to the management of the division in taking short-term decisions on production and pricing, but it is inappropriate as a measure of performance because it does not take into account the fixed costs which are controllable by the division. The management of the division may accept that performance is best measured by profit controllable by the division, but the management of the organisation as a whole may be reluctant to accept this figure on the grounds that, at the end of the day, all costs must be covered, including the fixed costs incurred centrally which are beyond divisional control. (The term 'contribution' is applied to the difference between revenue and variable cost of sales. It is a term which is dealt with in greater detail in Chapter 9.)

There may be some energetic debate as to which fixed costs are controllable and which are non-controllable so far as the division is concerned. Depreciation of fixed assets is a controllable cost for the division because the division has control of the investment in fixed assets. The division will take a share of head office service costs, such as personnel, accounting and legal services. To the

**Exhibit 8.3
Statement of divisional profit**

	£
Sales to external customers	xx
Transfers to other divisions	xx
Total revenue	xx
Variable costs of operations	xx
Contribution	*xx*
Fixed costs controllable by the division	xx
Profit controllable by the division	xx
Fixed costs not controllable by the division	xx
Total divisional profit	*xx*

extent that the divisional manager has a choice as to the extent to which such service costs are taken on, there should be a controllable fixed cost in respect of these items.

Because of the various conflicts that may arise in deciding on the best profit measure to use in performance measurement, the view is taken that divisional profit is not a satisfactory means of measuring the performance of management. It is also regarded as unsatisfactory because profit is an absolute measure and if managers think they are successful in making higher and higher profits, they may have no regard for the investment in fixed assets used in earning those profits. In a situation where it was discovered that stolen money had been used to finance the purchase and refurbishment of a hotel, the disgruntled manager of a rival hotel commented: 'It's not surprising that they could undercut our prices and take all our customers – they never had to worry about earning a return on their investment.'

8.5.5 Return on investment as a measure of divisional performance

A better measure of divisional performance is to relate the profit earned by a division to the investment in assets which produced that profit. This is referred to as the *profitability* of the division (where 'profitability' means the rate of profit per unit of investment).

Definition

Return on investment (ROI) of a division is calculated by taking profit controllable by the division as a percentage of the investment in assets which produces that profit.

8.5.6 Illustration: advantages and disadvantages of return on investment

Exhibit 8.4 compares the ROI for new projects with the existing ROI for each division.

Exhibit 8.4
Return on investment for each division

	Division A	Division B
Investment in assets for project	£2m	£2m
Profit controllable by the division, to be generated by each project	£400,000	£260,000
ROI of each project	20%	13%
ROI of division at present	22%	12%

The calculation in exhibit 8.4 shows that the return on investment is higher for division A. However, it is possible that division A will decide not to take up the new project because it has a lower ROI than the division's existing performance. Division B will be pleased that the new project has a higher ROI than the existing average.

There may be technical problems in deciding on the division's investment in assets because the assets are owned by the organisation as a whole, rather than the division. It will usually require assets to be traced to a division, either on the basis that they are physically located there or on the basis that they are used by the division. It may be that use of assets is shared by more than one division, so that a portion of asset value is assigned to each division. The investment in assets may include an element of investment in working capital.

There may also be problems in deciding how to value the assets. Historical cost could be used, taking the net book value as applied for financial accounting purposes. However, in times of rising prices this could allow the highest return on capital employed to arise in the division having the oldest assets, because these would have a low value. It could discourage a division from investing in new assets. If all divisions have to use the current value of the assets used, then the valuation base is comparable across all divisions.

There could be more than one view of which measure of profit to apply. There are no specific rules as to the choice to be made, but there should be regard for the general principle that performance measurement should take account of relevant costs. If the focus of the ROI calculation is the motivation of divisional managers, then allocation of non-controllable costs may have a negative effect. If the focus is economic performance of divisions within the organisation as a whole, then it may be important to include the impact of apportioned costs.

Advantages of return on investment

ROI is the most widely used measure of divisional performance. An advantage, therefore, is its general acceptance. It is widely understood and it encourages managers to concentrate on projects which make best use of resources.

Disadvantages of return on investment

There are practical difficulties in deciding on the data to be used in the formula. Both the numerator and denominator have more than one possible definition. It could distort performance where a manager of one division avoids a project which lowers the average ROI for that division but would nevertheless be of benefit to the organisation as a whole. It is undesirable to have the entire performance of a division taken down to a single measure. It is always valuable to look at a situation from more than one angle.

8.5.7 Residual income

Residual income (RI) is another method of measuring divisional performance. It is calculated by deducting from the operating profit an interest charge based on the assets used and controlled by the division. The view taken is that the assets are controlled by the company and therefore are financed from the company's resources. If the division were an independent entity it would have to borrow money to acquire equivalent assets, so it is reasonable to charge the division with an amount representing interest on borrowed funds. There is no actual interest payment within the company, so the figure has to be created using interest rates which might apply to borrowed funds. This created figure is called *imputed* interest. ('Imputed' used in this sense means 'thought to belong to'.)

Definition

> *Residual income (RI)* is defined as operating profit less an interest charge based on the assets used and controlled by the division.

8.5.8 Example

Exhibit 8.5 continues with the new project proposed in exhibit 8.4.

Exhibit 8.5
Residual income for each division

	Division A	Division B
Investment in assets for project	£2m	£2m
Profit controllable by the division, to be generated by each project	£400,000	£260,000
Interest charge applied to projects: 9% of investment	£180,000	£180,000
Residual income	£220,000	£80,000

The calculation in exhibit 8.5 shows that the residual income of both divisions would increase if the investment of £2m was made. Division A has the higher residual income and might therefore be preferred if there were a limited amount of funding so that only one division could receive investment funding.

Advantages of residual income

The main advantage of using residual income is that managers will be more readily encouraged to act in the best interests of the organisation because this will match their own best interests in terms of performance measurement. If a new project is undertaken the residual income is affected only by the additional profit as compared with interest on the additional investment. It does not average out the new project with the existing projects as happens with the return on investment calculation.

A second advantage is that the interest charge may be varied according to the risk of the investment project. The return on investment calculation allows only one overall percentage to be calculated.

Disadvantage of residual income

A disadvantage of residual income is that it provides an absolute measure rather than a relative measure. A large division produces more residual income in total than does a small division. To avoid any problems of relative size, the target residual income for a division needs to match, in order of magnitude, the investment in assets.

8.5.9 Which to use – return on investment or residual income?

Both return on investment and residual income could be criticised as placing too much emphasis on the short term. They both emphasise profit when it may be that other factors of a more qualitative nature are important. They both suffer from the problem of identifying the asset base used and controlled by the division. As a result, either of them could lead to inappropriate comparisons across divisions.

It has been suggested that residual income is more appropriate where the divisional manager has considerable freedom to determine the investment in assets. The return on investment may be more appropriate where the divisional manager has little or no control over the level of investment in the division. If return on investment is calculated, it is important that an imputed interest charge is *not* deducted from the operating profit, since to do so would involve double-counting. Between these two extremes it may be appropriate to use both techniques and compare the outcome.

Evidence from research shows that the dominant measure used in practice is return on investment, but it is also common to find return on investment and residual income used together. Residual income is rarely used alone, but this may be a reflection of the dominance of central control, rather than divisional control, of asset investment.

8.5.10 Case study: return on investment and residual income

Here is Fiona McTaggart to explain a situation where she compared the impact of return on investment with that of residual income as a measure of performance.

FIONA: *I was called in to discuss performance measurement with the washing powder division and the toothpaste division of a large chemical company. They provided the following data:*

	Washing powder £	Toothpaste £
Investment in assets	5,000,000	15,000,000
Profit controllable by the division	1,000,000	5,000,000
Return on investment	20%	33.3%

Their problem was that they had done what the textbooks recommend in calculating *the return on investment, but the management team in the washing powder division was now feeling aggrieved about being shown as underperforming in comparison with the toothpaste division. To improve the return on capital employed, the washing powder division proposed closing down an operation at a remote branch where there was an investment of £500,000 in assets, earning a return of 15 per cent to yield a profit of £75,000. If that disappeared, then they would have a divisional profit of £925,000 on assets of £4,500,000, improving the ROI to 23.1 per cent. Although senior management could see the potential for improving ROI, they were of the view that closing down did not seem logical or sensible.*

My reply was that of course it was not a logical action. The branch operation was yielding 15 per cent at a time when the company's cost of capital was 13 per cent. If the company pulled out of that area, a competitor would jump in with a replacement. Where the divisional managers have discretion over levels of investment, then residual income may be preferred as giving a relative measure of performance which will not lead to actions against the company's interest. I recalculated the performance measures using residual income as follows:

	Washing powder £	Toothpaste £
Investment in assets	5,000,000	15,000,000
Profit controllable by the division	1,000,000	5,000,000
Charge for cost of capital at 13%	650,000	1,950,000
Residual income	350,000	3,050,000

If the washing powder division were to dispose of its branch as tentatively suggested, then the residual income would fall:

Washing powder division

	Before disposal £	After disposal £
Investment in assets	5,000,000	4,500,000
Profit controllable by the division	1,000,000	925,000
Charge for cost of capital at 13%	650,000	585,000
Residual income	350,000	340,000

On this comparison the performance measure would worsen because the division's total residual income would fall and it would be seen to be contributing less to the overall wellbeing of the company.

I explained that where the managers of a profit centre have discretion to acquire and dispose of substantial amounts of assets, the residual income is a preferable method of performance measurement. It is an absolute measure and leads to the conclusion that the higher the residual income, the better for the organisation as a whole. The only condition on expanding into new assets or retaining existing ones is that these should earn a profit which exceeds the cost of capital. If the profit earned is less than the cost of capital, then the activity should cease.

I also pointed out the dangers of relying on one performance measure only. I recommended that in future the divisional performance should be assessed by reference to all the following criteria, as a starting point:

- *Is the target cash flow being achieved?*
- *Is the target ROI being met?*
- *Is the actual profit within the budget?*
- *Is the residual income maximised, subject to any organisational constraints?*

I explained that I was emphasising meeting targets rather than making comparisons between divisions. There could be good reasons for the different ROI in the two divisions, the most likely of which is relative competition in the industry. Targets should be set in advance, having regard to the economic conditions, so that the division is measured against its own statement of achievable performance rather than against a comparison which may not be valid.

8.5.11 Comment

Return on investment and residual income are competing as alternative methods of performance evaluation for divisions of a business, but the usefulness of each should be considered in the light of all the circumstances. It is more important to think carefully about the interpretation of results from calculations and to cross-check by more than one evaluation, as Fiona did for the washing powder division.

Activity 8.5

Write a 300-word summary of the relative merits of ROI and RI as measures of divisional performance.

8.6 Non-financial performance measures

Within an organisation, people are employed to carry out specific activities. The only aspect of their work over which they have direct control may well be the volume and the quality of tasks they undertake. Applying revenues and costs to these activities may be important for the organisation as a whole, but will have little meaning for the individual employee who does not sell the goods or services directly and does not purchase the input materials.

To ensure that the motivation of employees is consistent with the profit objectives of the organisation, it may be necessary to use non-financial performance measures to indicate what is required to achieve the overall financial targets. Using non-financial performance measures does not mean that the financial performance measures may be disregarded. They are ways of translating financial targets and measures into something that is more readily identifiable by a particular employee or group of employees.

The non-financial performance measures should cover both quantity and quality.

8.6.1 Quantity measures

This chapter has augmented Chapter 7 in showing the importance of flexible budgeting in ensuring that the cost targets used as a basis for comparison are flexible as levels of output change. That is essential in order to avoid a sense of injustice in the application of management accounting techniques. However, it may not be sufficient to motivate employees directly in understanding and meeting the targets expected of them. The accounting numbers have to be converted to some measure of quantity which relates more closely to the individual. If the employees are involved in the entire productive process, then the financial target may be converted to units of product per period. That approach may be more difficult when a service activity is involved or a group of employees is involved in only part of a production process.

As an illustration of the problems of performance measurement in a service business, take an example of a school where activities are subdivided by subject area. The primary measure of activity will be the number of pupils taught, but the individual departments will have no control over the number of pupils taught. If teaching staff are appointed on permanent contracts, so that salary costs are largely fixed costs, then the cost per student will vary depending on the number of students taught in any period. A performance measure of cost per student may be attractive to the management accountant but will have little impact on the staff of the history department whose main aim is to ensure that their pupils achieve high grades in the end-of-year examinations. For them, examination success rates are the prime performance measure and they will be concerned to ensure that fluctuations in pupil numbers do not affect that success rate. A performance report on the history department would therefore emphasise first of all the non-financial performance, in terms of examination success, but would then additionally report the cost implications so that the consequences of achieving a high, or a low, success rate could be linked to the cost of that activity.

8.6.2 Quality measures

The ultimate measure of quality is customer satisfaction. Companies will invest time and effort in measuring customer satisfaction, perhaps by questionnaire survey, or possibly by telephone interview. Indirect measures of customer satisfaction may be found in complaints records, frequency of repairs under warranty and level of goods being returned as unwanted.

Another important aspect of quality is the process undertaken by the organisation. This is so important that an external agency (often the auditors) may be employed to provide independent certification of the quality of the process and the controls within the process.

Finally, quality is measured also in terms of the inputs to the process, where inputs may be materials, labour and capital equipment. Quality of inputs may be controlled directly by imposing standards on suppliers, or may be monitored by reviewing the rate of return of unsatisfactory goods, the non-productive time incurred because of faulty equipment, or the reliability of delivery dates and quantities.

Some examples of non-financial performance measures are:

1 in respect of demand for products:
    (a) number of enquiries per advertisement placed; and
    (b) percentage of customers who remember the advertisement;

2 in respect of delivering the products:
    (a) error free deliveries as a percentage of total deliveries;
    (b) number of complaints as a percentage of units sold; and
    (c) time between receiving customer order and supplying the goods or service.

An electricity supply company provided the following information about non-financial performance over a one-year period:

Restore supply in three hours	Target **Performance**	80% **83.8%**
Restore supply in 24 hours	Target **Performance**	99% **99.9%**
Moving a meter inside 15 working days	Target **Performance**	95% **96.7%**
Reply to telephone calls within 10 seconds	Target **Performance**	90% **91.1%**

Activity 8.6

Write out five non-financial performance measures which could be reported by an organisation which delivers parcels to the general public and to businesses.

8.7 Summary

This chapter has distinguished feedback from feed forward control and has introduced the concept of a responsibility centre. It has also explored the principles of preparing a relevant and useful report on performance evaluation. Measurement of short-term performance against budget and the assessment of performance of divisionalised companies have been used as practical illustrations of performance evaluation and reporting in practice.

The management accountant should be aware of the behavioural aspects of performance evaluation. If performance evaluation is resisted by those on whom it is targeted, then any attempts at improvement are unlikely to be successful.

Performance of divisionalised companies may be measured either by the return on investment (ROI) or by the residual income (RI). While ROI is more frequently encountered in practice, it may discourage investment that would be in the best interests of the organisation as a whole. In situations where the divisional manager has discretion to decide long-term investment in assets, RI may lead to a more useful and relevant measure of performance.

Further reading

Emmanuel, C. R., Otley, D. T. and Merchant, K. (1990), *Accounting for Management Control*, Chapman & Hall.

Emmanuel, C. R., Otley, D. T. and Merchant, K. (eds) (1991), *Readings in Accounting for Management Control*, Chapman & Hall.

Ezzamel, M. (1992), *Business Unit and Divisional Performance Measurement*, Advanced Management Accounting and Finance Series, ed. D. Otley, Harcourt Brace, in association with CIMA.

Fitzgerald, L., Johnston, R., Brignall, S., Silvestro, R. and Voss, C. (1991), *Performance Measurement in Service Businesses*, Chartered Institute of Management Accountants (UK).

Morse, W. J. and Roth, H. P. (1986), *Cost Accounting: Processing, Evaluating and Using Cost Data*, Addison-Wesley.

Northcott, D. (1992), *Capital Investment Decision-Making*, Advanced Management Accounting and Finance Series, ed. D. Otley, Harcourt Brace & Company, in association with CIMA.

Wilson, R. M. S. and Chua, W. F. (1992), *Managerial Accounting: Method and Meaning*, Chapman & Hall.

Self-testing on the chapter

1 What are the essential features of a management accounting report addressed to a manager of a responsibility centre?

2 What are the issues to be considered in applying variance analysis to evaluate the performance of a responsibility centre?

3 What are the advantages of divisionalisation?

4 What are the disadvantages of divisionalisation?

5 Why is profit not a suitable measure of divisional performance?

6 Explain, in terms of divisional performance evaluation, the difference between using 'profit' and 'profitability'.

7 Define, and explain the use of, return on investment as a measure of divisional performance.

8 Define, and explain the use of, residual income, as a measure of divisional performance.

9 Explain the circumstances in which return on investment and residual income are preferable as measures of divisional performance.

10 Explain the significance of non-financial performance indicators.

11 The following table sets out information in respect of Division X and Division Y.

	Division X	*Division Y*
Amount to be invested in new project	£4m	£4m
Sales	£2m	£2m
Net profit	£1.2m	£0.8m
ROI of existing investment	33%	4%

The cost of borrowing new finance is 10 per cent per annum.

Explain what view the managers of each division might take, depending on the method of performance evaluation applied.

Activities for study groups

1 Obtain the annual report of a large listed company which has divisions undertaking different activities. Read the divisional reports in the section of the annual report describing business operations. Based upon those divisional reports, and using what information exists in the financial statements, write a programme for a management audit of each division. Your programme should consist of a series of questions, the purpose of asking the question and the type of answer expected being explained in each case.

2 Obtain the annual report of a large listed company. Look throughout the report for mention of non-financial performance indicators. Having read the report, prepare a list of non-financial performance indicators which you think would be useful to readers in understanding more about the company. For each indicator suggested, you should give a reason. The aim should be to have a table of indicators covering no more than one side of A4 paper in printed form.

Case studies

Case 8.1

Standard pine benches are assembled and packed in the bench assembly department of Furniture Manufacture Ltd. The department is treated as a cost centre. Control reports prepared every month consist of a statement comparing actual costs incurred in the department with the level of costs which was budgeted at the start of the month.

For the month of June 19X6 the following control report was produced, and received favourable comment from the directors of the company.

Bench Assembly Department
Control Report for June 19X6

	Budgeted cost			Actual cost	Variance[1]	
	Fixed	Variable	Total			
	£	£	£	£	£	
Direct labour	–	36,000	36,000	30,000	6,000	(F)
Indirect labour	6,000	8,000	14,000	14,000	–	
Indirect materials	–	4,000	4,000	3,500	500	(F)
Power	3,000	12,000	15,000	9,000	6,000	(F)
Maintenance materials	–	5,000	5,000	3,000	2,000	(F)
Maintenance labour	5,000	4,000	9,000	15,000	6,000	(A)
Depreciation	85,000	–	85,000	75,000	10,000	(F)
Production overhead	–	20,000	20,000	15,000	5,000	(F)

Note: [1](F) = favourable; (A) = adverse.

Due to a power failure, the level of production achieved was only 75 per cent of that expected when the budget was prepared. No adjustment has been made to the original budget because the departmental manager claims that the power failure which caused the loss of production was beyond his control.

Required

Prepare a memorandum to the directors of the company:

1 Explaining the weaknesses in the existing form of control report.

2 Presenting the control report in such a way as to give a more meaningful analysis of the costs.

3 Assessing the performance of the Bench Assembly Department during the month.

Case 8.2

Musical Productions Ltd, a client of your firm, has two divisions. The Compact Disc division (CD) assembles and markets portable compact disc players. The Portable Stereo division (PS) assembles and markets portable tape players.

Budgets for the coming year have been prepared by the managers of each division and agreed by the head office, as follows:

	CD £000s	PS £000s
Investment in fixed assets	840	700
Revenue	420	210
Operating expenses	210	140
Profit	210	70

A new investment opportunity has arisen. It could be adopted by either division. The initial investment in fixed assets will be £140,000 and the expected annual operating profits from this investment are £28,000.

Musical Productions Ltd presently uses return on investment (ROI) as a criterion for evaluating divisional performance, but the finance director is aware that a close competitor applies the residual income (RI) method, using a required rate of return of 18 per cent per annum.

Required

Write a report to the finance director explaining:

1   The relative merits and limitations of ROI, as compared with RI, as a criterion for evaluation of divisional performance.

2   The acceptability of the new investment opportunity from the viewpoint of each divisional manager and of Musical Productions Ltd as an entity, using both ROI and RI methods.

Case 8.3

You are the management accountant at the head office of a company which owns retail shoe shops throughout the country. The shops are grouped into areas, each having an area manager. Goods for sale are bought through a central purchasing scheme administered by head office. Shop managers have discretion to vary sales prices subject to the approval of the area manager. It is the responsibility of shop managers to record on a wastage sheet any shoes which are discarded because of damage in the shop. Shop managers have total control over the number of staff they employ and the mix of permanent and casual staff, subject to interview in the presence of the area manager. Shop managers also arrange for cleaning of the premises and are responsible for heat and light and other overhead costs.

The head office accounting system has produced the following information with regard to the Southern area:

	Shop A £	Shop B £	Shop C £	Area target %
Turnover	450,000	480,000	420,000	100
Costs:				
Cost of goods sold	355,000	356,000	278,000	69
Wastage	5,000	4,000	2,000	
	360,000	360,000	280,000	
Salaries and wages:				
Branch manager	15,000	16,000	16,000	
Bonus for manager	1,000	1,500	1,500	
Permanent assistants	9,000	7,000	7,000	
Bonus for assistants	450	480	420	
Casual workers	3,000	4,000	5,000	
	28,450	28,980	29,920	6
Heat, light, cleaning and other overheads	7,600	8,500	8,200	2
Operating profit before area office recharges	53,950	82,520	101,880	
Area office recharges	3,000	3,000	3,000	
	50,950	79,520	98,880	22

Further information

(a) The Southern area has an overall operating profit target of 20 per cent of sales. The area office has a target allowance of 2 per cent of sales to cover its expenses other than those recharged to shops.

(b) Details of area office expenses are:

	£
Area manager's salary	18,000
Area manager's bonus	3,000
Other office expenses	2,400
	23,400
Area office recharges	(9,000)
	14,400

(c) It is the policy of the company to disclose sufficient information to motivate and inform the appropriate level of management or staff, but to avoid reporting excessive detail, particularly where such detail would unnecessarily disclose information about wages or salaries of individual employees.

Required

Prepare three separate reports including comments on and interpretation of the quantitative performance data as follows:

1 To the area manager on the overall performance of the area and the relative performance of each shop within the area.

2 To the manager of shop A on the performance of that shop relative to the rest of the area and to the area target.

3 To the employees of shop B showing them how their shop performed relative to the rest of the area.

Case 8.4

Dairies Ltd operates a milk processing and delivery business. The retail distribution of milk is controlled by a regional head office which has overall responsibility for five geographical distribution areas. Each area is run by an area manager who has responsibility for ten depots. At each depot there is a depot manager in charge of 20 drivers and their milk floats. Milk is bottled at a central processing plant and sent to depots by lorry.

All information regarding the operation of each depot and each area office is sent to the divisional head office accounting department. This department produces weekly reports to be sent to each depot manager, each area manager and the manager of the distribution division.

A pyramidal system of reporting is in operation whereby each manager receives an appropriate weekly report containing the financial information on the operations for which he is responsible.

Required

1 Explain what is meant by responsibility accounting.

2 List, giving reasons, the information which should be contained in the weekly reports to each of the three levels of manager specified.

Part 4

Profit, performance and current developments

Chapter 9

Profit measurement and short-term decision making

| Learning objectives | After studying this chapter you should be able to: |

After studying this chapter you should be able to:

1 Explain how the accountant's view of cost behaviour differs from that of the economist.

2 Prepare a breakeven chart.

3 Prepare a profit–volume graph.

4 Understand the usefulness and limitations of breakeven analysis.

5 Apply contribution analysis in short-term decision-making problems.

6 Understand and explain the factors affecting pricing policy in business organisations.

7 Compare the effect on profit of absorption costing and variable costing.

8 Understand the usefulness of variable costing in short-term decision making and the dangers of taking a short-term perspective.

9.1 Introduction

In Chapter 1 the role of management accounting was explained in terms of directing attention, keeping the score and solving problems. Chapters 6, 7 and 8 have concentrated primarily on the planning and control aspects of management and the score-keeping and attention-directing role of the management accountant. This chapter turns to the problem-solving aspect of the management accountant's work and in particular to the use of management accounting information to help with decisions in the short term (where the short term is typically a period of weeks or months, extending to twelve months at the most, in which some costs are fixed and others are variable, depending on the level of activity). Chapter 10 looks at decisions about the longer term.

| Activity 9.1 | *The classification of costs was explained at length in Chapter 2. If you have any doubts about that chapter, go back and work through it again. It is essential that Chapter 2 is understood before this chapter is attempted.* |

This chapter will first explain how costs and revenues behave in the short term as the volume of activity increases. This is called *cost–volume–profit analysis*. It makes use of graphs which will help you follow the analysis of costs, revenues and profits.

It will then show how the distinction between variable cost and fixed cost may be used in short-term decision making in situations of special orders, abandonment of a product line, and the existence of limiting factors. They are set out as case studies so that you will see that each problem, while using the same principles of contribution analysis, requires some adaptability in using the analysis in the specific circumstances.

Pricing decisions will often require management accounting information about how the price charged for a product or service matches up to the cost of that product or service. Note, however, that the price which consumers are willing to pay may be decided by economic forces rather than by the costs incurred. You will see in this chapter the main approaches to pricing and the role of costs in those approaches.

Finally, the chapter considers a decision about the valuation of goods and services. Should the value include a portion of overhead cost (absorption costing) or is it preferable, for decision-making purposes, to avoid overhead allocation problems and use only the direct materials, direct labour and direct expenses (variable costing)?

9.2 Cost behaviour: fixed and variable costs

In Chapter 2 we explained that the cost classification systems are as varied as the businesses they serve. Types of cost classification system were identified in that chapter by reference to questions which needed answers. Chapter 2 also provided definitions of variable cost and fixed cost, while exhibits 2.2, 2.5 and 2.7 showed different types of cost behaviour as activity increased.

Definitions

> A *variable cost* is one which varies directly with changes in the level of activity, over a defined period of time.
>
> A *fixed cost* is one which is not affected by changes in the level of activity, over a defined period of time.

This chapter now moves on from that starting point outlined in Chapter 2 to ask more questions about the relationships between cost, volume of output and profit.

9.2.1 Cost related to activity level: the economist's view and the accountant's view

There are two ways of viewing the behaviour of cost in relation to activity level. One is referred to as *the economist's view* and the other is referred to as *the accountant's view*. Each is discussed here, and the use of the accountant's view is then justified as a reasonable short-term approximation.

The economist's view

Exhibit 9.1 shows total cost related to activity level over a wide range of activity within a business. Starting at zero activity, there is a total cost of £200,000 shown representing the fixed cost of the operations, including items such as rent of premises, business rates, administration salaries and any similar costs incurred to allow operations to commence. Initially, the slope of the graph rises relatively steeply because high levels of costs are incurred as activity begins. Then the

Exhibit 9.1
Total cost varying with activity

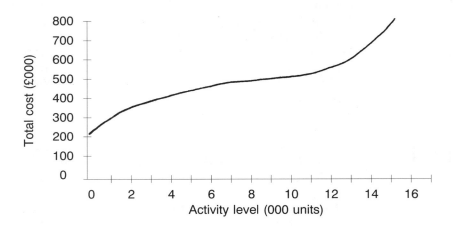

slope becomes less steep as the business begins to enjoy the economies of scale, sharing fixed-costs over a wider range of activity so that the marginal cost of producing an extra item becomes progressively less. At the extreme right-hand side of the graph the slope begins to rise more steeply again as further fixed costs are incurred. Perhaps high rental has to be paid for new premises at this point to allow expansion, or labour resources become more scarce and higher labour rates have to be paid to employ staff.

To calculate profit, a business must compare its cost with its revenue. The economist's portrayal of revenue is superimposed on the cost line in Exhibit 9.2.

Exhibit 9.2
Revenue and costs: the economist's view

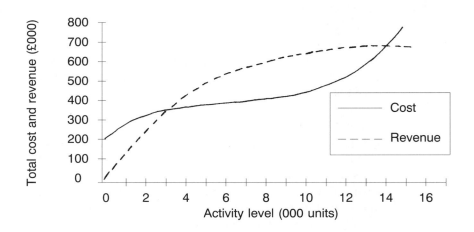

The total revenue starts at zero when there is zero activity. It rises rapidly when supply begins and customers are willing to pay relatively high prices for the goods. Then, as supply increases, the marginal selling price of each item decreases progressively as it becomes more difficult to sell larger volumes of output. Where the total revenue line is below the total cost line the business is making a loss, and where the total revenue line is above the total cost line the business is making a profit. The business represented by the graph in exhibit 9.2 shows losses at the left-hand and right-hand sides of the diagram and a profit in the centre. Successful businesses aim to stay in the profit-making region.

The accountant's view

The graph in exhibit 9.2 represents activity level changes which could take some time to achieve as the business grows. The accountant takes a much shorter time perspective and looks at a relatively limited range of activity that might be achieved within that time period. In those circumstances, it may be reasonable to use straight line graphs rather than curves, although great care is needed before assuming it is safe to use straight lines.

Exhibit 9.3
Variable cost

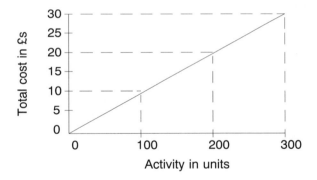

Exhibit 9.4
Fixed cost

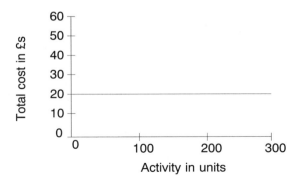

In exhibits 9.3 and 9.4 there are set out graphs for fixed cost and variable cost. The data from which each of these graphs was constructed is shown in exhibit 9.5.

Exhibit 9.5
Table of data showing variable and fixed costs

Activity level	0 units	100 units	200 units	300 units
	£	£	£	£
Variable cost	0	10	20	30
Fixed cost	20	20	20	20
Total cost	20	30	40	50

In exhibit 9.6, these two graphs are added together to give a graph of total cost. The total cost starts at £20 and increases by £10 for every 100 units of activity. The total cost line meets the vertical axis at the fixed cost amount of £20. The slope of the total cost line gives a picture of how fast the variable costs are rising as activity level increases.

Exhibit 9.6
Total cost

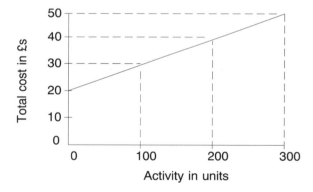

The profit of the business is measured by comparing costs with revenues. Here again, the accountant takes the view that it may be reasonable, over a short time-scale and relatively limited range of activity, to use a straight line. In exhibit 9.7, a sales line is added based on a selling price of 30 pence per unit, so that total sales are £30 for 100 units, £60 for 200 units and £90 for 300 units.

The sales line is below the cost line at the left-hand side of the graph, crossing the cost line when the activity is 100 units. This shows that for activity levels below 100 units the business will make a loss. At 100 units of activity the business makes neither profit nor loss. This is called the *breakeven point*. Beyond

100 units of activity the business makes a profit and the amount of profit is measured by the vertical difference between the sales and cost lines.

The graph shown in exhibit 9.7 is more commonly called a *breakeven* chart. It shows the activity level at which total costs equal total sales and at which the business makes neither a profit nor a loss. It also shows what happens to costs and revenues on either side of this breakeven point. If activity falls below the breakeven level, then the amount of loss will be measured by the vertical distance between the cost and sales line.

Exhibit 9.7
Total cost and total sales

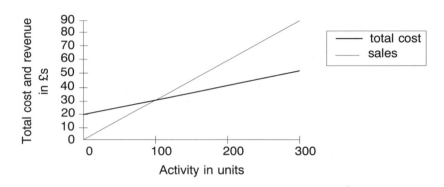

| Definition | The *breakeven point* is that point of activity (measured as sales volume) where total sales and total cost are equal, so that there is neither profit nor loss. |

If activity rises above the breakeven level then the amount of profit will be measured by the vertical distance between the sales and cost line. If the business is operating at an activity level higher than the breakeven point, the distance between these two points is called the *margin of safety*. The margin of safety indicates how much activity has to fall from its present level before profit becomes zero.

| Definition | The *margin of safety* is the difference between the breakeven sales and the normal level of sales (measured in units or in £s of sales). |

Exhibit 9.8
The features of a breakeven chart

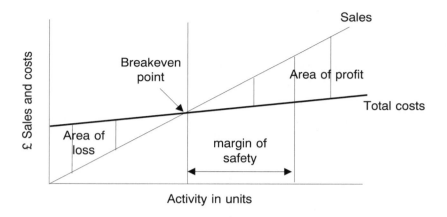

Exhibit 9.8 summarises the various features of a breakeven chart. The use of a chart of this type to depict the behaviour of costs and sales over a range of activity in the short-term has been found extremely helpful in presenting management accounting information to non-financial managers who are involved in making decisions which have financial consequences.

9.3   Breakeven analysis

Breakeven analysis is a technique of management accounting which is based on calculating the breakeven point and analysing the consequences of changes in various factors calculating the breakeven point. Before moving on to aspects of that analysis, this section will first indicate ways of finding the breakeven point. The following case study shows how the breakeven point may be determined by algebra, by formula or by a graph.

9.3.1   Case study: market trader

Case study data
A market trader rents a stall at a fixed price of £200 for a day and sells souvenirs. These cost the trader 50 pence each to buy and have a selling price of 90 pence each. How many souvenirs must be sold to break even?

Activity 9.2

> Hopefully, you will find the case study so easy to solve that you will already have computed the answer. If so, then analyse how you arrived at the answer before you read the next paragraphs and compare your method with the descriptions given there. It is always better to work out a method for yourself, if it is a good one, than to try remembering something from a book.

Algebraic method

The equation for the breakeven point is:

Sales	equals	**Fixed costs + Variable costs**

If the number of souvenirs sold at the breakeven point is n, then the total sales revenue is $0.9n$ and the total variable cost is $0.5n$:

$$0.9n = 200 + 0.5n$$
$$0.4n = 200$$

Solving the equation, $n = 500$ souvenirs to be sold to break even.

Formula method

In Chapter 8, the word 'contribution' was used. The *contribution* from a product is the amount by which its selling price exceeds its variable cost. The idea of contribution is central to breakeven analysis in evaluating the effects of various decisions.

Definition

> *Contribution per unit* is the sales price per unit minus the variable cost per unit. It measures the contribution made by each item of output to the fixed costs and profit of the organisation.

Once the contribution per unit is known it can be compared with the fixed costs. The business does not begin to make a profit until the fixed costs are covered, so the formula is applied as:

Breakeven point	equals	**Fixed costs** / **Contribution per unit**

Taking the data from the illustration, the contribution is 40 pence per souvenir (selling price 90 pence minus variable cost 50 pence) and the fixed costs are £200:

$$\text{Breakeven point} = \frac{200}{0.40} = 500 \text{ units}$$

Graphical method

The general appearance of a breakeven chart has already been shown in exhibit 9.8. To plot the graph some points on each line are necessary. Because they are all straight lines only two points are needed, together with a ruler and pencil to join them. Points on a graph may be defined by specifying two co-ordinates in the form (x, y). A point defined as (10, 100) means that it lies at the intersection of a line up from 10 on the horizontal (x) axis and a line across from 100 on the vertical (y) axis. In Exhibit 9.9, two points are plotted, namely, (10,100) and (30,300). These may then be joined by a straight line.

Exhibit 9.9
Plotting points for a graph

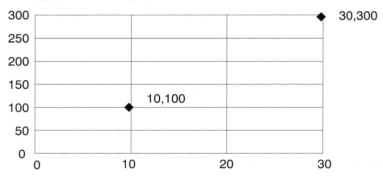

The graph needs to cover an activity scale wide enough to show both sides of the breakeven point, so it is a useful idea to work round the breakeven point by choosing one point which is loss-making and one point which is profit-making. The point of zero activity will usually be loss-making because there is nil revenue but there are fixed costs. So the start of the sales line can be plotted at (0, 0) and the start of the cost line at (0, £200). For a position of profit, the sales and total cost must be calculated for a higher activity level, which in this case might be 900 souvenirs:

Sales of 900 souvenirs at 90 pence each = £810

The sales line will therefore join the points (0, £0) and (900, £810):

		£
Variable cost of 900 souvenirs at 50 pence each	=	450
Fixed cost	=	200
Total cost		650

The total cost line joins (0, £200) and (900, £650). Exhibit 9.10 shows the breakeven chart with a breakeven point at 500 units sold. Gridlines are added to show the points plotted.

**Exhibit 9.10
Breakeven chart**

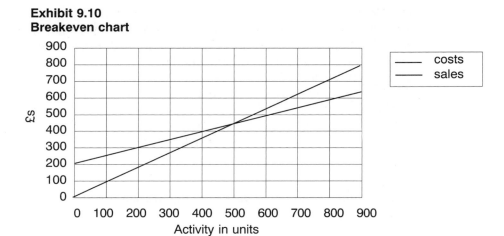

9.3.2 Profit–volume graph

Profit is an important aspect of most management accounting reports. However, the breakeven chart does not show directly the amount of profit. It has to be estimated by measuring the vertical distance between the sales and total cost lines. There is another form of graph used in management accounting called a *profit–volume* graph. On the horizontal axis is plotted the volume, measured by activity level in £s of sales, and on the vertical axis is plotted the profit at that activity level.

The activity level is measured in £s of sales in order that the slope of the graph matches the *profit/volume ratio*, a slightly confusing name for the ratio which calculates contribution as a percentage of sales value:

Profit/volume ratio	equals	$\dfrac{\text{Contribution per unit}}{\text{Selling price per unit}} \times 100$

Exhibit 9.11 sets out a diagram showing the main features of a profit–volume chart.

**Exhibit 9.11
Profit–volume chart**

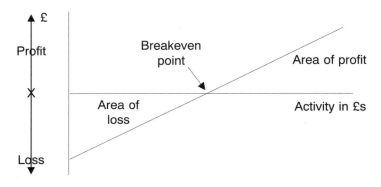

Illustration

Taking the data used in preparing exhibit 9.10, the preparation of a profit–volume graph requires only the profit line to be drawn. When sales are zero, there will be a loss equal to the fixed cost, which gives the first point to plot at (£0, £–200). When 900 units are sold the sales are £810 and the profit is £160, giving the second point to plot at (£810, £160). The result is shown in Exhibit 9.12.The gridlines are included to show where the profit line has been plotted. The breakeven point of zero profit or loss is at a sales level of £450. The graph rises by £40 of profit for every £90 increase in sales activity, giving a slope of 44.4 per cent.

Exhibit 9.12
Profit–volume chart using data from the 'Market trader' case study

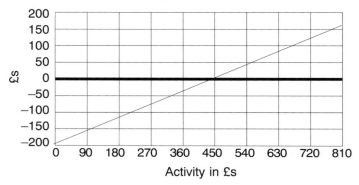

The profit/volume ratio is calculated by formula as:

$$\frac{\text{Contribution per unit}}{\text{Sales price per unit}} = \frac{40 \text{ pence}}{90 \text{ pence}} = 44.4\%$$

9.4 Using breakeven analysis

It was stated earlier that breakeven analysis is a very useful tool. It may be used to answer questions of the following type:

- What level of sales is necessary to cover fixed costs and make a specified profit?
- What is the effect of contribution per unit beyond the breakeven point?
- What happens to the breakeven point when the selling price of one unit changes?
- What happens to the breakeven point when the variable cost per unit changes?
- What happens to the breakeven point when the fixed costs change?

Each of these questions is now dealt with in this section by an illustration and an explanation following the illustration.

9.4.1 Covering fixed costs and making a profit

To find the level of sales necessary to cover fixed costs and make a specified profit requires a knowledge of selling price per unit, variable cost per unit, and the fixed costs together with the desired profit. These are set out in the data table.

Data	
Selling price per unit	80 pence
Variable cost per unit	30 pence
Fixed cost	£300
Desired level of profit	£400

The contribution per unit is 50 pence (80 pence – 30 pence). To find the breakeven point, the fixed costs of £300 are divided by the contribution per unit to obtain a breakeven point of 600 units.

To meet fixed costs of £300 and desired profit of £400 requires the contribution to cover £700 in all. This is achieved by selling 1,400 units.

$$\text{Volume of sales required} = \frac{700}{0.5} = 1,400 \text{ units}$$

Activity 9.3

Check that 1,400 units at a contribution of 50 pence each gives a total contribution of £700. It is always a useful precaution to check the arithmetic of a calculation as a safeguard against carelessness.

9.4.2 Beyond the breakeven point

Beyond the breakeven point the fixed costs are covered and the sales of further units are making a contribution to profit. The higher the contribution per unit, the greater the profit from any particular level of activity. The data table sets out some information on selling prices, variable costs and fixed costs of two products.

Data

A dry-cleaning shop takes two types of clothing. Jackets cost £6 to clean and the customer is charged £9 per garment. Coats cost £10 to clean and the customer is charged £12 per garment. The monthly fixed costs are £600 for each type of garment (representing the rental costs of two different types of machine). The shop expects to clean 500 jackets and 500 coats each month.

Activity 9.4

Before reading the analysis in exhibit 9.13, calculate the contribution made by each product, work out the breakeven point of each, and then explore the effect on the breakeven point of:

(a) changes in the price charged to customers;
(b) changes in the variable costs; and
(c) changes in the fixed costs.

If you have access to a spreadsheet package this is the kind of problem for which spreadsheets are highly suitable.

The calculations set out in exhibit 9.13 show that, although both products have the same fixed costs, the jackets have a lower breakeven point because they make a higher contribution per unit. Beyond the breakeven point they continue to contribute more per unit. The profits at any given level of activity are therefore higher for jackets.

Exhibit 9.13
Calculation of breakeven point and of sales beyond the breakeven point

	Jackets	Coats
	£	£
Selling price	9	12
Variable cost	6	10
Contribution per item	3	2
Fixed costs	600	600
Breakeven point	200 units	300 units
Profit for sales of 500 units	900	400

9.4.3 Change in selling price

If the selling price per unit increases and costs remain constant, then the contribution per unit will increase and the breakeven volume will be lower. Take as an example the dry-cleaning business of the previous illustration. If the selling price of cleaning a coat rises to £15, then the contribution per unit will rise to £5. That will require cleaning only 120 coats to break even. The risk of raising the price is that customers may move elsewhere, so that while it may not be difficult to exceed the breakeven point at a selling price of £12 it may be extremely difficult at a selling price of £15.

9.4.4 Change in variable cost

The effect of a change in variable cost is very similar to the effect of a change in selling price. If the variable cost per unit increases, then the contribution per unit will decrease, with the result that more items will have to be sold in order to reach the breakeven point. If it is possible to reduce variable costs, then the contribution per unit will increase. The enterprise will reach the breakeven point at a lower level of activity and will then be earning profits at a faster rate.

9.4.5 Change in fixed costs

If fixed costs increase, then more units have to be sold in order to reach the breakeven point. Where the fixed costs of an operation are relatively high, there is a perception of greater risk because a cutback in activity for any reason is more likely to lead to a loss. Where an organisation has relatively low fixed costs, there may be less concern about margins of safety because the breakeven point is correspondingly lower.

9.5 Limitations of breakeven analysis

Breakeven analysis is a useful tool for problem solving and decision making, but some of the limitations should be noted:

1 the breakeven analysis assumes that cost and revenue behaviour patterns are known and that the change in activity levels can be represented by a straight line;
2 it may not always be feasible to split costs neatly into variable and fixed categories. Some costs show mixed behaviour;
3 the breakeven analysis assumes that fixed costs remain constant over the volume range under consideration. If that is not the case, then the graph of total costs will have a step in it where the fixed costs are expected to increase;
4 breakeven analysis, as described so far in this book, assumes input and output volumes are the same, so that there is no build-up of stocks and work-in-progress;
5 breakeven charts and simple analyses can only deal with one product at a time;
6 it is assumed that cost behaviour depends entirely on volume.

These limitations may be overcome by modifying the breakeven analysis. However, that would involve considerably more computation work and is beyond the scope of this textbook.

9.6 Applications of contribution analysis

Breakeven analysis is a particular example of the more general technique of contribution analysis. This analysis emphasises the relationship between sales

245

revenue, costs and profit in the short term. In this context the short term is a period of time over which some costs are fixed, whatever the level of output within a range limited by the existing capacity of the business. In the longer term, all costs become variable because the capacity of a business can be altered by acquiring new premises, hiring more employees or investing in more equipment.

In using contribution analysis, management accounting is meeting the needs of directing attention and solving problems. In the short term, decisions have to be made within the existing constraints of the capacity of the business and the aim of that decision making will be to maximise short-term profit. Typical decision-making situations requiring contribution analysis would be:

- accepting a special order to use up spare capacity
- abandoning a line of business
- the existence of a limiting factor
- carrying out an activity in-house rather than buy in a service under contract.

Each of these situations is now considered in turn.

Activity 9.5	*Those who comment on the applications of contribution analysis always emphasise that it is a short-run decision making tool. Write a 200-word note explaining this view.*

9.6.1 Special order to use up spare capacity

In the short term, a business must ensure that the revenue from each item of activity at least covers variable costs and makes a contribution to fixed costs. Once the fixed costs are covered by contribution, the greater the level of activity, the higher the profit. When the business reaches full capacity there will be a new element of fixed cost to consider should the business decide to increase its capacity. If there is no increase in capacity, then the business should concentrate on those activities producing the highest contribution per unit or per item.

But supposing the business is *not* operating at full capacity. Should it lower its sales price in an attempt to increase the volume of activity? The question may arise in the form of a request from a customer for a special price for a particular order. (Customers may well know that the business is not operating at full capacity and may therefore try to use their bargaining power to force a lower sales price.) Should the business accept the special order? Contribution analysis gives the answer that the special order is acceptable provided the sales price per item covers the variable costs per item and provided there is no alternative use for the spare capacity which could result in a higher contribution per item.

9.6.2 Abandonment of a line of business

The management of a business may be concerned because one line of business appears not to be covering all its costs. This situation may arise particularly where costs are being used for score-keeping purposes and all fixed costs have been allocated to products. As was shown in Chapter 3, the allocation of fixed costs to products is a process which is somewhat arbitrary in nature, and is not relevant to decision making because the fixed costs are incurred irrespective of whether any business activity takes place.

When a line of business comes under scrutiny as to its profitability, contribution analysis shows that in the short term it is worth continuing if it makes a contribution to fixed costs. If the line of business is abandoned and nothing better takes its place, then that contribution is lost but the fixed costs run on regardless.

9.6.3 Existence of a limiting factor

In the short term, it may be that one of the inputs to a business activity is restricted in its availability. There may be a shortage of raw materials or a limited supply of skilled labour. There may be a delivery delay on machinery or a planning restriction which prevents the extension of a building on the business premises. There may then be a need to choose from a range of possible activities so as to maximise short-term profit. The item which is restricted in availability is called the *limiting factor*.

Contribution analysis shows that maximisation of profit will occur if the activity is chosen which gives the highest contribution per unit of limiting factor.

9.6.4 In-house activity versus bought-in contract

For a manufacturing business, there may be a decision between making a component in-house as compared with buying the item ready-made. For a service business there may be a decision between employing staff in-house and using the services of an agency which supplies staff as and when required. Contribution analysis shows that the decision should be based on comparison of variable costs per unit, relating this to the difference in fixed costs between the options.

9.7 Short-term decision making

Contribution analysis is particularly well suited to management needs in short-term decision making. Fiona McTaggart now discusses four cases she has come across where contribution analysis has been relevant. The first relates to a decision about taking on a special order to fill a gap where the business was not running at full capacity. The second relates to a potential abandonment of a line of business, the third deals with a limiting factor causing scarcity of an input to the production process, and the fourth relates to buying in services.

9.7.1 Decisions on special orders

FIONA: *My first story is about a car hire business in a holiday resort which was experiencing a temporary fall in activity in the run up to the start of the tourist season. Their normal charge was £1.50 per mile, to cover all costs including the driver's wages.*

Exhibit 9.14
Analysis of variable and fixed costs of car hire firm

Variable costs:	
Petrol	60 pence per litre
Fuel consumption	6 miles per litre
Tyre costs	£800 per set of four tyres
Tyre replacement	every 20,000 miles
Fixed costs:	£42,000
These covered:	
Driver's wages	
Insurance	
Licence fee for airport waiting	
Licence fee to town council	
Depreciation of vehicle	
Annual testing	
Radio control membership	
Average annual mileage per car:	40,000 miles

A telephone installation company offered a three-month contract to run engineers between two towns on a return journey of 100 miles, at a fixed price of £90 per journey. The car hire company asked my advice about accepting this offer of 90 pence per mile.

I asked the company what the drivers and cars would be doing each day if the contract was not taken up and the answer was that they would not be doing anything other than waiting at the depot and cleaning their cars. My advice was that, on that basis, the contract would be worth undertaking if it covered the variable costs of each journey and made a contribution to fixed costs and profit.

We sat down to look at the fixed costs and produced the statement shown in exhibit 9.14. Quite deliberately I did not write any amounts against the separate items of fixed costs because I wanted to emphasise that these are the unavoidable element which will arise whether or not the contract is taken up.

From the data provided, I calculated the variable cost per mile as 10 pence for petrol and 4 pence for tyres, giving 14 pence in all. The normal charge of £1.50 per mile is intended to cover this 14 pence per mile plus the fixed cost per mile, amounting to £1.05 per mile using the average annual mileage per car. That total cost of £1.19 per mile leaves a profit of 31 pence per mile or £12,400 per annum if the average mileage is achieved.

It is clear that to cover all costs the charge of £1.50 is probably about right, but if the drivers and cars are otherwise unoccupied, extra journeys contribute £1.36 per mile (£1.50 − £0.14) to fixed costs and profit. I advised them to take up the contract on two conditions:

1 they must be as sure as they could be that there will not be an upturn in business during the hire period which would mean they were turning down the possibility of carrying passengers who would pay £1.50 per mile; and

2 *if the journeys involve extra payments to drivers for overtime or late-night work, those extra payments should be regarded as part of the variable cost of the contract and the costings recalculated on that basis.*

They took my advice and carried out the contract. It fitted perfectly into the quiet period of business and the company realised later that the contract had made a useful contribution to profit at a time when drivers and cars would otherwise have been inactive.

In Fiona's example, the company made use of the idea that, in the short term, any contract is worth taking on if it covers variable costs and makes some contribution to fixed costs and profit. Care needs to be taken that the special order does not create a precedent for future work, particularly if existing customers find that special treatment is being given which appears to undercut the price they are paying. The company may find it difficult in future to return to the price which covers all costs. In the long term, the company must charge a price which covers fixed costs as well as variable costs if it is to survive.

Fiona's second illustration relates to a decision on abandoning a line of activity.

9.7.2 Abandonment decisions

FIONA: *A private tuition college was providing two types of secretarial training course. The first was teaching wordprocessing and the second was teaching office skills. The college had produced the profit and loss statement shown in exhibit 9.15.*

Exhibit 9.15
Information for abandonment decision

	Wordprocessing £000s	Office skills £000s	Total £000s
Tuition fee income	485	500	985
Variable costs	200	330	530
Fixed overhead	120	220	340
Total costs	320	550	870
Profit/(loss)	165	(50)	115

On the basis of this profit and loss statement the owners of the business were on the point of cancelling all further courses in office skills. I asked them how they had decided on the allocation of fixed overheads and they explained that these comprised primarily administrative staff costs and permanent teaching staff, plus items such as rent and business rates as well as depreciation of wordprocessors and of the equipment used in the cabin which had been set up to simulate the most up-to-date office conditions. The cabin itself was depreciated over twenty years. Fixed overhead which could be allocated directly to the relevant courses, such as depreciation of equipment, was allocated in its entirety to the relevant course type. This approach was also used for teaching costs where these were specific to one course type. Fixed overhead which could apply to each type of course, such as administrative staff salaries, was spread in proportion to the number of courses given.

I pointed out to the owners that their profit and loss statement would be more informative if it were set out in the format shown in exhibit 9.16.

Exhibit 9.16
Revised data for abandonment decision

	Wordprocessing £000s	Office skills £000s	Total £000s
Tuition fee income	485	500	985
Variable costs	200	330	530
Contribution	285	170	455
Fixed overhead			340
Profit			115

From exhibit 9.16 it is relatively straightforward to see that the office skills programme is making a contribution of £170,000 to fixed costs and profit, after covering its own variable costs. If the programme were not offered, then the business would have only the contribution of £285,000 from word processing which would not cover the fixed overhead of £340,000. Far from abandoning the office skills programme, it was essential to retain it. The allocation of fixed overheads was, for short-term analysis purposes, irrelevant. The cabin and office equipment had already been purchased and would continue to depreciate whether used or not. If put up for sale, these assets would have a negligible value. Administrative and permanent staff were also in place and could not instantly be disengaged.

I advised them that while it was preferable in the short term to keep both programmes running, there were some questions they should ask themselves for longer-term planning:

1   To what extent do clients take up the wordprocessing courses because office skills may be learned at the same time and in the same place?
2   How much fixed cost could be avoided in the longer term if either course ceased to exist?
3   Would it be a more effective use of resources to concentrate only on one type of course so that the fixed costs are restricted to one type of equipment and perhaps relatively fewer administrative staff?

The answers might lead to reorganisation towards one type of course only. On the other hand, it might be found that the two programmes are so interrelated that each needs the other and the fixed costs are effectively essential to both, whatever the accounting allocation process.

Fiona's third story concerns a business where there was a restriction in the amount of a factor of input to the production process.

9.7.3 Existence of limiting factors

FIONA: *A kitchen equipment service company had come across a problem of a shortage of trained engineers in a district because new oil exploration activity had attracted the best staff by making offers of high salaries.*

On a short-term basis the company felt it could not continue to service washing machines, dishwashers and built-in ovens in that area and would prefer to concentrate the most profitable use of its labour resource. Exhibit 9.17 shows the most recent annual data available, based on the situation before the employee shortage crisis arose. However, the total labour force now available was estimated in cost terms at £20,000 in total.

Exhibit 9.17
Data for limiting factor problem

	Washing machines £000s	Dishwashers £000s	Built-in ovens £000s
Sales	40	60	90
Direct materials	5	10	9
Direct labour	15	15	30
Variable overhead	5	15	15
Total variable cost	25	40	54
Contribution	15	20	36

I advised them that, in these circumstances, the limiting factor of labour should be used so as to maximise the contribution from every £ of labour used. First, I calculated the contribution per £ of scarce resource for each of the three types of service contract (see exhibit 9.18).

Exhibit 9.18
Calculation of contribution per £ of limiting factor

	Washing machines £000s	Dishwashers £000s	Built-in ovens £000s
Contribution	15	20	36
Direct labour	15	15	30
Contribution per £ of labour	£1.00	£1.33	£1.20

The highest contribution per £ of labour is therefore provided by dishwashers, followed by built-in ovens. So I explained that it would be best to use the scarce labour resource first of all to service dishwashers. At the existing level of sales that would take up £15,000 worth of labour, leaving the balance of £5,000 worth of labour to service built-in ovens on a restricted basis. If more dishwasher work became available, that would be the preferred choice for profit generation.

This would be a short-term solution, but in the longer term it would be essential to consider whether the market could stand higher charges for servicing equipment, which would allow higher wage rates to be paid and thus permit all three types of work to continue.

Fiona has used in this example a particular case of a general principle that where limiting factors apply, profit is made as high as possible where the greatest contribution is obtained each time the scarce resource is used.

In her fourth example, Fiona describes a situation where a company was considering buying in services rather than employing its own staff.

9.7.4 In-house activity versus bought-in services

FIONA: *A company had been employing its own legal department, comprising a qualified solicitor and two assistants. The solicitor was about to retire and the company had to decide whether to advertise for a replacement or to use a commercial law service as and when required. There would be no redundancy costs in respect of the two assistants because the younger one could be redeployed to a vacancy elsewhere in the organisation and the other would continue to be required as the internal contact with the commercial law service.*

I showed the management that, because the commercial law service would charge on an hourly basis, the costs to be compared were the variable costs per hour charged by the commercial service and the fixed costs per annum of the in-house solicitor's salary. We compared the hourly charge rate of £200 with the solicitor's salary of £30,000 and the assistant's salary of £18,000 and worked out that the breakeven point would be 240 hours of the commercial law service each year. If more than 240 hours are requested next year, it would be worth continuing the in-house service.

9.8 Pricing decisions

One of the most important decisions taken by a business is that of pricing its product. If the price is too high, there will be no demand. If the price is too low, the organisation will be making a lower profit than could be achieved.

9.8.1 Economic factors affecting pricing

The method of arriving at a price depends on economic factors. If the business has a monopoly position (where one supplier has control of the market), it will be able to dictate its own price. However, the higher the price, the greater the attraction to incomers to break down the monopoly powers in seeking to share the benefits enjoyed by the monopolist.

Where the business is a market leader, it may be able to set its price by reference to covering its full costs and making a satisfactory profit. If there are only a few large sellers, each with a significant share of the market, the situation is described as an oligopoly. These few large sellers may compete with each other on price or they may prefer to set their prices at a level which covers all costs and to keep the price reasonably constant while competing on non-price factors such as quality of the product.

In the perfectly competitive market, no one supplier is in a position to dictate prices. Economic theory shows that the optimal price will be achieved where marginal cost equals marginal revenue. In other words, the additional cost of producing one more item of output equals the additional revenue obtained by selling that item. While the additional revenue exceeds the additional cost, the economist argues that it is worth producing more. When the additional revenue is less than the additional cost, production will not take place in the perfectly competitive market.

Pricing policy therefore depends primarily on the circumstances of the business. In many situations there is strong competition and the organisation must accept the market price and try to maximise its profit by controlling cost. In that situation, the most efficient organisation will achieve the highest profit as a percentage of sales. Sometimes the organisation may be faced with pressure from customers to reduce selling price. The decision to do so will require an evaluation of the lower price against costs. In other cases, the organisation may have some ability to control price and therefore has to decide on a price related to what the market will bear and related to covering its costs.

There are therefore some situations in which a cost-based pricing formula may be appropriate. These are now considered.

9.8.2 Cost-based pricing

The most readily available cost-based approach to pricing is to calculate the total cost per unit of output and add a percentage to that cost called the *percentage mark-up on cost.*

Calculation of total cost requires allocation of overhead costs. It was shown in Chapter 3 that there is more than one method of allocating production overhead costs. The same variety of method may be found in allocation of non-production overhead. Different organisations will have different ideas on which costs they want to cover in a cost-based pricing approach. What really matters is that the organisation understands its cost structure and ensures that all overhead costs are covered in some way by revenue in the longer term.

When the company is a price taker and is asked to take a lower price, or not to raise its existing price, then cost-plus pricing is still important, but it is also important for the organisation to ensure that it makes a decision using *relevant costs.* If the pricing decision is based on a short-term perspective, then the organisation may decide to accept any price provided that the additional revenue covers the variable costs. That is the accountant's version of the economist's rule that marginal cost should equal marginal revenue. In management accounting terms, the item should make a *contribution* to fixed costs but does not necessarily need to cover all fixed costs. In the longer term, the business must cover all costs, whether fixed or variable, but it is possible that some fixed costs may be avoidable. If, for example, a reduced price is forced upon the business, it may accept this in the short term but also take a long-term decision to cut back on permanent staff and rental of premises. Such a decision may be unpleasant to take, in terms of human consequences for staff, but may allow the business to survive in a harsher economic situation.

Definition	*Relevant costs* are those future costs which will be affected by a decision to be taken. Non-relevant costs will not be affected by the decision.

9.8.3 Mark-up percentages

The cost-based approach to pricing requires a percentage to be added to cost. Where does this percentage come from? The answer is that it depends very much on the type of business and the type of product. Where the market is competitive, mark-up percentages will be low and the organisation relies for its success on a high volume of sales activity. This may be seen in the operation of supermarkets, which charge lower prices than the small shops and therefore have lower margins on the items sold, but customers take away their purchases by the car load rather than in small parcels. In the case of supermarket chains there is another aspect to pricing in that they themselves buy from suppliers. The supermarkets may use the strength of their position to dictate price terms to the suppliers, so that the margins are not as low as they would seem from the prices charged to the customers.

In some industries, or for some products, there appears to be a 'normal' for the mark-up which all companies apply fairly closely. This 'normal' mark-up may be so characteristic that it is used by the auditor as a check on how reasonable the gross profit amount appears and is also used by the tax authorities as a check on whether all sales and profit are being declared for taxation purposes.

For those businesses which are in a position to apply cost-plus pricing, it may encourage stability in the pricing structure because other businesses in the same industry may be in a position to predict the behaviour of competitors. Companies in an industry will know the mix of variable and fixed costs in the industry and will therefore have a good idea of how competitors' profits will be affected by a change of price.

9.8.4 Limitations of cost-plus pricing

Cost-plus pricing, used without sufficient care, may not take into account the demand for the product. A business may charge a mark-up of 20 per cent on sales when market research could have shown that the potential customers would have accepted up to 25 per cent as a mark-up and still bought the goods or services.

Apportionment of fixed costs is an arbitrary process, with more than one approach being available. The profit estimated using the cost-plus basis will depend on the apportionment of fixed costs. If the price is distorted by the costing process, an optimal level of sales may not be achieved.

There may be a lack of benefit to customers where businesses are able to set prices on a cost-plus basis and, as a consequence, a group of companies works together to 'agree' a price. Such a situation is described in economics as a 'cartel', and in some situations a government will legislate against price-fixing by cartels because it creates a monopoly position in a situation which appears at first sight to be competitive.

Activity 9.6

> *Write down two products or services where the pricing might be based on cost plus a percentage to cover profits. Write down two products or services where the prices are determined in a highly competitite market. Write a short explanation (200 words) for an employee newsletter in a soap manufacturing business explaining why your product price is always a few pence higher in the shops than that of other leading brands.*

9.9 Absorption costing and variable costing

In discussing pricing policy the problem of allocating overhead costs has been mentioned. The problems of allocating fixed production overheads were explained in detail in Chapter 3. Because of the allocation problems, there are situations in management accounting where it is preferable to avoid the problem by allocating only variable costs to products. Fixed costs are regarded as costs of the period rather than costs of the product. The question to be addressed in this section is how the choice between absorption costing (which means absorbing all costs into products) and variable costing (which means allocating only to the variable costs of production) may be dependent on the purpose to which management accounting is being applied.

Definitions

> In *absorption costing*, all production costs are allocated to products and the unsold stock is measured at total cost of production.
>
> In *variable costing*, only variable costs of production are allocated to products and the unsold stock is measured at variable cost of production. Fixed production costs are treated as a cost of the period in which they are incurred.

9.9.1 A note on terminology

Some authors refer to 'marginal costing' rather than 'variable costing' but that is potentially a confusing term because the economists use 'marginal costing' to refer to the extra cost of making one more item. From the economists' viewpoint, that extra cost could include fixed cost if capacity has to be expanded or a new employee is required. It is safer to refer to 'variable cost' throughout a management accounting approach.

9.9.2 Illustration of the two approaches

Take the example of a business planning its operations for five trading periods. Data regarding budgeted selling price, budgeted variable cost per unit and fixed production overheads is given in exhibit 9.19, together with budgeted volumes of production and sales over the next five periods of production. The question to be answered is, 'How much profit is expected for each of the five trading periods?'

Exhibit 9.19
Data for illustration of absorption versus variable costing

	£
Selling price per unit	20
Variable cost per unit	9
Fixed costs for each period	500

	Period 1 units	Period 2 units	Period 3 units	Period 4 units	Period 5 units
Produced	230	270	260	240	250
Sold	200	210	260	280	300
Held in stock at end of period	30	90	90	50	nil

Under absorption costing the first task is to decide how the fixed costs for each period should be allocated to products. Where production volume is varying in the manner shown in exhibit 9.19, a common practice is to base the predetermined overhead cost rate on the normal level of activity. In this case, it might be reasonable to take a normal level of activity as the average production level, which is 250 units per period. The predetermined fixed overhead cost rate is therefore £2 per unit.

9.9.3 Absorption costing

Under absorption costing the opening and closing stock is valued at total cost of £11 per unit, comprising variable cost per unit of £9 and fixed cost per unit of £2. Exhibit 9.20 illustrates the absorption costing approach.

Activity 9.7

Go back to the data of exhibit 9.19. Cover up the answer in exhibit 9.20 and then attempt to write out the profit calculation under absorption costing. Add a note of narrative explanation to each line as a means of helping understanding by yourself and others. Make sure that you understand the absorption costing approach fully.

Exhibit 9.20
Profit per period under absorption costing

	Period 1	Period 2	Period 3	Period 4	Period 5	Total
	£	£	£	£	£	£
Opening stock	nil	330	990	990	550	nil
Cost of production:						
Variable cost	2,070	2,430	2,340	2,160	2,250	11,250
Fixed cost	500	500	500	500	500	2,500
Closing stock	(330)	(990)	(990)	(550)	nil	nil
Cost of goods sold	2,240	2,270	2,840	3,100	3,300	13,750
Sales	4,000	4,200	5,200	5,600	6,000	25,000
Gross profit	1,760	1,930	2,360	2,500	2,700	11,250

9.9.4 Variable costing

Using variable costing, the stock of unsold output at the end of each period would be valued at the variable cost of £9 per unit. The fixed cost would be regarded as a cost of the period, without allocation to products. Exhibit 9.21 illustrates the variable costing approach.

Exhibit 9.21
Profit per period under variable costing

	Period 1	Period 2	Period 3	Period 4	Period 5	Total
	£	£	£	£	£	£
Opening stock	nil	270	810	810	450	nil
Cost of production	2,070	2,430	2,340	2,160	2,250	11,250
Closing stock	(270)	(810)	(810)	(450)	nil	nil
Cost of goods sold	1,800	1,890	2,340	2,520	2,700	11,250
Fixed costs of period	500	500	500	500	500	2500
Total costs	2,300	2,390	2,840	3,020	3,200	13,750
Sales	4,000	4,200	5,200	5,600	6,000	25,000
Gross profit	1,700	1,810	2,360	2,580	2,800	11,250

Activity 9.8

Look back at the data of exhibit 9.19. Before turning to the answer in exhibit 9.21 attempt to write out the profit calculation under variable costing. Add a note of narrative explanation to each line as a means of helping understanding by yourself and others. Make sure that you understand the variable costing approach fully before proceeding to absorption costing.

9.9.5 Comparison of profit under each approach

Exhibit 9.22 compares the profit calculated under each approach. The first point to note from exhibit 9.22 is that over the total period of time, where total production equals total sales, there is no difference in total profit. The difference between absorption costing and variable costing is purely a result of timing of the matching of fixed overhead with products.

Exhibit 9.22
Comparison of profit, using variable costing and absorption costing

	Period 1 £	Period 2 £	Period 3 £	Period 4 £	Period 5 £	Total £
Variable costing	1,700	1,810	2,360	2,580	2,800	11,250
Absorption costing	1,760	1,930	2,360	2,500	2,700	11,250
Difference	+60	+120	0	−80	−100	0

Activity 9.9

Before reading the rest of this section, write a brief commentary on the most significant features of exhibit 9.22.

The second point to note is that the differences between the two profit calculations are based entirely on the *change* in volume of stock during the period, multiplied by the fixed overhead cost rate of £2 per unit. During period 1, stock increases by 30 units over the period and, as a consequence, profit under absorption costing is £60 higher than under variable costing. During period 2, stock increases by 60 units over the period and, as a consequence, profit under absorption costing is £120 higher. During period 3 stock levels remain constant and therefore both approaches give the same answer. During period 4, stock levels decrease by 40 units so that profit under absorption costing is £80 lower. During period 5, stock levels decrease by 50 units and therefore profit under absorption costing is £100 lower.

The third point to note is that the overall effect of the positive and negative differences over the business life is zero, provided the allocation process is applied consistently. Different allocation processes will cause costs to fall in different time periods, but they cannot create or destroy costs in the total.

Finally, the effect of the change in stock levels may be understood using exhibit 9.22. Making a general statement from this specific example, it appears safe to say that when stock levels are increasing, profit under absorption costing is higher than it is under variable costing. That is because a portion of the fixed production cost incurred in the period is carried forward to the next period as part of the closing stock valuation.

Generalising further from the analysis, it may be said that when stock levels are decreasing, profit under absorption costing is lower than it is under variable costing. That is because fixed costs incurred in earlier periods are brought to the current period as part of the opening stock, to be sold during the period.

When stock levels are constant, both approaches give the same answer.

9.9.6 Why is it necessary to understand the difference?

In Chapter 1 it was shown that management accounting has three major roles in directing attention, keeping the score and solving problems. The particular role which applies in any situation will depend upon the management function which is being served. That management function could relate to the formation of a judgement or to making a decision about a course of action. In Chapter 2 it was shown that the classification of costs is very much dependent on which of the three management accounting roles is the dominant one in any specific situation and on the type of management function.

Where the management function relates to planning and control, the management accountant is carrying out a score-keeping function and it is usually necessary to account for fixed costs of production as a part of the product cost. That means absorption costing is the appropriate approach. In this situation there is a strong overlap with financial accounting and with external reporting to stakeholders in a business. If the stakeholders are company shareholders, then the external reporting will be regulated by company law and accounting standards that require fixed costs of production to be treated as product costs and provide guidance on the allocation process. Where the stakeholders are the electorate, in the case of a public sector body, or partners in a business partnership, the rules may be more flexible, but in many cases they conventionally follow the practice recommended for companies.

9.9.7 Arguments in favour of absorption costing

The arguments put forward in favour of absorption costing are:

1 since all production costs are incurred with a view to creating a product for sale, all costs should attach to products until they are sold;
2 in the longer term, fixed overhead costs must be recovered through sales if the business is to survive. Setting the stock value by reference to full costs encourages a pricing policy which covers full cost;
3 if fixed production costs are treated as period costs (as happens in variable costing) and there is a low level of sales activity in a period, then a relatively low profit or a loss will be reported. If there is a high level of sales activity, there will be a relatively high profit. Absorption costing creates a smoothing of these fluctuations by carrying the fixed costs forward until the goods are sold.

9.9.8 Arguments in favour of variable costing

Where the management accounting role is primarily that of directing attention and the management function is primarily one of decision making, it may be dangerous to regard fixed production costs as product costs. The attractions of using variable costing in such a situation are as follows:

(a) in the short term, relevant costs are required for decision making and fixed overheads are largely non-relevant because they cannot be avoided. They are best seen as a committed cost of the period;

(b) profit calculation is not dependent on changes in stock levels. The illustration in exhibits 9.20 to 9.22 shows the practical effect of disentangling fixed costs from stock values;

(c) there is no risk of carrying forward in stock an element of fixed production overhead cost which may not be recovered through sales;

(d) allocating all production costs to products and then applying full-cost pricing may result in loss of sales which would have made a contribution to fixed production costs and profit;

(e) where sales volumes are declining but output is sustained, variable costing provides the profit warning more rapidly than does absorption costing in a situation where attention needs to be drawn urgently to the profit implications.

Activity 9.10

Now that you understand the difference between variable costing and absorption costing, write a short evaluation of the two approaches.

9.10 Dangers of short-termism

Variable costing is essentially a useful tool of management accounting in relation to short-term management decisions. It is popular with management accounting experts because it avoids the allocation problems of absorption costing, which can be shown to cause incorrect decisions in some short-term situations.

There is a fear, outside the immediate world of management accounting, that business is too dependent on short-term attitudes. Some have blamed this on the influence of financial markets where investors in companies are seeking short-term gains from their investments. Those appointed by them to run the business are therefore presumed to act with the same short-term perspective. Others have said that it is not the fault of the market. Institutional investors may well take a longer-term perspective of an investment. In that case, it is possible that managers are serving their own purpose by taking short-term views, either because their remuneration is dependent on their performance or because they feel under pressure to show improving results in order to justify their appointment.

While this debate on the dangers of short-termism has been taking place in the realm of finance and external reporting, the techniques of management accounting have been moving forward. New approaches have been devised which claim to allow assignment of all costs to products while providing cost information that is relevant to decision making. The best publicised of these new approaches is activity-based costing (ABC), strongly publicised by two US authors, Johnson and Kaplan, as a more refined method of allocating costs to products based on the activity or activities which drive those costs. This will be explained further in Chapter 11.

Other approaches to the short-term problem have been to change the manufacturing systems, strategies and technologies. Many of these ideas have originated in countries which are relatively new to manufacturing activity and which have had to build up an international competitive advantage very quickly. These advances in manufacturing technology have been given various titles, such as just-in-time (JIT), optimised production technology (OPT) and materials requirement and resource planning (MRP). Whatever the title, the common feature is that they are all directed towards reducing the time lag between production and sale. Management accounting debates on variable versus absorption costing then become largely irrelevant. New management accounting techniques are required to trace the costs of these new approaches through to product cost. Chapter 11 will review these recent developments and their effect on management accounting.

9.11 Summary

This chapter has considered the decision-making function of management and has explained some of the techniques used traditionally in management accounting to provide information for decision-making purposes. It has consistently made use of the distinction between fixed costs and variable costs. The concept of contribution has been central to the chapter.

The breakeven point – making neither profit nor loss – has been shown by graphical representation and by calculation. Profit–volume charts have been presented as another way of depicting the relationships between costs, revenues and the breakeven point.

Wider applications of contribution analysis in short-term decision making have been illustrated and explained, taking as examples decisions such as: accepting a special order to use up spare capacity; abandonment of a line of business; existence of a limiting factor; and in-house activity versus a bought-in contract.

Pricing decisions may sometimes be related to cost and the chapter has therefore covered those situations where management may have a decision to make on pricing the product or service. Finally, the problem of valuing stock, and its impact on periodic profit, is dealt with by comparing absorption costing with variable costing. The problem is shown to be short-term rather than permanent, but there is a danger that the short-term focus of those who observe the performance of companies may encourage short-termism in accounting methods and presentation. The chapter concluded with some thoughts on short-termism and some indications of the new directions being taken by management accounting.

Further reading

Drury, C. (1992), *Management and Cost Accounting*, Chapman & Hall.

Horngren, C. T., Foster, G. and Datar, S. (1993), *Cost Accounting: A Managerial Emphasis*, Prentice Hall.

Morse, W. J. and Roth, H. P. (1986), *Cost Accounting: Processing, Evaluating and Using Cost Data*, Addison-Wesley.

Wilson, R. M. S. and Chua, W. F. (1992), *Managerial Accounting: Method and Meaning*, Chapman & Hall.

Self-testing on the chapter

1 Define *variable cost* and *fixed cost*.

2 Contrast the economist's view of costs and revenues with that taken in management accounting.

3 Sketch, and explain the main features of, a breakeven chart.

4 Explain the algebraic method for determining the breakeven point.

5 Explain the formula method for determining the breakeven point.

6 Sketch, and explain the main features of, a breakeven chart.

7 What happens to the breakeven point when the sales price per unit falls?

8 What happens to the breakeven point when the variable cost per unit falls?

9 What happens to the breakeven point when fixed overheads increase?

10 State the limitations of breakeven analysis.

11 Give three examples of applications of contribution analysis.

12 Explain how contribution analysis may help in:
   (a) decisions on special orders;
   (b) abandonment decisions;
   (c) situations of limiting factors; and
   (d) a decision on buying in services.

13 Explain how economic factors usually dictate prices of goods and services.

14 Explain the situations where cost-based pricing may be appropriate.

15 Define absorption costing.

16 Define variable costing.

17 Explain why absorption costing and variable costing may lead to different measures of profit in a period.

18 Set out the arguments in favour of absorption costing.

19 Set out the arguments in favour of variable costing.

20 Outline the perceived dangers of short-termism.

21 Plot a breakeven chart based on the following data and label the features of interest on the chart:

Number of units	Fixed cost £	Variable cost £	Total cost £	Sales £
10	200	100	300	150
20	200	200	400	300
30	200	300	500	450
40	200	400	600	600
50	200	500	700	750

22 Fixed costs are £5,000. Variable cost per unit is £3 and the unit selling price is £5.50. What is the breakeven volume of sales?

23 Stationery Co Ltd produces envelopes and writing pads. Weekly sales and costs are as follows:

	Envelopes (Dept E)	Writing pads (Dept W)
Quantity sold	20,000 packets	15,000 packs
Selling price	£1.05 per packet	95 pence per pad
Variable cost	60 pence per packet	54 pence per pad
Allocated fixed cost	£5,400 per week	£3,690 per week

The volume of production always equals the volume of sales.

Draw separate breakeven charts for:
(a) envelopes; and
(b) writing pads.

24 A business manufactures two products, namely, chairs and tables, in a fixed ratio of four chairs to every one table. Sales and production volume are always equal.

The following selling prices and costs are specified:

	Chair £	Table £
Selling price per item	60	75
Variable cost per item	35	40

Total fixed costs of production are expected to be £135,000 per month.

Required

Present a breakeven chart showing this information in a form which will be useful to the management of the business.

25 A valve refurbishing business wishes to compare the cost of buying a component outside the business with the cost of making the component themselves.

The cost of outside components is £6 per item.

The cost of manufacturing internally is calculated as follows:

	£
Direct materials	1.20
Direct labour	1.40
Variable overhead	1.40
Fixed overhead[1]	2.00
Cost per item	6.00

Note: [1]This cost estimate is based on production of 1 million items.

It is expected that, at the present time, production would not require more than 800,000 components in one year but, if the economy improves, this usage could increase by 50 per cent or more.

You are asked to present this information in a breakeven chart in a manner which will assist the owners of the business in deciding whether to manufacture their own components, or buy from an outside supplier. Your answer should also mention other points to be considered before a final decision is taken.

26 Farthing Ltd manufactures bicycle frames which it sells for £40. The present machinery has a maximum capacity of 20,000 frames per year at which level net profit is £3 per frame and the contribution to sales ratio is 20 per cent. A replacement machine is to be purchased with a capacity of 30,000 frames per year which will increase fixed costs by £20,000. Variable costs will be reduced by £6 per frame and to achieve the maximum sales, selling price will be reduced by £5 per frame.

Required

Present all the above information in the form of a graph noting the level of production required from the replacement machine to give a 50 per cent increase in profit compared with that achieved by full production on the old machine.

Activities for study groups

1 In groups of three, take the role of finance director, production director and sales director in a company manufacturing pressure diecastings, gravity diecastings and sand castings. The three types of casting are manufactured in different locations but each is no more than twenty miles from either of the other locations. All castings are brought to central premises for finishing treatment. The costs of materials are around 56 per cent of final sales price and the costs of labour are around 30 per cent of sales price.

The finance director has been asked to explain to the production director and the sales director the effect of measuring profit using variable costing rather than absorption costing. It is important to keep separate the profit on each of the three product types. The finance director should provide a short explanation and the production director and sales director should ask questions about anything which is unclear or omitted from the explanation. After the discussion is completed (say, 30 minutes in all) the group should make a presentation to the class outlining the nature of their discussion and the conclusion reached as to how profit for each product should be measured.

2 Your company manufactures furniture units to customers' specifications. In groups of three, take the role of sales director, production director and finance director. You have met to decide on the price to be charged for each contract. The sales director aims to maximise revenue, the finance director seeks to maximise profit and the production director wishes to continue operating at full capacity. Discuss the approach you will take to deciding the company's pricing policy for the year ahead. Present to the rest of the class the arguments you will present to the entire board of directors.

Case studies

Case 9.1

Supertoys Ltd is the sole manufacturer in Scotland of the Super-robot toy. The current level of production and sales is 40,000 toys per annum. The selling price of each Super-robot is £20. The contribution from each toy is 20 per cent of selling price. Fixed costs of current operations are £100,000 per annum.

A feasibility study based on new methods of working, which include making greater use of part-time workers, has shown that production and sales could be increased to 60,000 toys per annum. This would increase fixed costs by £20,000 but would reduce variable costs by £4.50 per toy. In order to sell 60,000 toys per annum the selling price would have to be reduced by £2.50 per toy.

The managing director has expressed concern that the new methods of working will leave his company more vulnerable to fluctuations in demand. He has set a target of a 50 per cent increase in profit during the coming year. He is uncertain as to whether implementing the findings of the feasibility study would be compatible with achieving this target.

Required

Prepare a report to the managing director of Supertoys Ltd analysing and interpreting the information provided in the feasibility study. Your report should include a response to his concern about the vulnerability of the company if the new methods of working were adopted.

Case 9.2

Dairyproducts Ltd has recently developed sales of cream in aerosol dispensers which are sold alongside the company's traditional products of cartons of cream and packets of cheese. The company is now considering the sale of cream cheese in aerosol dispensers.

It is company policy that any new product must be capable of generating sufficient profit to cover all costs, including estimated initial marketing and advertising expenditure of £1,000,000.

Current weekly production, with unit costs and selling prices, is as follows:

	Units of output	Variable cost (£)	Fixed cost (£)	Selling price (£)
Cartons of cream	400,000	0.45	0.15	0.75
Aerosol cans of cream	96,000	0.50	0.25	1.05
Packets of cheese	280,000	1.00	0.20	1.30

Sales volume is equal to production volume. A fifty-week trading year is assumed. Rates of absorption of fixed costs are based on current levels of output.

In order to produce cream cheese in aerosol dispensers, the aerosol machine would require modification at a cost of £400,000 which is to be recovered through sales within one year. Additional annual fixed costs of £500,000 would be incurred in manufacturing the new product. Variable cost of production would be 50 pence per can. Initial research has estimated demand as follows:

Price per can (£)	Maximum weekly demand (cans)
1.50	60,000
1.40	80,000
1.15	100,000

There is adequate capacity on the aerosol machine, but the factory is operating near capacity in other areas. The new product would have to be produced by reducing production elsewhere and two alternatives have been identified:

(a) reduce production of cream cartons by 20 per cent per annum; or
(b) reduce production of packet cheese by 25 per cent per annum.

The directors consider that the new product must cover any loss of profit caused by this reduction in volume. They are also aware that market research has shown growing customer dissatisfaction because of wastage with cream sold in cartons.

Required

Prepare a memorandum to the board of directors of Dairyproducts Ltd showing the outcome of the alternative courses of action open to the company and make a recommendation on the most profitable course open to the company.

Case 9.3

Woollens Ltd manufactures high-quality sweaters. At present the company sells direct to retail stores, but sales through those outlets have been declining due to overseas competition. The profit last year was only £160,000 compared with the company's target of £250,000. You are the company's newly appointed management accountant. The following information has been provided to you:

Profit and loss account for the year ended 31 August 19X8:

	£	£	£
Sales (100,000 sweaters at £30)			3,000,000
Production costs (100,000 sweaters)			
Direct materials	300,000		
Direct labour	1,050,000		
Variable overhead	180,000		
Fixed overhead	660,000		
		2,190,000	
Fixed administration overhead		320,000	
Selling and distribution costs:			
Sales commission (2% of sales)	60,000		
Variable distribution costs	150,000		
Fixed advertising costs	120,000		
		330,000	
			2,840,000
Profit			160,000

Further information

(a) Sales and production volumes are always equal. There was no stock of unsold sweaters at 31 August 19X8.
(b) It is anticipated that costs can be held at the 19X8 level during 19X9.

The following proposals have been made for the coming year:

(a) *Proposal I:* Reduce selling price by 10 per cent. Market research has shown this would increase demand by 40 per cent over the year ahead.

(b) *Proposal II:* Continue to sell to shops at £30 per sweater but also take up an enquiry from a mail order company regarding a possible sale of a further 50,000 sweaters.

Market research indicates that sales of 90,000 sweaters could be made through shops in the coming year if the price is maintained at £30 per item. The mail order company would collect finished goods at no cost to Woollens Ltd. A payment of £180,000 towards the cost of the mail order catalogue and special packaging costing 75 pence per sweater would have to be provided by Woollens Ltd. The sales commission would not be payable in respect of mail order sales. Competition for mail order business is considerable and

Woollens Ltd will need to charge the lowest price possible within the constraint of achieving an overall profit of £250,000.

(c) *Proposal III:* Reduce selling price by 10 per cent and carry out a special advertising campaign costing £50,000. The sales director believes this will achieve sales of 160,000 sweaters per annum.

Required

Evaluate each of these three proposals, commenting in particular on the breakeven point and margin of safety of each proposal.

Case 9.4

Resistor Ltd manufactures electrical units. All units are identical. The following information relates to June and July 19X5:

(a) Budgeted costs and selling prices were:

	June £	July £
Variable manufacturing cost per unit	2.00	2.20
Total fixed manufacturing costs (based on budgeted output of 25,000 units per month)	40,000	44,000
Total fixed marketing cost (based on budgeted sales of 25,000 units per month)	14,000	15,400
Selling price per unit	5.00	5.50

(b) Actual production and sales recorded were:

	Units	Units
Production	24,000	24,000
Sales	21,000	26,500

(c) There was no stock of finished goods at the start of June 19X5. There was no wastage or loss of finished goods during either June or July 19X5.
(d) Actual costs incurred corresponded to those budgeted for each month.

Required

Calculate the relative effects on the monthly operating profits of applying the undernoted techniques:

1 absorption costing;

2 variable costing.

Case 9.5

Leisure Furniture Ltd produces furniture for hotels and public houses using specific designs prepared by firms of interior design consultants. Business is brisk and the market is highly competitive with a number of rival companies tendering for work. The company's pricing policy, based on marginal costing (variable costing) techniques, is generating high sales.

The main activity of Home Furniture Ltd is the production of a limited range of standard lounge suites for household use. The company also offers a service constructing furniture to customers' designs. This work is undertaken to utilise any spare capacity. The main customers of the company are the major chains of furniture retailers. Due to recession, consumer spending on household durables has decreased recently and, as a result, the company is experiencing a significant reduction in orders for its standard lounge suites. The market is unlikely to improve within the next year. The company's pricing policy is to add a percentage mark-up to total cost.

Required

Explain why different pricing policies may be appropriate in different circumstances, illustrating your answer by reference to Leisure Furniture Ltd and Home Furniture Ltd.

Chapter 10

Capital budgeting

<table>
<tr>
<td>

Learning objectives

</td>
<td>

After studying this chapter you should be able to:

1 Explain the purpose of capital budgeting.

2 Explain the process by which a decision is made on capital expenditure.

3 Apply the payback method of project evaluation and understand its limitations.

4 Apply the accounting rate of return method of project evaluation and understand its limitations.

5 Understand the concept of present value and calculate present values.

6 Calculate and interpret the net present value of a project.

7 Calculate and interpret the internal rate of return of a project.

8 Explain how to evaluate competing projects.

9 Understand the importance of controls over projects before and after the project is undertaken.

</td>
</tr>
</table>

10.1 Purpose of capital budgeting

The word 'capital' can have more than one meaning in accounting. In financial reporting in particular it is used to denote the finance provided to the business by owners and long-term lenders. Economists use the term 'capital' to refer to the fixed assets and working capital of a business which are purchased with the money provided by the owners and lenders. This chapter uses the term 'capital' in a manner similar to that used by the economists.

When the managers of a business make plans for the long term they have to decide whether, and how much, to invest in fixed assets and working capital to maintain or increase the productive capacity of the business. They will usually be faced with choices of projects available, each requiring a different type of investment, and only a limited amount of finance available. They have to ask themselves a number of questions, including:

1 How many of the proposed projects are worth undertaking?

2 How much finance, in total, should we commit to new projects?

3 Where should the finance be obtained?

4 After the event, was the investment in the proposed project successful?

These questions cross an academic spectrum of study which begins in management accounting and ends in finance. The first and fourth of these questions are normally dealt with in management accounting textbooks, while the second and third form the focus of finance textbooks. Some books in either discipline will attempt to deal with all the questions. To make matters even more difficult for students, some textbooks use the term *capital budgeting* and some use the term *capital investment appraisal*, without agreeing on how the terms should be defined.

For this text the term *capital investment appraisal* will be applied to dealing with all four issues, namely the entire process of planning: which projects to take up; how much to invest; how to finance them; and how to evaluate their success. The more restricted process of dealing with the first and fourth issues only will be called *capital budgeting*. This will be the focus of the chapter.

Definition	*Capital budgeting* is a process of management accounting which assists management decision making by providing information on the investment in a project and the benefits to be obtained from that project, and by monitoring the performance of the project subsequent to its implementation.

10.2 The role of the management accountant in capital budgeting

The process of budget planning and relationships is set out in diagrammatic form in Exhibit 6.2 of Chapter 6. That exhibit shows that the objectives and assumptions lead into the necessity for a capital projects budget to cover the fixed assets and working capital needed to support the plans for operations. It also shows that the capital projects budget must be taken into the finance plan and the master budget. Chapter 6 dealt with the short-term aspects of the budgetary process. This chapter looks to the longer term.

The management accountant's role was set out in Chapter 1 as directing attention, keeping the score and solving problems. In capital budgeting it is the attention-directing role which is important. Information about proposed capital projects must be presented in a way which will direct management's attention towards the significant information for decision-making purposes. There will most probably be problems to solve in terms of gathering and presenting the information. After the project is implemented there will be a score-keeping aspect in terms of comparing the actual outcome with the plans and expectations.

This chapter concentrates on the techniques of presenting information so as to direct attention to the significant aspects of the capital project for decision-making purposes. It concludes with an explanation of the retrospective evaluation of a project by a post-completion audit.

10.3 The assumptions adopted

This chapter makes an assumption that all future cash inflows and outflows of a long-term project may be predicted with certainty. It also assumes that there are no taxes and there is no inflation to cause prices to increase over the life of the project. Making an assumption of certainty may seem a rather unrealistic starting point, but it is necessary to do so in order to analyse the principles of capital budgeting without having too many real-world complications crowding in. At the end of the chapter there are references to textbooks and readings which show what happens when the assumption of certainty is relaxed. Those further readings also deal with the added real-world complications of taxes and inflation.

10.4 Making a decision on a capital investment

Chapter 1 contains a specification of the processes of planning and control which are necessary for a systematic approach to making an investment decision in locating a new retail outlet. In general terms, that process is as shown in exhibit 10.1.

Exhibit 10.1
Planning and control for a capital investment decision

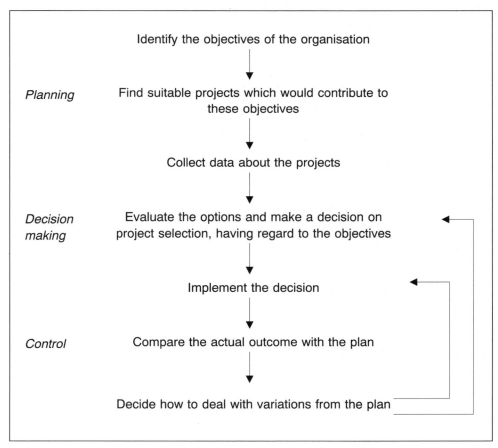

To be successful the business must first of all discover projects which have the potential for success. All the management accounting in the world will not create a successful project. The successful entrepreneur is the person who has the flair and imagination to identify projects and to see how they might successfully operate. The role of management accounting, through the capital budgeting process, is to ensure that the excitement of creating new investment opportunities does not cause management to lose sight of the need to meet the organisation's objectives.

10.5 Selecting acceptable projects

Suppose there has been a meeting of the board of directors of a company at which the managing director has said: *'We want to ensure that any cash we invest in a project comes back as soon as possible in the form of cash flows which give us a profit overall and provide the cash to reinvest in the next project.'*

A second director has replied by saying: *'It's fine for you to talk about cash flows but the outside world judges our success by our profit record. I would like to see us choosing projects which maximise the return on assets invested in the project.'*

A third member of the board has joined in with: *'I agree with the cash flow perspective but I want to be sure that, at the minimum, we cover the interest charges we have to pay on the money we borrow to finance the project. Ideally, there should be cash flows generated which exceed the cost of borrowing, so that we have surplus funds to use for investment in further projects or for increasing dividends to our shareholders.'*

Reading carefully what each has said, it is apparent that there are similarities and differences in the targets they would like to set. They are all looking to cash flows from the project, but the first director is emphasising the speed of collecting cash flows, while the second director wants to convert cash flows to profit by deducting depreciation, and the third director is more concerned about the amount of cash flows in total and whether they provide a surplus after covering all costs.

Management accounting can provide information for capital budgeting purposes which would satisfy the criteria set by any one of the three directors, but there would remain the question as to which of the three directors is using the best approach so far as the business is concerned. Three methods of capital budgeting will now be explained. These are: the payback method; the accounting rate of return; and the net present value method. Each management accounting technique will be described in turn and the advantages and disadvantages of each will be discussed.

Activity 10.1	*You might like to decide now which of the three directors you think has the most desirable approach and why you think that way. You can then monitor the development of your views as you read the chapter.*

10.6 Payback method

The first director wanted cash invested in a project to come back as quickly as possible in the form of cash flows. To test whether this objective has been met by a capital project, the payback method of project appraisal is used. It provides a calculation of the length of time required for the stream of cash inflows from a project to equal the original cash outlay. The most desirable project, under the payback method, is the one which pays back the cash outlay in the shortest time. Data is set out in exhibit 10.2 which will be used to illustrate all the capital budgeting methods explained in this chapter. An illustration of the payback calculation is provided in exhibit 10.3, and from this table of calculations it may be seen that project C offers the shortest payback period. Thus if the most important measure of success in investment is the recovery of the cash investment, then Project C is the preferred choice.

Definition

The *payback period* is the length of time required for a stream of net cash inflows from a project to equal the original cash outlay.

Exhibit 10.2
Data for illustration of methods of capital budgeting

Data

A haulage company has three potential projects planned. Each will require investment in two refrigerated vehicles at a total cost of £120,000. Each vehicle has a four-year life. The three projects are:

A Lease the vehicles to a meat-processing factory which will take the risks of finding loads to transport and will bear all driver costs for a three-year period. Expected net cash inflows, after deducting all expected cash outflows, are £60,000 per annum.

B Enter into a fixed price contract for three years to carry frozen foods from processing plants in the UK to markets in Continental Europe, returning with empty vehicles. This will require employing drivers on permanent contracts. Expected cash inflows, after deducting all expected cash outflows, are £50,000 per annum.

C Employ a contracts manager to find loads for outward and return journeys but avoid any contract for longer than a six-month period, so as to have the freedom to take up opportunities as they arise. Drivers will be hired on short-term contracts of three months. Expected cash inflows, after deducting all expected cash outflows, are £40,000 in year 1, £100,000 in year 2 and £110,000 in year 3.

Exhibit 10.3
Calculations for payback method

Cash flows	Project A	Project B	Project C
	£	£	£
Outlay	120,000	120,000	120,000
Cash inflows, after deducting all outflows of the year			
Year 1	60,000	50,000	40,000
Year 2	60,000	50,000	100,000
Year 3	60,000	50,000	110,000
Payback period	2 years	2.4 years	1.8 years
Workings	*60+60 = 120*	*50 + 50 + 20/50*	*40 + 80/100*

10.6.1 Impact of uncertainty in real life

This calculation assumes certainty about the cash flows predicted for each project, but hopefully, as you were reading the conditions of the three different contracts set out in exhibit 10.2, you had some thoughts about the relative commercial risk of each project and the risks attached to the cash flows. In this chapter we do not make allowance for the relative risks of each project, because we make an assumption of certainty of predicted cash flows, but in real life, Project C would be regarded as the high-risk option, while projects A and B provide greater certainty through having contracts in place for the three-year period. Of these two, project B looks the least attractive but leaves opportunities for casual earnings if loads can be found for the return journey.

10.6.2 Usefulness and limitations of the payback approach

The payback method of capital budgeting is widely used in practice, possibly because it is relatively painless in its arithmetic. Furthermore, there is a reflection of commercial realism in concentrating on projects which give early returns of cash flow. That may be important to organisations which face cash flow constraints. It may also be seen as a cautious approach to take where product markets are uncertain and it is difficult to predict the longer-term cash flows expected from a product.

One major limitation of using the payback method of capital budgeting as described here is that it ignores the fact that investing funds in a long-term project has a cost in terms of the interest charges on borrowed funds (or interest foregone when money is tied up in fixed assets). Economists refer to this interest cost as the *time value of money*. The cash flows earned from a project should repay the capital sum invested, but they should also be sufficient to provide a reward to investors which equals the interest cost of capital.

A second major limitation is that, in concentrating on the speed of recovery of cash flows, the method ignores any cash flows arising after the payback date. A project which would make a long-term contribution to the overall cash flows of the business could be sacrificed for short-term benefits in a project with a limited time horizon.

Activity 10.2

> *Check that you understand fully the calculation of the payback period and its interpretation. Write a 200-word note on the meaning and usefulness of the payback period as a means of evaluating the suitability of a project.*

10.7 Accounting rate of return

The accounting rate of return differs from the payback method in using accounting profits rather than cash flows. As you will by now have realised, the calculation of profits includes depreciation, which is an accounting allocation but has no cash flow effect. The attraction of using profit in a method of capital budgeting is that it links long-term decision making to profit as the conventional measure of success in business.

Definition

> The *accounting rate of return* is calculated by taking the average annual profits expected from a project as a percentage of the capital invested.

Some textbooks recommend as denominator the initial amount of capital invested while others suggest the use of the average capital invested. Calculation of the average involves making some arbitrary assumptions about the way capital is used up over the project. A simple pattern is to assume it is used up evenly. Suppose a project requires £1,000 invested at the start, there will be nothing left at the end and the capital is used up equally each year. Then the average investment is £500 (which is the average of £1,000 at the start and £nil at the end). This textbook will use the initial investment for illustrative purposes, but you should be aware that different definitions will be used in practice and it is important to know how any return on capital has been defined.

The data in exhibit 10.2 may be used to illustrate the accounting rate of return as a method of capital budgeting. A straight line method of depreciation is applied, assuming a zero residual value, so that depreciation of £30,000 per annum is deducted from cash flows. The resulting profits and accounting rate of return are shown in exhibit 10.4.

Perhaps not surprisingly, the accounting rate of return gives a ranking of the three projects which is the same as that obtained by the payback method. It is possible to envisage cash flow patterns which might lead to apparent conflicts between the two methods, but in many cases there will be no conflict.

Exhibit 10.4
Calculations for the accounting rate of return

Cash flows	Project A	Project B	Project C
	£	£	£
Outlay (a)	120,000	120,000	120,000
Profits, after deducting depreciation from cash flows			
Year 1	30,000	20,000	10,000
Year 2	30,000	20,000	70,000
Year 3	30,000	20,000	80,000
Average annual profit (b)	30,000	20,000	53,000
Accounting rate of return (b × 100/a)	25%	16.7%	44.2%

10.7.1 Usefulness and limitations of accounting rate of return

The accounting rate of return is regarded as a useful measure of the likely success of a project because it is based on the familiar accounting measure of profit. It is also regarded as useful because it takes into the calculation all the profits expected over the project life (in contrast to the payback method which ignores all cash flows beyond the payback date).

A major defect of the accounting rate of return is that it ignores the time value of money. It makes no distinction between two projects of the same average profit, one of which gives most of its profits at an early stage and the other of which gives most of its profits at a later stage.

A less serious defect, but nevertheless a limitation, is that the accounting rate of return depends on profit which, in turn, includes a subjective accounting estimate of depreciation. That may not matter too much in an example of the type illustrated in exhibit 10.4, where average profits are used and straight line depreciation is applied across all projects, but there could be situations where different depreciation policies could distort a decision based on accounting rate of return.

Activity 10.3

Before proceeding further, make sure that you understand fully the calculation and usefulness of the accounting rate of return. Write a 200-word note on the limitations of relying on the accounting rate of return when evaluating a project.

10.8 Net present value method

The net present value (NPV) method of capital budgeting is a technique which seeks to remedy some of the defects of payback and the accounting rate of return. In particular it takes into account all cash flows over the life of the project and makes allowance for the time value of money. Before the net present value method can be explained further, it is necessary to make a short digression into the time value of money.

10.8.1 Time value of money

If £100 is invested at 10 per cent per annum, then it will grow to £110 by the end of the year. If the £100 is spent on an item of business machinery, then the interest is lost. So the act of investing leads to a lost opportunity of earning investment. The idea of applying calculations of the time value of money is a way of recognising the reward needed from a project to compensate for the lost opportunity.

Suppose now that you have been given a written promise of £100 to be received in one year's time. Interest rates are 10 per cent. You do not want to wait one year to receive cash and would like the money now. What is the price for which you could sell that promise? Most students see the answer as £90.91 intuitively, but they do not all see immediately how they arrived at that answer. (It might be useful for you to think out your own approach before you read the next few paragraphs. It is much easier to work something out for yourself than to try remembering formulae which you will forget in a crisis.)

The intuitive answer is that £90.91 is the amount which, invested now at 10 per cent, would grow to £100 in one year's time. Provided the promise is a good one, there would be no problem in selling the £100 promise for £90.91 now. Both the buyer and the seller would be equally satisfied that the price reflected the time value of money.

Now make it a little harder. Suppose the promise of £100 was for payment in *two* years' time. What is the price for which you could sell that promise now? The answer is £82.64 because that would grow at 10 per cent to £90.91 at the end of one year and to £100 at the end of two years.

The calculation of the value of the promise today can be conveniently represented in mathematical notation as follows:

Definition

The *present value* of a sum of £1 receivable at the end of n years when the rate of interest is r per cent per annum equals:

$$\frac{1}{(1+r)^n}$$

where r represents the annual rate of interest, expressed in decimal form, and n represents the time period when the cash flow will be received.

The process of calculating present value is called *discounting*. The interest rate used is called the *discount rate*.

Using this calculation to illustrate the two calculations already carried out intuitively, the present value of a sum of £100, due one year hence, when the discount rate (interest rate) is 10 per cent, is calculated as:

$$\frac{£100}{(1 + 0.1)^1}$$
$$= £90.91$$

The present value of a sum of £100, due two years' hence, when the interest rate is 10 per cent, is calculated as:

$$\frac{£100}{(1 + 0.1)^2}$$
$$= £82.64$$

The calculation using this formula is no problem if a financial calculator or a spreadsheet package is available, but can be tedious if resources are limited to a basic pocket calculator. In such circumstances, some people prefer to use tables of discount factors which give the present value of £1 for every possible rate of interest and every possible time period ahead. A full table of discount factors is set out in the supplement at the end of this chapter.

In this supplement, the column for the discount rate of 10 per cent has the following discount factors:

At end of period	Present value of £1
1	0.909
2	0.826
3	0.751

Using the tables, for the discount rate of 10 per cent, it may be calculated that the present value of £100 receivable at the end of year 1 is £100 × 0.909 = £90.90, while the present value of £100 receivable at the end of year 2 is £100 × 0.826 = £82.60. (There is a difference in the second place of decimals when this answer is compared with the result of using the formula. The difference is due to rounding in the discount tables.)

Now that you are familiar with the calculation of the present value of a promised future cash flow, the explanation of the net present value method of capital budgeting may be given.

Activity 10.4

Use your calculator to check the discount factors for the present value of £1 at the end of one year, two years and three years for a discount rate of 10 per cent. Write a parallel table for 8 per cent and 12 per cent. Show that the discount factor decreases as the discount rate increases.

10.8.2 Net present value calculation

The net present value method of capital budgeting is based on the view that a project will be regarded as successful if the present value of all expected cash inflows is greater than, or equal to, the capital invested at the outset. It is called net present value because, in calculation, the capital invested is deducted from the present value of the future cash flows. (Use of the word 'net' always means that one item is being deducted from another.) If the present value of the expected cash flows is greater than the capital invested, then the net present value will be positive. If the present value of the expected cash flows is less than the capital invested, then the net present value will be negative. A positive net present value indicates that the project should be accepted, while a negative net present value indicates that it should be rejected.

Definition

The *net present value* of a project is equal to the present value of the cash inflows minus the present value of the cash outflows, all discounted at the cost of capital.

The illustration in exhibit 10.5 sets out the data for project A taken from exhibit 10.2. Exhibit 10.6 sets out the net present value calculation, assuming a discount rate of 10 per cent.

Exhibit 10.5
Data for net present value illustration

Cash flows	Project A £
Outlay	120,000
Cash inflows, after deducting all outflows of the year:	
Year 1	60,000
Year 2	60,000
Year 3	60,000

Exhibit 10.6
Calculation of net present value

Using the formula approach the net present value is calculated as:

$$\frac{£60,000}{(1.10)} + \frac{£60,000}{(1.10)^2} + \frac{£60,000}{(1.10)^3} - £120,000$$

$$= £54,550 + £49,590 + £45,080 - £120,000 = £29,220$$

Continued overleaf

Exhibit 10.6 continued

Using the discount tables the net present value is calculated as:

End of year	Cash flow £	Discount factor	Present value £
1	60,000	0.909	54,540
2	60,000	0.826	49,560
3	60,000	0.751	45,060
			149,160
Less initial outlay			(120,000)
Net present value			29,160

Rounding errors

The answer obtained from the discount tables (£29,160) differs marginally from that obtained from the formula (£29,220), because the discount factors are rounded to three decimal places. In many cases, such differences are marginal to the overall calculation and you should not worry about them. If, in any particular case, the rounding errors are likely to have an impact, then the formula should be used rather than the tables of discount factors. In real life it is questionable whether any decision should be based on fine-tuning of rounding errors. The conclusion should be clear from the overall magnitudes being calculated and should not be dependent on differences of very small magnitude.

Activity 10.5

> *If you have access to a spreadsheet package, find out whether it has a net present value (NPV) function. If so, use the data in exhibit 10.5 to satisfy yourself that the spreadsheet produces answers similar to those derived here.*

Cash flow patterns assumed by the net present value calculation

It is worth pausing to analyse the cash flow patterns which are assumed by the net present value calculation. This analysis helps in understanding when it is safe to use the net present value approach to capital budgeting and when it should be applied with caution.

Assume the investor who has provided the capital of £120,000 requires 10 per cent interest at the end of each year, to be paid out of the cash flows. Assume that any surplus cash flows are retained in the business and reinvested at 10 per cent. The accumulation of cash generated by the project is shown in exhibit 10.7. The cash balance at the end of year 3 is £159,000, out of which the original capital of £120,000 is repaid, leaving an actual surplus of £39,000. That surplus at the end of year 3 has a present value of £29,000 (£39,000 × 0.751) which is the answer derived earlier by the net present value calculation (allowing for rounding differences).

Exhibit 10.7
Accumulation of cash during a project

Year	Balance of cash at start of year (1) £000s	Interest earned on balance invested (2) £000s	Cash flow (3) £000s	Interest paid (4) £000s	Balance of cash at end of year (1+2+3-4) £000s
1	nil	–	60	12	48
2	48	5	60	12	101
3	101	10	60	12	159

Exhibit 10.7 is provided here to illustrate one of the assumptions of the net present value calculation which requires some thought. It assumes that surplus cash generated during the project can be invested at the cost of capital. Whether or not that is the case for a particular project is more an issue for study in the area of finance, but in real life it is rare that the interest earned on deposited funds is as high as that paid on borrowings. What is possible in many situations is that the surplus cash is used to start further projects in the business and those new projects are also successful in creating positive net present values of cash flows at the organisation's cost of capital.

10.8.3 The net present value decision rule

The NPV decision rule is as follows:

Definition

1 Where the net present value of the project is *positive*, accept the project.
2 Where the net present value of the project is *negative*, reject the project.
3 Where the net present value of the project is zero, the project is acceptable in meeting the cost of capital but gives no surplus to its owners.

If an organisation seeks to maximise the wealth of its owners, then it should accept any project which has a positive net present value. If finance markets are working efficiently, funds will always be available to finance projects which meet or exceed their cost of capital.

In real life, obtaining finance may be difficult because of temporary imbalance in the capital markets or because the supply of capital within the organisation is constrained. If the organisation is in the public sector it may be subject to a cash limit of capital expenditure. If it is in the private sector and is a subsidiary or a division within a group, it may be restricted by the group's plans for total fund-raising by the group. Such practical problems are sometimes referred to as *capital rationing* and will lead to organisations devising decision rules for ranking projects. These ranking decisions will not be explored in detail here but it is important to note that any project which is rejected, when it has a positive net present value, will be a loss to the potential wealth of the owners of the business.

10.9 Internal rate of return

Net present value is only one method in capital budgeting which takes into account the time value of money. The decision rule is based on the absolute amount of the net present value of the surplus generated by the project. There is some evidence from research into practical use of capital budgeting techniques that decision makers feel more comfortable with a percentage rather than an absolute amount. (The reason is not so clear but could be linked to the historical reliance on the accounting rate of return as a percentage.)

The internal rate of return (IRR) is another method in capital budgeting which uses the time value of money but results in an answer expressed in percentage form. It is a discount rate which leads to a net present value of zero, where the present value of the cash inflows exactly equals the cash outflows.

Definition

> The *internal rate of return* (IRR) is the discount rate at which the present value of the cash flows generated by the project is equal to the present value of the capital invested, so that the net present value of the project is zero.

10.9.1 Method of calculation

The calculation of the internal rate of return involves a process of repeated guessing at the discount rate until the present value of the cash flows generated is equal to the capital investment. That guessing may be carried out by computer, asking the computer to try values of the discount factor in the formula. Most spreadsheet computer packages have the facility to perform a calculation of internal rate of return once the initial investment and cash flows have been entered on the spreadsheet.

$$\text{Initial investment} = \frac{C_1}{(1+d)} + \frac{C_2}{(1+d)^2} + \frac{C_3}{(1+d)^3} + \ldots + \frac{C_n}{(1+d)^n}$$

That process of repeated guessing is extremely time-consuming if a computer is not used. Even where a computer is used, it needs to be provided with a first guess which is reasonably close. For a manual process of estimation it may be easier to use discount tables, with an aim of arriving at a reasonably close answer, rather than worrying too much about figures beyond the decimal point.

Take, as an illustration, the data on project A of exhibit 10.2, repeated in exhibit 10.5. The starting point for calculating IRR is to find two values of NPV using discount rates lying either side of the IRR. Exhibit 10.8 sets out two such calculations. A first guess of 20 per cent produces a net present value which is positive. The aim is to find the discount rate which gives a zero net present value, so the first guess must have been too low and a higher discount rate of 24 per cent is used for the second guess.

Exhibit 10.8
Calculation of net present value at 20 per cent and at 24 per cent

	Cash flows £	Discount rate 20%	£	Discount rate 24%	£
End of year 1	60,000	0.833	49,980	0.806	48,360
End of year 2	60,000	0.694	41,640	0.650	39,000
End of year 3	60,000	0.579	34,740	0.524	31,440
			126,360		118,800
Outlay			(120,000)		(120,000)
Net present value			6,360		(1,200)

The second guess was a fortunate one because the net present value changed from being positive at 20 per cent to being negative at 24 per cent. That means that the net present value of zero must be found at a discount rate between these two rates. If the second guess had failed to give a negative net present value, a further guess would have been required.

The actual discount rate which gives a zero net present value may now be found by assuming a linear interval between 20 per cent and 24 per cent. (The interval is not exactly linear but may be taken as approximately so over a narrow difference in rates.)

The difference between the two net present values is £6,360 – (–£1,200), that is £7,560. The difference between the two discount rates is 4 per cent and therefore, using simple proportion calculations, the net present value of zero lies at:

$$20\% + \left(\frac{6,360}{7,560} \times 4\right) = 23.365\%$$

Exhibit 10.9 sets out the linear relationship which is assumed in the calculation. The process of estimation shown there is called *interpolation*. In words, the formula used in this calculation is:

$$\text{Lower of the pair of discount rates} + \left(\frac{\text{NPV at lower rate}}{\text{difference between the NPVs}} \times \text{difference in rates}\right)$$

The internal rate of return answer, as produced by a computer package, is 23.375 per cent. The use of a simple proportion calculation appears to provide a good approximation.

Activity 10.6

If you have access to a computer spreadsheet package which has an internal rate of return function, test the data used in the chapter. It will ask you for a first guess and will then proceed to repeat the calculation of IRR until it arrives at a net present value of zero.

Exhibit 10.9
Locating the internal rate of return between two discount rates of known net present value

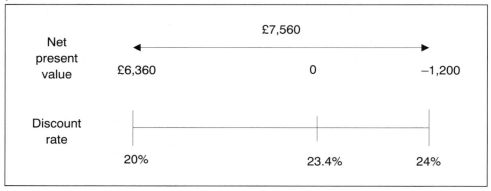

It is also possible to plot a graph of net present value against discount rate, as shown in exhibit 10.10. The internal rate of return is the discount rate at which the graph crosses the horizontal line representing zero net present value. That point is designated with a letter P in the graph and is shown to be around 23.4 per cent by a vertical dotted line from P to the horizontal axis.

Exhibit 10.10
Graph of net present value against discount rate showing internal rate of return

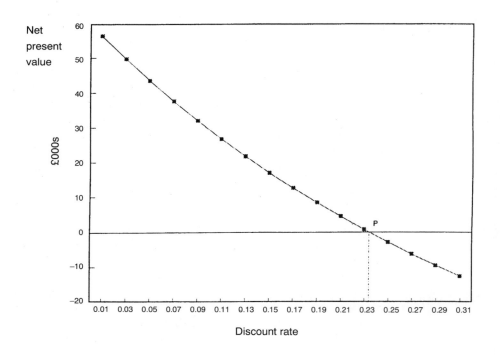

10.9.2 The internal rate of return decision rule

The decision rule is that a project is acceptable where the internal rate of return is greater than the cost of capital. Under those conditions the net present value of the project will be positive. A project is not acceptable where the internal rate of return is less than the cost of capital. Under those conditions the net present value of the project will be negative.

Definition

1 Where the IRR of the project is greater than the cost of capital, accept the project.
2 Where the IRR of the project is less than the cost of capital, reject the project.
3 Where the IRR of the project equals the cost of capital, the project is acceptable in meeting the required rate of return of those investing in the business but gives no surplus to its owners.

When the net present value and the internal rate of return criteria are applied to an isolated project, they will lead to the same accept/reject decision because they both use the discounting method of calculation applied to the same cash flows. For an isolated project the use of either technique is a matter of personal preference. Where a choice of competing projects has to be made, the practice may be more complicated. The techniques available for dealing with that problem are beyond the scope of this book, but the next section outlines the nature of the problem.

10.10 Mutually exclusive projects

An organisation may need to make a choice between two projects which are mutually exclusive (perhaps because there is only sufficient demand in the market for the output of one of the projects, or because there is a limited physical capacity which will not allow both). Some care is then required in using the net present value and the internal rate of return as decision criteria. In many cases they give the same answer on relative ranking, but occasionally they may give different answers, as shown in the following case example.

10.10.1 Case study: whisky distillery

A distillery is planning to invest in a new still. There are two plans, one of which involves continuing to produce the traditional mix of output blends and the second of which involves experimentation with new blends. The second plan will produce lower cash flows in the earlier years of the life of the still, but it is planned that these cash flows will overtake the traditional pattern within a short space of time. Only one plan may be implemented. The project is to be appraised on the basis of cash flows over three years. The cash flows expected are shown in exhibit 10.11. The cost of capital is 12 per cent per annum. At this discount rate the net present values are shown in the second table of exhibit 10.11. The internal rates of return are also shown in that table.

Exhibit 10.11
Cash flows, NPV and IRR for two mutually exclusive projects

Project	Initial investment	Cash flows Year 1	Year 2	Year 3
	£	£	£	£
A	120,000	96,000	48,000	12,000
B	120,000	12,000	60,000	108,000

Project	NPV at 12% £	IRR
A	12,521	20.2%
B	15,419	17.6%

It may be seen from exhibit 10.11 that, looking at the net present value at the cost of capital, project B appears the more attractive with the higher net present value. Looking at the internal rate of return, project A appears most attractive. Both are acceptable because they give a positive net present value and the ideal answer would be to find the resources to undertake both projects. In this example, the two are mutually exclusive (which means that taking on one project excludes the possibility of the other).

If the business has the aim of maximising net present value, then one further decision rule may be helpful, based on the *profitability index*.

Definition

The *profitability index* is the present value of cash flows (discounted at the cost of capital) divided by the present value of the investment intended to produce those cash flows.

The project with the highest profitability index will give the highest net present value for the amount of investment funding available. Taking the data in exhibit 10.11, the profitability index calculations are:

Project A: Profitability index $= \dfrac{132,521}{120,000} = 1.10$

Project B: Profitability index $= \dfrac{135,419}{120,000} = 1.13$

This confirms that, of the two, project B is preferable at a cost of capital of 12 per cent. Where the investment in both projects is of the same amount, as in this case, the profitability index confirms what is already obvious, but where there are competing projects of differing initial investment, it is a useful device for ranking projects to maximise net present value.

10.10.2 Sensitivity to changes in the discount rate

To understand the apparently different conclusions from the NPV and IRR approaches, it is helpful to plot a graph of the net present value of each project against a range of discount rates. The graph is shown in exhibit 10.12.

Exhibit 10.12
Net present value of competing projects using a range of discount rates

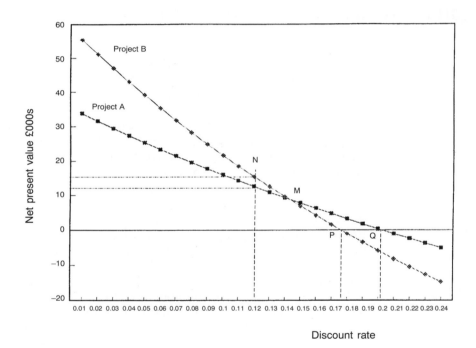

From exhibit 10.12, it will be seen that, for both projects, the net present value decreases as the discount rate increases but that the net present value of project B decreases more rapidly. Starting at the left-hand side of the graph, the net present value of project B is higher than that of project A at all discount rates above the point, M, at which they intersect (around 14.2 per cent). In particular project B has a higher net present value than project A at the cost of capital 12 per cent (point N on the graph). For discount rates above 14.2 per cent, the net present value of project B is always higher than that of project A. The internal rate of return of each project is the discount rate at which they cross the line of zero net present value (i.e. at point P for project B and point Q for project A).

How does this help the decision maker? If it is absolutely certain that the cost of capital will remain at 12 per cent throughout the life of the project, then the net present value method correctly leads to a choice of project B in preference to project A. On the other hand, 12 per cent is quite close to the point of intersection at 14.2 per cent, where project A takes over. If there is a chance that the cost of capital will in reality be higher than the 12 per cent expected, then it might be safer to choose project A. The line of the graph for project A is less steep and this project is said to be less sensitive to changes in the discount rate. There is therefore no clear-cut answer to the problem and the final decision will be based on an assessment of sensitivity. Looking at exhibit 10.12, the different ranking by net present value and by internal rate of return was a useful clue to the need to consider the relative sensitivities as shown in the graph.

10.11 Which methods are used in practice?

This chapter has now explained the capital budgeting techniques of payback, accounting rate of return, net present value and internal rate of return. The benefits and limitations of each have been discussed in the respective sections. It could be argued that the proof of the value of each technique lies in the extent to which it is used in practice. There exists a considerable volume of survey research seeking an answer to the question of which methods are most commonly used in practice. The conclusions from each project are not totally unanimous because they depend on the time period covered by the research, the nature of the sample chosen, the country in which the questions are asked, and the questions asked. There are themes which may be discerned in the research results, the first of which is that the payback method appears to be the most frequently used technique in the UK but discounted cash flow methods are found more commonly in the USA. It is also found that organisations will use more than one method of capital budgeting. Where discounting methods are used, internal rate of return appears more popular than net present value.

Research investigations are able to collect information of this type. Once the patterns are known, it is interesting is to speculate on the motives behind these patterns of choice. Perhaps the payback method is most frequently used because there are many small businesses undertaking lots of small projects. It might not matter that discounting methods are used less frequently provided they are used on the larger projects in larger organisations. This issue has also been tested in research and it has been shown that larger companies do make relatively more use of discounting techniques. Perhaps the payback method, in many cases, shows so clearly that a project is acceptable that it would be a waste of time to carry out lengthy discounting calculations to arrive at the same conclusion. Perhaps those using payback realise that, in some instances, its emphasis on early cash flows is not so different from that of the net present value approach in situations where the later cash flows are relatively low.

10.12   Control of investment projects: authorisation and review

The capital investment projects of an organisation represent major commitments of resources. It would be a mistake to be overenthusiastic about decision making techniques without considering also how management accounting may help in the subsequent implementation of the project.

The organisation should have in place a procedure by which new project suggestions are investigated and evaluated using the techniques described in this chapter, or suitable alternatives. There should then be a decision-making group, perhaps called the capital budgeting committee or the management review committee, which makes decisions on the projects to be selected. Once the decision has been made and the capital budgeting committee has authorised the project to proceed, the management accountant is again needed in implementing a system for reviewing and controlling the project.

The two important aspects of control and review are:

1   controlling the amount of the expenditure needed to make the project operational;
2   post-completion audit of cash inflows and outflows.

10.12.1   Controlling capital expenditure

The specification of the project will have included an estimate of the initial outlay required and the timing of that outlay. For simplification, the illustrations used in this chapter assumed a single amount being paid out at the start of the project, but in real life the capital expenditure will be spread over a period of time on an agreed schedule. If the capital expenditure involves constructing a building, there will be a contract for the building work which sets out the dates for completion of each stage and the amount of cash to be paid at that point. The payment will only be made when an expert (such as the architect supervising the project) has confirmed that the work has been carried out according to the specification. If a contract has been drawn up with care, it will contain safeguards to ensure that the work is completed on time and within the original cost estimates. There may be a penalty clause, so that a part of the cash payment may be withheld if the contract is not performed as promised.

Activity 10.7

> Write a list of key points to be made in a recommendation to the board of directors on the implementation of an expenditure control process for capital investment plans.

10.12.2   Post-completion audit

A post-completion audit involves a review of the actual results of a project in order to compare these with the expectations contained in the project proposals.

It is called an audit because it requires a more flexible approach than would be found in management accounting evaluations of short-term plans (as covered in Chapter 9). The post-completion audit might require a view of the wider implications of the project rather than concentrating too much on annual cash flows item by item. A project might take a different turn from that envisaged at the outset and a longer-term view would be required of the likely outcome of that different turn. In real life, uncertainty is a factor which cannot easily be built into the project plans and the audit may have to take account of factors which could not have been foreseen at the outset.

There could be dangers in such an audit process if managers of projects see themselves as being held to blame for a subsequent failure to meet expectations. They might be motivated to put forward only those projects which they saw as safe but unadventurous. The review process has to be flexible to allow for the unknown but also to discourage unrealistic or overenthusiastic plans.

10.13   Advanced manufacturing technologies

It has been argued in some quarters that the heavy academic emphasis on discounting techniques of NPV and IRR may have hampered the introduction of innovative techniques in manufacturing processes. The conventional presentation of the NPV and IRR calculations implies that it is necessary to identify a specific outlay and then a series of cash flows attributable to that outlay. Advanced manufacturing technology may result in a continuous process of change and a blurring of the line between capital expenditure and recurring expenditure which has an investment purpose. The kind of recurring expenditure which might be creating benefits for the future could include quality improvement measures, delivery time reductions, operating cost savings, stock controls and flexibility of product switching. It is argued that these create a form of benefit which extends beyond the immediate period of the expenditure, but that the benefit is difficult to incorporate in a discounted cash flow calculation of the NPV and IRR type.

Rather than abandon the technique because it is difficult, a better answer from management accounting is to rise to the challenge and modify the net present value approach. The cash flows may need to be estimated with more care and the benefits may have to be identified more specifically. Where the benefits do not translate directly into cash flows, they may be capable of being used to identify cut-off points to be applied after the cash flows have been discounted at the cost of capital. The amount of the net present value, as quantified, can be evaluated against the qualitative description of the benefits, and a form of sensitivity analysis used to establish a level of NPV required to equate to the expected benefits.

The specific debate on the role of capital budgeting techniques in relation to advanced manufacturing technologies is a useful example of the wider point that management accounting must continually be changing to adapt to changed circumstances. A textbook can present basic ideas, but those ideas will only work effectively in a practical situation if moulded to meet the needs of the situation.

10.14 Summary

This chapter has explained the role of capital budgeting in the management process and the ways in which management accounting contributes to that process. It has set out techniques for project appraisal, covering: payback period; accounting rate of return; net present value; and internal rate of return. The use of formulae, discount tables and graphical representations has been explained. The problems of mutually exclusive projects are outlined but extensive exploration is left for more advanced study. Finally, it has dealt with post-completion audit of capital projects, and also touched on the developments of advanced manufacturing technologies where there will be challenges to the conventional application of discounting techniques.

Further reading

Drury, C. (1992), *Management and Cost Accounting*, Chapman & Hall.

Northcott, D. (1992), *Capital Investment Decision Making*, Advanced Management Accounting and Finance Series, ed. D. Otley, Harcourt Brace in association with CIMA.

Wilson, R. M. S. and Chua, W. F. (1992), *Managerial Accounting: Method and Meaning*, Chapman & Hall.

Self-testing on the chapter

1 What is the purpose of capital budgeting?

2 What is meant by the assumption of certainty of cash flows?

3 What are the main steps in making a decision about a capital investment?

4 What is the payback method of evaluating a project?

5 What are the advantages and limitations of the payback method?

6 What is the accounting rate of return?

7 What are the advantages and limitations of the accounting rate of return as a technique for use in capital budgeting?

8 What is meant by the time value of money?

9 What is meant by the present value of a cash flow?

10 What is meant by the term 'discounting'?

11 Define net present value and explain how it is calculated.

12 State the net present value decision rule to be used in capital budgeting.

13 Define internal rate of return and explain how it is calculated.

14 State the internal rate of return decision rule to be used in capital budgeting.

15 Explain the problems which may arise in choosing between mutually exclusive projects.

16 Explain the processes necessary for authorisation and review of capital projects.

17 Projects Ltd intends to acquire a new machine costing £50,000 which is expected to have a life of five years, with a scrap value of £10,000 at the end of that time.

Cash flows arising from operation of the machine are expected to arise on the last day of each year as follows:

End of year	£
1	10,000
2	15,000
3	20,000
4	25,000
5	25,000

Calculate the payback period, the accounting rate of return and the net present value, explaining the meaning of each answer you produce. (Assume a discount rate of 10 per cent per annum.)

Activities for study groups

1 Using a suitable computer spreadsheet package, set up a spreadsheet which will calculate net present values and internal rates of return for projects having cash flows for a ten-year period. Test the spreadsheet with sample data and then write a brief instruction sheet. Save the spreadsheet to a disk and exchange disks and instruction sheets with another group in the class.

2 Now write an evaluation of the spreadsheet you have received from another group. Consider the following:

(a) Does it deal with all possible types of cash flows (e.g. a negative flow at some point)?
(b) Does it provide a recommendation on accept/reject (e.g. using a conditional function)?
(c) Does it allow for relatively easy variation of the discount rate?
(e) Does the instruction sheet explain how to produce graphs of net present value plotted against discount rate?

List any other features of the spreadsheet which you would use in evaluating its effectiveness and user-friendliness.

Case studies

Case 10.1

Offshore Services Ltd is an oil-related company providing specialist firefighting and rescue services to oil rigs. The board of directors is considering a number of investment projects to improve the cash flow situation in the face of strong competition from international companies in the same field.

The proposed projects are:

Project	Description
ALPHA	Commission an additional firefighting vessel.
BRAVO	Replace two existing standby boats.
CHARLIE	Establish a new survival training course for the staff of client companies.
DELTA	Install latest communications equipment on all vessels.

Each project is expected to produce a reduction in cash outflows over the next five years. The outlays and cash benefits are set out below:

	End of year	ALPHA £000s	BRAVO £000s	CHARLIE £000s	DELTA £000s
Outlay	–	(600)	(300)	(120)	(210)
Cash flow benefits:					
	1	435	–	48	81
	2	435	–	48	81
	3	–	219	48	81
	4	–	219	48	81
	5	–	219	48	81
Internal rate of return		28.8%	22.0%	28.6%	26.8%

Any project may be postponed indefinitely. Investment capital is limited to £1,000,000. The board wishes to maximise net present value of projects undertaken and requires a return of 10 per cent per annum.

Required

Prepare a report to the board of directors containing:

1   calculations of net present value for each project, and

2   a reasoned recommendation on maximisation of net present value within the £1,000,000 investment limit.

Case 10.2

The directors of Advanced plc are currently considering an investment in new production machinery to replace existing machinery. The new machinery would produce goods more efficiently, leading to increased sales volume. The investment required will be £1,150,000 payable at the start of the project. The alternative course of action would be to continue using the existing machinery for a further five years, at the end of which time it would have to be replaced.

The following forecasts of sales and production volumes have been made:

Sales (in units)

Year	Using existing machinery	Using new machinery
19X1	400,000	560,000
19X2	450,000	630,000
19X3	500,000	700,000
19X4	600,000	840,000
19X5	750,000	1,050,000

Production (in units)

Year	Using existing machinery	Using new machinery
19X1	420,000	564,000
19X2	435,000	637,000
19X3	505,000	695,000
19X4	610,000	840,000
19X5	730,000	1,044,000

Further information

(a) The new machinery will reduce production costs from their present level of £7.50 per unit to £6.20 per unit. These production costs exclude depreciation.

(b) The increased sales volume will be achieved by reducing unit selling prices from their present level of £10.00 per unit to £8.50 per unit.

(c) The new machinery will have a scrap value of £150,000 after five years.

(d) The existing machinery will have a scrap value of £30,000 at the start of 19X1. Its scrap value will be £20,000 at the end of 19X5.

(e) The cost of capital to the company, in money terms, is presently 12 per cent per annum.

Required

1 Prepare a report to the directors of Advanced plc on the proposed investment decision.

2 List any further matters which the directors should consider before making their decision.

Case 10.3

The board of directors of Kirkside Glassware Ltd is considering the following proposed investment projects:

Project	Nature
A	Establishment of a staff training scheme.
B	Major improvements to the electrical system.
C	Installation of a computer.
D	Development of a new product.
E	Purchase of a warehouse space, presently leased.

It is estimated that each product will provide benefits in terms of reduced cash outflows, measured over the coming five years. The outlays and cash flow benefits, net of taxation, are set out below:

	End of year	Project A £000s	Project B £000s	Project C £000s	Project D £000s	Project E £000s
Outlay	–	(40,000)	(70,000)	(180,000)	(100,000)	(200,000)
Cash flow benefits:						
	1	16,000	27,000	66,000	–	145,000
	2	16,000	27,000	66,000	–	145,000
	3	16,000	27,000	66,000	73,000	–
	4	16,000	27,000	66,000	73,000	–
	5	16,000	27,000	66,000	73,000	–
Internal rate of return		28.65%	26.82%	24.32%	22.05%	28.79%

Each project has two separate phases of equal cost and providing equal cash flow benefits. The board is willing to consider adopting the first phase of any project without the second, if this appears necessary. Any project or phase not undertaken immediately may be postponed indefinitely. Capital available for investment is limited to £300,000. The board aims, as far as possible, to maximise the net present value of projects undertaken.

The company requires a return of 10 per cent per annum based on the net cash flows of any project.

Required

Prepare a report to the board of directors:
1 setting out a decision rule which could be applied in ranking the investment projects, and

2 listing other factors which the board of directors might wish to consider when selecting projects for implementation.

Supplement: Table of discount factors

Number of years	1%	2%	3%	4%	5%	6%	7%	8%	9%	10%	11%	12%	13%	14%	15%
1	0.990	0.980	0.971	0.962	0.952	0.943	0.935	0.926	0.917	0.909	0.901	0.893	0.885	0.877	0.870
2	0.980	0.961	0.943	0.925	0.907	0.890	0.873	0.857	0.842	0.826	0.812	0.797	0.783	0.769	0.756
3	0.971	0.942	0.915	0.889	0.864	0.840	0.816	0.794	0.772	0.751	0.731	0.712	0.693	0.675	0.658
4	0.961	0.924	0.888	0.855	0.823	0.792	0.763	0.735	0.708	0.683	0.659	0.636	0.613	0.592	0.572
5	0.951	0.906	0.863	0.822	0.784	0.747	0.713	0.681	0.650	0.621	0.593	0.567	0.543	0.519	0.497
6	0.942	0.888	0.837	0.790	0.746	0.705	0.666	0.630	0.596	0.564	0.535	0.507	0.480	0.456	0.432
7	0.933	0.871	0.813	0.760	0.711	0.665	0.623	0.583	0.547	0.513	0.482	0.452	0.425	0.400	0.376
8	0.923	0.853	0.789	0.731	0.677	0.627	0.582	0.540	0.502	0.467	0.434	0.404	0.376	0.351	0.327
9	0.914	0.837	0.766	0.703	0.645	0.592	0.544	0.500	0.460	0.424	0.391	0.361	0.333	0.308	0.284
10	0.905	0.820	0.744	0.676	0.614	0.558	0.508	0.463	0.422	0.386	0.352	0.322	0.295	0.270	0.247
11	0.896	0.804	0.722	0.650	0.585	0.527	0.475	0.429	0.388	0.350	0.317	0.287	0.261	0.237	0.215
12	0.887	0.788	0.701	0.625	0.557	0.497	0.444	0.397	0.356	0.319	0.286	0.257	0.231	0.208	0.187
13	0.879	0.773	0.681	0.601	0.530	0.469	0.415	0.368	0.326	0.290	0.258	0.229	0.204	0.182	0.163
14	0.870	0.758	0.661	0.577	0.505	0.442	0.388	0.340	0.299	0.263	0.232	0.205	0.181	0.160	0.141
15	0.861	0.743	0.642	0.555	0.481	0.417	0.362	0.315	0.275	0.239	0.209	0.183	0.160	0.140	0.123
16	0.853	0.728	0.623	0.534	0.458	0.394	0.339	0.292	0.252	0.218	0.188	0.163	0.141	0.123	0.107
17	0.844	0.714	0.605	0.513	0.436	0.371	0.317	0.270	0.231	0.198	0.170	0.146	0.125	0.108	0.093
18	0.836	0.700	0.587	0.494	0.416	0.350	0.296	0.250	0.212	0.180	0.153	0.130	0.111	0.095	0.081
19	0.828	0.686	0.570	0.475	0.396	0.331	0.277	0.232	0.194	0.164	0.138	0.116	0.098	0.083	0.070
20	0.820	0.673	0.554	0.456	0.377	0.312	0.258	0.215	0.178	0.149	0.124	0.104	0.087	0.073	0.061
21	0.811	0.660	0.538	0.439	0.359	0.294	0.242	0.199	0.164	0.135	0.112	0.093	0.077	0.064	0.053
22	0.803	0.647	0.522	0.422	0.342	0.278	0.226	0.184	0.150	0.123	0.101	0.083	0.068	0.056	0.046
23	0.795	0.634	0.507	0.406	0.326	0.262	0.211	0.170	0.138	0.112	0.091	0.074	0.060	0.049	0.040
24	0.788	0.622	0.492	0.390	0.310	0.247	0.197	0.158	0.126	0.102	0.082	0.066	0.053	0.043	0.035
25	0.780	0.610	0.478	0.375	0.295	0.233	0.184	0.146	0.116	0.092	0.074	0.059	0.047	0.038	0.030
26	0.772	0.598	0.464	0.361	0.281	0.220	0.172	0.135	0.106	0.084	0.066	0.053	0.042	0.033	0.026
27	0.764	0.586	0.450	0.347	0.268	0.207	0.161	0.125	0.098	0.076	0.060	0.047	0.037	0.029	0.023
28	0.757	0.574	0.437	0.333	0.255	0.196	0.150	0.116	0.090	0.069	0.054	0.042	0.033	0.026	0.020
29	0.749	0.563	0.424	0.321	0.243	0.185	0.141	0.107	0.082	0.063	0.048	0.037	0.029	0.022	0.017
30	0.742	0.552	0.412	0.308	0.231	0.174	0.131	0.099	0.075	0.057	0.044	0.033	0.026	0.020	0.015

Note: Present value of £1 to be received after n years when the rate of interest is r % per annum equals $1/(1 + r)^n$.

Number of years	16%	17%	18%	19%	20%	21%	22%	23%	24%	25%	26%	27%	28%	29%	30%
1	0.862	0.855	0.847	0.840	0.833	0.826	0.820	0.813	0.806	0.800	0.794	0.787	0.781	0.775	0.769
2	0.743	0.731	0.718	0.706	0.694	0.683	0.672	0.661	0.650	0.640	0.630	0.620	0.610	0.601	0.592
3	0.641	0.624	0.609	0.593	0.579	0.564	0.551	0.537	0.524	0.512	0.500	0.488	0.477	0.466	0.455
4	0.552	0.534	0.516	0.499	0.482	0.467	0.451	0.437	0.423	0.410	0.397	0.384	0.373	0.361	0.350
5	0.476	0.456	0.437	0.419	0.402	0.386	0.370	0.355	0.341	0.328	0.315	0.303	0.291	0.280	0.269
6	0.410	0.390	0.370	0.352	0.335	0.319	0.303	0.289	0.275	0.262	0.250	0.238	0.227	0.217	0.207
7	0.354	0.333	0.314	0.296	0.279	0.263	0.249	0.235	0.222	0.210	0.198	0.188	0.178	0.168	0.159
8	0.305	0.285	0.266	0.249	0.233	0.218	0.204	0.191	0.179	0.168	0.157	0.148	0.139	0.130	0.123
9	0.263	0.243	0.225	0.209	0.194	0.180	0.167	0.155	0.144	0.134	0.125	0.116	0.108	0.101	0.094
10	0.227	0.208	0.191	0176	0162	0149	0.137	0.126	0.116	0.107	0.099	0.092	0.085	0.078	0.073
11	0.195	0.178	0.162	0.148	0.135	0.123	0.112	0.103	0.094	0.086	0.079	0.072	0.066	0.061	0.056
12	0.168	0.152	0.137	0.124	0.112	0.102	0.092	0.083	0.076	0.069	0.062	0.057	0.052	0.047	0.043
13	0.145	0.130	0.116	0.104	0.093	0.084	0.075	0.068	0.061	0.055	0.050	0.045	0.040	0.037	0.033
14	0.125	0.111	0.099	0.088	0.078	0.069	0.062	0.055	0.049	0.044	0.039	0.035	0.032	0.028	0.025
15	0.108	0.095	0.084	0.074	0.065	0.057	0.051	0.045	0.040	0.035	0.031	0.028	0.025	0.022	0.020
16	0.093	0.081	0.071	0.062	0.054	0.047	0.042	0.036	0.032	0.028	0.025	0.022	0.019	0.017	0.015
17	0.080	0.069	0.060	0.052	0.045	0.039	0.034	0.030	0.026	0.023	0.020	0.017	0.015	0.013	0.012
18	0.069	0.059	0.051	0.044	0.038	0.032	0.028	0.024	0.021	0.018	0.016	0.014	0.012	0.010	0.009
19	0.060	0.051	0.043	0.037	0.031	0027	0.023	0.020	0.017	0.014	0.012	0.011	0.009	0.008	0.007
20	0.051	0.043	0.037	0.031	0.026	0.022	0.019	0.016	0.014	0.012	0.010	0.008	0.007	0.006	0.005
21	0.044	0.037	0.031	0.026	0.022	0.018	0.015	0.013	0.011	0.009	0.008	0.007	0.006	0.005	0.004
22	0.038	0.032	0.026	0.022	0.018	0.015	0.013	0.011	0.009	0.007	0.006	0.005	0.004	0.004	0.003
23	0.033	0.027	0.022	0.018	0.015	0.012	0.010	0.009	0.007	0.006	0.005	0.004	0.003	0.003	0.002
24	0.028	0.023	0.019	0.015	0.013	0.010	0.008	0.007	0.006	0.005	0.004	0.003	0.003	0.002	0.002
25	0.024	0.020	0.016	0.013	0.010	0.009	0.007	0.006	0.005	0.004	0.003	0.003	0.002	0.002	0.001
26	0.021	0.017	0.014	0.011	0.009	0.007	0.006	0.005	0.004	0.003	0.002	0.002	0.002	0.001	0.001
27	0.018	0.014	0.011	0.009	0.007	0.006	0.005	0.004	0.003	0.002	0.002	0.002	0.001	0.001	0.001
28	0.016	0.012	0.010	0.008	0.006	0.005	0.004	0.003	0.002	0.002	0.002	0.001	0.001	0.001	0.001
29	0.014	0.011	0.008	0.006	0.005	0.004	0.003	0.002	0.002	0.002	0.001	0.001	0.001	0.001	0.000
30	0.012	0.009	0.007	0.005	0.004	0.003	0.003	0.002	0.002	0.001	0.001	0.001	0.001	0.000	0.000

Chapter 11

The frontiers of management accounting

| Learning objectives |

After studying this chapter you should be able to:

1　Understand the development of activity-based costing.

2　Explain the main features of activity-based costing.

3　Compare activity-based costing with traditional approaches to cost allocation.

4　Explain in outline total quality management and life-cycle costing.

5　Understand the impact of advanced manufacturing technologies on traditional approaches to management accounting.

6　Be aware that developments such as strategic management accounting and business process re-engineering will provide scope for considerable further study of management accounting once you have mastered the basic, traditionally oriented, approach taken in this textbook.

11.1　Introduction

In Chapters 1 to 10 we have set out aspects of management accounting which have a history dating back to the early years of the nineteenth century. That history gives such management accounting techniques a respectable pedigree of being well tried and tested, but it also raises the question of how long an accounting technique can remain relevant to the changing needs of business.

The question of the relevance of management accounting practices was raised in a dramatic fashion in the 1980s by Johnson and Kaplan, two US authors who have written widely during recent years but whose views are most conveniently encapsulated in their book *Relevance Lost: The Rise and Fall of Management Accounting* (1987).

They analyse the development of management accounting in terms of the industrial revolution, arguing that management accounting developed to evaluate the efficiency of internal processes in the business, while financial accounting developed to measure the overall profit of the organisation. Financial accounting developed to meet the demands of stewardship and, in particular, developed accounting standards which required particular approaches to product costing and the treatment of overhead costs. These rules are most obvious in the financial accounting standards which deal with stock and long-term contracts, but rules on the allocation of costs may be found in other financial accounting standards such as those dealing with research and development expenditure and with depreciation.

In the opinion of Johnson and Kaplan this split between management and financial accounting was the root cause of the lost relevance as the century progressed, because the nature of businesses changed and non-manufacturing organisations became more significant to the economy as a whole. For such organisations, where service is the essential feature, there is little relevance in applying management accounting techniques which are derived from needs for product costing. Yet that is what they did.

In the 1960s, while financial accounting standards were developing around the world, management accounting research was being driven by an economic perspective and was developing rigorous mathematical techniques to refine the traditional product costing methods. These mathematical models were very satisfying to the theoreticians who produced them, but they were complex and found only limited acceptance in practice.

The 1970s saw management accounting research move into a different area, emphasising the need to balance the costs and benefits of information. The academic literature was labelled the 'information economics' approach because it regarded information as an item subject to the forces of supply and demand like any other product. The simple picture of supply and demand was modified by another group of academic literature which considered the relationship between the managers of an organisation and the owners of the organisation. Because the managers are the agents of the owners, there may be questions as to how far the agents act in the best interests of the owners and how far they protect their own interests as agents. This academic literature has been called 'agency theory'.

While all these academic developments were taking place there was considerable study of the behavioural aspects of management accounting. Such study has concentrated on the limitations of traditional management accounting techniques by showing that, when properly used, they may have positive motivational effects but, when used inappropriately, they may have a demotivating effect on employees. These motivational aspects have been referred to in earlier chapters.

By the early 1980s it had become apparent that a great deal of this academic activity had produced very little impact on management accounting practice. Scapens, in his book entitled *Management Accounting: A Review of Recent Developments* (1991), referred to the empirical research which had shown that the traditional, and relatively unsophisticated, methods persisted in practice despite the academic offerings of more sophisticated techniques. His conclusion was that the simple techniques might be arriving at the optimal solution to a problem and that they should not be rejected solely on the grounds that they are simple techniques. It was necessary to concentrate on explaining existing practice rather than promoting the academic models at all costs.

Into this arena stepped Kaplan, the US academic, who did exactly what Scapens and others were advising. Kaplan, together with his colleagues, found organisations which were forward-looking in their attitudes to management and then he observed their practices. As he did this, he wrote case studies for use by his management students, and from these case studies he saw a pattern emerging to which he gave the title *activity-based costing* (ABC). This attracted unprecedented interest from business managers, who were eagerly looking for new approaches to management accounting but had not been enthused by previous academic literature.

11.2 Activity-based costing

ABC is a new approach to assigning overhead costs to products. The proponents of the subject claim that ABC provides product cost information which is useful for decision making. That is quite a different claim from the message given throughout the previous ten chapters of this textbook, which repeatedly gave warnings about the dangers of making decisions based on accounting data that included an overhead allocation. The claims of ABC will be explored in this chapter by outlining the principles and then examining a case study.

There are four stages to establishing an activity-based costing system. These are:

1 identify the major activities which take place in an organisation;
2 identify the factors which most closely influence the cost of an activity. These factors are called the 'cost drivers' and are a direct indication of how the activity demands cost;
3 create a cost pool for each activity;
4 trace costs to activities according to how the activities demand costs.

11.2.1 Contrasting activity-based costing and traditional product cost allocation

Allocating direct costs to products is not a problem. In traditional costing, the direct costs are allocated to the products, while in the activity-based approach these direct costs are directly driven by the product and identifiable with the product.

The particular need for activity-based costing lies in the area of allocating overhead costs to products. The traditional approach to allocating overhead costs to products was explained in Chapter 3. In that chapter it was shown that, traditionally, costs are allocated first to cost centres and then to products which pass through those cost centres. Activity-based costing follows a different route to channelling costs towards products. Exhibit 11.1 sets out the contrasting approaches.

11.2.2 Nature of an activity

An activity, in its broadest sense, is something which happens in the business. An activity could be using materials to make a physical product or using labour to carry out a service operation. In ABC language, that would be an example of a *unit activity*, which is performed each time a product is produced. Other activities are performed to enable output of products but are not so closely dependent on how many units are produced. These are called *product-sustaining activities*. Examples would be product design, product testing and marketing. Some activities are classified as *batch-related activities* which are fixed for a given batch of products. This would include costs of the buying department, costs of moving stores from the warehouse to the factory floor, and costs of planning a

Exhibit 11.1
Contrasting activity-based costing and traditional product cost allocation

Traditional product cost allocation	Activity-based costing
Identify *cost centres* in which costs may be accumulated. Cost centres are determined by the nature of their function (e.g. production or service department cost centres).	Identify the way in which products drive the activity of the business and define suitable *cost pools* for collecting the costs relating to each activity. Activity pools are determined by the activities which drive the costs (e.g. obtaining new customers, negotiating customer contracts).
↓	↓
Collect costs in cost centres.	Collect costs in activity cost pools.
↓	↓
Determine an *overhead cost rate* for each production cost centre (e.g. cost per direct labour hour).	Determine a *cost driver rate* for each activity cost pool (e.g. a cost per customer contract, cost per customer order received).
↓	↓
Allocate cost to products using the calculated cost rate and the measure of the *product's consumption of that department's cost* (e.g. number of labour hours required).	Allocate cost to products according to the *product's demand for the activity* which drives cost.

production schedule. Where there are expenses such as rent or insurance which are not driven by making products, they are designated as *facility-sustaining activities* and no attempt is made to allocate these to products. They are charged as a total cost against all products after the separate profit margins on each product are determined.

Because activity-based costing requires a very thorough analysis of how products drive the costs of various activities, it is not feasible to work through a full illustration here. Instead, one activity, that of purchasing materials for use in a hotel restaurant, will be explored by case study in some detail. Hopefully, that will give you a flavour of the complexity and fascination of ABC and encourage you to read further.

11.2.3 Role of the management accountant

Activity-based costing allows the attention-directing functions of the management accountant to come to the fore. The management accountant takes a key role in understanding the operation of the business and translating into cost terms the activities as perceived by those who carry them out.

11.2.4 Case study: Glen Lyon Hotel

The Glen Lyon Hotel has two main product lines, with quite different characteristics. In the restaurant, meals are provided on a daily basis to the chef's high standards of perfection. In the conference suite, banquets are arranged for special functions such as weddings. There is a restaurant manager, responsible for restaurant meals, and a functions manager, responsible for banquets. The hotel seeks to offer competitive prices subject to meeting all costs and earning an adequate profit.

The hotel has a purchasing department which purchases the food required by the hotel restaurant and all supplies required for special functions, including crockery and cutlery. The purchasing officer is concerned that the restaurant manager insists on buying food in relatively small quantities, because the chef is very particular about monitoring the continued high quality of supplies. The functions manager also creates problems for the purchasing department because she insists on buying crockery and cutlery in bulk, to save cost, which requires time being taken by the purchasing officer to negotiate the best terms with the supplier. Even the suppliers can create a great deal of work because they are constantly changing their prices and this has to be recorded on the computer system of the purchasing department. The purchasing officer would like to show that these activities are all costly because they drive the amount of work undertaken by the purchasing department.

Fiona McTaggart has been called in to help, and she now explains how she went about the task of applying activity-based costing in relation to the activities of the purchasing department.

FIONA: *First of all I asked for a list of all the costs incurred by the department in a year (see exhibit 11.2).*

Exhibit 11.2
List of costs incurred by resources used in the purchasing department

Resource cost	£
Salary of purchasing officer	15,000
Wages of data processing clerk	9,000
Telephone calls	3,000
Total costs to be allocated	27,000

Identifying the cost drivers

Then I sat down with the purchasing officer for a long meeting during which we talked about how the purchasing process worked. From those discussions I found that a number of activities were driving the work of purchasing and I listed all those (see exhibit 11.3).

I explained to the purchasing officer that, although the purchasing department was an identifiable unit of the organisation for staff management purposes, it would no longer be treated as a cost centre under activity-based costing. The purchasing process would be regarded as a set of activities consuming 'resources' such as salaries, wages and telephone calls. Each activity would collect a 'pool' of cost as the resources were used up.

Exhibit 11.3
List of activities in the purchasing department

- Agreeing terms with supplier
- processing an order
- updating the price lists
- updating the supplier records
- processing queries about invoices.

The pool of costs would be passed on to those other departments drawing on the services of the purchasing department and from those departments the costs would find their way into products.

Creating the cost pools

The next stage was to decide how much of each resource cost was attributable to the activity driving that cost. This part was quite tricky because the purchasing officer only had a 'feel' for the relative impact in some cases. Take as an example the processing of an order. When the restaurant manager asks for food to be ordered, the purchasing officer first has to phone the supplier to check availability and likely delivery time. Then she checks that someone will be available to open the cold store when the delivery arrives. She is then able to fax the order to the supplier who will phone back to confirm that the goods are available and that delivery will be as requested. Once the goods arrive, the purchasing officer has to check that the delivery note agrees with what was ordered. That whole process takes about 20 minutes for each order.

We carried on talking and I was able to identify, for each resource cost, some measure of how the activity was being driven. The starting point was salaries. We estimated that the purchasing officer spent the equivalent of two days per week agreeing terms with suppliers. The remaining three days were divided equally over the other activities listed. The data processing clerk spent three days per week in processing orders, half a day each week on updating price lists and updating suppliers' records, and one day per week on checking and processing questions from the accounts department about invoices received for payment. The final cost heading was telephone calls. The destination and duration of each call is logged by the telephone system so we took a sample of one week's calls and decided that 60 per cent of telephone calls were routine calls to place an order, 20 per cent were dealing with queries over price changes and the remainder were spread equally over agreeing terms, updating the supplier records and dealing with invoice queries. Following these discussions I sketched a diagram of the ABC approach (see exhibit 11.4) and then drew up a table showing how each cost item could be allocated to the various activities so that a cost pool is created for each activity (see exhibit 11.5).

Demand for each activity

The next stage was to determine how many times each activity driver was put into action. This involved measuring the volume of each activity, as a measure of the demand for that activity. Agreeing terms with the supplier is not easy to quantify, but we were aware that there are discussions with each supplier at some time during the year, so we

Exhibit 11.4
Sketch of the ABC approach applied to the activity of purchasing

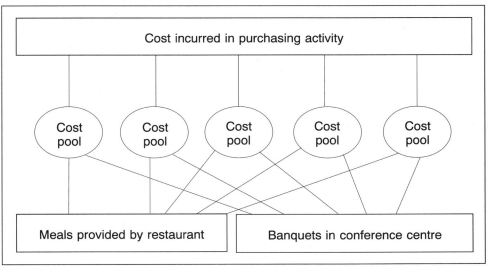

Exhibit 11.5
Creating a cost pool: allocation of resource costs to activities

Resource	Resource cost	Activity cost pools				
		Agreeing terms with supplier	Processing an order	Updating the price list	Updating the supplier records	Processing invoice queries
	£	£	£	£	£	£
Salary	15,000	6,000	2,250	2,250	2,250	2,250
Wages	9,000		5,400	900	900	1,800
Telephone	3,000	200	1,800	600	200	200
	27,000	6,200	9,450	3,750	3,350	4,250

took the number of suppliers as the measure of volume driving that activity. It was relatively easy to establish the number of orders processed at the request of the restaurant manager. The price list has to be updated every time the supplier changes the price of any items, and they all change at least twice per month, so we decided that the number of items on the order list was a reasonable measure. Updating supplier records involves changing minor details for existing suppliers but takes more time to record a new supplier. So we used the number of new suppliers as the measure of the volume of that activity. Processing invoice queries depends on the number of such queries.

Cost driver rates

My final accounting statement was a calculation of the cost per unit for each activity (see *exhibit 11.6*). This was determined by dividing the cost in the pool by the measure of how that activity was being driven by products.

Exhibit 11.6
Calculation of cost per activity unit for each activity

	Activity cost pools				
	Agreeing terms with supplier	Processing an order	Updating the price list	Updating the supplier records	Processing invoice queries
Cost per exhibit 11.5	£6,200	£9,450	£3,750	£3,350	£4,250
Activity driver	Number of suppliers	Number of orders	Number of items listed	Number of suppliers updated	Number of queries
Activity volume	60	1,600	7,000	60	150
Cost per activity unit	£103.333	£5.06	£0.536	£55.833	£28.333

Using the calculation of cost per activity unit for each activity I was able to explain the benefits of activity-based costing. The purchasing department is providing a service to the rest of the organisation, but at a cost. That cost could be made more visible using activity-based costing because the factors driving the cost could be quantified in their effect. Looking at exhibit 11.6, it is not difficult to see that the most significant cost drivers are the activities of agreeing terms with suppliers and of updating the suppliers' records. Each new supplier causes a further £159.166 (£103.333 + £55.833) to be incurred at an early stage. The restaurant manager needs to be aware that placing large numbers of low-volume orders causes cost to be incurred on each order. The total cost incurred could be reduced by moving to a lower number of orders, each being of higher volume. (Someone would need to check that that did not create larger new costs in storage of the goods.) The next most costly activity, in terms of cost per unit, is that of answering queries about invoices. The accounts department should be made aware that each enquiry costs £28.333.

I also looked back to the old way of allocating the cost of the purchasing department (see *exhibit 11.7*). Before activity-based costing was considered, the organisation charged the purchasing costs to products as a percentage of the value of materials ordered. Looking back to exhibit 11.5, the total purchasing department costs are shown as £27,000. The purchasing department handles goods to the value of £800,000 in a year. The purchasing department costs were therefore charged to products at 3.375 per cent of cost.

Why was this not the best approach? The answer is that there were two main product lines, having quite different characteristics. One was restaurant meals provided on a routine basis and the other was special banquets for functions such as weddings. My further enquiries revealed that the high-price purchases required for special functions

Exhibit 11.7
Previous methods of allocation, based on percentage of value of items requested

	Restaurant manager	Functions manager	Accounts department
	£	£	£
Goods purchased through purchasing department	300,000	500,000	–
3.375% of goods purchased	10,125	16,875	nil

Note: Allocation base equals 3.375 per cent of goods purchased.

caused relatively few problems in agreeing terms with suppliers and relatively few queries arose over the invoices. Where problems of negotiation and invoicing did arise was in the low-price, high-volume ingredients used routinely in the dining room meals. The information on cost per unit of each activity allowed a much more precise allocation of cost, although I was now in for even more work in tracing the costs from the various activity pools through to the products.

Tracing costs through to products

To trace costs through to products I obtained estimates of the quantity of each activity demanded by the restaurant manager and the function manager (see exhibit 11.8) and multiplied each quantity by the cost per activity unit calculated in exhibit 11.6. The result is shown in exhibit 11.9.

Exhibit 11.8
Quantity of activity demanded by each function

Activity	Demanded by restaurant manager	Demanded by functions manager
Agreeing terms with supplier	10 new suppliers	50 new suppliers
Processing an order	1,200 orders	400 orders
Updating the price list	4,000 items	3,000 items
Updating the supplier records	10 new suppliers	50 new suppliers
Processing invoice queries	All 150 demanded by accounts department	

Compare this with the cost allocation under the traditional system which is shown in exhibit 11.7.

My conclusions were that the accounts department had previously been unaware of the costs it was causing the purchasing manager whenever an invoice query was raised. Using activity-based costing would allow the allocation of cost to the accounts

Exhibit 11.9
Allocation of purchasing cost to restaurant manager, functions manager and accounts department

Activity	Restaurant manager	Functions manager	Accounts department	Total
	£	£	£	£
Agreeing terms with supplier	1,033	5,167		6,200
Processing an order	7,088	2,362		9,450
Updating the price list	2,143	1,607		3,750
Updating the supplier records	558	2,792		3,350
Processing invoice queries			4,250	4,250
Total cost allocated	10,822	11,928	4,250	27,000

department each time a question was raised. Some care might need to be taken to examine the size and significance of the invoice query in relation to the cost allocation. It would not be a good idea for the accounts department to allow a £50,000 error to go unchecked because they feared a charge of £28.33. The implementation of activity-based costing might need to be accompanied by the use of performance measures which show how the benefits of an activity exceed the costs incurred.

The functions manager would incur less overhead cost under the activity-based system than under the previous approach. The recorded cost of functions would therefore decrease. As I explained earlier, the high-priced purchases of food for special functions cause relatively few problems in processing a smaller number of orders. The functions manager seems to have a relatively high number of new suppliers. Cost could be controlled further if fewer suppliers were used for functions. Less purchasing effort would be required.

The restaurant manager experiences little difference in cost under either approach. To improve overhead costs there would need to be a quantum leap in practice, such as reducing the order frequency to the stage where one less person was employed in the purchasing department, or else where a part-time employee could do the work presently undertaken full-time. Merely reducing the order frequency would not be enough if the purchasing staff are still present full-time and the same cost is being spread over a lower volume of activity. Although there is little impact, these figures give the restaurant manager food for thought.

Product costs

In the full application of ABC, the costs would be taken into the final product cost. I have not done that here because the purchasing department's costs are only one small corner of the total business. Activity-based costing creates a lot of work, but a well coded computerised accounting system can handle that. I spent the best part of one day dealing only with the analysis of the purchasing department costs, so it would take a few weeks *of consultancy to cover the entire range of activities which contribute to the cost of the products. My consultancy fees would be another overhead to be allocated, but I believe the hotel would find the effort well worth it in terms of more effective management over a period of years.*

11.2.5 The benefits claimed for activity-based costing

Activity-based costing appeared first in the academic literature during the late 1980s. It had reached the professional accountancy journals by the early 1990s and by that time was already being used (or tested) by companies with progressive attitudes. The main benefits claimed are that it provides product cost information which, although it includes an allocation of overheads, is nevertheless useful for decision making purposes. It is useful because the overhead costs are allocated to the products in a way that reflects the factor driving the cost. If a product cost is thought to be too high, then it can be controlled by controlling the factors driving the most significant elements of its cost. Attention is directed towards problem areas. Activity-based costing is seen as a valuable management tool because it collects and reports on the significant activities of the business. It is also attractive for service-based organisations which have found the traditional, manufacturing-based costing methods not suited to the different nature of the service sector.

You may ask at this point, 'If activity-based costing is the best approach, why is it not in the first chapter?' The answer to that question is, first, that the technique is still relatively rare in practical application, despite the amount written about it. Secondly, no allocating mechanism can produce accurate results unless the cost item which is being processed is of high reliability and its behaviour is well understood. The successful application of activity-based costing depends on a thorough understanding of basic principles of cost behaviour and the ability to record and process costs accurately.

Activity-based costing will not solve all problems of forward planning. The analytical method relies on historical data and therefore shares with many other aspects of accounting the disadvantage of being a backward-looking measure which must be used with caution in forward-looking decisions.

Finally, activity-based costing requires detailed accounting records and a well-structured cost coding system so that costs are allocated correctly to cost pools and from there to products. There may need to be a considerable investment in discovering and installing the best information system for the job.

Activity 11.1

Imagine you are the owner of a business which rents ice-cream stalls from the local council. You employ persons to run each stall. Write down a list of the costs you would expect to incur. Write another list of the drivers of cost. How could activity-based costing help you understand and control the costs of your business?

11.3 Total quality management and cost of quality

The success of Japanese companies in recent years has caused intense interest in Japanese styles of management. One aspect of Japanese management is the approach of 'get it right first time'. In this spirit, total quality management (TQM) has the customer as its focal point.

Quality is defined as fully satisfying agreed customer requirements at the lowest internal price. TQM is therefore a management function which could be added to those explained in Chapter 1. It straddles the traditional management functions of planning and control. The use of the TQM approach is seen as the key to improving profitability because there is a cost associated with failing to meet quality standards in products and services. Such costs could arise through loss of customers, claims for refunds in respect of defective supplies, and the work of putting right mistakes. If costs can be controlled through TQM, then profits will increase.

Those who are enthusiastic for TQM believe that it is possible to obtain defect-free work first time on a consistent basis. That may be an idealistic target but to have such a target encourages a culture where prevention of error is a key feature of the operations.

This activity of improving quality to improve profits will itself cause cost to be incurred. The term *cost of quality* is a collective name for all costs incurred in achieving a quality product or service.

Cost of quality may be defined by the 'prevention-appraisal-failure' model. *Prevention costs* are the costs of designing, implementing and maintaining the TQM system. They include: quality planning; quality assurance; training; and determining specifications for incoming materials, for processes carried out in the operations of the business and for finished products. *Appraisal costs* are the costs of evaluating suppliers and obtaining an evaluation by customers. They include checking incoming materials and supplies, inspecting equipment and collecting information from customers on satisfaction with goods and services. *Failure costs* are of two main types: *internal failure costs* are the costs incurred when it is found, before delivery to customers, that the work does not reach the desired specification; *external failure costs* are the costs incurred when poor quality work is discovered after the supply to the customer has taken place. Examples of internal failure costs are: waste; scrap; rectification; re-inspection of rectified work; and analysis of the causes of failure. External failure costs include: repairs; warranty claims; complaints; returns; product liability litigation; and loss of customer goodwill.

The traditional picture of quality control is that in the absence of quality control, failures occur which create *failure costs*. Detection of failure relies on checking after the failure has occurred. The checking process involves further *checking costs*. With quality controls in place, as prevention work is undertaken, the costs of failure should begin to fall. At the outset, the prevention costs will be additional to the costs of checking for failures, but as confidence grows, and the frequency of failure decreases, the need for checking should diminish. The quality exercise will be successful in cost terms if there is a reduction in total cost over the three headings of prevention, appraisal and failure costs.

TQM ideas are widely practised and there are many non-financial performance measures being used in business organisations. Measuring the cost of quality is a relatively undeveloped area although a few businesses have a well-developed approach. The management accountant as scorekeeper is ideally placed to record and monitor cost of quality, but many of the initiatives emerging are in special units within an organisation which are separate from the 'traditional' management accounting functions. Management accountants may need to be proactive in seeking out new ways of applying their generic skills.

Activity 11.2

Look through the feature pages of a newspaper such as the Financial Times *for articles about management. Make a file of any articles relating to total quality management (TQM). To what extent is accounting measurement mentioned in these articles? Do they show an awareness of the cost of maintaining high quality?*

11.4 Benchmarking

In order to obtain a feel for relative success in TQM, or other developments in business activity, companies are increasingly turning to *benchmarking*. This is the name given to the process of measuring the organisation's operations, products and services against those of competitors recognised as market leaders, in order to establish targets which will provide a competitive advantage.

The stages of benchmarking are:

1   decide what area of activity to benchmark (e.g. customer services, business processes in particular departments, quality of employees, standard of training);
2   select a competitor who is reputedly the best in the area of activity to be benchmarked. Major companies in one country may target an international competitor rather than a domestic company. In some benchmarking situations the competitor may agree to an exchange of information because both parties believe they can benefit from the exchange;
3   decide on the appropriate measurements to be used in defining performance levels;
4   determine the competitor's strengths and compare these with the company's own record;
5   use the information collected as the basis for an action plan. To be effective, this action plan must involve all grades of employee working in the area of activity.

The management accountant has a role throughout this process because the emphasis is on improving profit and measuring performance. The management accounting role starts with directing attention, by producing the performance measures and showing the relationship with profit improvement. It moves into problem solving as the information on comparative performance measures is collected and has to be transformed into an action plan for the organisation. It then takes on the scorekeeping aspect as the achievement of total quality is monitored.

11.5 Life-cycle costing

The life-cycle of a product starts with the design stage, moving on through development and market-testing, design of the process and acquisition of equipment. Commercial production then begins and the remainder of the product's life is dependent on the continued demand.

Particular attention has to be paid to the early stages of the product life-cycle because decisions made at that stage tend to have an effect on all subsequent stages. Management accounting reporting tends to be based on short time periods such as a year, a half-year, a month or a week. The life-cycle may have a place in the budgetary process when a new product or service is being planned, but it does not feature in management accounting reports once the activity has commenced.

Life-cycle costing is a process which evaluates the performance of the product against previously determined expectations, over its life-cycle, and also evaluates the total revenues against total costs. Those costs will include the costs of investment in plant and equipment, research and development, design and marketing, as well as the operating costs which are matched against revenue in the conventional measurement of short-term profit. This emphasis on the life-cycle sees the product as an entity within the activity of the business and helps to focus on the desirability of continuing or discontinuing the product line. The term *post-completion product audit* has been used to describe this life-cycle approach.

11.6 Advanced manufacturing technologies

Advanced technologies in manufacturing (AMTs) have been developed by engineers as a means of competing more effectively. To compete, organisations need to manufacture innovative products of high quality at low cost. The product life-cycle may be short, demand may be changing more rapidly, and international competition creates a further element of uncertainty. As with any business activity, these changes represent new approaches to the management of the business, and management accounting must keep pace with the change in management approach.

Engineers have produced new technology of four main types:

1 design innovations;
2 planning and control techniques;

3 execution; and
4 overarching technologies.

Each of these new technologies is considered in turn.

The *design innovations* have covered computer-aided design (CAD), computer-aided engineering (CAE), computer-aided process planning (CAPP) and design for manufacture and assembly. CAD uses computers to evaluate various designs of the product, while CAE includes design but also encompasses evaluation and testing so that the initial design becomes a working product. CAPP uses computers to plan the detailed processes required to manufacture the design proposed. Finally, the computer can also be used to design a system which makes the manufacture and assembly process meet the demand for the output.

Planning and control techniques have covered materials requirements planning (MRP), manufacturing resource planning (MRP II), and statistical process control (SPC). MRP involves matching stock levels to the production process and controlling incoming customer orders to match the availability of materials. MRP II applies similar controls to all resources used in the manufacturing process. They both use computers to break down a customer's order into various stages which can be matched against resource availability. SPC uses statistical analysis to identify the most likely causes of bottlenecks in the manufacturing process, which can then be corrected before a crisis arises.

Execution means converting raw materials and components into finished goods. The technologies have included robotics, automated guided vehicles (AGVs), flexible manufacturing systems (FMS) and automated storage and retrieval system (ASRS). These titles are self-descriptive of the activities involved.

The *overarching technologies* are those which take a total perspective of the organisation. They include total quality management (TQM), just-in-time (JIT), focused factory, and computer-integrated manufacturing (CIM). The management approach involved in TQM has been described earlier in this chapter. Just-in-time (JIT) is a methodical manner of reducing machine set-up times, accepting only perfect incoming resources, allowing no deviation from standards, and matching output exactly to the demands of the customer. Every activity occurs exactly at the time needed for effective execution and always happens exactly as planned. TQM, JIT, focused factory and CIM are all types of management philosophy, as well as being sophisticated new management techniques.

11.6.1 The role of management accounting

The traditional role of management accounting, as described in Chapters 1–10, has focused on transactions-oriented data. Advanced manufacturing technologies concentrate on quality of product, quantity of product that may be produced within specified constraints, improving on-time delivery, or the effective timing of production runs. A focus on costs which have been developed by a traditional costing system may be unhelpful in such a management approach.

Traditional accounting systems focus on making plans, observing the outcome and giving feedback that is used to modify the next round of plans. AMTs work in the opposite manner. They seek to prevent problems by anticipating them or by taking action as they arise. There is no benefit seen in letting the problem happen and then calculating what it cost.

The crisis for management accounting has been the question of whether to adapt to these AMTs or carry on with the traditional approach not being integrated to the management technology. Some organisations have attempted the integration process. The number of data items used in AMTs is considerably higher than the number of data items used in traditional management accounting, so the management accounting recording system has to be adapted to allow exchange of information with the manufacturing system. There is no clearly prescribed way of carrying out such integration. It is very much dependent on the nature of the business. In the following case study, Fiona McTaggart describes the very early stages of the process.

11.6.2 Case study: accounting aspects of just-in-time

FIONA: *I recently participated in a pilot project involving a leading company manufacturing car engines. There were two shifts planned, one using manual labour and one entirely operated by robots. A just-in-time (JIT) philosophy applied throughout. Each item required for the manufacture of an engine was planned to arrive on the production line at exactly the right time. Delivery from suppliers was similarly timed with care. The computer recording system was designed so that the arrival of the component was recorded and bar coding allowed the cost to be recorded at the same time. There was no need to wait for an invoice to arrive before the cost of the component could be ascertained. Reports on direct costs could therefore be generated simultaneously with reports on physical activity. Dealing with overhead costs was more difficult, but a system was proposed where overhead costs were applied to activities using an activity-based approach and a focus on machine hours as the main measure of use of an activity.*

The JIT approach emphasises elimination of waste. The management accounting report for the two shifts had a waste exception report section which allowed rapid identification of departure from accepted waste levels on each shift. Linking the accounting records to the physical activity meant that each shift could be identified separately.

The pilot project was receiving a cautious welcome by the technical managers. They had regarded traditional management accounting as an unavoidable nuisance but they could see that the pilot scheme was bringing the accounting information closer to their perspective of the operation.

Activity 11.3

> *Read the feature pages of a business newspaper such as the* Financial Times. *Look for headings such as Production and Operations Management, or Information Management. Find articles on benchmarking, life-cycle costing and advanced manufacturing technologies. To what extent is the accounting aspect of each subject discussed?*
>
> *Note also that you will rarely find articles on management accounting as a separate topic. The management accounting applications will usually be discussed in the context of the management purpose featuring in the article.*

11.7   Strategic management accounting

The successful management of a business depends on having a successful business strategy. It has been argued that if the business strategy gives the organisation its competitive edge, then the management accounting should reflect that strategy as closely as possible. The traditional emphasis on costs and revenues may not achieve this aim. What really matters is the influence of the external environment.

Strategy usually includes planning to achieve a better performance than competitors. It is argued that management accounting should show the extent to which the organisation is beating its competitors. Market share, market prospects and the impact of product mix would all be useful information to include in a management accounting report as factors contributing to sales, profits and cash flows.

Another way of looking at the influence of the external environment is to consider competitive advantage in costs. If the business has an influential position as a purchaser of goods and services, then its strategy may include an aggressive policy of negotiating contracts for those goods and services. The JIT strategy of ordering goods from suppliers to arrive exactly when they are needed may put strains on the suppliers and force up their costs, increasing the price of the goods. The concept of a *value chain* has been proposed to describe how the corporate strategy affects the entire chain of value-creating activities. Strategic management accounting might show that £1 saved at one point in the chain has been offset by an extra £2 incurred at another stage.

Turning to capital budgeting, as explained in Chapter 10, the advocates of strategic management accounting would argue for abandoning such techniques in advanced manufacturing technologies. The reason given is that many of the strategic benefits of the AMTs, such as greater flexibility, are not readily reflected in cash flow forecasts for net present value calculations. Payback methods of capital budgeting are even more problematic with their strong emphasis on the short term. The manager using AMTs needs a longer-term perspective. The danger of abandoning the discounted cash flow approach is that the discipline of a rigorous analysis may be lost, to be replaced by intuition and impressions. A more fruitful route for the development of management accounting in such situations might be to make greater efforts to quantify all the cash flow effects, rather than allowing the practical difficulties to become an excuse for not trying.

11.8   Business process re-engineering

Those who are at the forefront of developing new approaches to improving business operations now claim to have moved on to a new stage, called business process re-engineering. This involves a dramatic redesign of business processes, organisation structures and use of technology, to achieve breakthroughs in business competitiveness. The benefits claimed are that operations can be streamlined, and consequently costs can be cut, while creating process excellence in all key aspects of the organisation.

The phrase 'breaking the china' has been used by those who describe the technique. They are looking for a quantum leap into being a world leader. They draw the analogy of passing a treasured set of family china from one generation to the next. One day the entire collection falls to the floor in pieces. Putting it together again produces a totally different pattern in the china. In a similar way, if the whole business process is broken up and then restructured with the aim of being a world leader, an entirely new policy will emerge.

The advances in management techniques during the 1980s are now seen as only a development within the overall pattern of handing the collection down the family intact. The advocates of business process re-engineering explain that, while concentrating on MRP, MRP II, TQM and JIT, businesses were retaining the traditional ways of working in functional groups. Quality teams were given the task of creating new ways of working within their specific areas or functions. In contrast, business process re-engineering concentrates on the process rather than the function.

Take an example of a company manufacturing engines for heavy goods vehicles. The castings provided by the supplier did not align exactly with the machine which carried them to the assembly line. This had always been accepted as a function of the business operation despite the fact that it caused a pause in production at regular intervals to allow maintenance work necessitated by wear and tear. As a re-engineering of the business process, the supplier was asked to manufacture the castings to a different specification which would align with the machine. This allowed the process to speed up by 30 per cent on previous activity levels and quickly recovered the extra costs charged by the supplier due to the redesign of the castings.

Take as a second example the processing of customer orders. In the traditional approach a sales representative visited the customer and took an order. The sales representative initiated the order documentation, giving it an order number and setting up a file on the computer. The product manager received the order, checked that the resources were available for implementation and rewrote the order so that the customer's description of what was required could be specified in terms of the operations carried out by the business. The customer's credit rating was checked by the credit controller. This process all took a considerable amount of time because it was not well co-ordinated and there were gaps of time between each stage. As a re-engineering move, the business process was shortened by giving the sales representative a portable computer and a modem to be taken out on visits to clients. This allowed credit rating to be checked on-line even while the job specification was being discussed with the customer. The computer also included a data sheet on which the sales representative could enter the customer's order in such a way as to match the specification required by the production department. The information passed directly to the manufacturing premises by way of the modem and the confirmed specification was returned by fax to the customer. The entire operation of specifying and confirming the order could be completed within one hour, while the sales representative was still on hand at the customer's premises.

The advocates of business process re-engineering emphasise three goals: customer satisfaction; market domination; and increased profitability. To win the claim to be a world leader requires success in all three. The business therefore has to identify the core business processes which drive it and to think in terms of process enhancement. Identifying the core business process and 'reading the market' helps the company to find a 'break point' where a change in the business process can cause a significant positive reaction in the market and take the company into a leadership position.

Where does all this leave the management accounting function? The books describing the new management techniques do not devote much space to the management accounting function. It is up to the management accountants to keep up with the new developments. One obvious way is to find new measures of costs and revenues which reflect the impact on profit, since increased profitability is a stated aim. Another way is perhaps to carry out some monitoring function to make sure that the non-financial goals do not cause a cash flow crisis before the benefits can be earned. That may sound somewhat heretical in a management accounting text, but, at the end of the day, someone is providing finance to the organisation and is looking for a return on that finance. That provider of finance has to be convinced that the returns will be achieved.

Activity 11.4	*Look through the management pages of a business newspaper such as the* Financial Times. *You should have little difficulty in finding articles on aspects of business process re-engineering. Select one article and identify the aspects on which management accounting ought to be offering a useful contribution. Write a short article (300 words) explaining how management accounting is relevant to changing management practices.*

11.9 Evolution or revolution?

You might ask, having read this chapter, why it is necessary to pay any attention to the previous ten chapters. The answer is that the ideas described in this chapter are exciting and forward-looking but they are being used primarily by a selection of the market leaders and the innovators. There is a vast range of businesses which are still using traditional management accounting techniques. That will necessitate an understanding of the traditional approach for some time yet. Bromwich and Bhimani, in a report written for the Chartered Institute of Management Accountants, used the phrase 'evolution not revolution'. So while you should read and think about the new ideas, you will also find it necessary to understand and apply the aspects of management accounting which have been taught traditionally. If you have a strong command of the approach to management accounting set out in the chapters of this book, then you will have the basis on which to build an understanding of the present practice in most business organisations. You will also be in a position to move on to an in-depth study of developments in management accounting in both the academic and the practical spheres.

Further reading	The following references provide a more detailed discussion of the developments which are mentioned in this chapter and provide further insight into the rich diversity of material awaiting those who decide to pursue the study of management accounting further.

Ashton, D., Hopper, T. and Scapens, R. (1990), *Issues in Management Accounting*, Prentice Hall.

Bank, J. (1992), *The Essence of Total Quality Management*, Prentice Hall International (UK).

Bromwich, M. and Bhimani, A. (1989), *Management Accounting: Evolution not Revolution*, 1st edn, Chartered Institute of Management Accountants (UK).

Bromwich, M. and Bhimani, A. (1993), *Management Accounting: Pathways to Progress*, 2nd edn, Chartered Institute of Management Accountants (UK).

Emmanuel, C. R., Otley, D. T. and Merchant, K. (1990), *Accounting for Management Control*, Chapman & Hall.

Emmanuel, C. R., Otley, D. T. and Merchant, K. (eds) (1991), *Readings in Accounting for Management Control*, Chapman & Hall.

Innes, J. and Mitchell, F. (1990), *Activity Based Costing – A Review with Case Studies*, Chartered Institute of Management Accountants (UK).

Innes, J. and Mitchell, F. (1991), *Activity Based Cost Management: A Study of Development and Implementation*, Chartered Institute of Management Accountants (UK).

Johansson, H. J., McHugh, P., Pendlebury, A. J. and Wheeler, W. A. (1993), *Business Process Re-Engineering*, Wiley (UK).

Johnson, T. and Kaplan, R. (1987), *Relevance Lost: The Rise and Fall of Management Accounting*, Harvard University Press.

Oakland, J. (1993), *Total Quality Management: The Route to Improving Performance*, Butterworth Heinemann.

Scapens, R. W. (1991), *Management Accounting: A Review of Recent Developments*, Macmillan.

Steedle, L. F. (ed.) (1990), *World-Class Accounting for World-Class Manufacturing*, National Association of Accountants, New Jersey.

Ward, K. (1992), *Strategic Management Accounting*, Butterworth-Heinemann in association with CIMA.

Wilson, R. M. S. and Chua, W. F. (1992), *Managerial Accounting: Method and Meaning*, Chapman & Hall.

The monthly professional journals *Management Accounting* (USA) and *Management Accountant* (UK) are excellent sources of description, discussion and commentary on topics of current interest.

Self-testing on the chapter

1   Explain the main stages of establishing an activity-based costing system.

2   How does activity-based costing differ from traditional product cost allocation?

3   What are the benefits claimed for activity-based costing?

4   What is the management philosophy represented by Total Quality Management?

5 How is the cost of quality measured?

6 What is meant by 'benchmarking'?

7 How does the concept of life-cycle costing differ from traditional approaches to management accounting?

8 What is the potential impact of advanced manufacturing technologies on management accounting practice?

9 What is meant by 'strategic management accounting'?

10 What is the stated purpose of 'business process re-engineering'?

Activities for study groups

1 Obtain recent issues of professional management accounting journals (six monthly issues would be sufficient). Prepare a chart of the following type:

Accounting issue	Type of article		
	Describing technique	Critical evaluation of technique	Stating a problem which is not yet fully solved

Using the chart make a short presentation to the class entitled 'Current issues in management accounting: the viewpoint in professional journals'.

2 Obtain recent issues of an academic management accounting journal (four quarterly issues would be sufficient). Prepare a chart of the following type:

Accounting issue	Type of paper			
	Describing technique	Critical evaluation of technique	Stating a problem which is not yet fully solved	Something else

Using the chart make a short presentation to the class entitled 'Current issues in management accounting: the viewpoint in an academic journal'.

3 Search the management feature pages of a business newspaper such as the *Financial Times* for a period of one month. Find articles about management which have a management accounting angle. Select one of the articles and write a response setting out the ways in which management accounting will contribute to the management purposes described in the article.

Glossary

Term	Definition
absorption costing	All production costs are allocated to products and the unsold stock is valued at total cost of production.
accounting	The process of identifying, measuring and communicating financial information about an entity to permit informed judgements and decisions by users of the information.
accounting policies	Accounting methods which have been judged by business enterprises to be most appropriate to their circumstances and adopted by them for the purpose of preparing their financial statements.
accounting rate of return	Calculated by taking the average annual profits expected from a project as a percentage of the capital invested.
accounting standards	Definitive statements of best practice issued by a body having suitable authority.
accruals concept	The accruals (or matching) concept states that revenues and expenses are recognised as they are earned or incurred and not as money is received or paid.
allocation	The process of spreading cost over more than one accounting period, or attributing cost to one period rather than another.
annual report	A document produced each year by limited liability companies containing the accounting information required by law. Larger companies also provide information and pictures of the activities of the company.
avoidable cost	One which may be eliminated by taking a particular action.
balance sheet	A statement of the financial position of an entity showing assets, liabilities and ownership claim.
breakeven point	That point of activity (measured as sales volume) where total sales and total costs are equal, so that there is neither profit nor loss.
budget	A detailed plan which sets out, in money terms, the plans for income and expenditure in respect of a future period of time. It is prepared in advance of that time period and is based on the agreed objectives for that period of time, together with the strategy planned to achieve those objectives.
business entity	A business which exists independently of its owners.
by-product	A product arising from a process where the sales value is insignificant by comparison with that of the main product or products.
capital	Amount of finance provided to enable a business to acquire assets and sustain its operations.

Term	Definition
Term	*Definition*
capital budgeting	A process of management accounting which assists management decision making by providing information on the investment in a project and the benefits to be obtained from that project, and by monitoring the performance of the project subsequent to its implementation.
cash flow projections	Statements of cash expected to flow into the business and cash expected to flow out over a particular period.
Companies Act	The Companies Act 1985 and 1989. Legislation to control the activities of limited liability companies.
contribution per unit	The sales price minus the variable cost per unit. It measures the contribution made by each item of output to fixed costs and profit.
controllable cost	A cost which is capable of being regulated by a manager within a defined boundary of responsibility.
cost centre	A unit of the organisation in respect of which a manager is responsible for costs under her or his control.
current asset	An asset that is expected to be converted into cash within the trading cycle.
depreciation	A measure of the wearing out, consumption or other reduction of the useful economic life of a fixed asset, from a range of causes.
direct costs	Directly traceable to an activity of the business for which costs are to be determined.
director(s)	Person(s) appointed by shareholders of a limited liability company to manage the affairs of the company.
discount rate	Most suitable rate of interest to be applied in calculating present value. Could be based on one particular type of finance but more usually is the cost of mixed sources.
discounting	The process of calculating present value of projected cash flows.
dividend	Amount paid to shareholder, usually in the form of cash, as a reward for investment in the company. The amount of dividend paid is proportionate to the number of shares held.
division	A part of the organisation where the manager has responsibility for generating revenues, controlling costs and producing a satisfactory return on capital invested in the division.
entity	Something that exists independently, such as a business which exists independently of the owner.
equivalent unit of output	The amount of output, expressed in terms of whole units, which is equivalent to the actual amount of partly or fully completed production.
external reporting	Reporting financial information to those users with a valid claim to receive it, but who are not allowed access to the day-to-day records of the business.
external users (of financial statements)	Users of financial statements who have valid interest but are not permitted access to the day-to-day records of the company.

Term	Definition
feed forward control	Means making predictions of outputs expected at some future time and then quantifying those predictions, in management accounting terms.
feedback control	Involves comparing outputs achieved against outputs desired and taking corrective action if necessary.
financial accounting	A term usually applied to external reporting by a business where that reporting is presented in financial terms.
financial adaptability	The ability of the company to respond to unexpected needs or opportunities.
financial information	Information which may be reported in money terms.
financial statements	Documents containing accounting information which is expected to have a useful purpose.
financial viability	The ability to survive on an ongoing basis.
fixed asset	An asset that: is held by an enterprise for use in the production or supply of goods and services, for rental to others, or for administrative purposes; has been acquired with the intention of being used on a continuing basis; and is not intended for sale in the ordinary course of the business.
fixed cost	One which is not affected by changes in the level of activity, over a defined period of time.
gross	Before making deductions.
incremental costs	The additional costs that arise from an activity of the organisation. To justify incurring incremental costs it is necessary to show they are exceeded by incremental revenue.
indirect costs	Spread over a number of activities of the business for which costs are to be determined.
interest (on loans)	The percentage return on capital required by the lender (usually expressed as a percentage per annum).
internal rate of return	The discount rate at which the present value of the cash flows generated by the product is equal to the present value of the capital invested, so that the net present value of the project is zero.
internal reporting	Reporting financial information to those users inside a business, at various levels of management, at a level of detail appropriate to the recipient.
investment centre	A unit of the organisation in respect of which a manager is responsible for capital investment decisions as well as revenue and costs.
investors	Persons or organisations which have provided money to a business in exchange for a share of ownership.
job costing system	A system of cost accumulation where there is an identifiable activity for which costs may be collected. The activity is usually specified in terms of a job of work or a group of tasks contributing to a stage in the production or service process.

Term	Definition
joint products	Two or more products arising from a process, each of which has a significant sales value.
liabilities	Obligations of an entity to transfer economic benefits as a result of past transactions or events.
limited liability	A phrase used to indicate that those having liability in respect of some amount due may be able to invoke some agreed limit on that liability.
limited liability company	Company where the liability of the owners is limited to the amount of *capital* they have agreed to contribute.
liquidity	The extent to which a business has access to cash or items which can readily be exchanged for cash.
loan creditors	Persons who have lent money to a business.
management	Collective term for those persons responsible for day-to-day running of a business.
management accounting	Reporting accounting information within a business, for management use only.
margin of safety	The difference between the breakeven sales and the normal level of sales (measured in units or in £s of sales).
matching concept	The matching (or accruals) concept states that revenues and expenses are recognised as they are earned or incurred and not as money is received or paid. Expenses are matched against revenues in the period they are incurred.
net	After making deductions.
net assets	*assets* minus *liabilities* [equals *ownership interest*].
net present value	The net present value (of a project) is equal to the present value of the cash inflows minus the present value of the cash outflows, all discounted at the cost of capital.
non-controllable cost	One which is not capable of being regulated by a manager within a defined boundary of responsibility, although it may be a cost incurred so that the responsibility may be exercised.
ownership interest	The residual amount found by deducting all of the entity's *liabilities* from all of the entity's *assets*.
payback period	The length of time required for a stream of cash inflows from a project to equal the original cash outlay.
period costs	Those costs which are treated as expenses in the period in which they are incurred.

Term	*Definition*
present value	A sum of £1 receivable at the end of n years when the rate of interest is r% per annum equals $$\frac{1}{(1+r)^n}$$ where r represents the annual rate of interest, expressed in decimal form, and n represents the time period when the cash flow will be received.
primary financial statements	The balance sheet, profit and loss account, statement of total recognised gains and losses and cash flow statement.
prime cost of production	Equal to the total of direct materials, direct labour and other *direct costs*.
process costing	Appropriate to a business or operation where there is a continuous flow of a relatively high volume of similar products during a reporting period.
product costs	Those costs associated with goods or services purchased, or produced, for sale to customers.
production overhead cost	Comprises indirect material, indirect labour and other indirect costs of production.
profit centre	A unit of the organisation in respect of which a manager is responsible for revenue as well as costs.
profitability index	The present value of cash flows (discounted at the cost of capital) divided by the present value of the investment intended to produce those cash flows.
public limited company (plc)	A company which has limited liability and offers its shares to the public.
relevant costs	Those future costs which will be affected by a decision to be taken. Non-relevant costs will not be affected by the decision.
reporting period	The period in respect of which the accounting information is prepared. In management accounting the period may be as frequent as the management chooses – weekly, monthly, quarterly and annual reporting are all used.
reserves	The claim which owners have on the *assets* of a company because the company has created new wealth for them over the period since it began.
residual income	Defined as operating profit less an interest charge based on the assets used and controlled by the division.
responsibility centre	An area of responsibility which is controlled by an individual. It might be a cost centre, a profit centre or an investment centre.
return (in relation to investment)	The reward earned for investing money in a business. Return may appear in the form of regular cash payments (dividends) to the investor, or in a growth in the value of the amount invested.
return on investment	Calculated by taking profit controllable by the division as a percentage of the investment in assets which produces that profit.
share capital	Name given to the total amount of cash which the shareholders have contributed to the company.

Term	*Definition*
shareholders	Owners of a limited company.
shares	The amount of share capital held by any shareholder is measured in terms of a number of shares in the total capital of the company.
short-term finance	Money lent to a business for a short period of time, usually repayable on demand and also repayable at the choice of the business if surplus to requirements.
standard costs	Target costs which should be attained under specified operating conditions. They are expressed in costs per unit.
total product cost	Comprises prime cost plus production overhead cost.
trade creditors	Persons who supply goods or services to a business in the normal course of trade and allow a period of credit before payment must be made.
turnover	The sales of a business or other form of revenue from operations of the business.
unavoidable cost	Not eliminated by taking a particular action.
variable cost	One which varies directly with changes in the level of activity, over a defined period of time.
variable costing	Only variable costs of production are allocated to products and the unsold stock is valued at variable cost of production. Fixed production costs are treated as a cost of the period in which they are incurred.
variance	Arises when an actual cost per unit differs from the standard cost set for that unit. An *adverse variance* arises when the actual cost is greater than the standard cost. A *favourable variance* arises when the actual cost is less than the standard cost.
working capital	Finance provided to support the short-term assets of the business (stocks and debtors) to the extent that these are not financed by short-term creditors.

Appendix

Solutions to numerical questions

Note that solutions are provided only for numerical material since other matters are covered either in the book or in the further reading indicated.

Chapters 1 and 11 have no separate solutions because there are no numerical questions.

Chapter 2

Q 1 (a) Cost X is a fixed cost because *total* cost does not vary with output

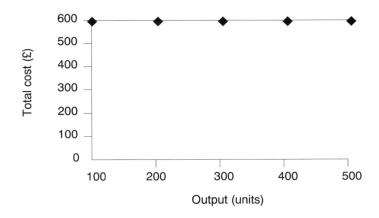

(b) Cost Y is a variable cost because total cost varies in direct proportion to output and is zero when output is zero

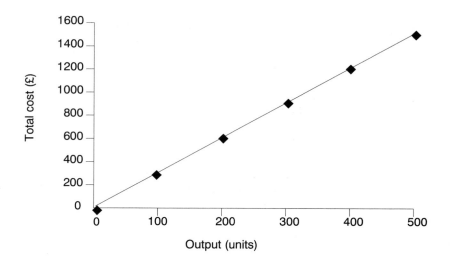

(c) Semi-variable cost because total cost varies in direct proportion to output but has a value of £600 when output is zero (seen by extending the graph until it meets the vertical axis). The fixed cost is £600.

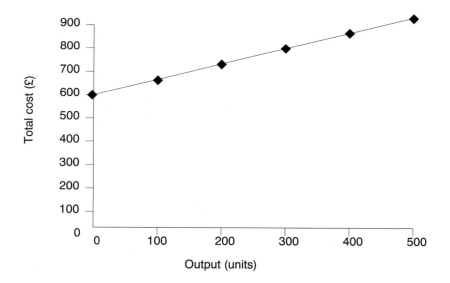

Q 3 **Table of costs for one year based on variable mileage within the year**

Mileage per annum	5,000	10,000	15,000	20,000	30,000
	£	£	£	£	£
Variable costs					
Spare parts	180	360	540	720	1,080
Fuel	700	1,400	2,100	2,800	4,200
Tyres	400	800	1,200	1,600	2,400
Total variable cost	1,280	2,560	3,840	5,120	7,680
Fixed costs					
Service costs per year	900	900	900	900	900
Insurance	800	800	800	800	800
Depreciation	4,800	4,800	4,800	4,800	4,800
Total fixed cost	6,500	6,500	6,500	6,500	6,500

(b) Note that in drawing the graph it is necessary to insert a point for 25,000 miles (although no calculation is required because the straight line is formed from the data already calculated).

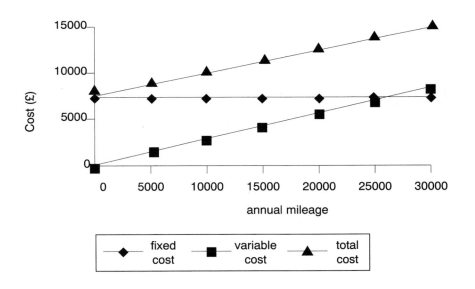

(c) Average cost per mile

Variable cost per mile (pence)	25.6	25.6	25.6	25.6	25.6
Fixed cost per mile (pence)	130.0	65.0	43.3	32.5	21.7
Average cost per mile (pence)	155.6	90.6	68.9	58.1	47.3

(d) All total costs follow a straight line. Total fixed costs do not depend on mileage. Total variable costs increase directly with mileage. Total fixed plus variable costs starts at £6,500 for zero miles and increases in direct proportion to mileage. The average cost per mile for each year falls as the annual mileage increases. Note that for tyres a proportionate cost has been calculated where the mileage is not exactly 15,000 miles. Note also that Depreciation has been included as a fixed cost because it does not depend on mileage covered.

Q 4

		£
Metal piping	Product	12,000
Wages to welders and painters	Product	9,000
Supplies for welding	Product	1,400
Advertising campaign	Period	2,000
Production manager's salary	Period	1,800
Accounts department computer costs for dealing with production records	Period	1,200

The costs incurred during May relate to 4,000 towel rails, so allocate costs on this basis. Product costs are £22,400 in total, or £5.60 per towel rail. There are 500 towel rails remaining in stock at the end of the month which would have a value of £(500 × 5.60) = £2,800.

Most business would use a value higher than £5.60 to take some of the period costs into account (e.g. a proportion of the production manager's salary). However, this is a matter of judgment where others would charge all period costs in the profit and loss account.

Chapter 3

Case 3.1

Statement of total cost of production
(In the absence of any information to the contrary it will be assumed that production equals sales so that there are no opening and closing stocks.)

		Cars 3,000 £		Tractors 6,000 £
Direct materials	3,000 × £16	48,000	6,000 × £10	60,000
Direct labour:				
Moulding department	3,000 × 5 hrs × £3	45,000	6,000 × 6 hrs × £3	108,000
Painting department	3,000 × 4 hrs × £3	36,000	6,000 × 4 hrs × £3	72,000
Production overhead (see below)				
Moulding department	£2.876 × 5hrs × 3,000	43,140	£2.876 × 6hrs × 6,000	103,526
Painting department	£2.759 × 4hrs × 3,000	33,108	£2.759 × 4hrs × 6,000	66,216
Total production cost*		205,248		409,742

*(£10 rounding error in totals)

Calculation of production overhead cost per unit of product

The canteen costs have first to be allocated to each of the production departments. Ideally this should be based on number of employees but that information is not available so some approximation is required. Tractors sell twice as many by volume as cars and the hours worked per toy are broadly similar, so it would be reasonable to allocate canteen costs on the basis 2:1.

Production overhead	*Moulding* £	*Painting* £	*Total* £
Variable costs	52,000	18,000	70,000
Fixed costs	84,000	60,000	144,000
Share of canteen (1:2)	10,667	21,333	32,000
	146,667	99,333	246,000
Number of hours (see below)	51,000	36,000	
Production overhead cost per hour	£2.876	£2.759	

Moulding: (3,000 × 5hrs) + (6,000 × 6 hrs) = 51,000 hrs
Painting: (3,000 × 4hrs) + (6,000 × 4 hrs) = 36,000 hrs

(b) Estimate of profit or loss on each product line

		Cars £		*Tractors* £
Sales	£120 × 3,000	360,000	£140 × 6,000	840,000
Total costs – per (a) above		205,248		409,742
Profit on product line		154,752		430,258

(c) Note that the profit on each product line depends on the way in which the canteen costs are allocated. If the proportions had been 1:1 rather than 1:2 then there would have been relatively more cost on moulding, with less cost on painting. Furthermore we are not told how the fixed costs were shared between moulding and painting departments. There is more in moulding (£84,000) than there is in painting (£60,000) but each unit spends more time in moulding than in painting so the split may appear reasonable.

The information on total cost and total profit may be used for showing segmental profit for each product line (subject to the warning about allocation of overhead costs). It may be used in reporting to managers in each department as part of the control process. The sales of tractors are twice those of cars but the profit is almost three times that of cars. This is primarily because of the higher sales price and lower materials cost. Labour costs per unit are marginally higher for tractors and the overheads follow a similar pattern.

Using the information for planning requires care, particularly in relation to the overhead costs. The relevant costs are first of all the variable costs, which must be covered by revenue earned. In the short term little can be done to avoid the fixed costs, so planning in the short term concentrates on selling prices and volumes and on variable costs.

Chapter 4

Q 1 (a) 16 components are charged to the job card and used as part of the value of work-in-progress.

    (b) The amount of £600 is added to work-in-progress, split as shown between the two jobs mentioned.

    (c) The job card is closed and the record is transferred to finished goods stock.

Q 2 *Direct costs*

Materials used:	£
500 drums of milk	75,000
Cartons	4,000
Cheesemakers' wages	6,000
Prime cost	85,000

Overhead costs

Cleaning and hygiene	1,200
Rent, rates, electricity	8,000
Cost of production	94,200

Q 3

Job cost record: Job 801		
3 May	Direct materials	112,000 †
30 May	Direct labour	10,000 ♥
	Prime cost	122,000
30 May	Production overhead:	20,600
	Total production cost	142,600
	To finished goods	(142,600)
	Work-in-progress	nil

Job cost record: Job 802		
3 May	Direct materials	32,000 †
30 May	Direct labour	5,000 ♥
	Prime cost	37,000
30 May	Production overhead:	10,300
	Total production cost	47,300
	Finished goods	(47,300)
	Work-in-progress	nil

Job cost record: Job 803		
3 June	Direct materials	12,800 †
30 June	Direct labour	5,000 ♥
	Prime cost	17,800
30 June	Production overhead:	10,300
	Total production cost	28,100
	Finished goods	28,100
1 May	*Work-in-progress*	nil

Note on production overheads:

	£
Rent, rates and electricity	18,000
Stain, varnish etc	22,500
Security	700
	41,200

Labour cost is £20,000 in total so production overhead is £2.06 per £ of labour.

Q 4 Statement of contract profit for year ended 31 December 19X1

Transactions during 19X1:		*£000s*
May	Materials purchased and delivered to site	91
May	Equipment delivered to site	14
July	Architect's fee	7
June-Dec	Materials issued from store	73
May-Dec	Wages paid on site	71
Sept	Payment to subcontractors	10
May-Dec	Direct costs	22
Dec	Head office charges	6
	Total costs incurred	294
	Deduct remaining at the end	
Dec	Value of equipment remaining on site	(9)
Dec	Value of material remaining on site	(15)
		270
	Add other costs of the period	
Dec	Amount due to subcontractors	3
Dec	Direct costs incurred but not yet paid	3
	Total costs for year	276
Dec	Sales value of work certified	280
	Less total costs	276
	Profit of the period	4

Case 4.1

430 packages (needs 2 shifts): Profit for 1 day

	£	£
Selling price 430 packages at £25.20		10,836
Cost of direct materials 430 at £23.75	10,213	
Cost of labour (£100 + £120)	220	
Supervision £40	40	
Other fixed overheads £280	280	
Depreciation £100	100	
		10,853
Net loss		(17)

880 packages (needs 3 shifts): Profit for 1 day

	£	£
Selling price 880 packages at £25.00		22,000
Cost of direct materials 880 at £23.75	20,900	
Cost of labour (£100 + £120 + £160)	380	
Supervision £40 + £40	80	
Other fixed overheads £280	280	
Depreciation £100	100	
		21,740
Net profit		260
Net profit per package		£3.38

1,350 packages (needs 3.8 shifts): Profit for 1 day

	£	£
Selling price 1,350 packages at £24.80		33,480
Cost of direct materials 1,350 at £23.75	32,063	
Cost of labour (£100 + £120 + £160 + £100)	480	
Supervision £40 + £40 + £20	100	
Other fixed overheads £280 + £100	380	
Depreciation £100 + £100	200	33,223
Net profit		257
Net profit per package		£0.19

Explanation. The 880 package option is the preferred one because it gives the benefit of a higher volume of profit without increasing the fixed costs. The 1,350 package option takes up more fixed costs and so reduces unit profit.

Chapter 5

Q 12 800 equivalent units at £3 = £2,400

Q 13 1,800 units with respect to materials and 600 units with respect to conversion and overhead

Q 14 Problem for allocation is the £2,000 of joint costs. These could be allocated by proportion to volume 3:1:2 or by sales value net of costs, i.e. £(15,000–4,000): £(4,000–1,800): £(6,000–2,400)

Q 15

	Physical flow (units)	Equivalent units of output
INPUT		
Work in progress at start	50,000	
Material introduced	80,000	
	130,000	
OUTPUT		
Goods finished this month	100,000	100,000
Work in progress at end (20% completed)	30,000	6,000
Total	130,000	106,000

	£
Opening work-in-progress brought forward	42,000
Incurred this month	140,000
Total costs to be accounted for	182,000

$$\text{Cost per equivalent unit} = \frac{£182,000}{106,000} = £1.717$$

	£
Value of finished output 100,000 × £1.717	171,700
Work-in-progress 6,000 × £1.717	10,300
Total costs accounted for	182,000

Q 16

	Physical flow (units)	Equivalent units of output
INPUT		
Work in progress at start	2,000	
Material introduced	6,200	
	8,200	
OUTPUT		
Goods finished this month	7,000	7,000
Work in progress at end (30% completed)	1,200	360
Total	8,200	7,360

	£
Opening work-in-progress brought forward	3,600
Incurred this month £14,700 + £12,820	27,520
Total costs to be accounted for	31,120

$$\text{Cost per equivalent unit} = \frac{£31{,}120}{7{,}360} = £4.228$$

	£
Value of finished output 7,000 × £4.228	29,600
Work-in-progress 360 × £4.228	1,520
Total costs accounted for	31,120

Case 5.1

(1)(a) Allocate joint costs by units of output

	Liquefied gas	Oil	Grease	Total
	£	£	£	£
Sales	20,000	230,000	8,000	258,000
Cost of crude oil*	2,038	101,942	1,020	105,000
Refining costs **	874	43,689	437	45,000
Additional processing costs	12,000	60,000		72,000
Total allocated costs	14,912	205,631	1,457	222,000
Profit	5,088	24,369	6,543	36,000

* Total output 515,000 units, crude oil cost £105,000, therefore unit cost was 20.39 pence per unit
** Total output 515,000, refining cost was £45,000, therefore unit cost was 8.74 pence per unit

(1)(b) Allocate joint costs by sales value

	Liquefied gas	Oil	Grease	Total
	£	£	£	£
Sales	20,000	230,000	8,000	258,000
Cost of crude oil*	8,140	93,604	3,256	105,000
Refining costs**	3,488	40,116	1,396	45,000
Additional processing costs	12,000	60,000		72,000
Total allocated costs	23,628	193,720	4,652	222,000
Profit/ (Loss)	(3,628)	36,280	3,348	36,000

* (20/258) × £105,000, (230/258) × £105,000, (8/258) × £105,000
** (20/258) × £45,000, (230/258) × £45,000, (8/258) × £45,000

(2) For decision-making purposes the previous cost allocations should not be used. Instead the extra revenue should be compared with the extra cost.

	Liquefied gas	Oil	Grease	Total
	£	£	£	£
Sales as recorded	20,000	230,000	8,000	258,000
Sales at split-off point	5,000	175,000	8,000	188,000
Additional sales through processing	15,000	55,000	nil	70,000
Additional processing costs	12,000	60,000		72,000

There has therefore been a net loss of £2,000 through processing further.

Case 5.2 (This solution follows the example set out in the chapter in which there is no opening work-in-progress.)

Assembly department
(i) Data in respect of month of July 19X2 (as per question)
(ii) Statement of physical flows and equivalent units of output for the month

	Physical flow (units)	Equivalent units of output	
		Material	Conversion
INPUT			
Units commenced	80,000		
	80,000		
OUTPUT			
Units completed in month	60,000	(100%) 60,000	(100%) 60,000
Work in progress at end	20,000	(100%) 20,000	(50%) 10,000
Total equivalent units	80,000	80,000	70,000

(iii) Ascertain total costs to be accounted for this period

	Material	Labour & prodn o/head	Total
	£	£	£
Incurred this month	240,000	205,000	445,000

(iv) Calculate cost per equivalent unit

	Material	Conversion
Total costs to be accounted for	£240,000	£205,000
Number of equivalent units	80,000	70,000
Cost per equivalent unit	£3	£2.93

(v) Apportion cost between finished output and work-in-progress

	£	£
Value of finished output 60,000 × £5.93		355,700
Work-in-progress:		
Material 20,000 × £3	60,000	
Labour & o/heads 10,000 × £2.93	29,300	
		89,300
Total costs accounted for		445,000

Finishing department

(i) Data in respect of month of July 19X2 (as per question)

(It is necessary to assume that the 60,000 units completed and transferred out of Assembly during the month were all transferred into Finishing)

(ii) Statement of physical flows and equivalent units of output for the month

	Physical flow (units)	Equivalent units of output	
		Material	*Conversion*
INPUT			
Transferred from Assembly	60,000		
	60,000		
OUTPUT			
Units completed in month	50,000	(100%) 50,000	(100%) 50,000
Work in progress at end	10,000	(100%) 10,000	(70%) 7,000
Total equivalent units	60,000	60,000	57,000

(iii) Ascertain total costs to be accounted for this period

	Material £	*Labour & prodn o/head* £	*Total* £
Transferred in from Assembly	355,700		355,700
Incurred this month	88,500	198,100	286,600
	444,200	198,100	642,300

(iv) Calculate cost per equivalent unit

	Material	*Conversion*
Total costs to be accounted for	£444,200	£198,100
Number of equivalent units	60,000	57,000
Cost per equivalent unit	£7.403	£3.475

(v) Apportion cost between finished output and work-in-progress

	£	£
Value of finished output 50,000 × £10.878		543,945
Work-in-progress:		
Material 10,000 × £7.403	74,030	
Labour & o/heads 7,000 × £3.475	24,325	
		98,355
Total costs accounted for*		642,300

*Rounding used where necessary to ensure all costs included

Chapter 6

Self-testing on the chapter

Q 16

	Jan	Feb	Mar	Apr	May	June
	£	£	£	£	£	£
Sales	12,000	13,000	14,000	13,500	12,600	11,100
Cash received – budget	nil	12,000	13,000	14,000	13,500	12,600

Q 17

	£
Goods purchased during January	18,000
Owing to creditors at end of January	13,600
Cash paid for January purchases	4,400
Payment for amounts owed at start	12,500
Total paid	16,900

Q 18 Cost of indirect materials in March £500, split £200 variable and £300 fixed.

During April direct labour hours will be 20 per cent higher and it is known that variable indirect material is proportionate to direct labour hours, so increase variable cost by 20 per cent from £200 to £240. Fixed cost remains constant so total budget is £540.

Q 19 Newtrend Ltd

(Note that in questions of this type there will often be more than one way of interpreting the information given. That is not a problem provided the total column is used to check for arithmetic consistency and the figure.)

Sales budget

Selling price £90 per unit

	Year 1				Total
	Quarter 1	Quarter 2	Quarter 3	Quarter 4	
Modified radio units	8,100	8,400	8,700	7,800	33,000
	£	£	£	£	£
Sales	729,000	756,000	783,000	702,000	2,970,000

Production budget for each quarter

By units, production must meet the sales of this quarter and 20 per cent of planned sales of the next quarter:

	Year 1				Total
	Quarter 1	Quarter 2	Quarter 3	Quarter 4	
Modified radio units	8,100	8,400	8,700	7,800	33,000
For sales of quarter	8,100	8,400	8,700	7,800	
Add 20% of next quarter sales	1,680	1,740	1,560	1,620	1,620
	9,780	10,140	10,260	9,420	
Less stock of previous quarter	–	1,680	1,740	1,560	
Production required	9,780	8,460	8,520	7,860	34,620

Converting from units of production to costs of production

	Year 1				Total
	Quarter 1	Quarter 2	Quarter 3	Quarter 4	
Units to be produced	9,780	8,460	8,520	7,860	34,620
	£	£	£	£	£
Direct materials	293,400	253,800	255,600	235,800	1,038,600
Direct labour	322,740	279,180	281,160	259,380	1,142,460
Fixed overhead *	117,360	101,520	102,240	94,320	415,440
	733,500	634,500	639,000	589,500	2,596,500
*Includes depreciation of	11,300	9,776	9,844	9,080	40,000

(Note that fixed overhead includes Depreciation of £40,000 per annum, allocated on the basis of a cost per unit produced. Total production is 34,620 units so depreciation is £1.155 per unit.)

Cash budget for each quarter

	Quarter 1 £	Quarter 2 £	Quarter 3 £	Quarter 4 £	Total £
		Year 1			Total
Cash from customers					
⅓ current quarter	243,000	252,000	261,000	234,000	
⅔ previous quarter	–	486,000	504,000	522,000	
Total cash received	243,000	738,000	765,000	756,000	2,502,000
Purchase of fixed assets	200,000				200,000
Payment to suppliers**	225,600	267,000	255,000	242,400	990,000
Wages	322,740	279,180	281,160	259,380	1,142,460
Fixed overhead (excl dep)	106,060	91,744	92,396	85,240	375,440
Total cash payments	854,400	637,924	628,556	587,020	2,707,900
Receipts less payments	(611,400)	100,076	136,444	168,980	(205,900)

**Schedule of payments to suppliers on one month's credit.*

The initial stock of 1,000 units will be paid for at the start of month 2, together with one-third of the units requires for month 1's production. Thereafter the payment is always on a one-third basis because the 1,000 units of stock remains constant.

	Quarter 1 £	Quarter 2 £	Quarter 3 £	Quarter 4 £	Total £
Direct materials purchased	293,400	253,800	255,600	235,800	1,038,600
Payment for initial stock	30,000				30,000
Two months' purchases	195,600	169,200	170,400	157,200	
One month from previous qtr	–	97,800	84,600	85,200	78,600
Total payment	225,600	267,000	255,000	242,400	990,000

Comment on cash flow statement

This is the type of statement which would be required by someone being asked to lend money to the business. The start-up situation requires cash but there is a positive cash flow from operations. The lender would want to add to the cash flow statement a schedule of loan repayments and interest payments to see whether the operational cash flows could meet the financing needs of the business.

Q 20 Tools Ltd

(Note that in questions of this type there will often be more than one way of interpreting the information given. That is not a problem provided the total column is used to check for arithmetic consistency.)

Sales budget

Selling price £90 per unit

	Year 1				Total
	Quarter 1	Quarter 2	Quarter 3	Quarter 4	
Modified tool units	4,050	4,200	4,350	3,900	16,500
	£	£	£	£	£
Sales	364,500	378,000	391,500	351,000	1,485,000

Production budget for each quarter

By units, production must meet the sales of this quarter and 100 per cent of planned sales of the next quarter:

	Year 1				Total
	Quarter 1	Quarter 2	Quarter 3	Quarter 4	
Modified tool units	*4,050*	*4,200*	*4,350*	*3,900*	*16,500*
For sales of quarter	4,050	4,200	4,350	3,900	
Add 10 per cent of next qtr sales	420	435	390	405	405
	4,470	4,635	4,740	4,305	
Less stock of previous qtr	–	420	435	390	
Production required	4,470	4,215	4,305	3,915	16,905

Converting from units of production to costs of production

	Year 1				Total
	Quarter 1	Quarter 2	Quarter 3	Quarter 4	
Units to be produced	4,470	4,215	4,305	3,915	16,905
	£	£	£	£	£
Direct materials	107,280	101,160	103,320	93,960	405,720
Direct labour	134,100	126,450	129,150	117,450	507,150
Fixed overhead *	44,700	42,150	43,050	39,150	169,050
	286,080	269,760	275,520	250,560	1,081,920
*Includes depreciation of	5,288	4,987	5,093	4,632	20,000

(Note that fixed overhead includes Depreciation of £20,000 per annum, allocated on the basis of a cost per unit produced. Total production is 16,905 units so depreciation is £1.183 per unit.)

Cash budget for each quarter

	Year 1				Total
	Quarter 1	Quarter 2	Quarter 3	Quarter 4	
Cash from customers					
⅓ current quarter	121,500	126,000	130,500	117,000	
⅔ previous quarter	–	243,000	252,000	261,000	
Total cash received	121,500	369,000	382,500	378,000	1,251,000
Purchase of fixed assets	100,000				100,000
Payment to suppliers**	83,520	103,200	102,600	97,080	386,400
Wages	134,100	126,450	129,150	117,450	507,150
Fixed overhead (excl dep)	39,412	37,163	37,957	34,518	149,050
Total cash payments	357,032	266,813	269,707	249,048	1,142,600
Receipts less payments	(235,532)	102,187	112,793	128,952	(108,400)

**Schedule of payments to suppliers on one month's credit.*

The initial stock of 500 units will be paid for at the start of month 2 together with one-third of the units required for month 1's production. Thereafter the payment is always on a one-third basis because the 500 units of stock remains constant.

	Quarter 1 £	Quarter 2 £	Quarter 3 £	Quarter 4 £	Total £
Direct materials purchased	107,280	101,160	103,320	93,960	405,720
Payment for initial stock	12,000				12,000
Two months' purchases	71,520	67,440	68,880	62,640	
One month from previous qtr	–	35,760	33,720	34,440	31,320
Total payment	83,520	103,200	102,600	97,080	386,400

Comment on cash flow statement

This is the type of statement which would be required by someone being asked to lend money to the business. The start-up situation requires cash but there is a positive cash flow from operations. The lender would want to add to the cash flow statement a schedule of loan repayments and interest payments to see whether the operational cash flows could meet the financing needs of the business.

Case 6.1 Garden Ornament Company

From the information presented in tables T 1 to T 5 the various detailed budgets are prepared as shown in tables T 6 to T 18. These lead to the master budget set out in tables T 19 to T 21.

Sales budget: sales and debtors

The sales budget sets out the volume of sales expected for each product, multiplied by the expected selling price, to obtain the total sales by value expected for each product. The total sales for the year ahead may then be calculated, shown in bold print in the sales budget.

(T 6)

Sales budget	Ref	Ducks	Herons	Total for year
Unit sales for year	T 1	8,000	15,000	
Unit selling price	T 1	£30	£45	
Total sales		£240,000	£675,000	**£915,000**

The year-end debtors are calculated as half of one month's sales (one-twenty-fourth of the total year's sales if these are spread evenly throughout the year)

(T 7)

Debtors budget	Ref	Ducks	Herons	Total for year
Total sales	T 6	£240,000	£675,000	£915,000
		divide by 24	divide by 24	
Debtors at year end		£10,000	£28,125	**£38,125**

Production plan

(T 8)

Production plan in units	Ref	Ducks	Herons
Planned sales volume	T 1	8,000	15,000
Add planned closing inventory of finished goods	T 3	–	–
Less opening inventory of finished goods	T 3	–	–
Planned unit production for year		8,000	15,000

Direct materials budget: Purchases, inventory and trade creditors

Once the production plan is decided, the costs of the various inputs to production may be calculated. Direct materials must be purchased to satisfy the production plans, but the purchases budget must also take into account the need to hold inventory of raw materials. After the purchases budget has been quantified in terms of cost, the impact on trade creditors may also be established.

The *purchases budget* is based on the units required for production in the period, making allowance for the opening and closing inventory of raw materials. The plan is to hold sufficient inventory at the end of the period to meet 60 per cent of the following month's production (*see* T3). The number of units to be purchased will equal the planned production for the period, plus the planned inventory of raw materials at the end of the period (shown in the opening balance sheet at T5), minus the planned inventory of raw materials at the end of the period (calculated in T8).

(T 9)

Purchases budget in units	Ref	Ducks	Herons
Production volume	T 8	8,000	15,000
Add raw materials inventory planned for end of period	T 3	400 60% of (8,000/12)	750 60% of (15,000/12)
Less raw materials inventory held at start of period	T 5	400	750
Purchases of raw materials planned		8,000	15,000

(T 10)

Purchases budget in £s	Ref	Ducks	Herons	Total for year
Volume of purchases	T 9	8,000	15,000	
		£	£	£
Cost per unit	T 1	14	16	
Total purchase cost		112,000	240,000	**352,000**

Trade creditors are calculated as one month's purchases, a relatively uncomplicated procedure in this instance because the purchases remain constant from month to month.

(T 11)

One month's purchases 352,000/12	£29,333

The direct materials cost of goods sold must also be calculated at this point, for use in the budgeted profit and loss account. The direct materials cost of goods sold is based on the materials used in production of the period (which in this example is all sold during the period).

(T 12)

Direct materials cost of goods sold	Ref	Ducks	Herons	Total for year
Production in units	T 8	8,000	15,000	
		£	£	
Materials cost per unit	T 1	14	16	
Total cost of goods to be sold		£112,000	£240,000	**£352,000**

Direct labour budget

The direct labour budget takes the volume of production in units and multiplies that by the expanded labour cost per unit to give a labour cost for each separate item of product and a total for the year, shown in bold print.

(T 13)

Direct labour budget	Ref	Evening dress	Costume dress	Total for year
Production in units	T 8	8,000	15,000	
		£	£	£
Labour cost per unit	T 1	12	13	
Total cost		96,000	195,000	**291,000**

It is also useful to check on the total resource requirement which corresponds to this total labour cost, since it takes time to plan increases or decreases in labour resources. The average direct labour cost was given in (T 1) as £15,000 per person per year. The following calculation assumes that the employees can work equally efficiently on any of the three product lines.

(T 14)

> *Resource requirement:*
>
> Based on an average cost of £15,000 per person per year, the total labour cost of £291,000 would require 19.4 full-time equivalent persons

Production overhead budget

Production overheads include all those overhead items which relate to the production activity. In this example it includes heat and light, business rates and depreciation. Depreciation is calculated at a rate of 20 per cent on the total cost of equipment held during the year (£190,000 at the start, as shown in (T 5), plus an additional £70,000 noted in (T 4)). (£260,000 × 20% = £52,000)

(T 15)

Production overhead budget	Ref	£
Heat and light	T 2	8,000
Production fixed overheads	T 2	4,000
Depreciation	T 4	52,000
Total		**64,000**

Total production cost budget

Total production cost budget comprises the cost of direct materials, direct labour and production overhead.

(T 16)

Production cost budget	Ref	£
Direct materials	T 12	352,000
Direct labour	T 13	291,000
Production overhead	T 15	64,000
Total		**707,000**

Administration expense budget

(T 17)

Administration budget	Ref	£
Partners' salaries (taken in cash)	T 2	55,000
Rent of premises	T 2	11,000
Office staff	T 2	48,450
Total		**114,450**

Marketing expense budget

The marketing expense budget relates to all aspects of the costs of advertising and selling the product. The information in (T 2) specifies a marketing cost which is dependent on sales, being estimated as 18 per cent of sales value.

(T 18)

Marketing expense budget	Ref	£
18% of £915,000	T 2 & T 6	**164,700**

Master budget

The master budget has three components: the budgeted profit and loss account for the year, the budgeted cash flow statement and the budgeted balance sheet. These are now set out using the foregoing separate budgets. Where the derivation of figures in the master budget should be evident from the earlier budgets, no explanation is given, but where further calculations have been performed these are shown as working notes.

Budgeted profit and loss account

(T 19)

Budgeted profit and loss account for the year ended 31 December 19X5

	Ref	Ducks £	Herons £	Total for year £
Total sales	T 6	240,000	675,000	915,000
Material cost	T 12	112,000	240,000	352,000
Labour cost	T 13	96,000	195,000	291,000
Total variable cost		208,000	435,000	643,000
Contribution		32,000	240,000	272,000
% on sales		13.3%	35.6%	
Production overhead	T 15			64,000
Gross profit				208,000
Administration cost	T 17			(114,450)
Marketing cost	T 18			(164,700)
Net loss				(71,150)

Budgeted cash flow statement

Where expenses are paid for as soon as they are incurred, the cash outflow equals the expense as shown in the budgeted profit and loss account. In the case of cash collected from customers, debtors at the start and end of the period must be taken into the calculation. In the case of cash paid to suppliers the creditors at the start and end of the period must be taken into account. The cash flow statement contains references to working notes which follow the statement and set out the necessary detail.

(T 20)

Budgeted cash flow statement for the year ended 31 December 19X5

	Note	£	£
Cash to be collected from customers	1		908,875
Cash to be paid to suppliers	2	352,667	
Direct labour	3	291,000	
Heat and light	3	8,000	
Production fixed overheads	3	4,000	
Partners' salaries	3	55,000	
Rent of premises	3	11,000	
Office staff costs	3	48,450	
Marketing costs	3	164,700	
			934,817
Net cash inflow from operations			25,942
New equipment to be purchased			70,000
Net cash outflow			(95,942)
Cash balance at start of year	T5		2,500
Cash balance at end of year			(93,442)

Working notes for budgeted cash flow statement

Note 1: Cash to be collected from customers:

	Ref	£
Sales during the period	T 6	915,000
Less credit sales which remain as		
debtors at the end of the year	T 7	38,125
		876,875
Add cash collected from debtors		
at the start of the year	T 5	32,000
Cash to be collected from customers		908,875

Note 2: Cash to be paid to suppliers:

	Ref	£
Purchases during the period	T 10	352,000
Less credit purchases which		
remain as creditors at the end		
of the year	T 11	29,333
		322,667
Add cash paid to creditors at the		
start of the year	T 5	30,000
Cash to be paid to suppliers		352,667

Note 3: Other cash payments

It has been assumed, for the convenience of this illustration, that all other expense items are paid for as they are incurred. In reality this would be unlikely and there would be further calculations of the type shown in Note 2, making allowance for creditors at the start and end of the period.

Budgeted balance sheet

(T 21)

Budgeted balance sheet at 31 December 19X5

	£	£
Equipment at cost (Note 1)		260,000
Accumulated depreciation (Note 2)		92,000
Net book value		168,000
Inventory of raw materials (Note 3)	17,600	
Trade debtors (T 7)	38,125	
	55,725	
Bank borrowing (T 20)	93,442	
Trade creditors (T 11)	29,333	
	122,775	
Net current liabilities		(67,050)
Total assets less current liabilities		100,950
Partners' capital (Note 4)		100,950

Working notes for budgeted balance sheet

Note 1
Equipment at cost = £190,000 + £70,000   =   £260,000

Note 2
Accumulated depreciation = £40,000 + £52,000   =   £92,000

Note 3
Inventory of raw material
   For 400 ducks @ £14 each   5,600
   For 750 herons @ £16 each   12,000
                                  17,600

Note 4
Partners' capital = £172,100 + (£71,150)   =   £100,950

Comment: Not a promising picture of where the business is likely to be heading but this amount of detail will help identify where action needs to be taken to improve profit and cash flow.

Case 6.2   Alpha Ltd

Budgeted profit and loss account

	Original for half year to 31 March £	Actual for half year to 31 March £	Note
Sales	7,800,000	6,240,000	down 20%
Cost of sales	(5,226,000)	(4,305,600)	
Gross profit (original budget at 33%)	2,574,000	1,934,400	31%
Fixed overheads–			
Selling and advertising	(750,000)	(650,000)	Advtg –50%
General administration	(547,250)	(492,525)	
Operating profit	1,276,750	791,875	
Interest payable on medium term loan	(67,500)	(73,750)	
Royalties payable on sales	(390,000)	(312,000)	
Net profit	819,250	406,125	

(Note the impact of the increase in stock levels has been ignored in this and the next statement because it is a temporary fluctuation which is put right by the end of the year)

	Actual for half year to 31 March £	Revised budget for half year to 30 Sept £
Sales	6,240,000	6,240,000
Cost of sales	(4,305,600)	(4,180,800)
Gross profit (original budget at 33%)	1,934,400	2,059,200
Fixed overheads–		
Selling and advertising	(650,000)	(650,000)
General administration	(492,525)	(492,525)
Operating profit	791,875	916,675
Interest payable on medium term loan	(73,750)	(80,000)
Royalties payable on sales	(312,000)	(312,000)
Net profit	406,125	524,675

The question asks only for the results at 31 March and the revised budget thereafter but the information may be used to reply to the question asked by the directors in relation to the cash flow impact. You may find this more difficult but it is something which you can at least think out in general terms. First of all the measures taken to restore the gross profit must have an impact. Then the directors are controlling the level of stock so that it is not using up resources in the form of cash. Reducing the period of credit given to trade debtors will improve cash flow (basing the calculation on the lower level of actual sales achieved and expected). Finally the cost of goods sold has been controlled better in the second half. This will reduce the amount owing to creditors, even although the period of credit remains unchanged.

Statement of cash flow:
Improvement through measures taken in second half

		£
Additional profit generated through measures taken		118,550
Reduction in stock level	200,000	
Reduction in debtors from two months to one month 6,240,000/6	1,040,000	
One month's creditors based on cost of goods sold: saving (4,305,600 – 4,180,800)/12	10,400	
		1,250,400
Improvement in cash flow due to measures taken at half-year		1,368,950

It may be seen that the most effective improvement in cash flow can be obtained by paying attention to collection of debts, but other measures also have a beneficial effect.

Case 6.3 Constructabus

Statement of budgeted profit for each product for the year ending 31 August 19X9

	Standard £	Luxury £
Sales	1,845,000	5,475,000
Cost of goods sold (Note 1)	1,860,000	3,805,000
Gross profit / (loss)	(15,000)	1,670,000
Variable selling costs	105,000	180,000
Net profit / (loss)	(120,000)	1,490,000

Note 1: Calculation of cost of goods sold

	Standard	Luxury
Production in units	60	145
	£	£
Direct material costs	240,000	725,000
Direct labour costs (Note 3)		
Assembly floor	720,000	870,000
Finishing shed	360,000	1,305,000
Variable overhead (Note 3)		
Assembly floor	360,000	435,000
Finishing shed	60,000	217,500
Total variable cost	1,740,000	3,552,500
Fixed overhead	200,000	220,000
Total cost of production	1,940,000	3,772,500
Add opening stock (Note 2)	500,000	645,000
	2,440,000	4,417,500
Less closing stock (Note 2)	580,000	612,500
Cost of goods sold	1,860,000	3,805,000

Note 2: Valuation of closing stock:

	Standard	Luxury
Units in stock at start	20	30
Stock value of one unit (Note 4)	£25,000	£21,500
Total stock at start	£500,000	£645,000
Production during year (planned)	60	145
Sales (planned)	(60)	(150)
Projected units in stock at end	20	25
Stock value of one unit (Note 4)	£29,000	£24,500
Variable cost per unit produced	£580,000	£612,500

Note 3: Calculation of cost rates for direct labour and variable overhead

Assembly

In 19X7/X8 the hours worked on the assembly floor were (90 × 2,000) hours plus (80 × 1,000) hours, i.e. 260,000 hours. Labour cost was £1,300,000 so labour rate was £5 per hour.

Variable overhead was £520,000 which was a rate of £2 per hour.

In 19X8/X9 the hours worked on the assembly floor are estimated as (60 × 2,000) plus (145 × 1,000) hours i.e. 265,000 hours. Estimated cost is £1,590,000 which is £6 per hour.

Variable overhead is estimated as £795,000 which is £3 per hour.

Finishing

In 19X7/X8 the hours worked in the finishing shed were (90 × 1,000) hours plus (80 × 1,500) hours i.e. 210,000 hours. Labour rate was 1,260/210 = £6 per hour.

Variable overhead was £210,000 which was a rate of £1 per hour.

In 19X8/X9 the hours worked in the finishing shed are estimated as (60 × 1,000) plus (145 × 1,500) hours i.e. 277,500 hours. Estimated cost of labour is £1,665,000 which is £6 per hour.

Variable overhead is estimated as £277,500 which is £1 per hour.

Note 4: Stock valuation at variable cost:

Standard bus

		at 1.9. X8 £		at 31.8.X9 £
Direct materials		4,000		4,000
Direct labour				
Assembly 2,000 hours	£5	10,000	£6	12,000
Finishing 1,000 hours	£6	6,000	£6	6,000
Variable overhead				
Assembly 2,000 hours	£2	4,000	£3	6,000
Finishing 1,000 hours	£1	1,000	£1	1,000
Total		25,000		29,000

Luxury coach

		at 1.9. X8 £		at 31.8.X9 £
Direct materials		4,000		5,000
Direct labour				
Assembly 1,000 hours	£5	5,000	£6	6,000
Finishing 1,500 hours	£6	9,000	£6	9,000
Variable overhead				
Assembly 1,000 hours	£2	2,000	£3	3,000
Finishing 1,500 hours	£1	1,500	£1	1,500
Total		21,500		24,500

Comments: The price of the standard bus is budgeted to stay the same at £30,750 but the variable cost is budgeted to rise to £29,000. This is marginally beneficial but uncomfortably narrow a gap. The contribution of £1,750 per bus produces only £105,000 profit on 60 buses which does not cover the fixed costs of £200,000. There is some benefit to the profit and loss account of bringing forward 20 buses in stock at the start at the lower valuation of £25,000. This 'saving' of £4,000 per bus or £80,000 in total means the gross loss is kept down to £15,000 but the selling costs make the overall results worse. The company must either sell more buses, or raise the price, to remain profitable.

Chapter 7

Self-testing on the chapter

Q 15 20,000 blocks require 100,000 kg of material so standard usage is 5 kg per block. 16,000 blocks should use 80,000 kg but actual usage is 80,080 kg. Adverse usage variance is 80kg at standard cost of £3 per kg, i.e. adverse variance £240.

Q 16 Total variance is £6,000 adverse less £2,500 favourable = £3,500 adverse. So actual costs was £3,500 higher than standard cost, i.e. £39,500.

Q 17 Fixed overhead expenditure variance is £1,500 adverse.

Q 18

	Budget for May	Actual for May	Variance	
Production in units	42,800	42,800		
	£	£	£	
Direct material	256,800	267,220	10,420	(A)
Direct labour	342,400	356,577	14,177	(A)
Variable overhead	171,200	165,243	5,957	(F)
Fixed overhead	90,000	95,000	5,000	(A)
Total production cost	860,400	884,040	23,640	(A)
Less stock at standard cost,				
2,800 units at £21	58,800	58,800		
Cost of goods sold	801,600	825,240		
Sales 40,000 × £70	2,800,000	2,800,000		
Net profit	1,998,400	1,974,760	23,640	(A)

Note on standard cost

Budgeted cost per unit	£
Direct material 5kg × £1.20	6
Direct labour 2 hours × £4	8
Variable overhead 2 hours × £2	4
Fixed overhead £90,000 / 30,000	3
	21

Analysis of variances

Direct materials (total variance £10,420 adverse)

Price variance = AQ (SP − AP)	Usage variance = SP (SQ − AQ)
= 213,776 kg (£1.20 − £1.25)	= £1.20 (214,000 − 213,776)
= £10,688 adverse variance	= £268 favourable variance

Direct labour (total variance £14,177 adverse)

Rate variance = AH (SR − AR)	Efficiency variance = SR (SH − AH)
= 86,970 hours (£4.00 − £4.10)	= £4.00 (85,600 − 86,970)
= £8,697 adverse variance	= £5,480 adverse variance

Variable overhead (total variance £5,957 favourable)

Rate variance = AH (SR − AR)	Efficiency variance = SR (SH − AH)
= 86,970 hours (£2.00 − £1.90)	= £2.00 (85,600 − 86,970)
= £8,697 favourable variance	= £2,740 adverse variance

Fixed overhead expenditure variance is £5,000 adverse, indicating overspending.

One possible interpretation of the variance analysis is that less wastage of material occurred through buying higher quality material at a higher unit price. Labour was paid more than expected, which may have been due to an unexpected pay award, but nevertheless worked less efficiently than expected. The inefficient working has a consequence also on the efficiency of using variable overheads although this was more than offset by a lower than expected rate of variable overhead cost.

Q 19 Budgeted and actual costs for the month of May

	Budget £	Actual £	Variance £	
Actual level of output (units)	120	120		
Direct materials	30,000	31,200	1,200	(A)
Direct labour	18,000	16,800	1,200	(F)
Fixed manufacturing overhead	12,000	9,600	2,400	(F)
Total costs of production	60,000	57,600	2,400	(F)

Analysis of variances

Direct materials (total variance £1,200 adverse)

Price variance = AQ (SP − AP)	Usage variance = SP (SQ − AQ)
= 1,300 kg (£25 − £24)	= £25 (1,200 − 1,300)
= £1,300 favourable variance	= £2,500 adverse variance

Direct labour (total variance £1,200 favourable)

Rate variance = AH (SR − AR)	Efficiency variance = SR (SH − AH)
= 1,400 hours (£12 − £10)	= £10 (1,800 − 1,400)
= £2,800 adverse variance	= £4,000 favourable variance

Fixed overhead variance is an expenditure variance reflecting less spent than expected.

One possible story here is that the company tried to save money by buying cheaper material but this had the wrong effect because it increased wastage and hence usage was greater. The rate variance indicates that the incentive payment was successful: it had a cost which was more than offset by greater efficiency.

Q 20 Cabinets Ltd

Reconstructed budget for May 19X4

Production units budgeted	1,800
	£
Direct materials £3.00 × (9,600 × 1,800/1,600)	32,400
Direct labour £8.00 × (4,800 × 1,800/1,600)	43,200
Fixed overhead	36,000
Total budgeted cost	111,600

In the following tables, the figures in italics are the items which have been calculated from a knowledge of the other items in the table.

Direct materials (total variance £2,560 adverse)

Price variance = AQ (SP − AP)	Usage variance = SP (SQ − AQ)
= 11,200 kg *(£ 3.00* − £2.80)	= £3.00 (*9,600* − 11,200)
= £2,240 favourable variance	= £4,800 adverse variance

Direct labour (total variance £12,000 adverse)

Rate variance = AH (SR − AR)	Efficiency variance = SR (SH − AH)
= 5,600 hours (£8.00 − £9.00)	= £8.00 (*4,800* − 5,600)
= £5,600 adverse variance	= £6,400 adverse variance

Fixed overhead expenditure variance is £3,000 adverse, indicating the budget was £36,000.

One possible interpretation is that cheaper material was bought but resulted in more wastage, the adverse effect on usage exceeding the price saving. The labour rate increased, possibly due to an agreed wage rise, but the efficiency worsened perhaps because of the cheaper material. The adverse fixed overhead expenditure indicates overspending which is not related to volume effects.

Q 21 Fixit Ltd

	Flexible budget	Actual	Variance	
Production in units	5,500	5,500		
	£	£	£	
Direct materials	22,000	22,764	764	(A)
Direct labour	66,000	75,900	9,900	(A)
Variable production overhead	15,400	14,950	450	(F)
Fixed production overhead	10,000	9,000	1,000	(F)
Depreciation	4,000	4,000	–	
	117,400	126,614	9,214	(A)

Analysis of variances

Direct materials (total variance £764 adverse)

Price variance = AQ (SP − AP)	Usage variance = SP (SQ − AQ)
= 54,200 kg (£0.40 − £0.42)	= £0.40 (55,000 − 54,200)
= £1,084 adverse variance	= £320 favourable variance

Direct labour (total variance £9,900 adverse)

Rate variance = AH (SR − AR)	Efficiency variance = SR (SH − AH)
= 11,500 hours (£6.00 − £6.60)	= £6.00 (11,000 − 11,500)
= £6,900 adverse variance	= £3,000 adverse variance

Variable overhead (total variance £450 favourable)

Rate variance = AH (SR − AR)	Efficiency variance = SR (SH − AH)
= 11,500 hours (£1.40 − £1.30)	= £1.40 (11,000 − 11,500)
= £1,150 favourable variance	= £700 adverse variance

Fixed overhead expenditure variance is £1,000 favourable, indicating underspending.

More expensive material may have produced better quality and caused some offsetting in less material wastage. However, efficiency of working was lower than expected, affecting both labour and variable overhead costs. The variable overhead rate was lower than expected, suggesting some saving on the cost of overheads, but the labour rate was higher than expected, suggesting an unexpected pay award.

Case 7.1 Concrete Products Ltd

Heavy paving

	Actual	Budget	Flexible budget	Variance
	tonnes	tonnes	tonnes	
Sales volume	29,000	27,500	29,000	
Production volume	29,000	27,500	29,000	
	£000s	£000s	£000s	£000s
Revenue	720	690	727	7 (A)
Variable cost of sales	280	270	285	5 (F)
Contribution	440	420	442	2 (A)

Garden paving

	Actual	Budget	Flexible budget	Variance
	tonnes	tonnes	tonnes	
Sales volume	10,500	8,500	10,500	
Production volume	10,500	8,500	10,500	
	£000s	£000s	£000s	£000s
Revenue	430	300	370	60 (F)
Variable cost of sales	170	127	157	13 (A)
Contribution	260	173	213	47 (F)

Comment: The comparison between budget and actual must be made on the basis of a flexible budget which allows for the revised levels of production and sales. In both cases the activity has been greater than was expected when the budget was set. Making comparison with a flexible budget shows that heavy paving made a contribution which was £2,000 less than expected while garden paving made a contribution which was £47,000 greater than expected.

Questions to ask:

1. Has there been a change in the sales price of these items? If so the budget should be revised to take account of the new price, and the variance for the period would be £8,000 adverse.

2. Has there been a change in the cost of direct materials? If so the budget should be revised to avoid giving the impression of an adverse variance of £8,000. The usefulness of variance analysis lies in identifying controllable variances, not in relating to outdated budgets.

3. On the presumption that there has been no change in the labour rate, is the supervisory team working effectively? One explanation of the adverse cost variance could be inefficient working in the production department.

Case 7.2   Nu-Line Ltd

Calculation of cost of production

	Flexible budget	Actual	Variance	
Units of production	140	140		
	£	£	£	
Cost of machine tools (for 140)	84,000	*67,510	16,490	(F)
Direct labour	42,000	47,500	5,500	(A)
Variable production overhead	14,000	13,000	1,000	(F)
	140,000	128,010	11,990	(F)
Fixed production overhead	**36,000	35,000	1,000	(F)
Total production cost	176,000	163,010	12,990	(F)
Less inventory, 5 items at £1,200 each	6,000	6,000		
Cost of goods sold	170,000	157,010	12,990	(F)
Sales 150 at £2,000 each	300,000	300,000		
	130,000	142,990	12,990	(F)

* Actual cost of £86,800 related to 180 units, but only 140 were used, so cost of 140 is taken proportionately as £67,510.
** Fixed production overhead of £200 per unit multiplied by budgeted production at 180 units because the fixed overhead budget is not flexible with volume of activity.

Calculation of units of inventory

	Original budget	Actual
Inventory of finished goods at start of year	15	15
Production	180	140
Sales	(130)	(150)
Inventory of finished goods at end of year	65	5

Comment: The original sales level expected was 130 units. Additional profit has been created by selling 150 units but beyond that there is a favourable variance of £12,990. This is primarily due to the cost of purchased machine tools being less than expected (£482 rather than £600 each). The direct labour variance was adverse but we are not provided with sufficient information to break this down into rate and efficiency variances. A similar limitation on analysis applies to the favourable variance on variable production overhead. The fixed production overhead shows a marginal saving on budget.

Case 7.3   Carrypack Ltd – month of April 19X6

	Flexible budget	*Actual*	*Variance*
	12,300 units	12,300 units	
	£	£	£
Sales: 12,300 units @ £50 each	615,000	615,000	nil
Production: 12,300 units			
	£	£	£
Direct materials	135,300	136,220	920 (A)
Direct labour	110,700	129,200	18,500 (A)
Variable overheads	73,800	72,200	1,600 (F)
Fixed overhead	48,000	49,400	1,400 (A)
Total cost	367,800	387,020	19,220 (A)
Actual profit	247,200	227,980	19,220 (A)

Direct materials (total variance £920 adverse)

Price variance = AQ (SP − AP)	Usage variance = SP (SQ − AQ)
= 27,800 kg (£5.00 − £4.90)	= £5 (*27,060 − 27,800)
= £2,780 favourable variance	= £3,700 adverse variance

*26,400 kg is standard for 12,000 units so proportionately 27,060 kg is standard for 12,300 units

Direct labour (total variance £18,500 adverse)

Rate variance = AH (SR − AR)	Efficiency variance = SR (SH − AH)
= 38,000 hours (£3.00 − £3.40)	= £3.00 (36,900 − 38,000)
= £15,200 adverse variance	= £3,300 adverse variance

Variable overhead (total variance £1,600 favourable)

Rate variance = AH (SR − AR)	Efficiency variance = SR (SH − AH)
= 38,000 hours (£2.00 − £1.90)	= £2.00 (36,900 − 38,000)
= £3,800 favourable variance	= £2,200 adverse variance

Fixed overhead expenditure variance is £1,400 adverse, indicating overspending.

Comment: Direct materials needs investigating for controllability of the usage variance and whether low price goods have been purchased with a consequence of more wastage. Direct labour is the variance of most concern because of its magnitude. If the labour rate has changed then the budget should be revised so that the non-controllable variance of £15,200 is not reported. The inefficiency of labour working is matched by inefficiency in use of variable overhead and the cause of the unexpected extra hours should be investigated.

Chapter 8

Self-testing on the chapter

Q 11   For Division X the new project would bring a ROI of £1.2m on £4m or 30 per cent, appearing unattractive in the context of the existing ROI of 33 per cent. The residual income would be (£1.2m – £0.4m) = £0.8m which is an addition to the profit of the division after rewarding investment and therefore would be attractive on RI measures.

 For Division Y the ROI of £0.8m on £4m is 20 per cent which looks attractive when compared with the existing level of 4 per cent. The residual income would be (£0.8m – £0.4m) = £0.4m. This is acceptable but if the company has only £4m to invest it would produce a higher RI in division X.

Case 8.1   Furniture Manufacture Ltd

A control report should emphasise the costs which are controllable within the organisation and which are most closely the responsibility of the manager concerned.

 Although the power failure was beyond the control of the departmental manager, the company needs to know the cost of that failure. If there was a power failure then there can have been no productive work from direct labour and it is likely that indirect labour, indirect materials and indirect production overhead would not have been incurred during that time. The fixed overheads will have been incurred irrespective but the variable maintenance costs may not have been incurred where there was no activity to maintain. So the budgeted cost should be re-calculated at 75 per cent of the expected cost and compared with actual. This may give a better comparison with the actual cost.

		Budgeted cost			*Actual cost*	*Variance*	
	Fixed	*Original Variable*	*Revised Variable*	*Total*		*(F) = favourable (A) = adverse*	
	£	£	£	£	£	£	
Direct labour	–	36,000	27,000	27,000	30,000	3,000	(A)
Indirect labour	6,000	8,000	6,000	12,000	14,000	2,000	(A)
Indirect materials	–	4,000	3,000	3,000	3,500	500	(A)
Power	3,000	12,000	9,000	12,000	9,000	3,000	(F)
Maintenance materials	–	5,000	3,750	3,750	3,000	750	(F)
Maintenance labour	5,000	4,000	3,000	8,000	15,000	7,000	(A)
Depreciation	85,000	–	–	85,000	75,000	10,000	(F)
Production overhead	–	20,000	15,000	15,000	15,000	–	

The revised table suggests that the bench assembly department manager should not be quite so complacent as was indicated from the earlier table. The labour costs appear to be higher than would be expected for a power failure period, unless the explanation is that they have been paid overtime rates to catch up on the work. Questions also need to be asked about the maintenance labour. It may be that the explanation is that additional maintenance was undertaken during the enforced idleness, although this explanation depends on being able to undertake maintenance without an electricity supply.

Case 8.2 Musical Productions Ltd

	CD £000s	PS £000s
Investment in fixed assets	840	700
Revenue	420	210
Operating expenses	210	140
Profit	210	70
ROI from budget	25%	10%
New investment	140	140
Expected profits	28	28
ROI from new project	20%	20%
Interest payable at 18%	25.2	25.2
Residual income from project	2.8	2.8

In ROI terms the project would be rejected by CD and accepted by PS. The residual income calculation is neutral to the decision, confirming only that the project can meet interest costs and leave a surplus.

The location of the project should therefore be based on other factors such as efficiency of management or suitability of workforce skills.

Case 8.4

(a) for explanation of responsibility accounting see chapter.

(b) Manager of distribution depot needs:
- area totals for demand (5 columns)
- area totals for running costs of floats
- area totals for drivers' wages and managers' salaries
- area totals for cash collection and note on areas of slow payment problems, with action taken
- copy of area returns as backup if required
- exception report from each area manager highlighting problem areas and action taken
- ratios identifying relationships of key variables

Area manager needs:
- depot totals for demand (10 columns)
- depot totals for running costs of floats
- depot totals for drivers' wages and mangers' salaries
- depot totals for cash collected and note on dealing with slow payers
- copy of depot returns as backup if required
- ratios identifing relationships of key variables.

Depot manager needs:
- delivery demand analysed by driver
- running costs of float analysed by driver
- drivers' wages for each employee
- cash collection analysed by driver
- ratios relating input to output.

Chapter 9

Self-testing on the chapter

Q 21

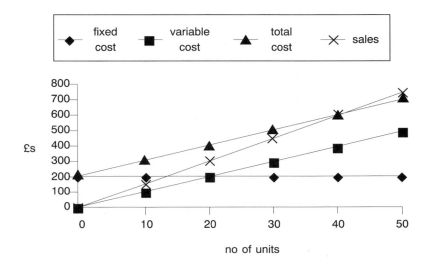

Q 22 Contribution is £5.50 − £3.00 = £2.50
Break-even point equals fixed cost/contribution = 5,000/2.50 = 2,000 units.

Q 23 First calculate some points for the graph (only two points are needed for a straight line)

Envelopes

Quantity	0	20,000
	£	£
Fixed cost	5,400	5,400
Variable cost	0	12,000
Total cost	5,400	17,400
Sales	0	21,000

Envelopes

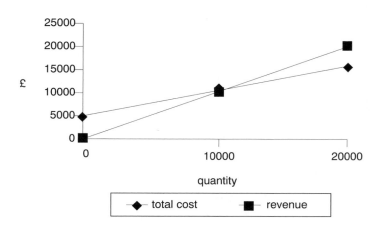

(Break-even point 5,400/ 0.45 = 12,000 units)

Writing pads

Quantity	0	15,000
	£	£
Fixed cost	3,690	3,690
Variable cost	0	8,100
Total cost	5,400	11,790
Sales	0	14,250

Writing pads

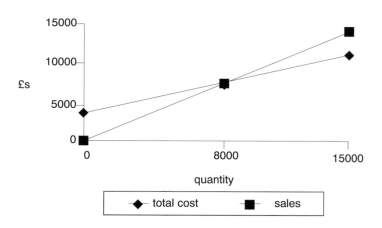

(Break-even point = 3690/0.41 = 9,000 units)

Q 24   Chairs and tables

A break-even chart can only show one product at a time but where there is a fixed proportion, as in this case, a 'product' can be created comprising bundles of one table plus four chairs.

	£
SP: 1 table £75 plus 4 chairs £240	315
VC: 1 table £40 plus 4 chairs £140	180
Contribution	135

(Break-even point is £135,000/135 = 1,000 sets of tables and chairs)

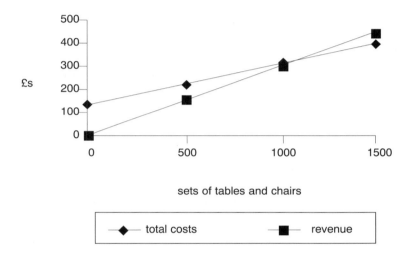

Q 25   Valve refurbishing business

Fixed overhead at £2 per unit based on 1m items = £2m total

Range of graph needs to cover up to 1,200,000 components

Total variable cost per unit is £4.

Draw graph to show where total cost of £4 per item plus £2m intersects with external cost of £6 per item. Graph shows break-even point at 1,000,000 items so that for 800,000 items it is better to purchase outside, but this would need to be a reversible decision if output does rise above 1,000,000 items.

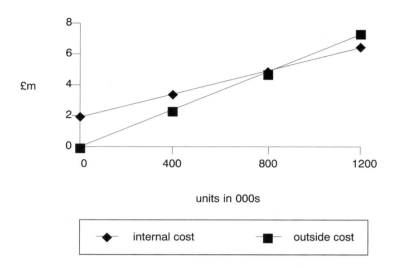

units in 000s

| internal cost | outside cost |

Q 26 Farthing Ltd

For existing machine:

	£
Selling price of one unit	40
Variable costs (by deduction)	32
Contribution at 20% of sales	8
Fixed cost per unit (based on 20,000 frames)	5
Net profit	3

Fixed cost is £100,000 in total

For new machine:

	£
Selling price of one unit (lower by £5)	35
Variable costs (lower by £1)	26
Contribution	9

Under new machine, fixed costs will be £120,000.

This information may be most appropriately shown on a profit–volume graph, plotting activity in units against overall profit or loss. This will allow more ready comparison between the products of the old and the new machines.

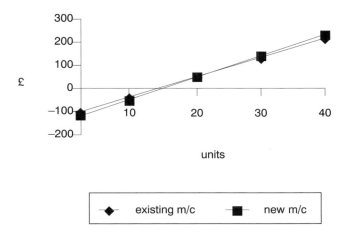

From the chart, the point of intersection is 20,000 units. Beyond that point the new machine gives higher profit.

Profit at full capacity on the old machine was £60,000. A 50 per cent increase in profit means £90,000 in total. The new machine must cover £120,000 fixed overhead plus £90,000 profit, i.e. £210,000 in total. Contribution per unit is £9 therefore 23,333 units are required to cover the required profit.

Case 9.1   Supertoys Ltd

	Current	*Projected*
Production and sales volume	40,000	60,000
	£	£
Selling price	20.00	17.50
Variable cost	16.00	11.50
Contribution	4.00	6.00
Fixed overhead	100,000	120,000
Break-even point	25,000 units	20,000 units
Profit at target volume	£60,000	£240,000
Profit at current volume, 40,000 units	60,000	£120,000

The contribution as a percentage of sales is 20 per cent under the current operation and 34.2 per cent under the projected methods of working. This means that beyond the break-even point the projected improvements will gain wealth faster. The break-even point under the projected method falls to 20,000 units and even at the current volume of 40,000 units produces a 50 per cent increase in profit reported previously.

Case 9.2 Dairyproducts Ltd

	Cartons of cream	*Aerosol cans of cream*	*Packets of cheese*	*Total*
Units of output	400,000	96,000	280,000	
	£	£	£	£
Selling price	0.75	1.05	1.30	
Variable cost	0.45	0.50	1.00	
Contribution per unit	0.30	0.55	0.30	
Total contribution	120,000	52,800	84,000	256,000
Fixed cost	60,000	24,000	56,000	140,000
Net profit of current prodn, per week				116,000
Annual profit				5,800,000

Range of demand for aerosol cream cheese

	£	£	£
Volume	60,000	80,000	100,000
	£	£	£
Sales price	1.50	1.40	1.15
Variable cost	0.50	0.50	0.50
Contribution per unit	1.00	0.90	0.65
Total contribution per week	60,000	72,000	65,000
Annual for 50 weeks		3,600,000	
Less:			
Additional advertising		(1,000,000)	
Modification cost		(400,000)	
Additional fixed cost		(500,000)	
Net benefit		1,700,000	

Reducing production of cream cartons by 20% per annum will lose
£120,000 × 50 × 20% i.e. £1,200,000.

Reducing production of packet cheese by 25% per annum will lose
£84,000 × 50 × 25% i.e. £1,050,000.

The net benefit of the new product is therefore greater than the loss on either of the options withdrawn.

The recommendation is to reduce packet cheese and replace with aerosol cream cheese. The only possible warning here is that there is only £150,000 of difference between withdrawing cream cartons and withdrawing packet cheese. If the growing customer dissatisfaction with cream in cartons is serious, the longer-term view might prevail over the short-term recommendation.

Case 9.3

Profit and loss account for the year ended 31 August 19X8:

	£	*Proposal I*	*Proposal II*	*Proposal III*
Volume of sales	100,000	140,000	90,000 + special	160,000
	£	£	£	£
Sales	3,000,000	3,780,000	2,700,000	4,320,000
Production costs				
Direct materials (£3 each)	300,000	420,000	270,000	480,000
Direct labour				
(£10.50 each)	1,050,000	1,470,000	945,000	1,680,000
Variable overhead				
(£1.80 each)	180,000	252,000	162,000	288,000
Fixed overhead	660,000	660,000	660,000	660,000
	2,190,000	2,802,000	2,037,000	3,108,000
Fixed administration				
overhead	320,000	320,000	320,000	320,000
Selling and distribution costs:				
Sales commission				
(2% of sales)	60,000	75,600	54,000	86,400
Variable distribution costs				
(£1.50 each)	150,000	210,000	135,000	240,000
Fixed advertising costs	120,000	120,000	120,000	170,000
	330,000	405,600	309,000	496,400
	2,840,000	3,527,600	2,666,000	3,924,400
Profit	160,000	252,400	34,000	395,600
Additional profit required			216,000	
Overall target			250,000	

For Proposal II a profit of £216,000 is required from the mail order activity. A payment of £180,000 is required for the catalogue, so the contribution must be at least £396,000.

Variable production cost is £15.30. Special packaging is £0.75 per unit.

Units sold are 50,000

Contribution required per unit is £396,000/50,000 = £7.92

So, for mail order, price would have to be £(16.05 + 7.92) = £23.97 each, say £24 each.

A neater way of addressing the problem

Statement of variable cost

	Original	Proposal I	Proposal II-mail order
	£	£	£
Direct materials	3.00	3.00	3.00
Direct labour	10.50	10.50	10.50
Variable overhead	1.80	1.80	1.80
	15.30	15.30	15.30
Sales commission	0.60	0.54	–
Variable distribution costs	1.50	1.50	–
Special packaging			0.75
Total variable cost	17.40	17.34	16.05

Original situation

Contribution from 100,000 selling at £30 is 100,000 (30 – 17.40) = £1,260,000

Break-even point is (660,000 + 320,000 + 120,000)/12.6   = 88,888 sweaters
Margin of safety   = 11,112 sweaters

Proposal I

Contribution from 140,000 selling at £27 is 140,000 (27 – 17.34) = £1,352,400

Net gain over existing   = £92,400

Break-even point is (660,000 + 320,000 + 120,000)/9.66   = 113,872 sweaters
Margin of safety   = 26,128 sweaters

Proposal II

	£
Contribution from 90,000 selling at £30 is 90,000 (30 – 17.40)	1,134,000
Shortfall over contribution from original situation	126,000
Additional profit required (250,000 – 160,000)	90,000
Amount sought from mail order to cover profit	216,000
Additional fixed cost of mail order	180,000
Fixed cost plus profit to be covered	396,000

Number sold by mail order is 50,000 so contribution per unit is	£7.92
Variable cost is £16.05 so minimum price to mail order is	£23.97

Break-even point on first tranche of 90,000 is
(660,000 + 320,000 + 120,000)/12.6   = 88,888 sweaters

If mail order is guaranteed then margin of safety   = 51,112 sweaters

Proposal III

Contribution from 160,000 selling at £27 is 160,000 (27 – 17.34) = £1,545,600

Improvement on original situation is   £ 285,600

But additional fixed costs are required   £   50,000

So net gain is   £ 235,600

Break-even point is
(660,000 + 320,000 + 120,000 + 50,000)/9.66 = 119,048 sweaters
Margin of safety is 40,952 sweaters.

Proposal III produces the highest profit but is marginally more risky in terms of a higher break-even point.

Case 9.5

The answer should use the headings discussed in the chapter, namely:

economic factors
cost-based pricing
mark-up percentages

In this question the important differences lie in the economic factors. You should underline each word or phrase which relates to economic factors and use these to explain why Leisure Furniture uses a price based on marginal cost while Home Furnishing applied a percentage mark-up to full cost.

Chapter 10

Self-testing on the chapter

Q 17 *Payback period*

The cumulative cash flows are:

End of year	£
1	10,000
2	25,000
3	45,000
4	70,000

The payback of £50,000 occurs one-fifth the way into year 4, i.e. payback is 3.2 years

Accounting rate of return

Total profit over 5 years is £95,000 less depreciation of £40,000, i.e. £55,000.

Average profit is therefore £11,000 per annum

Accounting rate of return is 11,000/50,000 = 22%

Net present value

(Using assumed discount rate of 10 per cent)

Using the formula approach the net present value is calculated as:

$$\frac{10{,}000}{(1.10)} + \frac{15{,}000}{(1.10)^2} + \frac{20{,}000}{(1.10)^3} + \frac{25{,}000}{(1.10)^4} + \frac{*35{,}000}{(1.10)^5} - 50{,}000$$

= 9,090 + 12,397 + 15,026 + 17,075 + 21,732 − 50,000
= 75,320 − 50,000
= 25,320

*Cash flow forecast for year 5 plus scrap value expected at end

Using the discount tables the net present value is calculated as:

End of year	Cash flow £	Discount factor	Present value £
1	10,000	0.909	9,090
2	15,000	0.826	12,390
3	20,000	0.751	15,020
4	25,000	0.683	17,075
5	35,000	0.621	21,735
			75,310
Less initial outlay			(50,000)
Net present value			25,310

(Difference from formula-based answer is due to rounding)

Case 10.1

	Yr	ALPHA £000s	Disct	BRAVO £000s	Disct	CHARLIE £000s	Disct	DELTA £000s	Disct
Outlay	–	(600)	(600)	(300)	(300)	(120)	(120)	(210)	(210)
Cash flow benefits:									
	1	435	395	–		48	43	81	74
	2	435	359	–		48	40	81	67
	3	–		219	164	48	36	81	61
	4	–		219	150	48	33	81	55
	5	–		219	136	48	30	81	50
Total PV			754		450		182		307
NPV			154		150		62		97
Total PV/outlay			1.26		1.50		1.52		1.46
Internal rate of return		28.8%		22.0%		28.6%		26.8%	

All the projects are acceptable because they all have a positive net present value but the maximisation of net present value from an investment of £1m requires selection of the projects which give the highest net present value per £ of investment. This is most conveniently estimated by comparing the total present value with the outlay (sometimes referred to as the *profitability index*). The order of preference is therefore:

Bravo, Charlie, Delta Alpha.

The highest net present value within a £1m limit would be £309,000 obtained from Bravo, Charlie and Delta. If the additional funding can be borrowed then Alpha is also desirable.

Case 10.2

This question requires evaluation of the investment of £1,150,000 as compared with continuing on the existing basis with no investment.

	19X1 £000s	*19X2* £000s	*19X3* £000s	*19X4* £000s	*19X5* £000s
Existing sales volume at £10 each	4,000	4,500	5,000	6,000	7,500
Proposed sales volume at £8.50	4,760	5,355	5,950	7,140	8,925
Incremental cash flow from sales	760	855	950	1,140	1,425
Existing production outflow at £7.50	3,150	3,263	3,788	4,575	5,475
New production outflow at £6.20	3,497	3,949	4,309	5,208	6,473
Incremental cash outflow on production	347	686	521	633	998
Excess inflow over outflow	413	169	429	507	427
Incremental scrap value					130
	413	169	429	507	557
Discount factors at 12%	0.893	0.797	0.712	0.636	0.567
Present value	458	135	305	322	316

Total present value = 1,447,000

Investment required is £1,447,000 and there is 'lost' scrap value of £30,000.
So compare present value of £1,447,000 with outlay of £1,180,000. Net present value is positive therefore investment is acceptable.

Other matters – is demand sustainable, are production costs controllable at lower level, is scrap value forecast realistic?

Index